HARDPRESS NET

ISBN: 9781290514767

Published by:
HardPress Publishing
8345 NW 66TH ST #2561
MIAMI FL 33166-2626

Email: info@hardpress.net
Web: http://www.hardpress.net

MEMOIRS

CORRESPONDENCE AND MANUSCRIPTS

OF

GENERAL LAFAYETTE

PUBLISHED BY HIS FAMILY.

VOL. I.

NEW YORK
SAUNDERS AND OTLEY ANN STREET
AND CONDUIT STREET LONDON.
MDCCCXXXVII.

NEW YORK:

CRAIGHEAD AND ALLEN,

PRINTERS.

MEMOIRS

CORRESPONDENCE AND MANUSCRIPTS

OF

GENERAL LAFAYETTE.

ADVERTISEMENT

OF THE AMERICAN EDITOR.

It was the desire of the late General Lafayette, that this edition of his Memoirs and Correspondence should be considered as a legacy to the American people. His representatives have accordingly pursued a course which they conceived the best adapted to give effect to his wishes, by furnishing a separate edition for this country, without any reservation for their own advantage, beyond the transfer of the copyright as an indemnity for the expense and risk of publication.

In this edition are inserted some letters which will not appear in the editions published in Paris and London. They contain details relating to the American Revolution, and render the present edition more complete, or, at least, more interesting to Americans. Although written during the first residence of General Lafayette in

America—when he was little accustomed to write in the English language—the letters in question are given exactly as they came from his pen—and as well as the others in the collection written by him in that language, are distinguished from those translated from the French, by having the word "Original" prefixed to them.

It was intended that these letters should have been arranged among those in the body of the work, in the order of their respective dates; but as the latter had been stereotyped before the former had been transmitted to the American editor, this design was rendered impracticable. They have therefore from necessity been added in a supplemental form with the marginal notes which seemed requisite for their explanation.

Columbia College, N. Y., July, 1837.

RESPECTFULLY to collect and scrupulously to arrange the manuscripts of which an irreparable misfortune has rendered them depositaries, have been for the Family of General Lafayette the accomplishment of a sacred duty.

To publish those manuscripts without any commentary, and place them, unaltered, in the hands of the friends of Liberty, is a pious and solemn homage which his children now offer with confidence to his memory.

GEORGE WASHINGTON LAFAYETTE.

NOTICE BY THE EDITORS.

Under the title of *Revolution of America*, are comprised eight years of M. de Lafayette's life,* from the commencement of 1771 until the end of 1784. His three voyages to the United States divide those eight years into three periods: 1777, 1778; 1779—1781; and 1782—1784.

1st. Circumstantial Memoirs, written for his friends after the peace of Versailles, and which were to have extended to 1780, open this collection.

2nd. These are continued and completed by two detached relations, composed between 1800 and 1814; the first, which has no title, and might be called *Notice of the American Life of General Lafayette*, appears to have been written for a person intending to publish the history of the war, or of General Washington; the second is entitled, *Observations on some portion of American History, by a friend of General Lafayette.*

As these two relations, both written by M. de Lafayette, and which we designate under the names

* M. de Lafayette (Marie-Paul-Joseph-Roch-Yois-Gilbert Motier) born at Chavaniac, in Auvergne, the 6th of September, 1757; married the 11th of April, 1774; set out for America the 26th of April, 1777. The other dates will be mentioned in proper order, with each particular event. All the notes which are not followed by the name of M. de Lafayette, may be attributed to the members of his family, sole editors of this work.

of Manuscript, No. 1, and Manuscript, No. 2, contain a second, and occasionally a third, account of events already mentioned in the Memoirs, we have only inserted quotations from them.

3rd. A relation of the campaign in Virginia, in 1781, shall be inserted in its complete state.

4th. Extracts from the collection of the general's speeches, begun by him in 1829, will give some details of his third voyage to America (1784).

5th. With the account of each particular period, that portion of the correspondence which may relate to it will be inserted. From a great number of letters, written from America, and addressed either to France or to America, or from France to America, those only have been suppressed whose repetitions, or details, purely military, would render them uninteresting to the public.

6th. In the Correspondence, some letters have been inserted from General Washington, and other contemporaries, and also some historical records, of which M. de Lafayette had taken copies, or which have been extracted from various collections published in the United States.

TO THE READER.*

WHEN, devoted from early youth to the ambition of liberty, I beheld no limit to the path that I had opened for myself, it appeared to me that I was sufficiently fulfilling my destiny, and satisfying my glory, by rushing incessantly forward, and leaving to others the care of collecting the recollections, as well as the fruits, of my labour.

After having enjoyed an uninterrupted course of good fortune for fifteen years, I presented myself, with a favourable prospect of success, before the coalition of kings, and the aristocracy of Europe: I was overthrown by the simultaneous fury of French jacobinism. My person was then given up to the vengeance of my natural enemies, and my reputation to the calumnies of those self-styled patriots who had so lately violated every sworn and national guarantee. It is well known that the regimen of my five years' imprisonment was not favourable to literary occupations, and when, on my deliverance from prison, I was advised to write an explanation of my conduct, I was disgusted with all works of the kind, by the numerous memoirs or notices by which so many persons had trespassed upon the attention

* Although this notice, written a short time before the 18th *Brumaire*, be anterior to a great number of events, in the midst of which General Lafayette continued his public life, we have placed it in this part of the work, as a sort of general introduction to the various materials it contains.

of the public. Events had also spoken for us; and many accusers, and many accusations, had fallen into oblivion.

As soon as I returned to France, my friends requested me to write memoirs: I found excuses for not doing so in my reluctance to judge with severity the first jacobin chiefs who have shared since in my proscription,—the *Girondins*, who have died for those very principles they had opposed and persecuted in me,—the king and queen, whose lamentable fate only allows me to pride myself upon some services I have rendered them,—and the vanquished royalists, who are at present deprived of fortune, and exposed to every arbitrary measure. I ought to add, likewise, that, happy in my retreat, in the bosom of my family, and occupied with agricultural pursuits, I know not how to purloin one moment from the enjoyments of my domestic life.

But my friends have renewed their request, and, to comply in some degree with it, I have consented to place in order the few papers that I still possess, assemble together some relations which have been already published, and unite, by notes, the whole collection, in which my children and friends may one day find materials for a less insignificant work.

As to myself, I acknowledge that my indolence in this respect is owing to the intimate conviction which I feel, that liberty will ultimately be established in the old as well as in the new world, and that then the history of our revolutions will put all things and all persons in their proper places.

CONTENTS

OF THE FIRST VOLUME.

AMERICAN REVOLUTION.

CONTENTS.

SECOND VOYAGE TO AMERICA, AND CAMPAIGNS OF 1780, 1781.

ADDITIONAL CORRESPONDENCE.

APPENDIX.

ERRATA.

Page i, line 1, (note,) *for* Yois *read* Yves.
— iii, — 1, (note,) *for* before *read* after.
— 3, — 7, *for* to *read* of.
— 4, — 6, *for* an *read* a.
— 10, — 15, *for* home *read* house.
— 16, — 11, *for* an *read* a.
— 22, — 11, *for* hardly *read* scarcely.
— 23, — 31, *for* his *read* their.
— 25, — 23, *for* his *read* their.
— 29, — 24, *for* was *read* were.
— 35, — 19, *for* neither *read* no; *for* nor *read* or.
— 38, — 5, *for* himself *read* himself such pretensions.
— 43, — 35, *for* was *read* were.
— 46, — 33, *for* an *read* a.
— 55, — 35, *for* Connecticut *read* Cannanicut.
— 64, — 18, *for* months *read* weeks.
— 67, — 19, *for* horrors *read* honors.
— 80, — 30, *for* Connecticut *read* Cannanicut.
— 86, — 22, *for* it and I *read* we.
— 91, — 21, *for* have forbidden some days since *read* I forbad some days ago.
— 92, — 17, *for* was *read* were.
—101, — 6, *for* an *read* a.
—104, — 28, *for* an *read* a.
—106, — 34, *for* and very *read* and a very.
—115, — 4, *for* you *read* I.
—131, — 26, *for* hope *read* trust.
—152, — 2, *for* inform *read* rejoin.
—152, — 5, *for* an *read* a.

Page 208, line 9, *for* no *read* us.
— 217, — 28, *for* heart, I admire *read* heart I admire.
— 247, — 6, *for* tie *read* connecting link.
— 257, — 30, *for* endeavored from circumstances, &c. *read* endeavored to draw the slightest pecuniary advantage from circumstances.
— 263, — 12, *for* who *read* which.
— 265, — 13, *for* every person was *read* all were.
— 285, — 27, *for* has *read* offer.
— 297, — 20, *for* The latter reasoning, &c., *read* The reasoning of the latter does not bring me over to.
— 299, — 12, *for* was *read* were.
— 299, — 15, *for* this sacrifice *read* than would be to me the sacrifice.
— 323, — 13, *for* there *read* it.
— 346, — 2, *for* Frenchman *read* Frenchmen.
— 347, — 5, *for* formed *read* form.
— 348, — 27, *for* either *read* one.
— 351, — 22, *for* Sesse *read* Tessé.
— 352, — 10, *for* monstrous *read* monotonous.
— 378, — 10, *for* neither pay, clothes, nor *read* no pay clothes, or.
— 378, — 28, *for* notion *read* opinion.
— 381, — 6, *for* of *read* with.
— :85, — 13, *for* come *read* came.
— 434, — 12, *for* the *read* its.
— 439, — (note) *for* Jefferson *read* Nelson.

FIRST VOYAGE

AND

FIRST CAMPAIGN IN AMERICA,

1777—1778.

MEMOIRS WRITTEN BY MYSELF,*

UNTIL THE YEAR 1780.

TO MY FRIENDS.

If I were to confound, as is too often done, obstinacy with firmness, I should blush at beginning these memoirs, after having so long refused to do so, and at even increasing their apparent egotism by my style, instead of sheltering myself under cover of the third person; but I will not yield a half compliance to the request of that tender friendship which is far more valuable to me than the ephemeral success which a journal might obtain. It is sufficient for me to know that this relation, intended for a few friends only, will never extend beyond their circle: it even possesses two very

* Note by M. de Lafayette upon the *Memoirs written by himself and his American correspondence*.—Many papers relating to the first years of my public life have been destroyed during the reign of terror. An imperfect copy of these memoirs has been saved: this ought to have been re-written; I have preferred copying it precisely as it was originally composed.

Several letters written from America had been copied by my wife for Dr. Dubrucil, (physician to the king and to *la Charité*, at St. Germain-en-laza, deceased 1785,) whose friendship was great advantages over many celebrated books; these are, that the public not being concerned in this work it cannot need a preface, and that the dedication of affection cannot require an epistle.

It would be too poetical to place myself at once in another hemisphere, and too minute to dwell upon the particulars of my birth, which soon followed the death of my father at Minden;* of my education in Auvergne, with tender and revered relations; of my removal, at twelve years of age, to a college at Paris,† where I soon lost my virtuous mother,‡ and where the death of her father rendered me rich, although I had been born, comparatively speaking, poor; of some schoolboy successes, inspired by the love of glory and somewhat disturbed by that of liberty; of my entrance into the regiment of the black musketeers, which

the pride of one portion of my life, and who has filled the remainder of it with a deep and tender recollection. Those papers have been preserved; it would be necessary to suppress some repetitions and insignificant details, but I have left them almost all untouched, because, whilst forming this collection, I felt pleasure in recalling the sentiments that had animated me at various periods of my existence.

The Duke d'Ayen, my father-in-law, was not one of the least hasty and severe censurers of my departure for America, but he restored to me his favour with all the kindness and sincerity which characterized him: his affectionate congratulations deeply touched my heart. The same feeling induces me at the present moment to repeat some details contained in the letters I addressed to him.

* Michel-Louis-Christophe-Roch-Gilbert de Motier, Marquis de Lafayette, colonel of the grenadiers of France, Chevalier de St. Louis, killed at the battle of Minden before the age of twenty-five.

† The college du Plessis.

‡ Marie-Louise-Julie de la Rivière, died at Paris the 12th of April, 1770, some days before her father Joseph-Yves-Thibauld-Hyacinthe, Marquis de la Rivière.

only interrupted my studies on review days; and finally, of my marriage, at the age of sixteen, preceded by a residence at the academy of Versailles. I have still less to say relating to my entrance into the world; to the short favour I enjoyed as constituting one member of a youthful society; to some promises to the regiment de Noailles; and to the unfavourable opinion entertained of me owing to my habitual silence when I did not think the subjects discussing worthy of being canvassed. The bad effects produced by disguised self-love and an observing disposition, were not softened by a natural simplicity of manner, which, without being improper on any great occasion, rendered it impossible for me to bend to the graces of the court, or to the charms of a supper in the capital.

You ask me at what period I first experienced

* Previous to the marriage of M. de Lafayette, we have only one letter written by him at fourteen years of age, the 8th of February, 1772, which will be read perhaps with some curiosity. It is addressed to his cousin, Mademoiselle de Chavaniac.

"I have just received, my dear cousin, your letter, and the good account you give me of my grandmother's health. After that, which was what first touched my heart, I was much interested by the account of the hunt of the proprietor of the forests of Lata. I should like very much to know whether those dogs that neither walk nor bark contributed to the success of the expedition? The details of that hunt would have amused me very much; if I had been speaking to you of a new-fashioned cap, I should have thought it my duty to have described to you its figure and proportions, with a compass in my hand.

"Our cousin's marriage is broken off; there is another one on the carpet, but they are obliged to lower their tone exceedingly. Mademoiselle de Roncherolles, a place with Madame de Bourbon, of a thousand crowns a-year, and five thousand small livres a-year—that is the whole amount. You see that this is a very short abridgment of the other intended matches. My uncle, who came to see me the other day, consents to the marriage, on condition that the Prince de Condé will promise one my ardent love of liberty and glory ? I recollect no time of my life anterior to my enthusiasm for anecdotes of glorious deeds, and to my projects of travelling over the world to acquire fame. At eight years of age, my heart beat when I heard of an hyæna that had done some injury, and caused still more alarm, in our neighbourhood, and the hope of meeting it was the object of all my walks. When I arrived at college, nothing ever interrupted my studies, except my ardent wish of studying without restraint. I never deserved to be chastised; but, in spite of my usual gentleness, it would have been dangerous to have attempted to do so; and I recollect with pleasure that, when I was to describe in rhetoric a perfect courser, I sacrificed the hope of obtaining a premium, and described the one who, on perceiving the whip, threw down his rider. Repub-

of his regiments of cavalry to the cousin. Madame de Montboissier thinks this is asking too much, and told M. le Marquis de Canillic that, in truth, if he were so difficult, her husband would no longer take any part in his affairs; this offended him, and some high words passed on both sides. The nephew does not care much about the marriage. He said, there were in his own province far better matches, which he named, that would not be refused him.

"I thought I had written you word that the Cardinal de La Roche-Aimon was abbé de St. Germain. It is said that M. de Briges has the barony de Mercœur. M. de la Vauguyon has died, little regretted either by the court or by the town. The ball of last Thursday is put off to the 15th, that is to say, for a week hence. I dined, the day before yesterday, Thursday, with M. de la Tour d'Auvergne, who is on a complimentary footing with M. de Turenne, now Duke de Bouillon. He told us he should lose perhaps a million from politeness. You will recognise him by that phrase.

"Adieu, dear cousin; my respects, if you please, to all the family; M. de Fayon presents his to you, and I remain your obedient servant,

"LAFAYETTE."

lican anecdotes always delighted me, and when my new connexions wished to obtain for me a place at court, I did not hesitate displeasing them to preserve my independence.* I was in that frame of mind when I first learnt the troubles in America; they only became thoroughly known in Europe in 1776, and the memorable declaration of the 4th of July reached France at the close of that same year.

After having crowned herself with laurels and enriched herself with conquests; after having become mistress of all seas; and after having insulted all nations, England had turned her pride against her own colonies. North America had long been displeasing to her; she wished to add new vexations to former injuries, and to destroy the most sacred privileges. The Americans, attached to the mother country, contented themselves at first with merely uttering complaints; they only accused the ministry, and the whole nation rose up against them; they were termed insolent and rebellious, and at length declared the enemies of their country: thus did the obstinacy of the king, the violence of the ministers, and the arrogance of the English nation, oblige thirteen of their colonies to render themselves independent. Such a glorious cause had never before attracted the attention of mankind; it was the last struggle of Liberty; and had she then been vanquished, neither hope nor asylum would have remained for

* A place in the household of a prince of royal blood. The Marshal de Noailles wished for this arrangement. To prevent it without openly opposing the will of those he loved, M. de Lafayette took an opportunity of displeasing, by a few words, the prince, to whose person they were desirous of attaching him, and all negotiations on the subject were thus broken off. We do not believe that since that period a reconciliation has ever taken place between him and Louis XVIII.

her. The oppressors and oppressed were to receive a powerful lesson; the great work was to be accomplished, or the rights of humanity were to fall beneath its ruin. The destiny of France and that of her rival were to be decided at the same moment; England was to lose, with the new states, an important commerce, of which she derived the sole advantage,—one quarter of her subjects, who were constantly augmenting by a rapid increase of population, and by emigration from all parts of Europe,—in a word, more than half of the most beautiful portion of the British territory. But if she retained possession of her thirteen colonies, all was ended for our West Indies, our possessions in Asia and Africa, our maritime commerce, and consequently our navy and our political existence.

(1776.) When I first learnt the subject of this quarrel, my heart espoused warmly the cause of liberty, and I thought of nothing but of adding also the aid of my banner. * Some circum-

* In 1828, Mr. Jared Sparks, a distinguished American author, intending to form a collection of the writings of Washington, which he is at present publishing at Boston, made a voyage to France to converse with M. de Lafayette, and consult the archives of foreign affairs. He obtained from the general many anecdotes, letters, and documents, of which extracts have enriched his publication. At the close of vol. v., he has placed an appendix, containing the account of the departure of M. de Lafayette from France, and his arrival in America. We doubt not but that the details of that narration were related, nay, perhaps even written, by the general himself. We shall therefore quote some extracts from it without hesitation, which, placed as notes, will completely elucidate the text of these memoirs.

"In the summer of 1776," says Mr. Sparks, "M. de Lafayette was stationed on military duty at Metz, being then an officer in the French army. It happened at this time that the Duke of Gloucester, brother to the King of England, was at stances, which it would be needless to relate, had taught me to expect only obstacles in this case from my own family; I depended, therefore, solely upon myself, and I ventured to adopt for a device on my arms these words—"*Cur non?*" that they might equally serve as an encouragement to myself, and as a reply to others. Silas Deane was then at Paris; but the ministers feared to receive him, and his voice was overpowered by the louder accents of Lord Stormont. He despatched privately to America some old arms, which were of little use, and some young officers, who did but little good, the whole directed by M. de Beaumarchais; and when the English ambassador spoke to our court, it denied having sent any cargoes, ordered those that were preparing to be discharged, and dismissed from our ports all American privateers. Whilst wishing to address myself in a direct manner to Mr. Deane, I became the friend of

Metz, and a dinner was given to him by the commandant of that place. Several officers were invited, and among others Lafayette. Despatches had just been received by the duke from England, and he made their contents the topic of conversation; they related to American affairs, the recent declaration of independence, the resistance of the colonists, and the strong measures adopted by the ministry to crush the rebellion.

"The details were new to Lafayette; he listened with eagerness to the conversation, and prolonged it by asking questions of the duke. His curiosity was deeply excited by what he heard, and the idea of a people fighting for liberty had a strong influence upon his imagination; the cause seemed to him just and noble, from the representations of the duke himself; and before he left the table, the thought came into his head that he would go to America, and offer his services to a people who were struggling for freedom and independence. From that hour he could think of nothing but this chivalrous enterprise. He resolved to return to Paris and make further inquiries.

"When he arrived in that city, he confided his scheme to two

Kalb, a German in our employ, who was applying for service with the *insurgents*, (the expression in use at that time,) and who became my interpreter. He was the person sent by M. de Choiseul to examine the English colonies; and on his return he received some money, but never succeeded in obtaining an audience, so little did that minister in reality think of the revolution whose retrograde movements some persons have inscribed to him! When I presented to Mr. Deane my boyish face, (for I was scarcely nineteen years of age,) I spoke more of my ardour in the cause than of my experience; but I dwelt much upon the effect my departure would excite in France, and he signed our mutual agreement. The secrecy with which this negotiation and my preparations were made appears almost a miracle; family, friends, ministers, French spies and English spies, all were kept completely in the dark as to my intentions. Amongst

young friends, Count Segur and Viscount de Noailles, and proposed that they should join him. They entered with enthusiasm into his views; but as they were dependent on their families, it was necessary to consult their parents, who reprobated the plan and refused their consent. The young men faithfully kept Lafayette's secret: his situation was more fortunate, as his property was at his own disposal, and he possessed an annual revenue of nearly two hundred thousand livres.

"He next explained his intentions to the Count de Broglie, who told him that his project was so chimerical, and fraught with so many hazards, without a prospect of the least advantage, that he could not for a moment regard it with favor, nor encourage him with any advice which should prevent him from abandoning it immediately. When Lafayette found him thus determined, he requested that at least he would not betray him, for he was resolved to go to America. The Count de Broglie assured him that his confidence was not misplaced; 'But,' said he, 'I have seen your uncle die in the wars of Italy; I witnessed your father's death at the battle of Minden; and I will my discreet confidants, I owe much to M. du Boismartin,* secretary of the Count de Broglie, and to the Count de Broglie himself, whose affectionate heart, when all his efforts to turn me from this project had proved in vain, entered into my views with even paternal tenderness.

Preparations were making to send a vessel to America, when very bad tidings arrived from thence. New York, Long Island, White Plains, Fort Washington, and the Jerseys, had seen the American forces successively destroyed by thirty-three thousand Englishmen or Germans. Three thousand Americans alone remained in arms, and these were closely pursued by General Howe. From that moment all the credit of the insurgents vanished; to obtain a vessel for them was impossible: the envoys themselves thought it right to express to me their own discouragement, and persuade me to abandon my project. I called upon Mr. Deane, and I thanked him for his frankness. "Until now, sir," said I, "you have only seen my ardour in your cause, and that may not prove at present wholly useless. I shall purchase a ship to carry out your officers; we must feel confidence in the future, and it is especially in the hour of

not be accessary to the ruin of the only remaining branch of the family.' He then used all his powers of argument and persuasion to divert Lafayette from his purpose, but in vain. Finding his determination unalterable, the Count de Broglie said, as he could render him no aid, he would introduce him to the Baron de Kalb, who he knew was seeking an opportunity to go to America, and whose experience and counsels might be valuable.—(The Writings of George Washington, vol. v. Appendix, No. 1, p. 445.)

* M. du Boismartin was the person sent to Bourdeaux to secure the purchase and equipment of the ship that M. de Lafayette intended for the United States.—(Sparks, loc. cit.)

danger that I wish to share your fortune."* My project was received with approbation; but it was necessary afterwards to find money, and to purchase and arm a vessel secretly: all this was accomplished with the greatest despatch.

The period was, however, approaching, which had been long fixed for my taking a journey to England;† I could not refuse to go without risking the discovery of my secret, and by consenting to take this journey I knew I could better conceal my preparations for a greater one. This last measure was also thought most expedient by MM. Franklin and Deane; for the doctor himself was then in France; and although I did not venture to go to his home, for fear of being seen, I corresponded with him through M. Carmichael, an American less generally known. I arrived in London with M. de Poix; and I first paid my respects to Bancroft, the American, and afterwards to his British Majesty. A youth of nineteen may be, perhaps, too fond of playing a trick upon the king he is going to fight with,—of dancing at the house of Lord Germain, minister for the English colonies, and at the house of Lord Rawdon, who had just returned from New York,—and of seeing at the opera that Clinton whom he was afterwards to meet at Monmouth. But whilst I concealed my intentions, I openly

* It is a singular coincidence that, at the same time that General Washington, who had never left America, reduced to a corps of two thousand men, did not despair of the common cause, the same sentiment was animating, two thousand leagues from thence, the breast of a youth of nineteen, who was destined to become one day his intimate friend, partake with him the vicissitudes and happy termination of that revolution, and afterwards carry back to another hemisphere the principles of liberty and equality which formed its basis.

† With the Prince de Poix. This journey lasted three weeks.

avowed my sentiments; I often defended the Americans; I rejoiced at their success at Trenton; and my spirit of opposition obtained for me an invitation to breakfast with Lord Shelbourne. I refused the offers made me to visit the sea ports, the vessels fitting out against the *rebels*, and everything that might be construed into an abuse of confidence. At the end of three weeks, when it became necessary for me to return home, whilst refusing my uncle,* the ambassador, to accompany him to court, I confided to him my strong desire to take a trip to Paris. He proposed saying that I was ill during my absence. I should not have made use of this stratagem myself, but I did not object to his doing so.

After having suffered dreadfully in the channel, and being reminded, as a consolation, how very short the voyage would be, I arrived at M. de Kalb's house in Paris, concealed myself three days at Chaillot, saw a few of my friends and some Americans, and set out for Bordeaux, where I was for some time unexpectedly delayed.† I took advantage of that delay to send to Paris, from whence the intelligence I received was by no means encouraging; but as my messenger was followed on his

* The Marquis de Noailles, brother to the Duke d'Aven, and uncle to Madame de Lafayette.

† M. de Lafayette learnt, at Bordeaux, that his intended departure was known at Versailles, and that the order to prevent it had been already issued. After having taken his ship to the port of the Passage, he returned himself to Bordeaux, and wrote to the ministers, to his family and friends. Amongst the latter was M. de Coigny, to whom he sent a confidential person, and who bade him entertain no hopes of obtaining the permission he wished for. Pretending to repair to Marseilles, where he had received an order to join his father-in-law, who was going into Italy, he set off in a postchaise with an officer named Mauroy, who was desirous of going to America. Some leagues

road by one from the government, I lost not a moment in setting sail, and the orders of my sovereign were only able to overtake me at Passage, a Spanish port, at which we stopped on our way. The letters from my own family were extremely violent, and those from the government were peremptory. I was forbidden to proceed to the American continent under the penalty of disobedience; I was enjoined to repair instantly to Marseilles, and await there further orders. A sufficient number of commentaries were not wanting upon the consequences of such an anathema, the laws of the state, and the power and displeasure of the government: but the grief of his wife, who was pregnant, and the thoughts of his family and friends, had far more effect upon M. de Lafayette.* As his vessel could no longer be stopped, he returned to Bordeaux to enter into a justification of his own conduct; and, in a declaration to M. de Fumel, he took upon himself all the consequences of his present evasion. As the court did not deign to relax in its determination, he wrote to M. de Maurepas that that silence was a tacit consent, and his own departure took place soon after that joking

from Bordeaux he got on horseback, disguised as a courier, and rode on before the carriage, which took the road to Bayonne. They remained two or three hours in that town, and whilst Mauroy was arranging some necessary affairs, M. de Lafayette remained lying on some straw in the stable. It was the postmaster's daughter who recognised the pretended courier at Saint Jean de Luz, from having seen him when returning from the Passage harbour to Bordeaux. (Sparks, loc. cit.)

* These memoirs, written until now in the first person, change here to the third person, in spite of the kind of engagement taken in the first page to continue them in the former manner. We are ignorant of the cause of the inconsistency thus offered by the manuscript, which is, however, completely written in the general's own hand.

despatch. After having set out on the road to Marseilles, he retraced his steps, and, disguised as a courier, he had almost escaped all danger, when, at Saint Jean de Luz, a young girl recognised him; but a sign from him silenced her, and her adroit fidelity turned away all suspicion. It was thus that M. de Lafayette rejoined his ship, the 26th of April 1777; and on that same day, after six months anxiety and labour, he set sail for the American continent.*

(1777.) As soon as M. de Lafayette had recovered from the effects of sea sickness, he studied the language and trade he was adopting. A heavy ship, two bad cannons, and some guns, could not have escaped from the smallest privateer. In his present situation, he resolved rather to blow up the vessel than to surrender; he concerted measures to achieve this end with a brave Dutchman named Bedaulx, whose sole alternative, if taken, would have been the gibbet. The captain insisted upon stopping at the islands; but government orders would have been found there, and he followed a direct course, less from choice than from compulsion.† At forty leagues from shore, they were met by a small vessel: the captain turned

* See, at the end of these memoirs, amongst the various fragments, fragment A.

† The court of France despatched orders to the Leeward and Windward Islands to stop him on his road, because the ship, not being able to take out papers for North America, was to have stopped in the Spanish islands. (Manuscript No. 1.) Mr. Sparks relates that M. de Lafayette declared to the captain that the ship belonged to him, and that if he offered the slightest resistance, he would take from him the command and give it to the mate. But as he soon discovered that the real motive of the captain's resistance was a cargo belonging to him of 8000 dollars, M. de Lafayette secured to him its full value upon his own private fortune, and thus succeeded in overcoming all his scruples. (Washington's writings, loc. cit.)

pale, but the crew were attached to M. de Lafayette, and the officers were numerous : they made a show of resistance. It turned out, fortunately, to be an American ship, whom they vainly endeavoured to keep up with ; but scarcely had the former lost sight of M. de Lafayette's vessel, when it fell in with two English frigates,—and this is not the only time when the elements seemed bent on opposing M. de Lafayette, as if with the intention of saving him. After having encountered for seven weeks various perils and chances, he arrived at Georgetown, in Carolina. Ascending the river in a canoe, his foot touched at length the American soil, and he swore that he would conquer or perish in that cause. Landing at midnight at Major Huger's house,* he found a vessel sailing for France, which appeared only waiting for his letters. Several of the officers landed, others remained on board, and all hastened to proceed to Charlestown.

This beautiful city is worthy of its inhabitants, and everything there announced not only comfort but even luxury. Without knowing much of M. de Lafayette, the generals Howe,† Moultrie, and

* When they landed, says Mr. Sparks, a distant light served to guide them. As they approached the house from whence it issued, the dogs barked, and the people took them for a band of marauders landing from an enemy's ship. They were asked who they were, and what they wanted. Baron Kalb replied, and all suspicions vanished. The next morning the weather was beautiful. The novelty of all that surrounded him,—the room, the bed covered with mosquito nets, the black servants who came to ask his commands, the beauty and foreign aspect of the country which he beheld from his windows, and which was covered by a rich vegetation,—all united to produce on M. de Lafayette a magical effect, and excite in him a variety of inexpressible sensations. (Sparks, appendix.)

† An American, who must not be confounded with the two brothers of that name who commanded the one the English army, the other the English fleet.

Gulden, received him with the utmost kindness and attention. The new works were shewn him, and also that battery which Moultrie afterwards defended so extremely well, and which the English appear, we must acknowledge, to have seized the only possible means of destroying. Several adventurers, the refuse of the islands, endeavoured vainly to unite themselves to M. de Lafayette, and to infuse into his mind their own feelings and prejudices. Having procured horses, he set out with six officers for Philadelphia. His vessel had arrived, but it was no longer protected by fortune, and on its return home it was lost on the bar of Charlestown. To repair to the congress of the United States, M. de Lafayette rode nearly nine hundred miles on horseback; before reaching the capital of Pennsylvania, he was obliged to travel through the two Carolinas, Virginia, Maryland, and Delaware. Whilst studying the language and customs of the inhabitants, he observed also new productions of nature, and new methods of cultivation: vast forests and immense rivers combine to give to that country an appearance of youth and majesty. After a fatiguing journey of one month, he beheld at length that Philadelphia, so well known in the present day, and whose future grandeur Penn appeared to designate when he laid the first stone of its foundation.

After having accomplished his noble manœuvres at Trenton and Princetown, General Washington had remained in his camp at Middlebrook. The English, finding themselves frustrated in their first hopes, combined to make a decisive campaign. Burgoyne was already advancing with ten thousand men, preceded by his proclamations and his savages. Ticonderoga, a famous stand of arms, was abandoned by Saint-Clair; he drew upon himself much public odium by this deed, but he saved the only corps whom the militia could rally round. Whilst the generals were busied assembling that militia, the congress recalled them, sent Gates in their place, and used all possible means to support him. At that same time the great English army, of about eighteen thousand men, had sailed from New York, and the two Howes were uniting their forces for a secret enterprise; Rhode Island was occupied by an hostile corps, and General Clinton, who had remained at New York, was there preparing for an expedition. To be able to withstand so many various blows, General Washington, leaving Putnam on the north river, crossed over the Delaware, and encamped, with eleven thousand men, within reach of Philadelphia.

It was under these circumstances that M. de Lafayette first arrived in America; but the moment, although important to the common cause, was peculiarly unfavourable to strangers. The Americans were displeased with the pretensions, and disgusted with the conduct, of many Frenchmen; the imprudent selections they had in some cases made, the extreme boldness of some foreign adventurers, the jealousy of the army, and strong national prejudices, all contributed to confound disinterested zeal with private ambition, and talents with quackery. Supported by the promises which had been given by Mr. Deane, a numerous band of foreigners besieged the congress; their chief was a clever but very imprudent man, and although a good officer, his excessive vanity amounted almost to madness. With M. de Lafayette, Mr. Deane had sent out a fresh detachment, and every day such crowds arrived, that the congress had finally adopted the plan of not listening to any stranger. The coldness with which M. de Lafayette was received, might have been taken as a dismissal; but, without appearing disconcerted by the manner in which the deputies addressed him,* he entreated them to return to congress, and read the following note:—

"After the sacrifices I have made, I have the right to exact two favours: one is, to serve at my own expense,—the other is, to serve at first as volunteer."

This style, to which they were so little accustomed, awakened their attention; the despatches from the envoys were read over, and, in a very flattering resolution, the rank of major-general was granted to M. de Lafayette. Amongst the various officers who accompanied him, several were strangers to him; he was interested, however, for them all, and to those whose services were not accepted an indemnity for their trouble was granted. Some months afterwards, M. —— drowned himself in

* When he arrived at Philadelphia, M. de Lafayette delivered his letters to Mr. Lovell, president of the committee for foreign affairs. The next day he proceeded to congress: Mr. Lovell came out of the meeting, and told him there was but little hope of his request being acceded to. Suspecting that his letters had not been read, M. de Lafayette wrote the note which will be found in the text. The resolution of the congress concerning him, deliberated the 31st of July, is expressed in the following manner: "Seeing that the Marquis de Lafayette, on account of his great zeal in the cause of liberty in which the United States are engaged, has quitted his family and country, and has come to offer his services to the United States, without demanding either pay or private indemnity, and that he desires to expose his life in our cause,—resolved, that his services be accepted, and that, on account of his zeal, illustrious family and connexions, he shall have the rank and commission of major-general in the army of the United States." The real

the Schuylkill, and the loss of that impetuous and imprudent man was perhaps a fortunate circumstance.

The two Howes having appeared before the capes of the Delaware, General Washington came to Philadelphia, and M. de Lafayette beheld for the first time that great man.* Although he was surrounded by officers and citizens, it was impossible to mistake for a moment his majestic figure and deportment; nor was he less distinguished by the noble affability of his manner. M. de Lafayette accompanied him in his examination of the fortifications. Invited by the General to establish himself in his house, he looked upon it from that moment as his own: with this perfect ease and simplicity was formed the tie that united two friends, whose confidence and attachment were to be cemented by the strongest interests of humanity.†

The American army, stationed some miles from Philadelphia, was waiting until the movements of the hostile army should be decided: the General

intention of this resolution was to give a rank to M. de Lafayette, and to leave to General Washington the right and care of confiding to him a command in unison with that rank. (Letters of Washington, 2nd part. V, p. 10, 35, and 128, and appendix No. I.)

* He was presented, for the first time, to Washington, says Mr. Sparks, at a dinner, at which several members of congress were present. When they were separating, Washington drew Lafayette aside, expressed much kindness for him, complimented him upon his zeal and his sacrifices, and invited him to consider the head quarters as his own house, adding, with a smile, that he could not promise him the luxuries of a court, but that, as he was become an American soldier, he would doubtless submit cheerfully to the customs and privations of a republican army. The next day Washington visited the forts of the Delaware, and invited Lafayette to accompany him. (Sparks, ibid.)

† See fragment B.

himself reviewed the troops ; M. de Lafayette arrived there the same day. About eleven thousand men, ill armed, and still worse clothed, presented a strange spectacle to the eye of the young Frenchman : their clothes were parti-coloured, and many of them were almost naked ; the best clad wore *hunting shirts*, large grey linen coats which were much used in Carolina. As to their military tactics, it will be sufficient to say that, for a regiment ranged in order of battle to move forward on the right of its line, it was necessary for the left to make a continued counter march. They were always arranged in two lines, the smallest men in the first line ; no other distinction as to height was ever observed. In spite of these disadvantages, the soldiers were fine, and the officers zealous ; virtue stood in place of science, and each day added both to experience and discipline. Lord Stirling, more courageous than judicious, another general, who was often intoxicated, and Greene, whose talents were only then known to his immediate friends, commanded as majors-general. General Knox, who had changed the profession of bookseller to that of artillery officer, was there also, and had himself formed other officers, and created an artillery. "We must feel embarrassed," said General Washington, on his arrival, "to exhibit ourselves before an officer who has just quitted French troops." "It is to learn, and not to teach, that I come hither," replied M. de Lafayette ; and that modest tone, which was not common in Europeans, produced a very good effect.

After having menaced the Delaware, the English fleet again disappeared, and during some days the Americans amused themselves by making jokes at its expense. These jokes, however, ceased when it reappeared in the Chesapeak; and, in order to approach it more closely during the disembarkation, the patriot army crossed through the town. Their heads covered with green branches, and marching to the sound of drums and fifes, these soldiers, in spite of their state of nudity, offered an agreeable spectacle to the eyes of all the citizens. General Washington was marching at their head, and M. de Lafayette was by his side. The army stationed itself upon the heights of Wilmington, and that of the enemy landed in the Elk river, at the bottom of Chesapeak bay. The very day they landed, General Washington exposed himself to danger in the most imprudent manner; after having reconnoitred for a long time the enemy's position, he was overtaken by a storm during a very dark night, entered a farm house close to the hostile army, and, from a reluctance to change his own opinion, remained there with General Greene, M. de Lafayette, and their aide-de-camp; but when at day break he quitted the farm, he acknowledged that any one traitor might have caused his ruin. Some days later, Sullivan's division joined the army, which augmented it in all to thirteen thousand men. This Major-General Sullivan made a good beginning, but a bad ending, in an intended surprise on Staten Island.

If, by making too extensive a plan of attack, the English committed a great error, it must also be acknowledged that the Americans were not irreproachable in their manner of defence. Burgoyne, leading his army, with their heads bent upon the ground, into woods from whence he could not extricate them, dragged on, upon a single road, his numerous cannons and rich military equipages. Certain of not being attacked from behind, the Americans could dispute every step they took: this kind of warfare attracted the militia, and Gates improved each day in strength. Every tree sheltered a skilful rifleman, and the resources offered by military tactics, and the talents even of their chiefs, had become useless to the English. The corps left in New York could, it is true, laugh at the corps of Putnam, but it was too feeble to succour Burgoyne; and instead of being able to secure his triumph, its own fate was even dependent upon his. During that time, Howe was only thinking of Philadelphia, and it was at the expense of the northern expedition that he was repairing thither by an enormous circuit. But, on the other side, why were the English permitted to land so tranquilly? Why was the moment allowed to pass when their army was divided by the river Elk? Why in the south were so many false movements and so much hesitation displayed? Because the Americans had hitherto had combats but not battles; because, instead of harassing an army and disputing hollows, they were obliged to protect an open city, and manœuvre in a plain, close to an hostile army, who, by attacking them from behind, might completely ruin them. General Washington, had he followed the advice of the people, would have enclosed his army in a city, and thus have entrusted to one hazard the fate of America; but, whilst refusing to commit such an act of folly, he was obliged to make some sacrifice, and gratify the nation by a battle. Europe even expected it; and although he had been created a dictator for six months, the General thought he ought to submit everything to the orders of congress, and to the deliberations of a council of war.

After having advanced as far as Wilmington, the general had detached a thousand men under Maxwell, the most ancient brigadier in the army. At the first march of the English, he was beaten by their advance guard near Christiana Bridge. During that time the army took but an indifferent station at Newport; they then removed a little south, waited two days for the enemy, and, at the moment when these were marching upon their right wing, a nocturnal council of war decided that the army was to proceed to the Brandywine. The stream, bearing that name covered its front; the ford called Chad's Ford, placed nearly in the centre, was defended by batteries. It was in that hardly examined station that, in obedience to a letter from congress, the Americans awaited the battle. The evening of the 10th of September, Howe advanced in two columns, and, by a very fine movement, the left column (about 8000 men under Lord Cornwallis, with the grenadiers and guards) directed themselves towards the fords of Birmingham, three miles on our right; the other column continued its road, and about nine o'clock in the morning it appeared on the other side of the stream. The enemy was so near the skirts of the wood that it was impossible to judge of his force; some time was lost in a mutual cannonading. General Washington walked along his two lines, and was received with acclamations which seemed to promise him success. The intelligence that was received of the movements of Cornwallis was both confused and contradictory; owing to the conformity of name betwixt two roads that were of equal length and parallel to each other, the best officers were mistaken in their reports. The only musket shots that had been fired were from Maxwell, who killed several of the enemy, but was driven back upon the left of the American army, across a ford by which he had before advanced. Three thousand militia had been added to the army, but they were placed in the rear to guard some still more distant militia, and took no part themselves in the action. Such was the situation of the troops when they learnt the march of Lord Cornwallis towards the scarcely known fords of Birmingham: they then detached three divisions, forming about five thousand men, under the generals Sullivan, Stirling, and Stephen. M. de Lafayette, as volunteer, had always accompanied the general. The left wing remaining in a state of tranquillity, and the right appearing fated to receive all the heavy blows, he obtained permission to join Sullivan. At his arrival, which seemed to inspirit the troops, he found that, the enemy having crossed the ford, the corps of Sullivan had scarcely had time to form itself on a line in front of a thinly-wooded forest. A few moments after, Lord Cornwallis formed in the finest order: advancing across the plain, his first line opened a brisk fire of musketry and artillery; the Americans returned the fire, and did much injury to the enemy; but their right and left wings having given way, the generals and several officers joined the central division, in which were M. de Lafayette and Stirling, and of which eight hundred men were commanded in a most brilliant manner by Conway, an Irishman, in the service of France. By separating that division from its two wings, and advancing through an open plain, in which they lost many men, the enemy united all his fire upon the centre: the confusion became extreme; and it was whilst M. de Lafayette was rallying the troops that a ball passed through his leg;—at that moment all those remaining on the field gave way. M. de Lafayette was indebted to Gimat, his aide-de-camp, for the happiness of getting upon his horse. General Washington arrived from a distance with fresh troops ; M. de Lafayette was preparing to join him, when loss of blood obliged him to stop and have his wound bandaged ; he was even very near being taken. Fugitives, cannon, and baggage now crowded without order into the road leading to Chester. The general employed the remaining daylight in checking the enemy: some regiments behaved extremely well, but the disorder was complete. During that time the ford of Chad was forced, the cannon taken, and the Chester road became the common retreat of the whole army. In the midst of that dreadful confusion, and during the darkness of the night, it was impossible to recover ; but at Chester, twelve miles from the field of battle, they met with a bridge which it was necessary to cross ; M. de Lafayette occupied himself in arresting the fugitives ; some degree of order was re-established ; the generals and the commander-in-chief arrived; and he had leisure to have his wound dressed.

It was thus, at twenty-six miles from Philadelphia, that the fate of that town was decided, (11th September, 1777.) The inhabitants had heard every cannon that was fired there ; the two parties, assembled in two distinct bands in all the squares and public places, had awaited the event in silence. The last courier at length arrived, and the friends of liberty were thrown into consternation. The Americans had lost from 1000 to 1200 men. Howe's army was composed of about 12,000 men ; their losses had been so considerable that their surgeons, and those in the country, were found insufficient, and they requested the American army to supply them with some for their prisoners. If the enemy had marched to Derby, the army would have been cut up and destroyed: they lost an all-important night;

and this was perhaps their greatest fault, during a war in which they committed so many errors.

M. de Lafayette, having been conveyed by water to Philadelphia, was carefully attended to by the citizens, who were all interested in his situation and extreme youth. That same evening the congress determined to quit the city: a vast number of the inhabitants deserted their own hearths—whole families, abandoning their possessions, and uncertain of the future, took refuge in the mountains. M. de Lafayette was carried to Bristol in a boat; he there saw the fugitive congress, who only assembled again on the other side of the Susquehannah; he was himself conducted to Bethlehem, a Moravian establishment, where the mild religion of the brotherhood, the community of fortune, education, and interests, amongst that large and simple family, formed a striking contrast to scenes of blood, and the convulsions occasioned by a civil war.

After the Brandywine defeat, the two armies manœuvered along the banks of the Schuylkill. General Washington still remained on a height above the enemy, and completely out of his reach; nor had they again an opportunity of cutting him off. Waine, an American brigadier, was detached to observe the English; but, being surprised during the night, near the White-Horse, by General Grey, he lost there the greatest part of his corps. At length Howe crossed the Schuylkill at Swede's Ford, and Lord Cornwallis entered Philadelphia.

In spite of the declaration of independence of the New States, everything there bore the appearance of a civil war. The names of Whig and Tory distinguished the republicans and royalists; the English army was still called the *regular troops;* the British sovereign was always designated by the name of *the king*. Provinces, towns, and families were divided by the violence of party spirit: brothers, officers in the two opposing armies, meeting by chance in their father's house, have seized their arms to fight with each other. Whilst, in all the rancour of their pride, the English committed horrible acts of licence and cruelty,—whilst discipline dragged in her train those venal Germans who knew only how to kill, burn, and pillage,—in that same army were seen regiments of Americans, who, trampling under foot their brethren, assisted in enslaving their wasted country. Each canton contained a still greater number whose sole object was to injure the friends of liberty, and give information to those of despotism. To these inveterate Tories must be added the number of those whom fear, private interest, or religion, rendered adverse to the war. If the Presbyterians, the children of Cromwell and Fairfax, detested royalty, the Lutherans, who had sprung from it, were divided among themselves: the Quakers hated slaughter, but served willingly as guides to the royal troops. Insurrections were by no means uncommon: near the enemy's stations, farmers often shot each other; robbers were even encouraged. The republican chiefs were exposed to great dangers when they travelled through the country; it was always necessary for them to declare that they should pass the night in one house, then take possession of another, barricade themselves in it, and only sleep with their arms by their side. In the midst of these troubles, M. de Lafayette was no longer considered as a stranger; never was any adoption more complete than his own: and whilst, in the councils of war, he trembled when he considered that his voice (at twenty years of age) might decide the fate of two worlds, he was also initiated in those deliberations in which, by reassuring the Whigs, intimidating the Tories, supporting an ideal money, and redoubling their firmness in the hour of adversity, the American chiefs conducted that revolution through so many obstacles.

Confined to his bed for six weeks, M. de Lafayette suffered from his wound, but still more severely from his inactivity. The good Moravian brothers loved him, and deplored his warlike folly. Whilst listening to their sermons, he planned setting Europe and Asia in a flame. As he was no longer able to do anything but write, he wrote to the commander of la Martinique, and proposed to him to make a descent upon the English islands under American colours. He wrote also to M. de Maurepas, and offered to conduct some Americans to the Isle of France, concerting previously with individuals an attack upon the English factories.* From the particulars which have since become known, that project in India would have succeeded; but it was rejected at Versailles, where no answers were yet vouchsafed to M. de Lafayette's letters. Bouillé, more ardent in temper, would have adopted the whole plan, but he could not act without permission;

* From Bethlehem he wrote to M. de Bouillé, governor of the Windward Islands, to propose to him to attack the English islands under American colours. That general approved of the project, and forwarded it to the court, who would not, however, accept it. At the same period, M. de Lafayette, although in disgrace himself at court, wrote to the Count de Maurepas, to propose to him a still more important enterprise against the English factories; but also under American colours. The old minister, from prudential motives, did not adopt this project, but he spoke publicly in praise of it, and expressed, ever after, a great partiality for Lafayette. "He will end, one day," said he, smiling, "by unfurnishing the palace of Versailles to serve the American cause; for when he has taken anything into his head, it is impossible to resist him."—(Note by M. de Lafayette.)

and these delays led to the period of the war which M. de Lafayette was so desirous of bringing on.

During his residence at Bethlehem, the English entrenched themselves at Philadelphia. The two rivers which encompassed the town were united by a chain of wooden palisades and good redoubts, partly covered by an inundation. A portion of their army was encamped at Germantown, five miles in advance of those lines; these were attacked, the 4th of October, by Washington, and although his left column was retarded by an absurd precedence of divisions, and misled by a thick fog,—although the advance guard of the right, under Conway, attacked in front what it ought to have attacked in flank, the enemy was not less taken by surprise and beaten; and the general, with his victorious wing, passed through the whole extent of the enemy's encampment. All things went on well until then; but a false movement of the left column, and still more the attack of a stone house which they should have turned, gave the enemy time to rally. Howe was thinking of a retreat, but Cornwallis arrived in haste with a reinforcement. The Americans repassed through the English encampment, and the action ended by a complete defeat. Many men were lost on both sides. General Agnew, an Englishman, and General Nash, an American, were killed. The Americans had some dragoons under Pulaski, the only one of the confederated Poles who had refused to accept a pardon. He was an intrepid knight, a libertine and devotee, and a better captain than general; he insisted on being a Pole on all occasions, and M. de Lafayette, after having contributed to his reception in the army, often exerted himself to effect a reconciliation betwixt him and the other officers.

Without waiting for his wound to be closed, M. de Lafayette returned to head-quarters, twenty-five miles from Philadelphia. The enemy, who had fallen back upon their lines, attacked Fort Mifflin, upon an island, and Fort Red-Bank, on the left side of the Delaware. Some *chevaux de frise*, protected by the forts, and some galleys, stopped the fleet, magazines, and detachments which had been sent from the Chesapeak. Amongst the skirmishes which took place betwixt small parties of soldiers, the most remarkable one was the surprise of a corps of militia at Cevoked-Billet,* in which the English burnt their wounded prisoners in a barn. Such was the situation of the south, when news was received of the capitulation of Burgoyne. That general, when he quitted Canada, had made a diversion on his right; but Saint Leger had failed in an operation against Fort Schuyler; and he himself, by advancing towards Albany, appeared to have lost much time. Gates was constantly adding numerous militia to his continental troops. All the citizens being armed militia, a signal of alarm assembled them, or an order of state summoned them to march. But if that crusade was rather a voluntary one, their residence at the camp was still more dependent on their own inclination: the discipline was suitable to the formation of the corps. The continentalists, on the contrary, belonged to the thirteen states, of which each one supplied some regiments; the soldiers were either engaged for the war or for three years, which improper alternative was occasioned by republican jealousy. These regular troops had military regulations, a severe discipline, and the officers of each state vied

* **This name is very illegible in the manuscript.**

with each other for promotion. Gates, placed in an entrenched position, in the centre of woods, on the road to Albany, and with the North river on his right, had assembled sixteen thousand men; and this invasion of the enemy, by threatening New England, had served as an instant summons to her brave militia. They had already proved their strength at Bennington, where Stark had surrounded and destroyed a detachment belonging to Burgoyne. The enemy, having arrived within three miles of Gates, and not being able to make a circuit round him without abandoning their cannon and military accoutrements, attempted twice to force him; but they had scarcely commenced their march when Arnold fell upon them with his division, and in those woods, lined with sharpshooters, it was only possible for them to reach the entrenchments. Arnold had his leg broken at the second affair; Lincoln, the other major-general, was wounded also. Four thousand men, who embarked at New York, had, it is true, ascended the Hudson. Whilst Vaughan was needlessly burning Esopus, Clinton had taken all the forts that defended the river. They were but little annoyed by Putnam, who, in the first breaking out of the troubles, had thrown aside his plough to bear to the army far more zeal than talent. But still that diversion was too weak; and by a note which a spy who had been taken swallowed, but which was recovered by an emetic, it was seen that Clinton was aware of his own weakness. Burgoyne, abandoned by the savages, regretting his best soldiers, and Frazer his best general, reduced to five thousand men, who were in want of provisions, wished to retreat; but it was then too late: his communications were no longer open; and it was at Saratoga, some miles in the rear of his army, that he signed the celebrated convention. A brilliant troop, covered with gold, filed out with Burgoyne: they encountered Gates and his officers, all clothed in plain grey cloth.' After a frugal repast, the two generals beheld the conquered army filing out; and, as a member of parliament said, "*five thousand men crossed the rebel country to take up their winter quarters near Boston.*" Clinton then redescended to New York, and the militia returned to their domestic hearths. Gates' chief merit consisted in his skilful choice of a position; Burgoyne's misfortune was owing to the nature of the country, which was impracticable and almost a desert. If the enemies of the former criticised the terms of the convention, M. de Lafayette loudly proclaimed how glorious he thought it; but he blamed Gates afterwards for rendering himself independent of his general, and for retaining the troops which he ought to have sent him. To obtain them, it was necessary to despatch Hamilton, a young man of great talents, whose counsels had justly acquired much credit.*

The forts of the Delaware had not yet yielded: that of Red-Bank, defended by four hundred men, was attacked, sword in hand, by sixteen hundred Hessians. The work having been reduced by Mauduit, a young Frenchman, the enemy engaged betwixt the old and new entrenchments. They were driven back with the loss of seven hundred men and Count Donop, their chief, whose last words were—"*I die the victim of my own ambition, and the avarice of my sovereign.*" That fort was commanded by an old and respected colonel, Greene,

* The celebrated Alexander Hamilton, one of the authors of the *Federalist*.

who, three years after, was massacred by the English, to whom he had surrendered, whilst, covering him with his own body, an old negro perished heroically by his side. Fort Mifflin, although attacked by land and water, did not defend itself less valiantly; the *Augusta*, an English ship of the line, had been already blown up; a frigate also perished; and Colonel Smith did not even think of surrendering: but the island being attacked from an unknown passage, the works were assaulted from the rear, and were obliged to be evacuated. Lord Cornwallis and five thousand men having fallen upon the Jerseys, it became also necessary to quit Red-Bank, which the Americans blew up before leaving it: General Greene, crossing the river at Trenton, opposed, with a precisely equal force, the detachment of Cornwallis.

Although M. de Lafayette's wound was not yet sufficiently closed for him to put on a boot, he accompanied Greene to Mount Holly; and detaching himself in order to reconnoitre, he found the enemy, November 25th, at Gloucester, opposite Philadelphia. The booty they had collected was crossing the river. To assure himself more fully on this point, M. de Lafayette advanced upon the strip of land called Sandy Point, and for this imprudence he would have paid dearly if those who had the power of killing him had not depended too much on those who had the power of taking him prisoner. After having succeeded in somewhat appeasing the terror of his guides, he found himself, about four o'clock, two miles from the English camp, before a post of four hundred Hessians with their cannon. Having only three hundred and fifty men, most of them militia, he suddenly attacked the enemy, who gave way before him. Lord Cornwallis came up with his grenadiers; but, supposing himself to be engaged with the corps of General Greene, he allowed himself to be driven back to the neighbourhood of Gloucester, with a loss of about sixty men. Greene arrived in the night, but would not attack the enemy. Lord Cornwallis passed over the river, and the American detachment rejoined the army at its station at Whitemarsh, twelve miles from Philadelphia. It had occupied, since the last month, some excellent heights; the general's accurate glance had discerned the situation of the encampment through an almost impenetrable wood.

The slight success of Gloucester gratified the army, and especially the militia. The congress resolved, that "it would be extremely agreeable to them to see the Marquis de Lafayette at the head of a division."* He quitted, therefore, his situation of volunteer, and succeeded Stephen in the command of the Virginians. The junction of Cornwallis having been the work of some hours, and that of Greene requiring several marches, it is difficult to imagine why Howe gave him time to arrive, and only proceeded with his army on the 5th of December to Chesnut Hill, three miles from Whitemarsh. After having felt his way with the right wing, of which he stood in some awe, he threatened to attack the extreme left; and that wing, following his own movements, stationed itself on the declivity of the heights. Some shots were exchanged betwixt the English light horsemen and the American riflemen, very skilful carabineers, who inhabit the frontiers of the savage tribes. Not being able to attack that position, and not wishing to make the circuit of it, Howe returned, on the fourth day, to Philadelphia. In

* Journal of Congress, 1st December, 1777.

spite of the northern reinforcements, the Americans were reduced to nine thousand, and the advanced season diminished their numbers rapidly. The protection of the country had cost the army dear. The 15th of December they marched towards Swedes' Ford, where Lord Cornwallis was accidentally foraging on the other side of the river. M. de Lafayette, being upon duty, was examining a position, when his escort and the enemy fired upon each other. The uncertainty being mutual, Lord Cornwallis and General Washington suspended their march; the former having retired during the night, the army crossed over the Schuylkill, and entrenched itself in the station of Valley-Forge, twenty-two miles from Philadelphia. Having skilfully erected there, in a few days, a city of wooden huts, the army established itself in its melancholy winter quarters. A small corps was detached to Wilmington, and fortified itself, under the command of Brigadier-General Smallwood.

Notwithstanding the success in the north, the situation of the Americans had never been more critical than at the present moment. A paper money, without any certain foundation, and unmixed with any specie, was both counterfeited by the enemy and discredited by their partizans. They feared to establish taxes, and had still less the power of levying them. The people, who had risen against the taxation of England, were astonished at paying still heavier taxes now; and the government was without any power to enforce them. On the other side, New York and Philadelphia were overstocked with gold and various merchandizes; the threatened penalty of death could not stop a communication that was but too easy. To refuse the payment of taxes, to depreciate the paper currency, and feed the enemy, was a certain method of attaining wealth; privations and misery were only experienced by good citizens. Each proclamation of the English was supported by their seductions, their riches, and the intrigues of the Tories. Whilst a numerous garrison lived sumptuously at New York, some hundreds of men, ill-clothed and ill-fed, wandered upon the shores of the Hudson. The army of Philadelphia, freshly recruited from Europe, abundantly supplied with everything they could require, consisted of eighteen thousand men: that of Valley-Forge was successively reduced to five thousand men; and two marches on the fine Lancaster road, (on which road also was a chain of magazines,) by establishing the English in the rear of their right flank, would have rendered their position untenable; from which, however, they had no means of retiring. The unfortunate soldiers were in want of everything; they had neither coats, hats, shirts, nor shoes; their feet and legs froze till they became black, and it was often necessary to amputate them. From want of money, they could neither obtain provisions nor any means of transport; the colonels were often reduced to two rations, and sometimes even to one. The army frequently remained whole days without provisions, and the patient endurance of both soldiers and officers was a miracle which each moment served to renew. But the sight of their misery prevented new engagements: it was almost impossible to levy recruits; it was easy to desert into the interior of the country. The sacred fire of liberty was not extinguished, it is true, and the majority of the citizens detested British tyranny; but the triumph of the north, and the tranquillity of the south, had lulled to sleep two-thirds of the continent. The remaining part was harassed by two armies; and, throughout this revolution, the greatest difficulty was, that, in order to conceal misfortunes from the enemy, it was necessary to conceal them from the nation also; that by awakening the one, information was likewise given to the other; and that fatal blows would have been struck upon the weakest points before democratic tardiness could have been roused to support them. It was from this cause that, during the whole war, the real force of the army was always kept a profound secret; even congress was not apprised of it, and the generals were often themselves deceived. General Washington never placed unlimited confidence in any person, except in M. de Lafayette; because for him alone, perhaps, confidence sprung from warm affection. As the situation grew more critical, discipline became more necessary. In the course of his nocturnal rounds, in the midst of heavy snows, M. de Lafayette was obliged to break some negligent officers. He adopted in every respect the American dress, habits, and food. He wished to be more simple, frugal, and austere than the Americans themselves. Brought up in the lap of luxury, he suddenly changed his whole manner of living, and his constitution bent itself to privation as well as to fatigue. He always took the liberty of freely writing his ideas to congress; or, in imitation of the prudence of the general, he gave his opinion to some members of a corps or state assembly, that, being adopted by them, it might be brought forward in the deliberations of congress.

In addition to the difficulties which lasted during the whole of the war, the winter of Valley-Forge recals others still more painful. At Yorktown, behind the Susquehannah, congress was divided into two factions, which, in spite of their distinction of south and east, did not the less occasion a separation between members of the same state. The deputies substituted their private intrigues for the wishes of the nation. Several impartial men had retired; several states had but one representative, and in some cases not even one. Party spirit was so strong, that three years afterwards congress still felt the effects of it. Any great event, however, would awaken their patriotism; and when Burgoyne declared that his treaty had been broken, means were found to stop the departure of his troops, which everything, even the few provisions for the transports, had foolishly betrayed. But all these divisions failed to produce the greatest of calamities—the loss of the only man capable of conducting the revolution.

Gates was at Yorktown, where he inspired respect by his manners, promises, and European acquirements. Amongst the deputies who united themselves to him, may be numbered the Lees, Virginians, enemies of Washington, and the two Adams. Mifflin, quarter-master-general, aided him with his talents and brilliant eloquence. They required a name to bring forward in the plot, and they selected Conway, who fancied himself the chief of a party. To praise Gates, with a certain portion of the continent and the troops, was a pretext for speaking of themselves. The people attach themselves to prosperous generals, and the commander-in-chief had been unsuccessful. His own character inspired respect and affection; but Greene, Hamilton, Knox, his best friends, were sadly defamed. The Tories fomented these dissensions. The presidency of the war-office, which had been created for Gates, restricted the power of the general. This was not the only inconvenience; a committee from congress arrived at the camp, and the attack of Philadelphia was daringly proposed. The most shrewd people did not believe that Gates was the real object of this intrigue. Though a good officer, he had not the power to assert himself. He would have given place to the famous General Lee, then a prisoner of the English, whose first care would have been to have made over to them his friends and all America.

Attached to the general, and still more so to the cause, M. de Lafayette did not hesitate for a moment; and, in spite of the caresses of one party, he remained faithful to the other, whose ruin seemed then impending. He saw and corresponded frequently with the general, and often discussed with him his own private situation, and the effect that various meliorations in the army might produce. Having sent for his wife to the camp, the general preserved in his deportment the noble composure which belongs to a strong and virtuous mind. "I have not sought for this place," said he to M. de Lafayette; "if I am displeasing to the nation, I will retire; but until then I will oppose all intrigues."

(1778.) The 22nd of January, congress resolved that Canada should be entered, and the choice fell upon M. de Lafayette. The Generals Conway and Stark were placed under him. Hoping to intoxicate and govern so young a commander, the war-office, without consulting the commander-in-chief, wrote to him to go and await his further instructions at Albany.* But after having won over by his arguments the committee which congress had sent to the camp, M. de Lafayette hastened to Yorktown, and declared there "that he required

* See fragment C, at the end of the Memoirs.

circumstantial orders, a statement of the means to be employed, the certainty of not deceiving the Canadians, an augmentation of generals, and rank for several Frenchmen, fully impressed," he added, "with the various duties and advantages they derived from their name; but the first condition he demanded was, not to be made, like Gates, independent of General Washington." At Gates' own house he braved the whole party, and threw them into confusion by making them drink the health of their general.* In congress he was supported by President Laurens, and he obtained all that he demanded. His instructions from the war-office promised that 2500 men should be assembled at Albany, and a large corps of militia at Coos; that he should have two millions in paper money, some hard specie, and all means supplied for crossing lake Champlain upon the ice, whence, after having burnt the English flotilla, he was to proceed to Montreal, and act there as circumstances might require.

Repassing then, not without some danger, the Susquehannah, which was filled with floating masses of ice, M. de Lafayette set out for Albany, and, in spite of the obstacles offered by ice and snow, rapidly traversed an extent of four hundred miles. Whilst travelling thus on horseback, he became thoroughly acquainted with the simplicity and purity of the inhabitants, their patriarchal mode of life, and their republican ideas. Devoted to their house-

* After having thus declared himself, he wrote to congress that "he could only accept the command on condition of remaining subordinate to General Washington, of being but considered as an officer detached from him, and of addressing all his letters to him, of which those received by congress would be but duplicates." These requests, and all the others he made, were granted. (Manuscript No. 2.)

hold cares, the women are happy, and afford to their husbands the calmest and truest felicity. To unmarried women alone is love spoken of, and their modesty enhances the charm of their innocent coquetry. In the chance marriages which take place in Paris, the fidelity of the wife is often repugnant to the voice of nature and of reason, one might almost say to the principles of justice. In America, a girl marries her lover, and it would be like having two lovers at the same time if she were to break that valid agreement; because both parties know equally how and in what manner they are bound to each other. In the bosom of their own families, the men occupy themselves with their private affairs, or assemble together to regulate those of the state. They talk politics over their glasses, and become animated by patriotism rather than strong liquor. Whilst the children shed tears at the name of Tory, the old men sent up prayers to Heaven that they might be permitted to see the end of that war. During his repeated and rapid journeys, M. de Lafayette, mixing with all classes of society, was not wholly useless to the good cause, to the interest of the French, and to the party of General Washington.

M. de Lafayette, on arriving at Albany, experienced some disappointments. Instead of 2500 men, there were not 1200. Stark's militia had not even received a summons. Clothes, provisions, magazines, sledges, all were insufficient for that glacial expedition. By making better preparations, and appointing the general earlier, success would probably have been secured. Several Canadians began to make a movement, and from that moment they testified great interest in M. de Lafayette; but two months were requisite to collect all that was necessary, and towards the middle of March the lakes begin to thaw. M. de Lafayette, general, at twenty years of age, of a small army, charged with an important and very difficult operation, authorized by the orders of congress, animated by the expectations now felt in America, and which, he knew, would ere long be felt likewise in Europe, had many motives for becoming adventurous; but, on the other hand, his resources were slender, the time allowed him was short, the enemy was in a good position, and Lieutenant-General Carleton was preparing for him another Saratoga. Forced to take a decisive step immediately, he wrote a calm letter to congress, and with a heavy sigh abandoned the enterprise. At the same period, congress, becoming a little less confident, despatched to him some wavering counsels, which, arriving too late, only served to compromise the general and justify the government. But the prudence of M. de Lafayette was at length rewarded by the approbation of congress and of the nation; and, until the opening of the campaign, he continued to command that department.* He found there that intrepid Arnold, who was still detained by his wound, and who since

* He had the discretion to renounce an expedition which, undertaken without proper means, would have produced fatal effects upon the whole northern part of the United States. At Georgetown, the present residence of congress, some anxiety was experienced, because they feared that M. de Lafayette had trusted himself upon the lakes in the season of the year when the ice begins to melt. The counter orders that were sent him would have arrived too late; and when it became known that he had himself renounced the expedition, he received the thanks of congress and of the minister of war, General Gates, who, in spite of the line of conduct Lafayette had pursued during his quarrel with General Washington, had always expressed great respect and esteem for him. (Manuscript No. 1.)

. . . . ; he became intimately acquainted with Schuyler, the predecessor of Gates, in disgrace as well as Saint-Clair, but who continued useful to the cause from the superiority of his talents, his importance in that part of the country, and the confidence he enjoyed in New York, of which state he was a citizen.

If Canada did not herself send an offensive army, all the savages were paid and protected by the English party: the Hurons and Iroquois committed their devastations on that whole frontier. Some baubles or a barrel of rum were sufficient to make them seize the tomahawk; they then rushed upon villages, burnt houses, destroyed harvests, massacred all, without regard to age or sex, and received on their return the price of each bloody scalp they could exhibit. A young American girl, whom her lover, an English officer, was expecting, that their marriage might take place, was killed by the very savages he had sent to escort her. Two Americans were actually eaten up by the Senecas, and a colonel of the English army was a guest at that horrible repast. "It is thus," was often said to the savages, whilst drinking with them at the councils, "it is thus we must drink the blood of rebels." M. de Lafayette, conscious that he could not protect such an immense extent of frontier, prepared quarters in every direction, and announced the speedy arrival of troops in all the counties; and this stratagem stopped the depredations of the savages, who do not usually attack those places in which they expect to find much resistance. But he kept the Albany troops close together, satisfied them a little as to payment, provisioned the forts, which had been hitherto neglected, and arrested a plot of which the particulars have never been precisely known. He found in George Clinton, governor of the state of New York, a firm and an enlightened co-operator.

Soon after, Schuyler and Duane, who were charged with the management of the affairs of the savages, appointed a general assembly at Johnson's Town, upon the Mohawk river. Recalling to them their former attachment to the French, M. de Lafayette repaired thither in a sledge to shew himself in person to those nations whom the English had endeavoured to prejudice against him. Five hundred men, women, and children, covered with various coloured paints and feathers, with their ears cut open, their noses ornamented with rings, and their half-naked bodies marked with different figures, were present at the councils. Their old men, whilst smoking, talked politics extremely well. Their object seemed to be to promote a balance of power; if the intoxication of rum, as that of ambition in Europe, had not often turned them aside from it. M. de Lafayette, adopted by them, received the name of *Kayewla*, which belonged formerly to one of their warriors; and under this name he is well known to all the savage tribes. Some louis which he distributed under the form of medals, and some stuffs from the state of New York, produced but little effect when compared to the presents they had received from England. A treaty was entered into, which some of them rigidly observed; and the course of the evil was at least arrested for the present. The Oneidas and Tuscaroras, the only real friends the Americans possessed, requested to have a fort; and M. de Lafayette left them M. de Gouvion, a French officer, whose talents and virtues rendered him of great value to the cause. Whenever savages were required at the army, whenever there was any dealings with these tribes, recourse was always had to the credit of M. de Lafayette, whose *necklaces* and *words* were equally respected.

On his return, he found that the form of a new oath had been established, which each civil and military officer was to take, according to his own religious belief. *An acknowledgment of the independence, liberty, and sovereignty of the United States; an eternal renunciation of George III., his successors, and heirs, and every King of England; a promise to defend the said states against the said George III.;* this was the purport of the oath administered by him to the whole northern department.* At the approach of spring, M. de Lafayette was recalled to the south. The affairs of General Washington were already in a more flourishing condition. Several of the states recommended him to their deputies; and from only suspecting one of them of being unfavourable to him, the New York assembly wished to recal one of their delegates. Congress had been a little recruited, and they were thinking of recruiting the army. At Valley-Forge, M. de Lafayette found some difficulty, not from the substance, but merely from the form of the oath; but that difficulty was easily obviated. A short time after, Simeon Deane arrived with the treaty of commerce between France and the United States.

By quitting France in so public a manner, M. de Lafayette had served the cause of the revolution. One portion of society was anxious for his success, and the attention of the other had become, to

* It is singular that the oath of renunciation to Great Britain and her king, which every one employed in the continental service was obliged to take at that time, should have been administered in one half of the United States by a Frenchman of twenty years of age. (Manuscript No. 2.)

say the least, somewhat occupied in the struggle. If a spirit of emulation made those connected with the court desirous of war, the rest of the nation supported the young rebel, and followed with interest all his movements; and it is well known that the rupture that ensued was truly a national one. Some circumstances relating to his departure having displeased the court of London, M. de Lafayette omitted nothing that could draw more closely together the nations whose union he so ardently desired. The incredible prejudices of the Americans had been augmented by the conduct of the first Frenchmen who had joined them. These men gradually disappeared, and all those who remained were remarkable for talents, or at least for probity. They became the friends of M. de Lafayette, who sincerely sought out all the national prejudices of the Americans against his countrymen for the purpose of overcoming them. Love and respect for the name of Frenchman animated his letters and speeches, and he wished the affection that was granted to him individually to become completely national. On the other side, when writing to Europe, he denied the reports made by discontented adventurers, by good officers who were piqued at not having been employed, and by those men who, serving themselves in the army, wished to be witty or amusing by the political contrasts they described in their letters. But, without giving a circumstantial account of what private influence achieved, it is certain that enthusiasm for the cause, and esteem for its defenders, had electrified all France, and that the affair of Saratoga decided the ministerial commotion. Bills of conciliation passed in the English house of parliament, and five commissioners were sent to offer far more than had been demanded until then. No longer waiting to see *how things would turn out*, M. de Maurepas yielded to the public wish, and what his luminous mind had projected, the more unchanging disposition of M. de Vergennes put in execution. A treaty was generously entered into with Franklin, Deane, and Arthur Lee, and that treaty was announced with more confidence than had been for some time displayed. But the war was not sufficiently foreseen, or at least sufficient preparations were not made. The most singular fact is, that at the very period when the firm resistance of the court of France had guided the conduct of two courts, America had fallen herself into such a state of weakness, that she was on the very brink of ruin. The 2nd of May, the army made a bonfire, and M. de Lafayette, ornamented with a white scarf, proceeded to the spot, accompanied by all the French. Since the arrival of the conciliatory bills, he had never ceased writing against the commission, and against every commissioner. The advances of these men were ill-received by congress; and, foreseeing a French co-operation, the enemy began to think of quitting Philadelphia.

General Washington sent two thousand chosen men across the Schuylkill to collect intelligence. M. de Lafayette, their commander, repaired, the 18th of May, to Barren Hill, eleven miles from the two armies. On a good elevation, his right resting upon some rocks and the river, on his left some excellent stone houses and a small wood, his front sustained by five pieces of cannon, and with roads in his rear, such was the position of M. de Lafayette. An hundred dragoons whom he was expecting did not arrive in sufficient time; but he stationed six hundred militia on his left at Whitemarsh, and their general, Porter, made himself answerable for those roads. On the evening of the 19th, Howe, who had just been recalled, and Clinton, who replaced him, sent out a detachment of seven thousand men, with fourteen pieces of cannon, under General Grant. Passing behind the inundation, that corps proceeded on the road to Francfort, and, by a circuitous movement, fell into that of Whitemarsh, from which the militia had just thought proper to retire. On the morning of the 20th, M. de Lafayette was conversing with a young lady, who, on pretence of seeing her relations, to oblige him had consented to go to Philadelphia, when he was informed that the red dragoons were at Whitemarsh. It was the uniform of those he was expecting; he had placed Porter there; he had promised to pay him a visit, and intended that very evening to carry thither his detachment. But, for greater security, he examined carefully into the truth of the report; and, ascertaining that a column was marching on the left, he changed his front, and covered it with the houses, the wood, and a small churchyard. Scarcely was that movement ended, when he found himself cut off by Grant on the Swedes' Ford road in his rear. It was in the presence of the troops that he first heard the cry that he was surrounded, and he was forced to smile at the unpleasant intelligence. Several officers, whom he had despatched to Valley-Forge, declared that they had been unable to find a passage. Every moment was precious, and M. de Lafayette proceeded on the road of Matson Ford, to which the enemy was nearer than himself. General Poor commanded his advance guard; and to him he sent Gimat, his own confidential aide-de-camp. He placed himself as the rear guard, and marched on with rapidity, but without precipitation. Grant had possession of the heights, and M. de Lafayette's road lay immediately beneath them. His apparent composure deceived his adversary; and perceiving that he was reconnoitring him, he presented to him, from among the trees and behind curtains, false heads of columns. The time that Grant occupied in reconnoitring, and discovering an imaginary ambuscade, M. de Lafayette employed in regaining the foreground; at length he passed by Grant's column. He managed to impose likewise on Grey's column, which followed him; and when the third division, under Howe and Clinton, reached Barren Hill, the Americans had already passed over Matson Ford. Forming themselves on the opposite shore, they awaited the enemy, who dared not attack them. Advancing on the ground, Howe was astonished at finding only one red line: the generals quarrelled; and although the commander in chief had invited some ladies to sup with M. de Lafayette, although the admiral, (Howe's brother,) knowing him to be surrounded, had prepared a frigate for him, the whole army, (of which half had made a march of forty miles,) returned, much fatigued, without having taken a single man. It was then that fifty savages, friends of the Americans, encountered fifty English dragoons; and the cries of war on one side, and the appearance of the cavalry on the other, surprised the parties so much that they both fled, with equal speed. The alarm had been likewise great at Valley-Forge; and the report of three pieces of cannon that were there fired appeared an additional mystery to Grant. The aim of the general being attained, the detachment returned to its quarters, and M. de Lafayette was well received by the general and army.*

An exchange of prisoners had long been talked of, and the cruelty of the English rendered this measure more necessary. Cooped up in a vessel at

* See, after these Memoirs, fragment D.

New York, and breathing a most noxious atmosphere, the American prisoners suffered all that gross insolence could add to famine, dirt, disease, and complete neglect. Their food was, to say the least, unwholesome. The officers, often confounded with their soldiers, appealed to former capitulations and to the right of nations; but they were only answered by fresh outrages. When one victim sunk beneath such treatment, "Tis well," was said to the survivors; "there is one rebel less." Acts of retaliation had been but rarely practised by the Americans; and the English, like other tyrants, mistook their mildness and generosity for timidity. Five hundred Americans, in a half-dying state, had been carried to the sea-shore, where the greatest number of them soon expired, and the general very properly refused to reckon them in exchange for his own prisoners of war. Another obstacle to the cartel was the capture of Lee, who had been taken prisoner in 1776; the congress insisted on his liberation, and, after much debating on both sides, he was at length exchanged for General Prescot. Lee, who had been formerly a colonel in the English service, a general in Poland, and a fellow-soldier of the Russians and Portuguese, was well acquainted with all countries, all services, and several languages. His features were plain, his turn of mind caustic, his feelings ambitious and avaricious, his temper uncomplying, and his whole appearance singular and unprepossessing. A temporary fit of generosity had induced him to quit the English service, and the Americans, at that period, listened to him as to an oracle. In his heart he detested the general, and felt a sincere affection for himself alone; but, in 1776, his advice had undoubtedly saved both the general and the army. He made many advances to M. de Lafayette, but the one was a violent Englishman, and the other an enthusiastic Frenchman, and their intimacy was often interrupted by their differences of opinion. Gates, whose great projects had been frustrated, was at that time commanding a corps at White Plains, upon the left side of the Hudson, opposite to the island of New York. Conway had retired from service, and the place of inspector, which had been created for him, was given to Steuben, an old Prussian, with moderate talents, but methodical habits, who organized the army and perfected their tactics. The congress received at that time some conciliatory epistles, and the sentiments their answers breathed, like all the other deliberations of that assembly, were nobly felt, and nobly expressed. Lord Carlisle was president of the commission, and Lord Howe, Sir Henry Clinton, Mr. Eden, and Governor Johnstone were its members. The last named person wrote to some friends, who published his letters.

On the 17th of June, Philadelphia was evacuated. The invalids, magazines, and heavy ammunition of the British were embarked with the general; the commissioners of conciliation alone remained behind. Passing over to Gloucester, the army marched, in two columns, each consisting of seven thousand men, commanded by Clinton and Knyphausen, towards New York. The army of the United States, which was of nearly equal force, directed itself from Valley Forge to Coryell's Ferry, and from thence to King's Town, within a march of the enemy; it was thus left at the option of the Americans, either to follow on their track, or to repair to White Plains. In a council held on this subject, Lee very eloquently endeavoured to prove that it was necessary to erect a bridge of gold for the enemy; that while on the very point of forming an alliance with them, every thing ought not to be placed at hazard; that the English army had never been so excellent and so well disciplined; he declared himself to be for White Plains: his speech influenced the opinion of Lord Stirling and of the brigadiers-general. M. de Lafayette, placed on the other side, spoke late, and asserted that it would be disgraceful for the chiefs, and humiliating for the troops, to allow the enemy to traverse the Jerseys tranquilly; that, without running any improper risk, the rear guard might be attacked; that it was necessary to follow the English, manœuvre with prudence, take advantage of a temporary separation, and, in short, seize the most favourable opportunities and situations. This advice was approved by many of the council, and above all by M. du Portail, chief of the engineers, and a very distinguished officer. The majority were, however, in favour of Lee; but M. de Lafayette spoke again to the general on this subject in the evening, and was seconded by Hamilton, and by Greene, who had been lately named quarter-master in place of Mifflin. Several of the general officers changed their opinion; and the troops having already begun their march, they were halted, in order to form a detachment. When united, there were 3,000 continentalists and 1,200 militia; the command fell to the share of Lee, but, by the express desire of the general, M. de Lafayette succeeded in obtaining it. Everything was going on extremely well, when Lee changed his mind, and chose to command the troops himself; having again yielded this point, he re-changed once more; and as the general wished him to adhere to his first decision—"It is my fortune and honour," said Lee, to M. de Lafayette, "that I place in your hands; you are too generous to cause the loss of both!" This tone succeeded better, and M. de Lafayette promised to ask for him the next day. The enemy, unfortunately, continued their march; M. de Lafayette was delayed by want of provisions; and it was not until the 26th, at a quarter to twelve at night, that he could ask for Lee, who was sent with a detachment of one thousand men to Englishtown, on the left side of the enemy. The first corps had advanced upon their right; and M. de Lafayette, by Lee's especial order, joined him at midday, within reach of the enemy, from whom he fortunately succeeded in concealing this movement. The two columns of the English army had united together at Monmouth Court-house, from whence they departed on the morning of the 28th. Whilst following them, the Americans marched rapidly through the woods of Freehold; and at eight o'clock the enemy's rear-guard was still in the vicinity of the court-house. If Lee had continued the direction he was then taking, he would have placed himself in an excellent position, especially as the American army was advancing on the road to Freehold; but the head of his column quitted the wood, into which it was again forced to retreat by the enemy's cannon. Lee then addressing himself to M. de Lafayette, told him to cross the plain, and attack the left flank of the enemy; and whilst this manœuvre, which exposed them to the fire of the English artillery, was executing, he sent him an order to fall back into the village in which he had placed the rest of the troops. From thence he drew back still farther, and, changing his attack into a retreat, he exposed himself to be driven back by Lord Cornwallis, and subsequently by the whole English army, to whom good space of time had been allowed to form themselves in proper order.

At the first retrograde movement, M. de Lafayette sent information to the general of what was passing, who, arriving speedily on the spot, found the troops retreating in confusion. "You know," said Lee, "that all this was against my advice." The general, sending Lee to the rear,* himself formed seven or eight hundred men, and stationed them, with some cannon, upon a chosen spot, and M. de Lafayette undertook to retard the enemy's march. The English dragoons made their first charge upon a small morass which sheltered him: the infantry marched round to attack him on the other side, but he had sufficient time to retire; and the army had by this time placed itself upon a height, where he took the command of the second line. A cannonade was kept up on both sides during the whole day, and two attacks of the enemy were repulsed. A battery, placed on their left, obliged them to change their position, and, when they presented their flank, the general attacked them and forced them to retreat, until darkness interrupted all operations. The American troops continued to gain ground, and Clinton retired during the night, leaving behind him more than three hundred dead and many wounded. The heat was so intense that the soldiers fell dead with-

* The two battalions formed to arrest the enemy's march were placed by General Washington himself. When, after having expressed his own feelings of dissatisfaction, he wished to give himself time to form his army on the heights behind the passage, he left there Major-General Lafayette, Brigadier-General Knox, commanding the artillery, and some officers of his staff. The colonels were good officers, and the battalions conducted themselves perfectly well. When the army was ranged in order of battle, General Greene commanded the right of the first line, Lord Stirling the left, and Lafayette the second line. (Manuscript No. 2.)

out having received a single wound, and the field of battle soon became untenable. During this affair, which ended so well, although begun so ill, General Washington appeared to arrest fortune by one glance, and his presence of mind, valour, and decision of character, were never displayed to greater advantage than at that moment.* Wayne distinguished himself; Greene and the brave Stirling led forward the first line in the ablest manner. From four o'clock in the morning until night M. de Lafayette was momentarily obliged to change his occupations. The general and he passed the night lying on the same mantle, talking over the conduct of Lee, who wrote the next morning a very improper letter, and was placed under arrest. He was afterwards suspended by a council of war, quitted the service, and was not regretted by the army. Clinton having retreated towards the hollows of Shrewsbury, the general contented himself with the success already gained, and marched towards White Plains; the second line, under M. de Lafayette, forming the right column. The 4th of July, being the anniversary of the declaration of independence, was celebrated at Brunswick; and a few days after the army learnt that the Count d'Estaing was before New York.†

Twelve French vessels, which sailed from Toulon, had been three months in reaching the Delaware:

* General Washington was never greater in battle than in this action. His presence stopped the retreat; his arrangements secured the victory. His graceful bearing on horseback, his calm and dignified deportment, which still retained some trace of the displeasure he had experienced in the morning, were all calculated to excite the highest degree of enthusiasm. (Manuscript No. 2.)

† See, after these Memoirs, the fragment E.

they arrived three days after the departure of the English fleet, and, following it to New York, M. d'Estaing anchored at Sandy-hook, outside the bar. He offered immense sums to be conveyed across that bar, but the pilots declared that the large vessels drew too much water, and the French finally agreed to attack Rhode Island, which the enemy then occupied with a force of 5000 men, who had entrenched themselves; whilst the state militia, under the command of Sullivan, were stationed at Providence. M. Girard, a French minister, arrived on board that squadron; he had been long most anxiously expected by the Americans, and M. de Lafayette called his delay a proof of confidence. The last mark of attention with which the court honoured M. de Lafayette, had been an order to arrest him in the West Indies; he was, in truth, out of favour in that quarter, and their displeasure had increased on receiving his letters, which were dictated less by the prudence of a philosopher than by the enthusiasm of a young lover of liberty: but although no letters were addressed to him, M. d'Estaing was not less kind and attentive in his conduct; and 2000 continentalists having been despatched from White-Plains to Providence, M. de Lafayette, who had exerted himself to hasten their departure, conducted them rapidly along the sound, across a smiling country, covered with villages, in which the evident equality of the population distinctly proved the democracy of the government. From the apparent prosperity of each colony, it was easy to judge of the degree of freedom which its constitution might enjoy.

By forcing the passage between Rhode Island and Connecticut, M. d' Estaing might easily have carried off as prisoners 1500 Hessians who were stationed on the latter island; but he yielded to Sullivans' entreaties, and waited until that general should be in readiness: but although the troops of M. de Lafayette had traversed 240 miles, he found on his arrival that no preparations were yet made. He repaired to the squadron, and was received with the greatest possible attention, especially by the general; and, as M. de Suffren was placed in front, he carried back to him an order from M. d'Estaing to attack three frigates, which, however, were burnt by their own crews. The American army repaired, on the 8th of August, to Howland's Ferry, during the time that the squadron was forcing its way between the two islands. General Greene having joined the army, M. de Lafayette yielded to him the command of half his corps; each then possessed a wing, of 1000 continentalists and 5000 militia. M. de Lafayette's corps was to receive the addition of the two battalions of Foix and Hainaut, with some marines. The English, fearing to be intercepted, evacuated the forts on the right of the island during the night of the 8th, and Sullivan landed with his troops the next day. M. de Lafayette was expecting the French that afternoon, and the boats were already under way, when a squadron appeared in sight on the south of the island, at M. d' Estaing's former anchorage. Lord Howe, brave even to audacity, having watched the movements of the French admiral and his fleet, collected a greater number of ships, of which the sizes were however too unequal: his position, and the southern wind, would enable him, he thought, to throw succours into Newport, where General Pigot had concentrated his force; but the wind changed during the night, and the next day M. d'Estaing, within sight of both armies, passed gallantly through the fire of the two batteries, whilst the enemy, cutting their cables, fled, under heavy press of sail. After a chace of eight hours the two squadrons at length met, and Lord Howe would have paid dearly for his temerity, had not a violent storm arisen; which dispersed the ships. By a singular chance, several of Byron's vessels came up at the same time on their return from Portsmouth; having been separated at the Azores by a violent gale of wind. The *Languedoc*, the admiral's ship, deprived of its masts and rudder, and driven by the tempest to a distance from the other vessels, was attacked by the *Isis*, of fifty guns, and owed its safety only to the courage and firmness of M. d'Estaing. At length he succeeded in rallying his squadron, and, faithful to his engagements, reappeared before Rhode Island; but as he no longer possessed the superiority of force, he announced his intention of repairing to Boston, where the *Cesar* had taken shelter after a combat. When the storm, which lasted three days, subsided, the American army drew near Newport. This town was defended by two lines of redoubts and batteries, surrounded by a wooden palisade, the two concentrated fronts of which rested on the sea-shore, and were supported by a ravine that it was necessary to cross. The trench was opened, the heavy batteries established, and General Greene and M. de Lafayette were deputed to go on board the French admiral ship, to endeavour to obtain time, and propose either to make an immediate attack, or to station vessels in the Providence river. If M. de Lafayette had felt consternation upon hearing of the dispersion of the fleet, the conduct of the sailors during the combat, which he learnt with tears in his eyes, inspired him with the deepest grief. In the council, where the question was agitated, M. de Brugnon (although five minutes before he had maintained the contrary) gave his voice in favour of Boston, and his opinion was unanimously adopted. Before they separated, the admiral offered his two battalions to M. de Lafayette, and appeared to feel great pleasure in being thus enabled to secure him his rank in the French army; but these troops were useful on board, and were not necessary on the island, and M. de Lafayette would not expose them to danger for his own private interest. At the departure of the vessels, there was but one unanimous feeling of regret and indignation. Their lost time, extinguished hopes, and embarrassed situation, all served to increase the irritation of the militia, and their discontent became contagious. The people of Boston already spoke of refusing the fleet admission into their port; the generals drew up a protestation, which M. de Lafayette refused to sign. Carried away by an impulse of passion, Sullivan inserted in an order "that our allies have abandoned us." His ill humour was encouraged by Hancock, a member of congress, formerly its president, and who then commanded the militia of Massachusets stationed on the island. To him M. de Lafayette first declared his intentions, and then, calling upon Sullivan, he insisted upon the words used in the order of the morning being retracted in that of the evening. Some hours after, the general returned his visit, and, drawing him aside, a very warm altercation took place; but although totally indifferent to the peril of a duel, Sullivan was neither indifferent to the loss of the intimacy of M. de Lafayette, nor to the influence this young Frenchman possessed at head-quarters, and over congress and the nation; and in the numerous letters which M. de Lafayette wrote on this occasion, he made ample use of his influence over those three important powers.

Dr. Cooper, a presbyterian minister, was extremely useful at Boston; and Hancock himself ended by repairing thither to receive the squadron. Rather than yield to the public torrent, M. de Lafayette had risked his own popularity; and in the fear of being guided by private interest, he had gone to the extreme in the opposite line of conduct. He lived in complete retirement, in his own military quarter, and was never seen but at the trench or the council, in which latter place he would not allow the slightest observation to be made against the French squadron. As hopes were still entertained of obtaining assistance from the latter, it was resolved to retreat to the north of the island; and M. de Lafayette was sent on an embassy to M. d'Estaing. After having travelled all night, he arrived at the moment when the general and his officers were entering Boston. A grand repast, given by the town, was followed by a conference between the council, the admiral, and himself, at which M. d'Estaing, while he clearly demonstrated the insufficiency of his naval force, offered to march himself with his troops. Every word was submitted to M. de Lafayette, and the admiral remarked this deference without appearing hurt by it. That same day, the 29th August, Sullivan retreated from his post; and although the discontent which the militia experienced had diminished the number of his troops, he conducted this movement, and the attack which it occasioned, with great ability.

The next morning, at the same time that M. de Lafayette was informed of the event, he learnt also that the two armies were in close contact at the north of the island, and that Clinton had arrived with a reinforcement. Traversing then eighty miles in less than eight hours, he repaired to Howland's Ferry, arriving there just as the army was re-crossing it. A corps of a thousand men had been left on the island, surrounded with divisions of the enemy: M. de Lafayette undertook the charge of them, and succeeded in withdrawing them without losing a single man. When congress returned thanks to him for his conduct during this retreat, they likewise expressed their gratitude for his journey to Boston, at the very period when he might so rationally have expected an engagement.* Sullivan returned to Providence, and left M. de Lafayette in the command of the posts around the island: the post of Bristol, in which his principal corps was placed, was exposed to an attack by water; he announced this to General Washington, to whom, Sullivan said, he thought the same idea had also occurred. It was at this place he learnt the affair of Ouessant, which he expected to celebrate as an important victory; but the welfare of the squadron recalled him to Boston, where he felt he could be useful to his countrymen. The general dissatisfaction was soon appeased; and although M. de Saint Sauveur had been killed accidentally in a tumult, the French had nevertheless full cause to acknowledge the kindness and moderation of the Bostonians. During a walk which he took with the Count d'Estaing, M. de Lafayette pointed out to him the remains of the army of Burgoyne: two soldiers of militia, stationed at each wing, alone constituted its guard. Feeling that his presence was no longer necessary to the squadron, and believing that it was his duty to return to France, M. de Lafayette set out to rejoin the principal corps of the army at Philadelphia.

During that time, the commissioners had made many addresses and proclamations. By endeavour-

* See fragment F.

ing to gain over one member, Johnstone had displeased the congress, who refused to treat with him. In a public letter, signed Carlisle, the French nation was taxed with *a perfidy too universally acknowledged to require any new proof.* With the effervescence of youth and patriotism, M. de Lafayette seized this opportunity of opposing the commission; and the first impulse of M. d'Estaing was to approve of his conduct. A haughty challenge was sent from head-quarters to Lord Carlisle: the answer was an ill-explained refusal; and the impetuosity of M. de Lafayette was attended with a good result, whilst the prudence of the president was ridiculed in every public paper.*

Soon afterwards, during M. de Lafayette's residence at Philadelphia, the commission received its death-blow; whilst he was breakfasting with the members of congress, the different measures proper to be pursued were frankly and cheerfully discussed. The correspondence which took place at that time is generally known; the congress remained ever noble, firm, and faithful to its allies: secretary Thomson, in his last letter to Sir Henry Clinton, informs him, that "*the congress does not answer impertinent letters.*" To conceal nothing from the people, all the proposals were invariably printed;

* The following was written by M. de Lafayette twenty years after the presumed date of the memoirs:—"Lord Carlisle refused,—and he was right. The challenge, however, excited some jokes against the commission and its president, which, whether well or ill founded, are always disadvantageous to those who become their objects."—(Manuscript No. 1.) "Lord Carlisle was right: but the challenge appearing the result of chivalric patriotism, party spirit took advantage of the circumstance, and the feeling which had inspired this irregular step was generally approved."—(Manuscript No. 2.)

but able writers were employed in pointing out the errors they contained. In that happy country, where each man understood and attended to public affairs, the newspapers became powerful instruments to aid the revolution. The same spirit was also breathed from the pulpit, for the Bible in many places favours republicanism. M. de Lafayette, having once reproached an Anglican minister with speaking only of heaven, went to hear him preach the following Sunday, and the words, *the execrable house of Hanover*, proved the docility of the minister.

M. de Lafayette addressed a polite letter to the French minister, and wrote also to the congress, that, "whilst he believed himself free, he had supported the cause under the American banner; that his country was now at war, and that his services were first due to her; that he hoped to return; and that he should always retain his zealous interest for the United States." The congress not only granted him an unlimited leave of absence, but added to it the most flattering expressions of gratitude. It was resolved that a sword, covered with emblems, should be presented to him, in the name of the United States, by their minister in France: they wrote to the king; and the *Alliance*, of thirty-six guns, their finest ship, was chosen to carry him back to Europe. M. de Lafayette would neither receive from them anything farther, nor allow them to ask any favour for him at the court of France. But the congress, when proposing a co-operation in Canada, expressed its wish of seeing the arrangement of the affair confided to him: this project was afterwards deferred from the general's not entertaining hopes of its ultimate success. But although old prejudices were much softened,—although the conduct of the admiral and the squadron had excited universal approbation,—the congress, the general, and, in short, every one, told M. de Lafayette that, in the whole circuit of the thirteen states, vessels only were required, and that the appearance of a French corps would alarm the nation. As M. de Lafayette was obliged to embark at Boston, he set out again on this journey of four hundred miles; he hoped, also, that he should be able to take leave of M. d'Estaing, who had offered to accompany him to the islands, and whose friendship and misfortunes affected him as deeply as his active genius and patriotic courage excited his admiration.

Heated by fatiguing journeys and over exertion, and still more by the grief he had experienced at Rhode Island; and having afterwards laboured hard, drank freely, and passed several sleepless nights at Philadelphia, M. de Lafayette proceeded on horseback, in a high state of fever, and during a pelting autumnal rain. Fetes were given in compliment to him throughout his journey, and he endeavoured to strengthen himself with wine, tea, and rum: but at Fishkill, eight miles from head-quarters, he was obliged to yield to the violence of an inflammatory fever. He was soon reduced to the last extremity, and the report of his approaching death distressed the army, by whom he was called *the soldier's friend*, and the whole nation were unanimous in expressing their good wishes and regrets for *the marquis*, the name by which he was exclusively designated. From the first moment, Cockran, director of the hospitals, left all his other occupations to attend to him alone. General Washington came every day to inquire after his friend; but, fearing to agitate him, he only conversed with the physician, and returned home with tearful eyes, and a heart oppressed with grief.* Suffering acutely from a raging fever and violent head-ache, M. de Lafayette felt convinced that he was dying, but did not lose for a moment the clearness of his understanding: having taken measures to be apprised of the approach of death, he regretted that he could not hope again to see his country and the dearest objects of his affection. Far from foreseeing the happy fate that awaited him, he would willingly have exchanged his future chance of life, in spite of his one and twenty years, for the certainty of living but for three months, on the condition of again seeing his friends, and witnessing the happy termination of the American war. But to the assistance of medical art, and the assiduous care of Dr. Cockran, nature added the alarming though salutary remedy of an hemorrhage. At the expiration of three months, M. de Lafayette's life was no longer in danger: he was at length allowed to see the general, and think of public affairs. By decyphering a letter from M. d'Estaing, he learnt that, in spite of twenty-one English vessels, the squadron had set out for la Martinique. After having spent some days together, and spoken of their past labours, present situations, and future projects, General Washington and he took a tender and painful leave of each other. At the same time that the enemies of this great man have accused him of insensibility, they have acknowledged his tenderness for M. de Lafayette; and how is it possible that he

* General Washington—who, when Lafayette was wounded at Brandywine, said to the surgeon, "*Take care of him as if he were my son, for I love him the same*"—expressed for him, during this illness, the most tender and paternal anxiety.—(Manuscript No. 1.)

should not have been warmly cherished by his disciple, he who, uniting all that is good to all that is great, is even more sublime from his virtues than from his talents? Had he been a common soldier, he would have been the bravest in the ranks; had he been an obscure citizen, all his neighbours would have respected him. With a heart and mind equally correctly formed, he judged both of himself and circumstances with strict impartiality. Nature, whilst creating him expressly for that revolution, conferred an honour upon herself; and, to shew her work to the greatest possible advantage, she constituted it in such a peculiar manner, that each distinct quality would have failed in producing the end required, had it not been sustained by all the others.

In spite of his extreme debility, M. de Lafayette, accompanied by his physician, repaired, on horseback, to Boston, where Madeira wine effectually restored his health. The crew of the *Alliance* was not complete, and the council offered to institute a press, but M. de Lafayette would not consent to this method of obtaining sailors, and it was at length resolved to make up the required number by embarking some English deserters, together with some volunteers from among the prisoners. After he had written to Canada, and sent some necklaces to a few of the savage tribes, Brice and Nevil, his aides-de-camp, bore his farewell addresses to the congress, the general, and his friends. The inhabitants of Boston, who had given him so many proofs of their kindness and attention, renewed their marks of affection at his departure; and the *Alliance* sailed on the 11th of January. A winter voyage is always boisterous in that latitude; but on approaching the banks of Newfoundland, the frigate experienced a violent storm: her main-top mast torn away, injured by a heavy sea, filling with water, during one long dark night she was in imminent danger; but a still greater peril awaited her, two hundred leagues from the coast of France. His British Majesty, encouraging the mutiny of crews, had issued a somewhat immoral proclamation, promising them the value of every *rebel* vessel that they should bring into an English port; which exploit could only be performed by the massacre of the officers and those who opposed the mutiny. This proclamation gave rise to a plot which was formed by the English deserters and volunteers, who had most imprudently been admitted, in great numbers, on board the ship: not one American or Frenchman (for some French sailors had been found at Boston, after the departure of the squadron) took part in this conspiracy. The cry of *Sail!* was to be raised, and when the passengers and officers came on deck, four cannon, loaded with canister shot, prepared by the gunner's mate, were to blow them into atoms. An English serjeant had also contrived to get possession of some loaded arms. The hour first named was four in the morning, but was changed to four in the afternoon. During that interim, the conspirators, deceived by the accent of an American who had lived a long time in Ireland, and traded on its coast, disclosed the plot to him, and offered him the command of the frigate: the worthy man pretended to accept it, and was only able to inform the captain and M. de Lafayette of the conspiracy one hour before the time fixed for its execution. They rushed, sword in hand, upon deck, followed by the other passengers and officers, called upon their own sailors to assist them, and seized thirty-one of the culprits, whom they placed in irons. Many others were accused in the depositions, but it was judged expedient to appear to rely upon the rest of the crew, although real confidence was only placed in the French and Americans. Eight days afterwards, the *Alliance* entered safely the port of Brest, February, 1779.

When I saw the port of Brest receive and salute the banner which floated on my frigate, I recalled to mind the state of my country and of America, and my peculiar situation when I quitted France. The conspirators were merely exchanged as English prisoners, and I only thought of rejoining my family and friends, of whom I had received no intelligence during the last eight months. When I repaired to a court which had hitherto only granted me *lettres de cachet*, M. de Poix made me acquainted with all the ministers. I was interrogated, complimented, and exiled, but to the good city of Paris; and the residence of the Hotel de Noailles was selected, instead of according me the horrors of the Bastille, which had been at first proposed. Some days afterwards, I wrote to the king to acknowledge an error of which the termination had been so fortunate: he permitted me to receive a gentle reprimand in person; and, when my liberty was restored to me, I was advised to avoid those places in which the public might consecrate my disobedience by its approbation. On my arrival, I had the honour of being consulted by all the ministers, and, what was far better, embraced by all the ladies. Those embraces lasted but one day; but I retained for a greater length of time the confidence of the cabinet, and I enjoyed both favour at the court of Versailles, and popularity at Paris. I was the theme of conversation in every circle, even after the queen's kind exertions had obtained for me the regiment of the king's dragoons. Times are widely changed;

but I have retained all that I most valued—popular favour and the affection of those I love.

Amidst the various tumultuous scenes that occupied my mind, I did not forget our revolution, of which the ultimate success still appeared uncertain. Accustomed to see great interests supported by slender means, I often said to myself that the expense of one *fête* would have organized the army of the United States; and to clothe that army I would willingly, according to the expression of M. de Maurepas, have unfurnished the palace of Versailles. In the meantime, the principal object of the quarrel, American independence, and the advantage our government and reputation would derive from seizing the first favourable opportunity, did not appear to me sufficiently promoted by those immense preparations for trifling conquests, and those projects conceived in the expectation of peace; for no person seriously believed in war, not even when it was declared, after the *hundredth injury* had induced Spain to enter into those co-operations which finally terminated in nothing more than noisy exercises.

FRAGMENTS

EXTRACTED FROM VARIOUS MANUSCRIPTS.*

A.

DEPARTURE FOR AMERICA IN 1777.

THE histories of the American war and revolution are, generally speaking, very favourable to M. de Lafayette; the life of Washington, by Mr. Marshall, is especially so. There is one phrase, however, (page 410 of the third volume of the London edition,) which requires some explanation. "*He left France ostensibly in opposition to his sovereign.*" This circumstance is treated in a more lucid and exact manner in the following works :—*The History, etc., by William Gordon, D.D.*, vol. ii., pages 499 and 500. *London*, 1788.—*The History of the American Revolution, by Dr. Ramsay*, vol. ii., page 11. *Philadelphia*, 1789.

The importance of this step was increased by a peculiar circumstance. The preparations for the

* We have already mentioned these manuscripts. The one we term *Manuscript No.* 1, consists of a rapid sketch of the American life of General Lafayette; the other one, or Manuscript 2, is entitled, *Observations on some portion of the American History, by a Friend of General Lafayette.* Both appear to have been written about the period of the empire. Fragment A is drawn from the Manuscript No. 2.

purchase and equipment of the vessel had delayed Lafayette's departure until the period which had been long previously fixed upon for an excursion of some weeks into England; this enabled him to conceal his departure; the American commissioners were well pleased to take advantage of this accident. Lafayette refused the proposals which were made him in London to visit the ports, or to do anything which could be construed into an abuse of confidence. He did not conceal his partiality for the American insurgents; but he endeavoured to profit by the parade with which, from political motives, the king and his ministry received at that period all persons coming from the court of France, and the attention which was paid them. The Marquis de Noailles, the ambassador, was his uncle. Lafayette felt no scruple in compromising the diplomatic character of this representation of the King of France, so that the *maximum* of the favourable effect that his departure could produce was obtained in England.

The same result took place in France. It would be difficult at this period to imagine into what a state of political and military insignificance the nation and government had been reduced during the war of seven years, and, above all, after the partition of Poland. The French ministry had personally, at that period, the reputation of great circumspection; the few indirect relations it permitted itself to hold with the agents of the insurgent colonies were only managed through the medium of unacknowledged agents, and were discovered the moment the ambassador pretended to become acquainted with them, or that the Americans could have drawn any advantage from them. Amongst the departures on which the ministers were kind enough to close their eyes, there were only four engineers for whom this toleration was in truth a secret mission.* One word from Lord Stormont was sufficient to procure the detention, discharge, and sometimes imprisonment of the Americans admitted into our ports: their liberty or property was only restored to them surreptitiously, and as if escaping from the vigilance of a superior.

Amidst this labyrinth of precautions, feebleness, and denials, the effect may be conceived that was produced at Versailles by the bold step taken by a youth of distinguished birth and fortune, allied to one of the first families of the court, by whom the King of England and his ministers would fancy themselves braved and even laughed at, and whose departure would leave no doubt as to the connivance of the ambassador and government of France. The displeasure of the rulers was roused to the highest pitch: a portion of Lafayette's family shared in this displeasure. He had secretly traversed France. Having met near Paris with Carmichael, secretary of the American agents, he had urged the immediate departure of his vessel from Bordeaux, preferring to complete the necessary arrangements at the Spanish port of Passage. He returned himself to Bordeaux, in the hope of obtaining a consent which he considered would be useful to his cause. The return of his courier having informed him that they would not condescend to give an answer to such an indiscreet request, he hastened to quit France himself in the disguise of a courier, and lost no time in setting sail.

The government, to appease as far as possible,

* MM. de Gouvion, Duportail, Laradière, and Laumoy.

the English ambassador, despatched two light vessels to the Leeward and Windward Islands to stop Lafayette. At that period, the French navigators did not risk steering straight towards the American continent; they first repaired to the West Indies, and, taking out papers for France, they ranged as close as possible to the American coast, and endeavoured to seize a favourable moment or pretext to steal into a harbour. Lafayette's vessel had followed the common course of all expeditions; but its youthful owner, who had several officers with him, and had won the affection of the crew, obliged the captain to take a straightforward direction. A lucky gale of wind drove off the frigates that had been cruising on the preceding day before Georgetown, and he sailed into that port, having been protected by fate against the various obstacles which had been opposed to his enterprise.

But whilst the French government thus seconded the views of the English government, the departure of young Lafayette produced, in Paris, in the commercial towns, in all societies, and even at court, a sensation that was very favourable to the American cause. The enthusiasm it excited was in a great measure owing to the state of political stagnation into which the country had so long been plunged, the resentment excited by the arrogance of England, her commissioner at Dunkirk, her naval pretensions, and the love inherent in all mankind of bold and extraordinary deeds, especially when they are in defiance of the powerful, and to protect the weak in their struggle for liberty. To these peculiar circumstances may be imputed the increased interest and attention, the strong national feeling, and the constantly augmenting force of public opinion to which the French government at length yielded, when, in its treaties with the United States, it formed engagements with them, and commenced a war with England, which were both equally opposed to its real character and inclination.

B.

FIRST INTERVIEW BETWEEN GENERAL WASHINGTON AND GENERAL LAFAYETTE.

The appearance of the two brothers Howe before the capes of the Delaware had given rise to the supposition that it was upon that side they intended to land. General Washington repaired with his army towards the neighbourhood of Philadelphia. That army had been recruiting during the winter. Washington went to Philadelphia to attend a public dinner given in honour of him. It was then Lafayette was introduced to him. This young foreigner had travelled by land over the southern states, and had made a direct application to the congress, requesting to serve at first as volunteer, and to serve at his own expense. The members were much struck with two requests differing so widely from those of several other officers, and of one in particular, an officer of artillery, who had made great pretensions on his arrival, and had soon afterwards drowned himself in the Schuylkill. The rank of major-general (the highest in the American army) was given to Lafayette. Washington received the young volunteer in the most friendly manner, and invited him to reside in his house as a member of his military family, which offer Lafayette accepted with the same frankness with which it was made.

He remained there until he was appointed to the command of a division. The court of France had required that the American envoys should write to America to prevent Lafayette from being employed in their army. They did not hasten to despatch that letter, and, when its contents became known, the popularity of Lafayette was so great that it could not produce any effect. It is thus evident, that from the first moment of his embracing the American cause every obstacle was thrown in his way; all of which, however, he encountered and surmounted. (Manuscript No. 1.)

C.

ON THE MILITARY COMMANDS DURING THE WINTER OF 1778, AND THE FRENCH IN THE SERVICE OF THE UNITED STATES.

Amongst the various means employed to deprive the general-in-chief of his friends, attempts were made to awaken the ambition of Lafayette, who already enjoyed much popularity in the army and in the country, and who besides appeared to the enemies of Washington, from his relations with Europe, one of the men whom it was most important to draw into their party. They fancied they should gain him over by offering him the government of the north, which Gates had just quitted, and by the hope of an expedition into Canada. General Washington received a packet from the minister of war, enclosing a commission for Lafayette as an independent commander-in-chief, with an order to repair to the congress to receive instructions. The general placed it in his hands, without allowing himself any observation on the subject. Lafayette immediately declared to three commissioners of congress, who happened to be at that moment in the camp, "that he would never accept any command independent of the general, and that the title of his aide-de-camp appeared to him preferable to any other that could be offered him." When General Washington received the order of congress, he only said to his young friend, whilst placing the letter in his hand, "I prefer its being for you rather than for any other person."

The military commands, during the winter of 1777 — 1778, were distributed in the following manner :—General Washington assembled in some huts at Valley-Forge what was termed the principal army, reduced at that time to four or five thousand half-clothed men General Mac-Dougal had the direction of a station at Peekskill. Lafayette commanded what was called the northern army, that is to say, a handful of men ; his head-quarters were at Albany. The enemy made a few incursions, but of slight importance ; and by the exercise of great vigilance, and a judicious choice of stations, the winter passed away tranquilly. Lafayette had under his orders two general officers, who had been engaged in the service of France, namely, General Kalb, a German by birth, who came over in the same vessel with himself ; and General Conway, an Irishman, who had been a major in a regiment of that nation, also in the service of France. Besides the four engineers who have been before named, and these two officers, we must also mention, amongst the foreigners employed in the service of the United States, Pulaski, a Polish nobleman, who had taken a conspicuous part in the confederation of his own country, and who, after the success of the Russians, had arrived in America with letters of introduction to the congress, General Washington, and General Lafayette; Kosciuszko, his countryman, who was a colonel of engineers in America, and who afterwards acted such a grand and noble part during the last revolutions in Poland; Ternant, by birth a Frenchman, who has served the United States, Holland, and France with great ability; La Colombe, aide-de-camp to Lafayette, who has been subsequently so usefully employed in the French revolution; the Marquis de la Royeric, whom disappointed love brought to the United States, and who has since taken part in the counter-revolution; Gimat, aide-de-camp to Lafayette, who has since had the command in the French islands; Fleury, who distinguished himself in the defence of Fort Mifflin, and in the attack of the fort of West-Point, and who afterwards died a field-marshal in France; Mauduit-Duplessis, an extremely brave officer of artillery, who has since taken part against the French revolution, and was massacred at Saint Domingo; Touzard, an officer of artillery, who lost his arm at Rhode Island, where he was acting as aide-de-camp to Lafayette; Major Lenfant, employed as engineer; Baron Steuben, a Prussian officer, a good tactician, who arrived at the commencement of 1778, and was of essential service in disciplining the American troops. These officers, and several others, obtained employment in America. The greatest number, however, of those who presented themselves were refused service, and returned to France, with some few exceptions, to bear thither their own prejudices against the Americans. Some of those who remained appear to have written home likewise in the same spirit. General Washington therefore observes very justly in one of his letters, that Lafayette, in his correspondence, by destroying the unfavourable impressions that were given of the Americans, and seeking, on the contrary, to excite the feelings of the French in their favour, rendered a new and very important service to their cause. (Manuscript No. 1.)

D.

RETREAT OF BARREN-HILL.

As the English army was preparing to evacuate Philadelphia, Lafayette was sent, with a detachment of two thousand chosen men, and five pieces of cannon, to a station half-way betwixt that city and Valley-Forge; this was Barren-hill. A corps of militia under General Porter had been placed on Lafayette's left wing; but he retired farther back, and the English took advantage of that movement to surround Lafayette's detachment. General Grant, with seven thousand men and fourteen pieces of cannon, was behind him, and nearer than himself to the only ford by which it was possible for him to pass the Schuylkill. General Grey, with two thousand men, arrived on his left at Barren-hill church; whilst the remainder of the English army, under the command of Generals Clinton and Howe, prepared to attack him in front. It is said that Admiral Lord Howe joined the army as a volunteer. The English generals felt so certain of the capture of Lafayette, that they sent to Philadelphia several invitations to a *fête*, at which they said Lafayette would be present. If he had not, in truth, manœuvred rather better than they did, the whole corps must inevitably have been lost. Alarm-guns were fired by the army; General Washington felt additional anxiety from the fact that, those troops being the flower of his army, their defeat would, he knew, have discouraged the rest. Lafayette instantly formed his plan of operation : he threw some troops into the churchyard, to check those of General Grey. He made a false attack upon General Grant, shewing him the heads of columns ; and whilst the latter halted, and formed his troops to receive him, he caused his detachment to file off. By these manœuvres he gained the ford, and passed it in presence of the enemy, without losing a single man. Two English lines met, and were on the point of attacking each other, for there was no longer anything between them ; the Americans had been for some time in safety at the other side of the Schuylkill. The English then returned to Philadelphia, much fatigued and ashamed, and were laughed at for their ill success. (Manuscript No. 1.)

E.

ARRIVAL OF THE FRENCH FLEET.

The treaty with France became known a short time before the opening of the campaign. The national enthusiasm for the Americans had much increased, but the ministry was afraid of war. Necker, in particular, did all he could to prevent the court of France from espousing the American cause, which may serve as an answer to the accusations of revolutionary ardour that were made against him by the aristocrats in France. Maurepas was very timid, but the news of the taking of Burgoyne inspired him with some courage. The Count de Vergennes flattered himself that he should succeed in avoiding war. The court of France shewed little sincerity in its proceedings with England. The treaty was at length concluded: Dr. Franklin, Silas Deane, and John Adams, accompanied by many other Americans then in Paris, were presented to the King and royal family. They repaired afterwards to the young Madame de Lafayette, who was at Versailles, wishing to testify by that public act how much they thought themselves indebted to Lafayette for the happy direction which their affairs had taken. The news of the treaty excited a great sensation in America, and, above all, in the army. Lafayette had long since returned from his command in the north to the head-quarters of General Washington. The manifesto of the French government to the British cabinet contained this expression: "The Americans having become independent by their declaration of such a day." "That," said Lafayette, smiling, "is a principle of national sovereignty which shall one day be recalled to them." The French revolution, and the part which he took in it, have doubly verified this prediction. (Manuscript No. 1.)

Mr. Marshall's work contains a curious dissertation upon the declaration of war between France and England, and gives also the extract of a memorial of M. Turgot, which it would be interesting to verify. It would then be seen what opinions were supported at that time, concerning the colonies in general, and the quarrel with the English colonies in particular, by one of the most liberal and enlightened men in regard to political and commercial questions. The idea that the queen supported the war party is not correct; her social tastes were rather of the Anglomania kind; her politics were completely Austrian, and the court of Vienna did not wish that France should have any pretext for refusing to fulfil the conditions of the treaty made with it, which were soon afterwards exacted; but the queen, like a true woman of the world, followed the impulse given by Paris, the commercial towns, and the public.

Dr. Ramsay alludes to the happiness which Lafayette must have experienced when, upon learning the happy news of the French alliance, he, with tears of joy, embraced his illustrious general. Several persons present have since recollected that when the message of the court of Versailles to that of London was read aloud, with all the justifications which dwelt upon the right of the American nation to give themselves a government, Lafayette exclaimed,—"That is a great truth which we will recall to them at home." (Manuscript No. 2.)

F.

DISSENSIONS BETWEEN THE FRENCH FLEET AND THE AMERICAN ARMY.

The history of Dr. Gordon, that of Ramsay, and of Mr. Marshall, give a detailed account of the arrival of Count d'Estaing at the entrance of the Delaware, his arrival at Sandyhook, and the expedition against Rhode Island. Lafayette conducted thither, from White Plains, two thousand men of the continental troops. He made that journey (two hundred and forty miles) very rapidly, and arrived before the remainder of the troops under Sullivan were in readiness. It is to be lamented that the latter general persuaded Count d'Estaing to await the cooperation of the Americans, whilst, had he encouraged him to force the passage between Rhode Island and Connecticut Island, he would have had time, at the first moment of his arrival, to have captured fifteen hundred Hessians who were upon the last-mentioned island. On the other hand, M. d'Estaing was wrong in being displeased with General Sullivan for effecting his passage and taking possession of the forts on the north of the island, as soon as he learnt that they had been abandoned by the enemy, and without having concerted any plan of operations with the admiral. Everything, however, went on extremely well. The Americans had twelve thousand men upon the island; their right was composed of the half of the continentalists brought by Lafayette from White Plains, and of five thousand militia, and was under the command of General Greene; the left consisted also of five thousand militia, with the other half of the continentalists, and was commanded by M. de Lafayette. On the 8th of August the American army proceeded to Howland's ferry, whilst the squadron forced the passage. The English set fire to three of their own frigates; they had six frigates, and several other vessels, burnt during this expedition. In the afternoon of the day that Sullivan's army landed, they were expecting the battalions of Foix and Hainaut, and the marines, which were to have joined Lafayette's corps, when Admiral Howe suddenly hove in sight, and took possession of the anchorage that Count d'Estaing had quitted, in order to force his passage between the islands. The French sailors feared that the enemy would take advantage of their situation, enclosed as they were between the islands, or that some reinforcements would at least be thrown upon the southern part of the island; but the wind having changed during the night, Count d'Estaing sailed out gallantly through the fire of the English batteries, and Lord Howe, cutting his cables, fled before him. This skilful admiral would have paid dearly for his bold manœuvre, if the storm had not come most opportunely to his aid.

Mr. Marshall, who had the letters of Washington and Lafayette before him, states the manner in which Lafayette, on the one side, exposed himself, without reserve, to the loss of his popularity, and on the other, zealously exerted himself in defending the honour of the French from the accusations that the dissatisfaction of the Americans had universally excited, especially at Rhode Island and Boston, against the officers of the squadron; and also to prevent that dissatisfaction from breaking into open disputes. Sullivan, the senior of the three majors-general, was commander-in-chief. It was after an explanation with Lafayette, his friend and comrade, that he softened, by a subsequent order of the day, the expressions which he had imprudently used in the one preceding. General Greene, a man of superior merit, contributed much to the reconciliation. The ex-president, Hancock, who had at first loudly expressed his displeasure, consented to repair to Boston to endeavour to calm the public mind, and to obtain provisions for the squadron. The popularity of Lafayette was usefully employed during his short visit to that town. The congress, and General Washington also, thought that this quarrel could not be too speedily appeased; but they were at a distance, and a proper mixture of firmness and persuasion was required from the first moment. Such a perfect understanding, however, was now established, that it was not even disturbed by the unfortunate event which, some time afterwards, cost M. de Saint Sauveur his life. Much was also due to Dr. Cooper, a distinguished minister of the Presbyterian church. (Manuscript No. 2.)

CORRESPONDENCE.

1777—1778.

TO THE DUKE D'AYEN.*

London, March 9, 1777.

You will be astonished, my dear father, at the news I am on the point of giving you: it has cost me far more than I can express not to consult you. My respect and affection for you, as well as my great confidence in you, must convince you of the truth of this assertion; but my word was given, and you would not have esteemed me had I broken it; the step I am now taking will at least prove to you, I hope, the goodness of my intentions. I have found a peculiar opportunity of distinguishing myself, and of learning a soldier's trade: I am a general officer in the army of the United States of America. The

* Jean Paul François de Noailles, Duke d'Ayen, afterwards Duke de Noailles, died a member of the House of Peers, in 1824, and was, as is well known, father-in-law to M. de Lafayette, who had been, we may say, brought up in the hotel de Noailles, and who looked upon all his wife's family as his own. It was at that time divided into two branches. The Marshal de Noailles, governor of Roussillon, and captain of the guards of the Scotch company, was the head of the eldest branch. He had four children: the Duke d'Ayen, the Marquis de Noailles, and Mesdames de Tessé and de Lesparre. The Duke d'Ayen, a general officer, captain of the guards in reversion, married Henriette Anne Louise Daguesseau, by whom he had daughters only. The eldest, who died in 1794, on the same

events, I must equally have been parted from you,—wandering about in Italy,* dragging on an inglorious life, surrounded by the persons most opposed to my projects, and to my manner of thinking? All these reflections did not prevent my experiencing the most bitter grief when the moment arrived for quitting my native shore. Your sorrow, that of my friends, Henrietta,† all rushed upon my thoughts, and my heart was torn by a thousand painful feelings. I could not at that instant find any excuse for my own conduct. If you could know all that I have suffered, and the melancholy days that I have passed, whilst thus flying from all that I love best in the world! Must I join to this affliction the grief of hearing that you do not pardon me? I should, in truth, my love, be too unhappy. But I am not speaking to you of myself and of my health, and I well know that these details will deeply interest you.

Since writing my last letter, I have been confined to the most dreary of all regions: the sea is so melancholy, that it and I mutually, I believe, sadden each other. I ought to have landed by this time, but the winds have been most provokingly contrary; I shall not arrive at Charlestown for eight or ten days. It will be a great pleasure to me to land, as I am expecting to do, in that city. When I am once on shore, I shall hope each day to receive news from France; I shall learn so many interesting things, both concerning the new country I am

* At the moment when M. de Lafayette's project of departure was taking place, he had been desired to join the Duke d'Ayen, and Madame de Tessé, his sister, who were setting out for Italy and Sicily.

† The first-born of M. de Lafayette, which died during his voyage. (See letter 16th June, 1778.)

seeking, and, above all, that home which I have quitted with so much regret! Provided I only learn that you are in good health, that you still love me, and that a certain number of my friends entertain the same feelings towards me, I can become a perfect philosopher with respect to all the rest, —whatever it may be, or whatever land it may concern. But if my heart be attacked in its most vulnerable part, if you were to love me less, I should feel, in truth, too miserable. But I need not fear this—need I, my dearest love? I was very ill during the first part of my voyage, and I might have enjoyed the pleasure of an ill-natured person, that of knowing that I had many fellow sufferers. I treated myself according to my own judgment, and recovered sooner than the other passengers; I am now nearly the same as if I were on shore. I am certain that, on my arrival, I shall be in a perfect state of health, and continue so for a long time. Do not fancy that I shall incur any real dangers by the occupations I am undertaking. The post of general officer has always been considered like a commission for immortality. The service will be very different from the one I must have performed if I had been, for example, a colonel in the French army. My attendance will only be required in the council. Ask the opinion of all general officers,—and these are very numerous, because, having once attained that height, they are no longer exposed to any hazards, and do not therefore yield their places to inferior officers, as is the case in other situations. To prove that I do not wish to deceive you, I will acknowledge that we are at this moment exposed to some danger, from the risk of being attacked by English vessels, and that my ship is not of sufficient force for defence. But when I have once landed, I shall be in perfect safety. You see that I tell you everything, my dearest love; confide therefore in me, and do not, I conjure you, give way to idle fears. I will not write you a journal of my voyage: days succeed each other, and, what is worse, resemble each other. Always sky, always water, and the next day a repetition of the same thing. In truth, those who write volumes upon a sea voyage must be incessant babblers; for my part, I have had contrary winds, as well as other people; I have made a long voyage, like other people; I have encountered storms; I have seen vessels, and they were far more interesting for me than for any other person: well! I have not observed one single event worth the trouble of relating, or that has not been described by many other persons.

Let us speak of more important things: of yourself, of dear Henriette, and of her brother or sister. Henriette is so delightful, that she has made me in love with little girls. To whichever sex our new infant may belong, I shall receive it with unbounded joy. Lose not a moment in hastening my happiness by apprising me of its birth. I know not if it be because I am twice a father, but my parental feelings are stronger than they ever were. Mr. Deane, and my friend Carmichael, will forward your letters, and will, I am sure, neglect nothing to promote my happiness as soon as possible. Write, and even send me a confidential person, it would give me such pleasure to question any one who has seen you: Landrin, for example; in short, whom you please. You do not know the warmth and extent of my affection, if you fancy that you may neglect anything relating to yourself. You will be, at first, a long time without hearing from me; but when I am once established you will receive letters constantly, and of a very recent date. There is no great difference of time between letters from America and letters from Sicily. I own that Sicily weighs heavily on my heart. I fancied myself near seeing you again! But let me break off at the word Sicily. Adieu, my dearest love; I shall write to you from Charlestown, and write to you also before I arrive there. Good night, for the present.

7th June.

I am still floating on this dreary plain, the most wearisome of all human habitations. To console myself a little, I think of you and of my friends: I think of the pleasure of seeing you again. How delightful will be the moment of my arrival! I shall hasten to surprise and embrace you. I shall perhaps find you with your children. To think, only, of that happy moment, is an inexpressible pleasure to me; do not fancy that it is distant; although the time of my absence will appear, I own, very long to me, yet we shall meet sooner than you can expect. Without being able myself to fix the day or the month of our reunion, without being aware even of the cause of our absence, the exile prescribed by the Duke d'Ayen, until the month of January, appeared to me so immeasurably long, that I certainly shall not inflict upon myself one of equal length. You must acknowledge, my love, that the occupation and situation I shall have are very different from those that were intended for me during that useless journey. Whilst defending the liberty I adore, I shall enjoy perfect freedom myself: I but offer my service to that interesting republic from motives of the purest kind, unmixed with ambition or private views; her happiness and my glory are my only incentives to the task. I hope that, for my sake, you will become a good American, for that feeling is worthy of every noble heart. The happiness of America is intimately connected with the happiness of all mankind; she will become the safe and respected asylum of virtue, integrity, toleration, equality, and tranquil happiness.

We have occasionally some slight alarms, but, with a little skill and good luck, I am certain of reaching the port in safety. I am more pleased with this prospect, because I feel that I am becoming, every day, extremely reasonable. You know that the viscount* has the habit of repeating, that "*travelling forms young men;*" if he said this but once every morning and once every evening, in truth it would not be too much, for I am constantly more strongly impressed with the justice of the observation. I know not where the poor viscount is at this present moment, nor the prince,† nor all my other friends. This state of uncertainty is a very painful one. Whenever you chance to meet any one whom I love, tell him a thousand and ten thousand things from me. Embrace tenderly my three sisters, and tell them that they must remember me, and love me; present my compliments to Mademoiselle Marin;‡ I recommend, also, poor Abbé Fayon to your care. As to the Marshal de Noailles, tell him that I do not write to him, for fear of tiring him, and because I should have nothing to announce to him but my arrival; that I am expecting his commis-

* The Viscount de Noailles, brother-in-law to M. de Lafayette.

† The Prince de Poix, son of the Marshal de Mouchy, and consequently uncle, according to the mode of Bretagne, to Madame de Lafayette.

‡ Mademoiselle Marin was governess to Mesdemoiselles de Noailles; and the Abbé Fayon was tutor to M. de Lafayette.

sions for trees or plants, or whatever else he may desire, and that I should wish my exactness in fulfilling his wishes to be a proof of my affection for him. Present, also, my respects to the Duchess de la Trémoïlle,* and tell her that I make the same offer to her as to the Marshal de Noailles, either for herself or her daughter-in-law, who has such a beautiful garden. Tell my old friend Desplaus,† also, that I am well. As to my aunts, Madame d'Ayen and the viscountess, I am myself writing to them.

These are my little commissions, my love; I have also written to Sicily. We have seen, to-day, several kinds of birds, which announce that we are not far from shore. The hope of arriving is very sweet, for a ship life is a most wearisome one. My health, fortunately, allows me to occupy myself a little; I divide my time between military books and English books. I have made some progress in this language, which will become very necessary to me. Adieu; night obliges me to discontinue my letter, as I have forbidden, some days since, any candles being used in my vessel: see how prudent I have become! Once more, adieu; if my fingers be at all guided by my heart, it is not necessary to see clearly to tell you that I love you, and that I shall love you all my life.

* Madame de Lafayette, author of the *Princess de Clèves*, had only one daughter, who became Madame de la Trémoïlle, and heiress to the property of the Lafayette family; and who cheerfully consented to restore to her cousins, who inhabited the province, those estates which a love of their family might make them wish to conserve to the heritors of the name of Lafayette. Since that period, the members of that branch, of which M. de Lafayette was the last scion, have constantly kept up feelings, not only of relationship, but of friendship, with the family of la Trémoïlle.

† An old valet de chambre.

15th June—At Major Hughes's.*

I have arrived, my dearest love, in perfect health, at the house of an American officer; and, by the most fortunate chance in the world, a French vessel is on the point of sailing; conceive how happy I am. I am going this evening to Charlestown, from whence I will write to you. There is no important news. The campaign is opened, but there is no fighting, or at least, very little. The manners in this part of the world are simple, polite, and worthy in every respect of the country in which the noble name of liberty is constantly repeated. I intended writing to Madame d'Ayen, but I find it is impossible. Adieu, adieu, my love. From Charlestown I shall repair, by land, to Philadelphia, to rejoin the army. Is it not true that you will always love me?

TO MADAME DE LAFAYETTE.

June 19th, 1777, Charlestown.

If my last letter, my dearest love, written five or six days ago, was closed hastily, I hope at least that the American captain, whom I then believed to be a French one, will remit it to you as soon as possible. That letter announced to you that I had landed safely in this country, after having suffered a little from sea-sickness during the first weeks of my voyage; that I was staying with a very kind officer, in whose house I was received upon my arrival; that I had been nearly two months at sea, and was

* The father of him who so generously devoted himself to save Lafayette from the prisons of Olmutz.—(Note of M. de Lafayette.)

anxious to continue my journey immediately; that letter spoke of everything which interests my heart most deeply, of my regret at having quitted you, of your pregnancy, and of our dear children; it told you, also, that I was in perfect health. I repeat this extract from it, because the English may very possibly amuse themselves by seizing it on its way. I place, however, so much confidence in my lucky star, that I hope it will reach you safely. That same star has protected me to the astonishment of every person; you may, therefore, trust a little to it in future, my love, and let this conviction tranquillize your fears. I landed after having sailed for several days along a coast swarming with hostile vessels. On my arrival here every one told me that my ship must undoubtedly be taken, because two English frigates had blockaded the harbour. I even sent, both by land and sea, orders to the captain to put the men on shore, and burn the vessel, if he had still the power of doing so. Well! by a most extraordinary piece of good fortune, a sudden gale of wind having blown away the frigates for a short time, my vessel arrived at noon-day, without having encountered friend or foe. At Charlestown I have met with General Howe, a general officer, now engaged in service. The governor of the state is expected this evening from the country. All the persons with whom I wished to be acquainted have shewn me the greatest attention and politeness (not European politeness merely); I can only feel gratitude for the reception I have met with, although I have not yet thought proper to enter into any detail respecting my future prospects and arrangements. I wish to see the congress first. I hope to set out in two days for Philadelphia, which is a land journey of more than two hundred and fifty leagues. We shall divide into small parties; I have already purchased horses and light carriages for this purpose. There are some French and American vessels at present here, who are to sail out of the harbour in company to-morrow morning, taking advantage of a moment when the frigates are out of sight: they are numerous and armed, and have promised me to defend themselves stoutly against the small privateers they will undoubtedly meet with. I shall distribute my letters amongst the different ships, in case any accident should happen to either one of them.

I shall now speak to you, my love, about the country and its inhabitants, who are as agreeable as my enthusiasm had led me to imagine. Simplicity of manner, kindness of heart, love of country and of liberty, and a delightful state of equality, are met with universally. The richest and the poorest man are completely on a level; and although there are some immense fortunes in this country, I may challenge any one to point out the slightest difference in their respective manner towards each other. I first saw and judged of a country life at Major Hughes's house: I am at present in the city, where everything somewhat resembles the English customs, except that you find more simplicity here than you would do in England. Charlestown is one of the best built, handsomest, and most agreeable cities that I have ever seen. The American women are very pretty, and have great simplicity of character; and the extreme neatness of their appearance is truly delightful: cleanliness is everywhere even more studiously attended to here than in England. What gives me most pleasure is to see how completely the citizens are all brethren of one family. In America there are none poor, and none even that can be called peasants. Each citizen has some property, and all citizens have the same rights as the richest individual, or landed proprietor, in the country. The inns are very different from those of Europe; the host and hostess sit at table with you, and do the honours of a comfortable meal; and when you depart, you pay your bill without being obliged to tax it. If you should dislike going to inns, you may always find country houses in which you will be received, as a good American, with the same attention that you might expect in a friend's house in Europe.

My own reception has been most peculiarly agreeable. To have been merely my travelling companion, suffices to secure the kindest welcome. I have just passed five hours at a large dinner given in compliment to me by an individual of this town. Generals Howe and Moultrie, and several officers of my suite, were present. We drank each other's health, and endeavoured to talk English, which I am beginning to speak a little. I shall pay a visit to-morrow, with these gentlemen, to the governor of the state, and make the last arrangements for my departure. The next day, the commanding officers here will take me to see the town and its environs, and I shall then set out to join the army. I must close and send my letter immediately, because the vessel goes to-night to the entrance of the harbour, and sails to-morrow at five o'clock. As all the ships are exposed to some risk, I shall divide my letters amongst them. I write to M M. de Coigny, de Poix, de Noailles, de Ségur, and to Madame d'Ayen.* If either of these

* The Viscount de Coigny, son of the last marshal of that name, was the intimate friend of M. de Lafayette in his youth. He died young, perhaps even during this voyage.—(See the letters of January the 6th, and February 13th, 1778.) The Count de Ségur, who had married the sister of the Duchess

should not receive my letter, be so kind as to mention this circumstance.

From the agreeable life I lead in this country, from the sympathy which makes me feel as much at ease with the inhabitants as if I had known them for twenty years, the similarity between their manner of thinking and of my own, my love of glory and of liberty, you might imagine that I am very happy: but you are not with me, my dearest love; my friends are not with me; and there is no happiness for me when far from you and them. I often ask you if you still love, but I put that question still more often to myself and my heart ever answers, yes: I trust that heart does not deceive me. I am inexpressibly anxious to hear from you; I hope to find some letters at Philadelphia. My only fear is that the privateer which was to bring them to me should have been captured on her way. Although I can easily imagine that I have excited the especial displeasure of the English, by taking the liberty of coming hither in spite of them, and landing before their very face, yet I must confess that we shall be even more than on a par if they succeed in catching that vessel, the object of my fondest hopes, by which I am expecting to receive your letters. I entreat you to send me both long and frequent letters. You are not sufficiently conscious of the joy with which I shall receive them. Embrace, most tenderly, my Henriette: may I add, embrace our children? The father of those poor children is a wanderer, but he is, nevertheless, a good, honest man,—a good father, warmly attached to his family, and

d'Ayen, and who was, therefore, the uncle of M. de Lafayette, continued, to the last, his friend.—(See the memoirs published before his death, which occurred in 1830.)

a good husband also, for he loves his wife most tenderly. Present my compliments to your friends and to mine; may I not say *our* friends? with the permission of the Countess Auguste and Madame de Fronsac.* By *my friends*, you know that I mean my own dear circle, formerly of the court, and which afterwards became the society of *the wooden sword*;† we republicans like it the better for the change. This letter will be given you by a French captain, who, I think, will deliver it into your own hands; but I must confide to you that I have an agreeable anticipation for to-morrow, which is to write to you by an American, who will sail on the same day, but at a later hour. Adieu, then, my dearest love; I must leave off for want of time and paper; and if I do not repeat ten thousand times that I love you, it is not from want of affection, but from my having the vanity to hope that I have already convinced you of it. The night is far advanced, the heat intense, and I am devoured by gnats; but the best countries, as you perceive, have their inconveniences. Adieu, my love, adieu.

TO MADAME DE LAFAYETTE.

Petersburg, July 17th, 1777.

I AM very happy, my dearest love, if the word happiness can truly be applied to me, whilst I am separated from all I love; there is a vessel on the

* The Countess Auguste d'Aremberg, the wife of Count de Lamark, the friend of Mirabeau, and the Duchess de Fronsac, daughter-in-law to the Marshal de Richelieu.

† A society of young men, who first assembled at Versailles, and afterwards at an inn at Paris.—(Note by M. de Lafayette.)

point of sailing for France, and I am enabled to tell you, before setting out for Philadelphia, that I love you, my dearest life, and that you may be perfectly tranquil respecting my health. I bore the fatigue of the journey without suffering from it; although the land expedition was long and wearisome, yet the confinement of my melancholy ship was far more so. I am now eight days' journey from Philadelphia, in the beautiful state of Virginia. All fatigue is over, and I fear that my martial labours will be very light, if it be true that General Howe has left New York, to go I know not whither. But all the accounts I receive are so uncertain, that I cannot form any fixed opinion until I reach my destination; from thence, my love, I shall write you a long letter. You must already have received four letters from me, if they have not fallen into the hands of the English. I have received no news of you, and my impatience to arrive at Philadelphia to hear from you cannot be compared to any other earthly feeling. Conceive the state of my mind, after having passed such an immense length of time without having received a line from any friend! I hope all this will soon end, for I cannot live in such a state of uncertainty. I have undertaken a task which is, in truth, beyond my power, for my heart was not formed for so much suffering.

You must have learnt the particulars of the commencement of my journey: you know that I set out in a brilliant manner in a carriage, and I must now tell you that we are all on horseback,—having broken the carriage, according to my usual praiseworthy custom,—and I hope soon to write to you that we have arrived on foot. The journey is somewhat fatiguing; but although several of my comrades have suffered a great deal, I have scarcely myself been conscious of fatigue. The captain who takes charge of this letter will, perhaps, pay you a visit; I beg you in that case to receive him with great kindness.

I scarcely dare think of the time of your confinement, and yet I think of it every moment of the day. I cannot dwell upon it without the most dreadful anxiety. I am, indeed, unfortunate, at being so distant from you; even if you did not love me, you ought to pity me; but you do love me, and we shall mutually render each other happy. This little note will be short in comparison to the volumes I have already sent you, but you shall receive another letter in a few days from me.

The farther I advance to the north, the better pleased am I with the country and inhabitants. There is no attention or kindness that I do not receive, although many scarcely know who I am. But I will write all this to you more in detail from Philadelphia. I have only time to intreat you, my dearest love, not to forget an unhappy man, who pays most dearly for the error he committed in parting from you, and who never felt before how tenderly he loved you.

My respectful compliments to Madame d'Ayen, and my affectionate regards to my sisters. Tell M. de Coigny and M. de Poix that I am in good health, in case some letters should miscarry which I shall send by another opportunity, by which I shall also send a line to you, although I do not consider it so secure as this one.

TO MADAME DE LAFAYETTE.

July 23rd, 1777.

I AM always meeting, my dearest love, with opportunities of sending letters; I have this time only a quarter of an hour to give you. The vessel is on the point of sailing, and I can only announce to you my safe arrival at Annapolis, forty leagues from Philadelphia. I can tell you nothing of the town, for, as I alighted from my horse, I armed myself with a little weapon dipt in invisible ink. You must already have received five letters from me, unless King George should have received some of them. The last one was despatched three days since; in it I announced to you that my health was perfectly good, and had not been even impaired by my anxiety to arrive at Philadelphia. I have received bad news here; Ticonderoga, the strongest American post, has been forced by the enemy; this is very unfortunate, and we must endeavour to repair the evil. Our troops have taken, in retaliation, an English general officer, near New York. I am each day more miserable from having quitted you, my dearest love; I hope to receive news of you at Philadelphia, and this hope adds much to the impatience I feel to arrive in that city. Adieu, my life; I am in such haste that I know not what I write, but I do know that I love you more tenderly than ever; that the pain of this separation was necessary to convince me how very dear you are to me, and that I would give at this moment half my existence for the pleasure of embracing you again, and telling you with my own lips how well I love you. My respects to Madame d'Ayen, my compliments to the viscountess, my sisters, and all my friends: to you only have I time to write. O! if you knew how much I sigh to see you, how much I suffer at being separated from you, and all that my heart has been called on to endure, you would think me somewhat worthy of your love! I have left no space for Henriette; may I say for my children? Give them an hundred thousand embraces; I shall most heartily share them with you.

TO MADAME DE LAFAYETTE.

Philadelphia, September 12th, 1777.

I WRITE you a line, my dearest love, by some French officers, my friends, who embarked with me, but, not having received any appointment in the American army, are returning to France. I must begin by telling you that I am perfectly well, because I must end by telling you that we fought seriously last night, and that we were not the strongest on the field of battle. Our Americans, after having stood their ground for some time, ended at length by being routed: whilst endeavouring to rally them, the English honoured me with a musket ball, which slightly wounded me in the leg,—but it is a trifle, my dearest love; the ball touched neither bone nor nerve, and I have escaped with the obligation of lying on my back for some time, which puts me much out of humour. I hope that you will feel no anxiety; this event ought, on the contrary, rather to reassure you, since I am incapacitated from appearing on the field for some time: I have resolved to take great care of myself; be convinced of this, my love. This affair, will, I fear, be attended with bad consequences for America. We will endeavour, if possible, to repair the evil. You must have received many letters from me, unless the English be equally ill-disposed towards my epistles as towards my legs. I have not yet received one letter, and I am most impatient to hear from you. Adieu; I am forbidden to write longer. For several days I have not had time to sleep. Our retreat, and my journey hither, took up the whole of last night; I am perfectly well taken care of in this place. Tell all my friends that I am in good health. My tender respects to Madame d'Ayen. A thousand compliments to the viscountess and my sisters. The officers will soon set out. They will see you; what pleasure! Good night, my dearest life! I love you better than ever.

TO MADAME DE LAFAYETTE.

October 1st, 1777.

I WROTE to you, my dearest love, the 12th of September; the twelfth was the day after the eleventh, and I have a little tale to relate to you concerning that eleventh day. To render my action more meritorious, I might tell you that prudent reflections induced me to remain for some weeks in my bed, safe sheltered from all danger; but I must acknowledge that I was encouraged to take this measure by a slight wound, which I met with I know not how, for I did not, in truth, expose myself to peril. It was the first conflict at which I had been present; so you see how very rare engagements are. It will be the last of this campaign, or, in all probability, at least, the last great battle; and if anything should occur, you see that I could not myself be present.

You may, therefore, my love, feel perfectly secure. I have much pleasure in thus reassuring you. While I am desiring you not to be alarmed on my account, I repeat to myself that you love me; and this little conversation with my own heart is inexpressibly delightful to me, for I love you more tenderly than I have ever done before. . . .

My first occupation was to write to you the day after that affair: I told you that it was a mere trifle; and I was right; all I fear is that you should not have received my letter. As General Howe is giving, in the meantime, rather pompous details of his American exploits to the king his master, if he should write word that I am wounded, he may also write word that I am killed, which would not cost him anything; but I hope that my friends, and you especially, will not give faith to the reports of those persons who last year dared to publish that General Washington, and all the general officers of his army, being in a boat together, had been upset, and every individual drowned. But let us speak about the wound: it is only a flesh-wound, and has neither touched bone nor nerve. The surgeons are astonished at the rapidity with which it heals; they are in an ecstasy of joy each time they dress it, and pretend it is the finest thing in the world: for my part, I think it most disagreeable, painful, and wearisome; but tastes often differ: if a man, however, wished to be wounded for his amusement only, he should come and examine how I have been struck, that he might be struck precisely in the same manner. This, my dearest love, is what I pompously style my wound, to give myself airs, and render myself interesting. . . . . . .

I must now give you your lesson, as wife of an American general officer. They will say to you,

"They have been beaten:" you must answer,—"That is true; but when two armies of *equal number* meet in the field; old soldiers have naturally the advantage over new ones; they have, besides, had the pleasure of killing a great many of the enemy, many more than they have lost." They will afterwards add: "All that is very well; but Philadelphia is taken, the capital of America, the rampart of liberty!" You must politely answer, "You are all great fools! Philadelphia is a poor forlorn town, exposed on every side, whose harbour was already closed; though the residence of congress lent it, I know not why, some degree of celebrity. This is the famous city which, be it added, we will, sooner or later, make them yield back to us." If they continue to persecute you with questions, you may send them about their business in terms which the Viscount de Noailles will teach you, for I cannot lose time by talking to you of politics.

I have delayed writing your letter till the last, in the hope of receiving one from you, answering it, and giving you the latest intelligence of my health; but I am told, if I do not send immediately to congress, twenty-five leagues from hence, my captain will have set out, and I shall lose the opportunity of writing to you. This is the cause of my scrawl being more unintelligible than usual; however, if I were to send you anything but an hurried scrawl, I ought, in that case, to beg your pardon, from the singularity of the case. Recollect, my dearest love, that I have only once heard of you, from Count Pulaski. I am much provoked, and am very miserable. Imagine how dreadful it is to be far from all I love, in this state of suspense and almost despair; it is impossible to support it; and I feel, at the same time, that I do not deserve to be pitied. Why was I so obstinately bent on coming hither? I have been well punished for my error; my affections are too strongly rooted for me to be able to perform such deeds. I hope you pity me; if you knew all I suffer, especially at this moment, when everything concerning you is so deeply interesting! I cannot, without shuddering, think of this. I am told that a parcel has arrived from France; I have despatched expresses on every road and in every corner; I have sent an officer to congress; I am expecting him every day, and you may conceive with what feelings of intense anxiety. My surgeon is also very anxious for his arrival, for this suspense keeps my blood in a state of effervescence, and he would fain require that it should flow calmly. O, my dearest life, if I receive good news from you, and all I love, —if those delightful letters arrive to-day, how happy I shall be!—but with what agitation, also, I shall open them!

Be perfectly at ease about my wound; all the faculty in America are engaged in my service. I have a friend, who has spoken to them in such a manner that I am certain of being well attended to; that friend is General Washington. This excellent man, whose talents and virtues I admired, and whom I have learnt to revere as I know him better, has now become my intimate friend: his affectionate interest in me instantly won my heart. I am established in his house, and we live together like two attached brothers, with mutual confidence and cordiality. This friendship renders me as happy as I can possibly be in this country. When he sent his best surgeon to me, he told him to take charge of me as if I were his son, because he loved me with the same affection. Having heard that I wished to rejoin the army too soon, he wrote me a letter full of tenderness, in which he requested me to attend to the perfect restoration of my health. I give you these details, my dearest love, that you may feel quite certain of the care that is taken of me. Amongst the French officers, who have all expressed the warmest interest for me, M. de Gimat, my aide-de-camp, has followed me about like my shadow, both before and since the battle, and has given me every possible proof of attachment. You may thus feel quite secure on this account, both for the present and for the future.

All the foreigners who are in the army,—for I do not speak only of those who have not been employed, and who, on their return to France, will naturally give an unjust account of America, because the discontented, anxious to revenge their fancied injuries, cannot be impartial,—all the foreigners, I say, who have been employed here are dissatisfied, complain, detest others, and are themselves detested: they do not understand why I am the only stranger beloved in America, and I cannot understand why they are so much hated. In the midst of the disputes and dissensions common to all armies, especially when there are officers of various nations, I, for my part, who am an easy and a good-tempered man, am so fortunate as to be loved by all parties, both foreigners and Americans: I love them all—I hope I deserve their esteem; and we are perfectly satisfied the one with the other. I am at present in the solitude of Bethlehem, which the Abbé Raynal has described so minutely. This establishment is a very interesting one; the fraternity lead an agreeable and very tranquil life: we will talk over all this on my return; and I intend to weary those I love, yourself, of course, in the first place, by the relation of my adventures, for you know that I was always a great prattler.

You must become a prattler also, my love, and say many things for me to Henriette—my poor little Henriette! embrace her a thousand times—talk of me to her, but do not tell her all I deserve to suffer; my punishment will be, not to be recognised by her on my arrival; that is the penance Henriette will impose on me. Has she a brother or a sister?—the choice is quite indifferent to me, provided I have a second time the pleasure of being a father, and that I may soon learn that circumstance. If I should have a son, I will tell him to examine his own heart carefully; and if that heart should be a tender one, if he should have a wife whom he loves as I love you, in that case I shall advise him not to give way to feelings of enthusiasm, which would separate him from the object of his affection, for that affection will afterwards give rise to a thousand dreadful fears.

I am writing, by a different opportunity, to various persons, and also to yourself. I think this letter will arrive first; if this vessel should accidentally arrive, and the other one be lost, I have given the viscount a list of the letters I have addressed to him. I forgot to mention my aunts;* give them news of me as soon as this reaches you. I have made no *duplicata* for you, because I write to you by every opportunity. Give news of me, also, to M. Margelay,† the Abbé Fayon, and Desplaces.

* Madame de Chavaniac and Madame de Motier, sisters of General Lafayette's father.

† An ancient officer, to whom M. de Lafayette was confided, on leaving college, as to a governor.

A thousand tender regards to my sisters; I permit them to despise me as an infamous deserter—but they must also love me at the same time. My respects to Madame la Comtesse Auguste, and Madame de Fronsac. If my grandfather's letters should not reach him, present to him my respectful and affectionate regards. Adieu, adieu, my dearest life; continue to love me, for I love you most tenderly.

Present my compliments to Dr. Franklin and Mr. Deane; I wished to write to them, but cannot find time.

TO M. DE VERGENNES,

MINISTER OF FOREIGN AFFAIRS.

Whitemarsh Camp, October 24, 1777.

Sir,—You were formerly annoyed, much against my wish, by the part you were called upon to take in my first projects; you will, perhaps, also feel annoyed by the attention I take the liberty of requesting you to give to the objects I have at present in view. They may appear to you as little worthy as the first of occupying your valuable time; but in this case, as in the previous one, my good intentions (even should they be ill-directed) may serve as my apology. My age might also, perhaps, have been one, formerly; I only request now that it may not prevent you from taking into consideration whether my opinions be rational.

I do not permit myself to examine what succour the glorious cause we are defending in America may have received; but my love for my own country makes me observe, with pleasure, under how many points of view the vexations of the family of England may be advantageous to her. There is; above all, one project which, in every case, and *at all events*, would present, I think, rational hopes of attaining any useful end, in exact proportion to the means employed in its execution; I allude to an expedition of greater or less importance against the East Indies; and I should fear to injure the cause by proposing myself to take charge of it.

Without pretending to the art of prophecy in relation to present events, but convinced in the sincerity of my heart that to injure England would be serving (shall I say revenging?) my country; I believe that this idea would powerfully excite the energy of each individual bearing the honourable name of Frenchman. I came hither without permission; I have obtained no approbation but that which may be implied by silence; I might also undertake another little voyage without having been authorized by government: if the success be uncertain, I should have the advantage of exposing only myself to danger,—and what should, therefore, prevent my being enterprising? If I could but succeed in the slightest degree, a flame kindled on the least important establishment of England, even if part of my own fortune were to be consumed also, would satisfy my heart by awakening hopes for a more propitious hour.

Guided by the slight knowledge which my ignorance has been able to obtain, I shall now state in what manner, Sir, I would undertake this enterprise. An American patent, to render my movements regular, the trifling succours by which it might be sustained, the assistance I might obtain at the French islands, the speculations of some merchants, the voluntary aid of a few of my fellow comrades,—such are the feeble resources which would enable me to land peacefully on the Isle of France. I should there find, I believe, privateers ready to assist me, and men to accompany me in sufficient numbers to lie in wait for the vessels returning from China, which would offer me a fresh supply of force, sufficient perhaps to enable me to fall upon one or two of their factories, and destroy them before they could be protected. With an aid, which I dare scarcely hope would be granted me, and, above all, with talents which I am far from having yet acquired, might not some advantage be taken of the jealousy of the different nabobs, the hatred of the Mahrattas, the venality of the sepoys, and the effeminacy of the English? Might not the crowd of Frenchmen dispersed at present on that coast be employed with advantage in the cause? As to myself personally, in any case, the fear of compromising my own country would prevent my acknowledging the pride I feel in being her son, even as the nobility in some provinces occasionally lay aside their marks of distinction to reassume them at a later period.

Although by no means blind as to the imprudence of the step, I would have hazarded this enterprise alone, if the fear of injuring the interests I wish to serve, by not sufficiently understanding them, or of proving a detriment to some better-concerted expedition, had not arrested my intended movements; for I have the vanity to believe that a project of this kind may one day be executed on a grander scale, and by far abler hands, than mine. Even now it might be executed in a manner that would, I think, insure success, if I could hope to receive from the government, not an order, not succours, not mere indifference,—but I know scarcely what, which I can find no language to express with sufficient delicacy.

In this case, an order from the king, should he deign to restore me for some time to my friends and family, without prohibiting my return hither, would give me a hint to prepare myself with American continental commissions; some preparations and instructions from France might also precede that pretended return, and conduct me straight to the East Indies: the silence which was formerly perhaps an error, would then become a sacred duty, and would serve to conceal my true destination, and above all the sort of approbation it might receive.

Such, Sir, are the ideas that, duly impressed with a sense of my incapacity and youth, I presume to submit to your better judgment, and, if you should think favourably of them, to the various modifications to which you may conceive them liable; I am certain, at least, that they cannot be deemed ridiculous, because they are inspired by a laudable motive—the love of my country. I only ask for the honour of serving her under other colours, and I rejoice at seeing her interest united to that of the republicans for whom I am combating; earnestly hoping, however, that I shall soon be allowed to fight under the French banner. A commission of grenadier in the king's army would, in that case, be more agreeable to me than the highest rank in a foreign army.

I reproach myself too much, Sir, for thus offering you my undigested ideas regarding Asia, to heighten my offence by presumptuously tracing a plan of America, embellished with my own reflections, which you do not require, and have not asked for: the zeal which led me hither, and, above all, the friendship which unites me to the general-in-chief, would render me liable to the accusation of partiality, from which feeling I flatter myself I am wholly free. I reserve till my return the honour of mentioning to you the names of those officers of merit whom the love of their profession has led to this continent. All those who are French, Sir, have a right to feel confidence in you. It is on this ground that I claim your indulgence; I have a second claim upon it from the respect with which I have the honour to be, Sir,

Your very humble and obedient servant,

LAFAYETTE.

If this letter should weary you, Sir, the manner in which it will reach you may be deemed perhaps but too secure. I entrust it to M. de Valfort, captain of the regiment of Aunis, with the commission of colonel in our islands, whom his talents, reputation, and researches, have rendered useful in this country, and whom the wishes of General Washington would have detained here, if his health had not rendered it absolutely necessary for him to return to France. I shall here await your orders, (which cannot, without difficulty, enter an American harbour,) or I shall go myself to receive them, as future circumstances may render proper; for, since my arrival, I have not received one order which could regulate my movements.

TO MADAME DE LAFAYETTE.

The Camp near Whitemarsh, Oct. 29th, 1777.

I SEND you an open letter, my dearest love, in the person of M. de Valfort, my friend, whom I entreat you to receive as such. He will tell you at length everything concerning me; but I must tell you myself how well I love you. I have too much pleasure in experiencing this sentiment not to have also pleasure in repeating it to you a thousand times, if that were possible. I have no resource left me, my love, but to write and write again, without even hoping that my letters will ever reach you, and I endeavour to console myself, by the pleasure of conversing with you, for the disappointment and anguish of not receiving one single line from France. It is impossible to describe to you how completely my heart is torn by anxiety and fear; nor should I wish to express all I feel, even if it were in my power to do so; for I would not disturb, by any painful impressions, the happiest moments of my exile—those in which I can speak to you of my tenderness. But do you, at least, pity me? Do you comprehend all that I endure? If I could only know at this moment where you are, and what you are doing! but in the course of time I shall learn all this, for I am not separated from you in reality, as if I were dead. I am expecting your letters with an impatience, from which nothing can for an instant divert my thoughts: every one tells me they must soon arrive; but can I rely on this? Neglect not one opportunity of writing to me, if my happiness be still dear to you. Repeat to me that you love me: the less I merit your affection, the more necessary to me are your consoling assurances of it.

You must have received so many accounts of my slight wound, that all repetitions on the subject would be useless; and if you ever believed it was anything serious, M. de Valfort can undeceive you. In a very short time I shall not even be lame.

Is it not dreadful, my love, to reflect that it is by the public, by English papers, by our enemy's gazettes, that I should receive intelligence concerning you? In an unimportant article relating to my arrival here, they ended by speaking of yourself, your situation, and approaching confinement; that source of all my fears, agitations, hopes, and joy. How happy I should feel if I could learn that I had become a second time a father, that you are in good health, that my two children and their mother are likely to constitute the felicity of my future life! This country is delightful for the growth of filial and paternal love: these feelings may even be termed passions, and give rise to the most assiduous and unremitting care. The news of your confinement will be received with joy by the whole army, and above all by its commander.

I shall find my poor little Henriette very amusing on my return. I hope she will deliver a long sermon of reproof, and that she will speak to me with all the frankness of friendship; for my daughter will be always, I trust, my most intimate friend; I will only be a father in affection, and paternal love shall unite in my heart with friendship. Embrace her, my love,—may I say embrace *them?*—for me! But I will not dwell upon all I suffer from this painful uncertainty. I know that you share all the sorrows of my heart, and I will not afflict you. I wrote by the last opportunity to Madame d'Ayen; since my wound I have written to everybody; but those letters have perhaps been lost. It is not my fault; I wish to return a little evil to those wicked letter-stealers when they are on land, but on the sea I have only the consolation of the weak, that of cursing heartily those of whom you cannot be revenged. A thousand tender respects to your mother; my kind regards to your sisters. Do not forget my compliments to the Marshal de Noailles, and to your paternal and maternal relations. I have received four foolish lines from the Marshal de Mouchy, who does not say one word of you; I swore at him in every language. Adieu, my love, adieu; ask questions of my good, excellent friend, M. de Valfort, for my paper is coming to a close. It is dreadful to be reduced to hold no communication but by letter with a person whom one loves as I love you, and as I shall ever love you, until I draw my latest breath.

I have not missed a single opportunity, not even the most indirect one, without writing to you. Do the same also on your side, my dearest life, if you love me; but I should indeed be unfeeling and ungrateful if I were to doubt your love.

TO MADAME DE LAFAYETTE.

Camp of Whitemarsh, November 6th, 1777.

You will perhaps receive this letter, my dearest love, at the expiration of five or six years, for I am writing to you by an accidental opportunity, in which I do not place great trust. See what a circuit my letter must make. An officer in the army will carry it to Fort Pitt, three hundred miles in the interior of the continent; it will then embark on the great Ohio river, and traverse regions inhabited only by savages; having reached New Orleans, a small vessel will transport it to the Spanish islands; a ship of that nation—God knows when!—will carry it with her on her return to Europe. But it will even then be very distant from you; and it is only after having been soiled by the dirty hands of all the Spanish post-masters that it will be allowed to pass the Pyrenees. It may very possibly be unsealed and resealed five or six times before it be finally placed in your hands; but it will prove to you that I neglect no opportunity, not even the most indirect one, of sending you news of myself, and of repeating how well I love you. It is, however, for my own satisfaction only that I delight to tell you so at present; I hope that I shall have the pleasure of throwing this letter in the fire when it arrives, for be it understood I shall be there also, and my presence will render this piece of paper very insignificant. The idea is most soothing to my heart, and I indulge it with rapture. How enchanting to think of the moments when we shall be together! but how painful also to recollect that my joy is only caused by an illusion, and that I am separated from the reality of my happiness by two thousand leagues, an immense ocean, and villanous English vessels! Those wretched vessels make me very unhappy. One letter, one letter only, have I yet received from you, my love; the others have been lost or taken, and are probably at the bottom of the sea. I must consider our enemy the cause of this dreadful loss; for I am certain you do not neglect to write to me from every port, and by all the despatches sent by Dr. Franklin and Mr. Deane. And yet some ships arrived; I have sent couriers to every corner of the continent; but all my hopes have been frustrated. Perhaps you have not been properly informed. I entreat you, my love, to inquire carefully in what manner you may best send your letters. It is so dreadful for me to be deprived of them, and I am so unhappy at being separated from all I love! I am guilty, it is true, of having caused my own calamity; but you would pity me if you knew all that my heart endured.

But why tell you news in a letter destined to travel about the world for years, which will reach you perhaps in shreds, and will represent antiquity personified? My other despatches must have informed you of the various events of the campaign. The battle of Brandywine, in which I most skilfully lost a small part of my leg; the taking possession of Philadelphia, which will by no means, however, be attended with the ill consequences which have been expected in Europe; the attack of a post at Germantown, at which I was not present, from having received a recent wound, and which did not prove successful; the surrender of General Burgoyne, with five thousand men—that same Burgoyne who wished to devour us all, last spring, but who finds himself this autumn the prisoner of war of our northern army; and finally, our present situation, stationed immediately opposite each other, at four leagues distance, and General Howe established at Philadelphia, making great exertion to take certain forts, and having already lost in the attempt one large and one small vessel. You are now quite as well informed on the subject as if you were general-in-chief of either army. I need only at this moment add, that the wound of the 11th of September, of which I have spoken to you a thousand times, is almost completely healed, although I am still a little lame, but that in a few days there will scarcely remain any traces of this accident. All these details will be given you very circumstantially by my friend

Mr. de Valfort, to whom I have given a letter for you, and on whose accounts you may implicitly rely. I have just learnt that he has sailed, not, as I expected, in a packet, but in a good frigate of thirty-five guns: it would be unlucky indeed if he were taken. From his lips, and the epistle which I confided to him five or six days ago, you will learn all that your affection for me may make you wish to know. I wish you also knew the precise day of my return, and I am most impatient to fix that day myself, and to be able to say to you, in the joy of my heart,—upon such a day I set out to rejoin you, and obtain all earthly happiness.

A little gentleman, in a blue coat, with lemon-coloured facings and a white waistcoat, a German, coming hither to solicit an employment, (which he will not obtain,) and speaking wretched French, told me that he quitted Europe in the month of August: he talked to me of politics and of the ministry; he upset all Europe generally, and every court individually; but he knew not a word of what was most interesting to my heart. I examined him in every way; I mentioned fifty names to him; his answer was always, "*Me not know them noblemen.*"

I will not weary you with a long account of the state of my finances. The accident which occurred to my vessel was a source of vexation to me, because that vessel would have been useful to me in the present settlement of my affairs; but it is no longer in being, and I should reproach myself with having sent it back, had I not been obliged to make its return a clause in my engagements, on account of my minority.* Everything here is incredibly dear. We feel the consolation of the malevolent in think-

* It will be seen by the memoirs that that vessel was wrecked on the bar of Charlestown.

ing that the scarcity is still greater in Philadelphia. In time of war, we become reconciled to all we may ourselves endure by making our enemies suffer ten times more. We have here an abundance of provisions, and we learn with pleasure that our English neighbours are not so fortunate.

Do not think at present of being uneasy on my account; all the hard blows are over, and there can be, at most, but some little miniature strokes, which cannot concern me; I am not less secure in this camp than I should be were I in the centre of Paris. If every possible advantage to be attained by serving here; if the friendship of the army in gross and in detail; if a tender union with the most respectable and admirable of men, General Washington, sustained by mutual confidence; if the affection of those Americans by whom I wish to be beloved; if all this were sufficient to constitute my happiness, I should indeed have nothing to desire. But my heart is far from being tranquil. You would compassionate me, if you knew how much that heart suffers, and how well it loves you!

The present season of the year makes me hope to receive some letters. What may they announce to me? what may I hope? O, my dearest love, how cruel it is to endure this painful anxiety, under circumstances which are so all-important to my happiness! Have I two children? have I another infant to share my tender affection with my dearest Henriette? Embrace my dear little girl a thousand times for me; embrace them both tenderly, my dearest life. I trust they will know one day how well I love them.

A thousand respectful compliments to Madame d'Ayen; a thousand tender ones to the viscountess and my sisters; to my friends a million of kind regards; remember me to every one. Adieu! take care of your own health; give me circumstantial details of all things; believe that I love you more than ever, that you are the first object of my affection, and the surest guarantee of my felicity. The sentiments so deeply engraven on a heart which belongs to you alonc, shall remain, whilst that heart continues to vibrate. Will you, too, always love me, my dearest life? I dare believe it, and that we shall mutually render each other happy by an affection equally tender and eternal. Adieu, adieu! how delightful would it be to embrace you at this moment, and say to you with my own lips, I love thee better than I have ever loved, and I shall love thee for the remainder of my life.

TO GENERAL WASHINGTON.*

(ORIGINAL.)

Haddonfield, the 26th November, 1777.

DEAR GENERAL,—I went down to this place since the day before yesterday, in order to be acquainted of all the roads and grounds around the enemy. I heard at my arrival that their main body was be-

* All the letters addressed to General Washington, as well as to other Americans, were written in English. Since the death of General Washington, his family have returned to General Lafayette the original letters he had addressed to him, and these are now in our possession. The originals of Washington's letters were almost all lost in the French revolution; but M. de Lafayette, during his last journey to the United States, had a great number of them copied from minutes preserved by Washington himself: they have been inserted in the collection we have so frequently quoted from, published by Mr. Sparks.

tween Great and Little Timber Creek since the same evening. Yesterday morning, in reconnoitering about, I have been told that they were very busy in crossing the Delaware. I saw them myself in their boats, and sent that intelligence to General Greene as soon as possible, as every other thing I heard of. But I want to acquaint your excellency of a little event of last evening, which, though not very considerable in itself, will certainly please you, on account of the bravery and alacrity a small party of ours shewed on that occasion. After having spent the most part of the day to make myself well acquainted with the certainty of their motions, I came pretty late into the Gloucester road, between the two creeks. I had ten light-horse with Mr. Lindsey, almost a hundred and fifty riflemen, under Colonel Buttler, and two piquets of the militia, commanded by Colonels Hite and Ellis: my whole body was not three hundred. Colonel Armand, Colonel Laumoy, the chevaliers Duplessis and Gimat, were the Frenchmen who went with me. A scout of my men, with whom was Mr. Duplessis, to see how near were the first piquets from Gloucester, found at two miles and a half of it a strong post of three hundred and fifty Hessians with field-pieces, (what number I did know, by the unanimous deposition of their prisoners,) and engaged immediately. As my little reconnoitering party was all in fine spirits, I supported them. We pushed the Hessians more than an half mile from the place where was their main body, and we made them run very fast: British reinforcements came twice to them, but, very far from recovering their ground, they went always back. The darkness of the night prevented us then to push that advantage, and, after standing upon the ground we had got, I ordered them to return very slow to Haddonfield. The enemy, knowing perhaps by our drums that we were not so near, came again to fire at us; but the brave Major Moriss, with a part of his riflemen, sent them back, and pushed them very fast. I understand that they have had between twenty-five and thirty wounded, at least that number killed, among whom I am certain, is an officer; some say more, and the prisoners told me they have lost the commandant of that body; we got yet, this day, fourteen prisoners. I sent you the most moderate account I had from themselves. We left one single man killed, a lieutenant of militia, and only five of ours were wounded. Such is the account of our little entertainment, which is indeed much too long for the matter, but I take the greatest pleasure to let you know that the conduct of our soldiers is above all praises: I never saw men so merry, so spirited, so desirous to go on to the enemy, whatever forces they could have, as that small party was in this little fight. I found the riflemen above even their reputation, and the militia above all expectations I could have: I returned to them my very sincere thanks this morning. I wish that this little success of ours may please you; though a very trifling one, I find it very interesting on account of the behaviour of our soldiers.

Some time after I came back, General Varnum arrived here; General Greene is, too, in this place since this morning; he engaged me to give you myself the account of the little advantage of that small part of the troops under his command. I have nothing more to say to your excellency about our business on this side, because he is writing himself: I should have been very glad, if circumstances had permitted me, to be useful to him upon a greater scale. As he is obliged to march slow in order to attend his troops, and as I am here only a volunteer, I will have the honour to wait upon your excellency as soon as possible, and I'll set out to-day: it will be a great pleasure for me to find myself again with you.

With the most tender affection and highest respect I have the honour to be,

LAFAYETTE.

I must tell, too, that the riflemen had been the whole day running before my horse, without eating or taking any rest.

I have just now a certain assurance that two British officers, besides those I spoke you of, have died this morning of their wounds in an house; this, and some other circumstances, let me believe that their lost may be greater than I told to your excellency.

TO THE DUKE D'AYEN.

Camp Gulph, Pennsylvania, Dec. 16th, 1777.

THIS letter, if it ever reaches you, will find you at least in France; some hazards are averted by this circumstance, but I must not indulge in many hopes. I never write a letter for Europe without deploring before hand the fate most probably awaiting it, and I labour, undoubtedly, more for Lord Howe than for any of my friends. The bad season is fortunately drawing near; the English ships will be obliged to quit their confounded cruising stations; I may then receive letters, and forward them from hence with some degree of security ; this will make me very happy, and will prevent my wearying you by a repetition of events which I wish you to be acquainted with, but which I do not wish to remind you of each time I write. I am very anxious for the account of your journey. I depend principally on Madame de Lafayette for its details; she well knows how interesting they will be to me. The Marshall de Noailles tells me, in general terms, that the letters he receives from Italy assure him the travellers are all in good health. From him I have also learnt the confinement of Madame Lafayette ; he does not speak of it as if it were the happiest of all possible circumstances ; but my anxiety was too keen to be able to make any distinction of sex ; and by kindly writing to me, and giving me an account of the event, he rendered me far, far happier than he imagined, when he announced to me that I had only a daughter.* The Rue de St. Honoré has now for ever lost its credit, whilst the other Hotel de Noailles has acquired new lustre by the birth of Adrian.† It is truly an ill-proceeding on my part to throw that disgrace on a family from whom I have received so much kindness. You must now be freezing on the high roads of France ; those of Pennsylvania are also very cold, and I endeavour vainly to persuade myself that the difference of latitude betwixt this and Paris ought to give us, comparatively speaking, a delightful winter : I am even told that it will be more severe. We are destined to pass it in huts, twenty miles from Philadelphia,

* Madame Charles de Latour-Maubourg.

† A son of the Viscount de Noailles, who was the son of Marshal de Mouchy, and married the eldest daughter of the Duke d'Ayen.

that we may protect the country, be enabled to take advantage of every favourable opportunity, and also have the power of instructing the troops by keeping them together. It would, perhaps, have been better to have entered quietly into real winter quarters; but political reasons induced General Washington to adopt this half-way measure.

I wish I had sufficient skill to give you a satisfactory account of the military events passing in this country; but, in addition to my own incapacity, reasons, of which you will understand the weight, prevent my hazarding in a letter, exposed to the capture of the English fleet, a relation which might explain many things, if I had the happiness of conversing with you in person. I will, however, endeavour to repeat to you, once more, the most important events that have occurred during this campaign. My gazette, which will be more valuable from not containing my own remarks, must be preferable to the gazettes of Europe; because the man who sees with his own eyes, even if he should not see quite correctly, must always merit more attention than the man who has seen nothing. As to the gazettes which the English shower upon us, they appear to me only fit to amuse chairmen over their mugs of ale; and even these men must have indulged in liberal potations, not to perceive the falsehoods they contain. It seems to me that the project of the English ministry was to cut in a line that part of America which extends from the bay of Chesapeak to Ticonderoga. General Howe was ordered to repair to Philadelphia by the Elk river; Burgoyne to descend to Albany, and Clinton to ascend from New York by the North river: the three generals might in this manner have joined hands; they would have received, or pretended to receive, the submission of the alleged conquered provinces; we should only have retained for our winter quarters the interior of the country, and have depended solely for our resources on the four southern states. An attack on Charlestown may also, perhaps, have been intended: in the opinion of the cabinet of the King of England, America was thus almost conquered. Providence fortunately permitted some alterations to take place in the execution of this finely-conceived project—to exercise, probably, for some time, the constancy of the British nation.

When I arrived at the army, in the month of August, I was much astonished at not finding any enemies. After having made some marches into Jersey, where nothing occurred, General Howe embarked at New York. We were encamped, and expecting their descent, on the Chester side, when we learnt that they were at the mouth of the Elk river. General Washington marched to meet them, and after having taken up several stations, resolved to wait their arrival upon some excellent heights on the Brandywine stream. The 11th of September the English marched to attack us; but whilst they were amusing us with their cannon, and several movements in front, they suddenly detached the greater part of their troops, the choicest men of their army, with the grenadiers, under the command of General Howe, and Lord Cornwallis, to pass a ford four miles distant on our right. As soon as General Washington became aware of this movement, he detached his whole right wing to march towards them. Some unfounded reports, which had all the appearance of truth, and which contradicted the first accounts received, arrested for a length of time the progress of that wing, and when it arrived, the enemy had already crossed the ford. Thus it became necessary to engage in an open field with an army superior in numbers to our own. After having for some time sustained a very brisk fire, though many were killed on the side of the English, the Americans were obliged to give way. A portion of them was rallied and brought back: it was then that I received my wound. In a word, to cut the matter short, everything went on badly on both sides, and General Washington was defeated—because he could not gain the first general battle which had been fought during the war. The army reassembled at Chester; but having been carried to a distance from it, I have not been able to follow its different movements. General Howe took advantage of the disorder which a tremendous rain had occasioned in our army to pass the Schuylkill: he repaired to Philadelphia, to take possession of it, and stationed himself between that town and Germantown. General Washington attacked him on the 4th of October; and we may assert that our general beat theirs, although their troops defeated ours, since he surprised him, and even drove back the English for some time; but their experience proved again triumphant over our unpractised officers and soldiers. Some time before this event, an American brigadier, placed in detachment on the other side of the river, had been attacked at night in his camp, and had lost some of his men. These are the only important events which took place on our side during the six weeks that I was absent from the camp, whilst obliged to keep my bed from my unclosed wound: at that time we received good news of General Burgoyne. When I first rejoined the army, whilst General Howe was on the water, I learnt that Ticonderoga had been precipitately abandoned by the Americans, leaving there several cannons and a quantity of ammunition. This success inflamed the pride of General Burgoyne, and he issued a pompous proclamation, for which he has since paid very dearly. His first act was to send a detachment, which was repulsed; he was not, however, discouraged, but marched on, through immense forests, in a country which contained but a single road. General Gates had under his orders fifteen or sixteen thousand men, who distressed the enemy by firing upon them from behind the trees. Whether conqueror or conquered, General Burgoyne's force became gradually weakened, and every quarter of a league cost him many men. At length, surrounded on all sides, and perishing with hunger, he was obliged to enter into a convention, in virtue of which he was conducted by the New England militia into that same state of Massachusets in which it had been asserted in London he was to take up his winter quarters. From thence he is to be conveyed, with whatever troops he may have remaining, to England, at the expense of the king his master. Ticonderoga has been since evacuated by the English.

General Clinton, who had set out rather late from New York, after having taken and destroyed Fort Montgomery, on the north river, endeavoured to reach the rear of Gates; but, hearing of the convention, he returned on the same road by which he had advanced. If he had been more rapid in his march, the affairs of General Gates would not have ended so fortunately.

When my wound permitted me, after the space of six weeks, to rejoin the army, I found it stationed fifteen miles from Philadelphia; our northern reinforcements had arrived; General Howe was much incommoded by two forts, one on the Jersey side, the other on the little Island of Mud, that you will find on your map, below the Schuylkill. Those two forts defended the chevaux de frise of the Delaware; they held out for a long time, against all the efforts of the English troops, both by sea and land. Two young Frenchmen, who were acting there as engineers, acquired much glory by their conduct; MM. de Fleury, of the regiment of Rouergue, and Mauduit Duplessis, who had also at the same time the command of the artillery: he is an artillery officer in France. Some Hessians, commanded by Count Donop, attacked the fort in which Mauduit was stationed, and were repulsed with considerable loss. Count Donop was taken and received a mortal wound. These forts, after having made a vigorous resistance, were at length evacuated. Lord Cornwallis then passed into Jersey with five thousand men. The same number of our troops was stationed there, under one of our majors-general. As I was only a volunteer, I went to reconnoitre the ground, and having met, accidentally, with a detachment near the enemy's post, the good conduct of my soldiers rendered an imprudent attack justifiable. We were told that his lordship had been wounded. He then again re-crossed the river, and we also did the same. Some days afterwards our army assembled at Whitemarsh, thirteen miles from Philadelphia. The whole army of General Howe advanced to attack us: but having examined our position on every side, they judged it more prudent to retire during the night, after four days of apparent hesitation. We then executed the project of crossing over on this side of the Schuylkill, and after having been delayed on the opposite side, from finding on this shore a part of the enemy's army, (although they only fired a few cannon balls at us,) they left us a free passage the next day, and we shall all repair unto our huts for the winter.

Whilst remaining there, the American army will endeavour to clothe itself, because it is almost in a state of nudity,—to form itself, because it requires instruction,—and to recruit itself, because it is feeble; but the thirteen states are going to rouse themselves and send us some men. My division will, I hope, be one of the strongest, and I will exert myself to make it one of the best. The actual situation of the enemy is by no means an unpleasant one; the army of Burgoyne is fed at the expense of the republic, and the few men they may obtain back, for many will be lost upon the road, will immediately be replaced by other troops; Clinton is quite at ease in New York, with a numerous garrison; General Howe is paying court to the belles of Philadelphia. The liberty the English take of stealing and pillaging from friends as well as foes, places them completely at their ease. Their ships at present sail up to the town, not, however, without some danger, for, without counting the ship of sixty-four guns and the frigate which were burnt before the forts, and without counting all those that I trust the ice will destroy, several are lost every day on the difficult passage they are obliged to undertake.

The loss of Philadelphia is far from being so important as it is conceived to be in Europe. If the differences of circumstances, of countries, and of proportion between the two armies, were not duly considered, the success of General Gates would appear surprising when compared to the events that have occurred with us,—taking into account the superiority of General Washington over General Gates. Our General is a man formed, in truth, for this revolution, which could not have been accomplished without him. I see him more intimately than any other man, and I see that he is worthy of the adoration of his country. His tender friendship for me, and his complete confidence in me, relating to all military and political subjects, great as well as small, enable me to judge of all the interests he has to conciliate, and all the difficulties he has to conquer. I admire each day more fully the excellence of his character, and the kindness of his heart. Some foreigners are displeased at not having been employed, (although it did not depend on him to employ them)—others, whose ambitious projects he would not serve,—and some intriguing, jealous men, have endeavoured to injure his reputation; but his name will be revered in every age, by all true lovers of liberty and humanity; and although I may appear to be eulogising my friend, I believe that the part he makes me act, gives me the right of avowing publicly how much I admire and respect him. There are many interesting things that I cannot write, but will one day relate to you, on which I entreat you to suspend your judgment, and which will redouble your esteem for him.

America is most impatiently expecting us to declare for her, and France will one day, I hope, determine to humble the pride of England. This hope, and the measures which America appears determined to pursue, give me great hopes for the glorious establishment of her independence. We are not, I confess, so strong as I expected, but we are strong enough to fight; we shall do so, I trust, with some degree of success; and, with the assistance of France, we shall gain, with costs, the cause that I cherish, because it is the cause of justice,—because it honors humanity,—because it is important to my country,—and because my American friends, and myself, are deeply engaged in it. The approaching campaign will be an interesting one. It is said that the English are sending us some Hanoverians; some time ago they threatened us with, what was far worse, the arrival of some Russians. A slight menace from France would lessen the number of these reinforcements. The more I see of the English, the more thoroughly convinced I am, that it is necessary to speak to them in a loud tone.

After having wearied you with public affairs, you must not expect to escape without being wearied also with my private affairs. It is impossible to be more agreeably situated than I am in a foreign country. I have only feelings of pleasure to express, and I have each day more reason to be satisfied with the conduct of the congress towards me, although my military occupations have allowed me to become personally acquainted with but few of its members. Those I do know have especially loaded me with marks of kindness and attention. The new president, Mr. Laurens, one of the most respectable men of America, is my particular friend. As to the army, I have had the happiness of obtaining the friendship of every individual; not one opportunity is lost of giving me proofs of it. I passed the whole summer without accepting a division, which you know had been my previous intention; I passed all that time at General Washington's house, where I felt as if I were with a friend of twenty years' standing. Since my return from Jersey, he has desired me to choose, amongst several brigades, the division which may please me best; but I have chosen one entirely composed of Virginians. It is weak in point of numbers at present, just in proportion, however, to the weakness of the whole army, and almost in a state of nakedness; but I am promised cloth, of which I shall make clothes, and recruits, of which soldiers must be made, about the same period; but, unfortunately, the last is the most difficult task, even for more skilful men than me. The task I am performing here, if I had acquired sufficient experience to perform it well, would improve exceedingly my future knowledge. The major-general replaces the lieutenant-general, and the field-marshal, in their most important functions, and I should have the power of employing to advantage, both my talents and experience, if Providence and my extreme youth allowed me to boast of possessing either. I read, I study, I examine, I listen, I reflect, and the result of all is the endeavour at forming an opinion, into which I infuse as much common sense as possible. I will not talk much, for fear of saying foolish things; I will still less risk acting much, for fear of doing foolish things; for I am not disposed to abuse the confidence which the Americans have kindly placed in me. Such is the plan of conduct which I have followed until now, and which I shall continue to follow; but when some ideas occur to me, which I believe may become useful when properly rectified, I hasten to impart them to a great judge, who is good enough to say that he is pleased with them. On the other hand, when my heart tells me that a favourable opportunity offers, I cannot refuse myself the pleasure of participating in the peril, but I do not think that the vanity of success ought to make us risk the safety of an army, or of any portion of it, which may not be formed or calculated for the offensive. If I could make an axiom, with the certainty of not saying a foolish thing, I should venture to add that, whatever may be our force, we must content ourselves with a completely defensive plan, with the exception, however, of the moment when we may be forced to action, because I think I have perceived that the English troops are more astonished by a brisk attack than by a firm resistance.

This letter will be given you by the celebrated Adams, whose name must undoubtedly be known to you. As I have never allowed myself to quit the army, I have not been able to see him. He wished that I should give him letters of introduction to France, especially to yourself. May I hope that you will have the goodness of receiving him kindly, and even of giving him some information respecting the present state of affairs. I fancied you would not be sorry to converse with a man whose merit is so universally acknowledged. He desires ardently to succeed in obtaining the esteem of our nation. One of his friends himself told me so.

TO GENERAL WASHINGTON.*

(ORIGINAL)

Camp, 30th December, 1777.

My Dear General,—I went yesterday morning to head-quarters with an intention of speaking to your excellency, but you were too busy, and I shall lay down in this letter what I wished to say.

* This letter was occasioned by the momentary success of an intrigue, known in American history under the name of Conway's cabal. Conway, who wished to oppose Gates to Washington, had written to the former a letter, in which he attacked the general-in-chief. An aide-de-camp of Lord Stirling gained

I don't need to tell you that I am sorry for all that has happened for some time past. It is a necessary dependence of my most tender and respectful friendship for you, which affection is as true and candid as the other sentiments of my heart, and much stronger than so new an acquaintance seems to admit; but another reason, to be concerned in the present circumstances, is my ardent and perhaps enthusiastic wishes for the happiness and liberty of this country. I see plainly that America can defend herself if proper measures are taken, and now I begin to fear lest she should be lost by herself and her own sons.

When I was in Europe I thought that here almost every man was a lover of liberty, and would rather die free than live a slave. You can conceive my astonishment when I saw that toryism was as openly professed as whiggism itself: however, at that time I believed that all good Americans were united together; that the confidence of congress in you was unbounded. Then I entertained the certitude that America would be independent in case she should not lose you. Take away, for an instant, that modest diffidence of yourself, (which, pardon my

knowledge of that letter, and communicated its contents to Washington, who entered immediately into an explanation with Conway, in consequence of which the latter sent in his resignation, and announced the intention of re-entering the service of France. The resignation was not accepted by congress, and Conway was, on the contrary, named inspector-general of the army, with the rank of major-general, and the formation of the war office in relation to the mercenary troops. We see, by a letter from General Washington, that M. de Lafayette was the only person to whom he shewed General Conway's letter, transmitted by Lord Stirling's aide-de-camp.—(Letter to Horatio Gates, of the 4th of January, 1778, written from Washington. V. 1st, Appendix No. 6.)

freedom, my dear General, is sometimes too great, and I wish you could know, as well as myself, what difference there is between you and any other man,) you would see very plainly that if you were lost for America, there is no body who could keep the army and the revolution for six months. There are open dissensions in congress, parties who hate one another as much as the common enemy; stupid men, who, without knowing a single word about war, undertake to judge you, to make ridiculous comparisons; they are infatuated with Gates, without thinking of the different circumstances, and believe that attacking is the only thing necessary to conquer. Those ideas are entertained in their minds by some jealous men, and perhaps secret friends to the British Government, who want to push you in a moment of ill humour to some rash enterprise upon the lines, or against a much stronger army. I should not take the liberty of mentioning these particulars to you if I did not receive a letter about this matter, from a young good-natured gentleman at York, whom Conway has ruined by his cunning, bad advice, but who entertains the greatest respect for you.

I have been surprised at first, to see the few establishments of this board of war, to see the difference made between northern and southern departments, to see resolves from congress about military operations; but the promotion of Conway is beyond all my expectations. I should be glad to have new major-generals, because, as I know, you take some interest in my happiness and reputation: it is, perhaps, an occasion for your excellency to give me more agreeable commands in some interesting instances. On the other hand, General Conway says he is entirely a man to be disposed of by me.

He calls himself my soldier, and the reason of such behaviour to me is, that he wishes to be well spoken of at the French court, and his protector, the Marquis de Castries, is an intimate acquaintance of mine; but since the letter of Lord Stirling I inquired in his character. I found that he was an ambitious and dangerous man. He has done all in his power, by cunning manœuvres, to take off my confidence and affection for you. His desire was to engage me to leave this country. Now I see all the general officers of the army against congress; such disputes, if known by the enemy, would be attended with the worst consequences. I am very sorry whenever I perceive troubles raised among the defenders of the same cause, but my concern is much greater when I find officers coming from France, officers of some character in my country, to whom any fault of that kind may be imputed. The reason of my fondness for Conway was his being by all means a very brave and very good officer. However, that talent for manœuvres, and which seems so extraordinary to congress, is not so very difficult a matter for any man of common sense who applies himself to it. I must pay to General Portail, and some French officers, who came to speak me, the justice to say, that I found them as I could wish upon this occasion; for it has made a great noise among many in the army. I wish, indeed, those matters could be soon pacified. I wish your excellency could let them know how necessary you are to them, and engage them at the same time to keep peace, and simulate love among themselves till the moment when those little disputes shall not be attended with such inconveniences. It would be, too, a great pity that slavery, dishonour, ruin, and unhappiness of a whole world, should issue from some trifling differences between a few men.

You will find, perhaps, this letter very useless, and even inopportune; but I was desirous of having a pretty long conversation with you upon the present circumstances, to explain you what I think of this matter. As a proper opportunity for it did not occur, I took the liberty of laying down some of my ideas in this letter, because it is for my satisfaction to be convinced that you, my dear general, who have been indulgent enough to permit me to look on you as upon a friend, should know the confession of my sentiments in a matter which I consider as a very important one. I have the warmest love for my country and for every good Frenchman; their success fills my heart with joy; but, sir, besides, Conway is an Irishman, I want countrymen, who deserve, in every point, to do honour to their country. That gentleman had engaged me by entertaining my head with ideas of glory and shining projects, and I must confess, to my shame, that it is a too certain way of deceiving me.

I wished to join to the few theories about war I can have, and the few dispositions nature gave, perhaps, to me, the experience of thirty campaigns, in hope that I should be able to be the more useful in the present circumstances. My desire of deserving your satisfaction is stronger than ever, and everywhere you will employ me you can be certain of my trying every exertion in my power to succeed. I am now fixed to your fate, and I shall follow it and sustain it as well by my sword as by all means in my power. You will pardon my importunity in favour of the sentiment which dictated it. Youth and friendship make me, perhaps, too warm, but I feel the greatest concern at all that has happened for some time since.

With the most tender and profound respect, I have the honour to be, &c.

FROM GENERAL WASHINGTON.

(ORIGINAL.)

Head-quarters, December 31st, 1777.

MY DEAR MARQUIS,—Your favour of yesterday conveyed to me fresh proof of that friendship and attachment, which I have happily experienced since the first of our acquaintance, and for which I entertain sentiments of the purest affection. It will ever constitute part of my happiness to know that I stand well in your opinion; because I am satisfied that you can have no views to answer by throwing out false colours, and that you possess a mind too exalted to condescend to low arts and intrigues to acquire a reputation. Happy, thrice happy, would it have been for this army and the cause we are embarked in, if the same generous spirit had pervaded all the actors in it. But one gentleman, whose name you have mentioned, had, I am confident, far different views; his ambition and great desire of being puffed off, as one of the first officers of the age, could only be equalled by the means which he used to obtain them. But finding that I was determined not to go beyond the line of my duty to indulge him in the first—nor to exceed the strictest rules of propriety to gratify him in the second—he became my inveterate enemy;

and he has, I am persuaded, practised every art to do me an injury, even at the expense of reprobating a measure that did not succeed, that he himself advised to. How far he may have accomplished his ends, I know not; and except for considerations of a public nature, I care not; for, it is well known, that neither ambitious nor lucrative motives, led me to accept my present appointments, in the discharge of which, I have endeavoured to observe one steady and uniform system of conduct, which I shall invariably pursue, while I have the honour to command, regardless of the tongue of slander, or the powers of detraction. The fatal tendency of disunion is so obvious, that I have, in earnest terms, exhorted such officers as have expressed their dissatisfaction at General Conway's promotion, to be cool and dispassionate in their decision about the matter; and I have hopes that they will not suffer any hasty determination to injure the service. At the same time, it must be acknowledged, that officers' feelings upon these occasions are not to be restrained, although you may control their actions.

The other observations contained in your letter have too much truth in them; and, it is much to be lamented, that things are not now as they formerly were. But we must not, in so great a contest, expect to meet with nothing but sunshine. I have no doubt that everything happens for the best, that we shall triumph over all our misfortunes, and, in the end, be happy; when, my dear marquis, if you will give me your company in Virginia, we will laugh at our past difficulties and the folly of others; and I will endeavour, by every civility in my power, to shew you how much, and how sincerely, I am your affectionate and obedient servant.

TO GENERAL WASHINGTON.

(ORIGINAL.)

Valley Forge, December 31st, 1777.

My Dear General,—I should have much reproached myself the liberty I took of writing to your excellency, if I had believed it could engage you in the trouble of answering that letter. But now, as you have written it, I must tell you that I received this favour with the greatest satisfaction and pleasure. Every assurance and proof of your affection fills my heart with joy, because that sentiment of yours is extremely dear and precious to me. A tender and respectful attachment for you, and an invariable frankness, will be found in my mind, as you know me better; but, after those merits, I must tell you, that very few others are to be found. I never wished so heartily to be intrusted by nature with an immensity of talents than on this occasion; I could be then of some use to your glory and happiness, as well as to my own.

What man do not join the pure ambition of glory with this other ambitious of advancement, rank, and fortune? As an ardent lover of laurels, I cannot bear the idea that so noble a sentiment should be mixed with any low one. In your preaching moderation to the brigadiers upon such an occasion, I am not surprised to recognise your virtuous character. As I hope my warm interest is known to your excellency, I dare entertain the idea that you will be so indulgent as to let me know everything concerning you, whenever you will not be under the law of secrecy or particular circumstances.

With the most tender and affectionate friendship—with the most profound respect—I have the honour to be, &c.

TO MADAME DE LAFAYETTE.

Camp, near Valley-Forge, January 6th, 1778.

WHAT a date, my dearest love, and from what a region I am now writing, in the month of January! It is in a camp, in the centre of woods, fifteen hundred leagues from you, that I find myself enclosed in the midst of winter. It is not very long since we were only separated from the enemy by a small river; we are at present stationed seven leagues from them, and it is on this spot that the American army will pass the whole winter, in small barracks, which are scarcely more cheerful than dungeons. I know not whether it will be agreeable to General Howe to visit our new city, in which case we would endeavour to receive him with all due honour. The bearer of this letter will describe to you the pleasant residence which I choose in preference to the happiness of being with you, with all my friends, in the midst of all possible enjoyments; in truth, my love, do you not believe that powerful reasons are requisite to induce a person to make such a sacrifice? Everything combined to urge me to depart,—honour alone told me to remain; and when you learn in detail the circumstances in which I am placed, those in which the army, my friend, its commander, and the whole American cause were placed, you will not only forgive me, but you will excuse, and I may almost venture to say, applaud me. What a pleasure I shall feel in explaining to you myself all the reasons of my conduct, and, in asking, whilst embracing you, a pardon, which I am very certain I shall then obtain! But do not condemn me before hearing my defence. In addition to the reasons I have given you, there is one other reason which I would not relate to every one, because it might appear like affecting airs of ridiculous importance. My presence is more necessary at this moment to the American cause, than you can possibly conceive ; many foreigners, who have been refused employment, or whose ambitious views have been frustrated, have raised up some powerful cabals ; they have endeavoured, by every sort of artifice, to make me discontented with this revolution, and with him who is its chief ; they have spread as widely as they could, the report that I was quitting the continent. The English have proclaimed also, loudly, the same intention on my side. I cannot in conscience appear to justify the malice of these people. If I were to depart, many Frenchmen who are useful here would follow my example. General Washington would feel very unhappy if I were to speak of quitting him ; his confidence in me is greater than I dare acknowledge, on account of my youth. In the place he occupies, he is liable to be surrounded by flatterers or secret enemies ; he finds in me a secure friend, in whose bosom he may always confide his most secret thoughts, and who will always speak the truth. Not one day passes without his holding long conversations with me, writing me long letters, and he has the kindness to consult me on the most important matters. A peculiar circumstance is occurring at this moment which renders my presence of some use to him : this is not the time to speak of my departure. I am also at present engaged in an interesting correspondence with the president of congress. The desire to debase England, to promote the advantage of my own country, and the happiness of humanity, which is strongly interested in the existence of one perfectly free nation, all induces me not to depart at the moment when my absence might prove injurious to the cause I have embraced. The General, also, after a slight success in Jersey, requested me, with the unanimous consent of congress, to accept a division in the army, and to form it according to my own judgment, as well as my feeble resources might permit; I ought not to have replied to such a mark of confidence, by asking what were his commissions for Europe. These are some of the reasons, which I confide to you, with an injunction of secrecy. I will repeat to you many more in person, which I dare not hazard in a letter. This letter will be given you by a good Frenchman, who has come a hundred miles to ask me for my commissions. I wrote to you a few days ago by the celebrated Mr. Adams; he will facilitate your sending me letters. You must have received those I sent you as soon as I heard of your confinement. How very happy that event has rendered me, my dearest love! I delight in speaking of it in all my letters, because I delight in occupying myself with it at every moment of my life! What a pleasure it will give me to embrace my two poor little girls, and make them request their mother to forgive me! You do not believe me so hard hearted, and at the same time so ridiculous, as to suppose that the sex of our new infant can have diminished in any degree my joy at its birth. Our age is not so far advanced, that we may not expect to have another child, without a miracle from Heaven. The next one must absolutely be a boy. However, if it be on account of the name that we are to regret not having a son, I declare that I have formed the project of living long enough to bear it many years myself, before I yield it to any other person. I am indebted to the Marshal de

Noailles for the joyful news. I am anxiously expecting a letter from you. I received the other day one from Desplaces, who mentioned having sent a preceding one; but the caprice of the winds, without speaking of English ships, often deranges the order of my correspondence. I was for some days very uneasy about the Viscount de Coigny, who, some of my letters announced, was in a precarious state of health. But that letter from Desplaces, who told me all were well, without mentioning the viscount's name, has quite reassured me. I have also received some other letters which do not speak of his health. When you write, I entreat you to send me many details of all the people whom I love, and even of all my acquaintance. It is very extraordinary that I have not heard of Madame de Fronsac's confinement. Say a thousand tender and respectful things from me to her, as well as to the Countess Auguste. If those ladies do not enter into the reasons which force me to remain here, they must indeed think me a most absurd being, more especially as they have opportunities of seeing clearly what a charming wife I am separated from; but even that may prove to them what powerful motives must guide my conduct. Several general officers have brought their wives to the camp; I envy them—not their wives—but the happiness they enjoy in being able to see them. General Washington has also resolved to send for his wife. As to the English, they have received a reinforcement of three hundred young ladies from New York; and we have captured a vessel filled with chaste officers' wives, who had come to rejoin their husbands: they were in great fear of being kept for the American army.

You will learn by the bearer of this letter that my health is very good, that my wound is healed, and that the change of country has produced no effect upon me. Do you not think that, at my return, we shall be old enough to establish ourselves in our own house, live there happily together, receive our friends, institute a delightful state of freedom, and read foreign newspapers, without feeling any curiosity to judge by ourselves of what may pass in foreign countries? I enjoy thus building, in France, castles of felicity and pleasure: you always share them with me, my dearest love, and when we are once united, nothing shall again separate us, or prevent our experiencing together, and through each other, the joy of mutual affection, and the sweetest and most tranquil happiness. Adieu, my love; I only wish this project could be executed on this present day. Would it not be agreeable to you also? Present my tender respects to Madame d'Ayen: embrace a thousand times the viscountess and my sisters. Adieu, adieu; continue to love me, and forget not for a moment the unhappy exile who thinks incessantly of thee with renewed ardour and tenderness.

TO GENERAL WASHINGTON.

(ORIGINAL.)

Dear General,—I shall make use, in this particular instance, of the liberty you gave me, of telling freely every idea of mine which could strike me as not being useless to a better order of things.

There were two gentlemen, same rank, same duty to perform, and same neglect of it, who have been arrested the same day by me. As I went in the night around the picquets, I found them in fault, and I gave an account of it the next day to your excellency. You answered, that I was much in wrong not to have had them relieved and arrested immediately. I objected that it was then very late for such a changement, and that I did not know which was the rule in this army, but that the gentlemen should be arrested in that very moment. The last answer of your excellency has been, "they are to have a court-martial, and you must give notice of it to the adjutant-general." Therefore, Major Nevil made two letters in order to arrest them, *one for having been surprised in his post*, and the other, for the same cause, *and allowing his sentries to have fires, which he could see in standing before the picquet.* I give you my word of honour, that there was not any exaggeration.

Now I see in the orders, the less guilty punished in a manner much too severe indeed, and dismissed from the service, (it is among all the delicate minds deprived of his honour,) when he was only to be severely reprimanded and kept for some time under arrest. But it can be attributed to a very severe discipline.

What must I think of the same court, when they unanimously acquit (it is to say that my accusation is not true) the officer who joins to the same fault, entirely the same this, of allowing his sentries to have fire in his own sight; for in every service *being surprised* or being found in the middle of his picquet without any challenging or stopping sentry, as Major Nevil, riding before me, found him, is entirely the same thing; and Major Nevil, riding before me, when I was busy to make a sentry pull off his fire, can swear that such was the case with that officer—he can do more than swearing, for he can give his word of honour, and I think that idea *honour* is the same in every country.

But the *préjugés* are not the same thing; for giving publicly the best of such a dispute (for here it becomes a trial for both parties) to an officer of the last military stage against one of the first, should be looked on as an affront to the rank, and acquitting a man, whom one other man accuses, looked upon as an affront to the person. It is the same in Poland, for Count de Pulaski was much affronted at the decision of a court-martial entirely acquitting Colonel Molens. However, as I know the English customs, I am nothing else but surprised to see such a partiality in a court-martial.

Your excellency will certainly approve my not arresting any officer for being brought before a court-martial for any neglect of duty; but when they will be robbers or cowards, or when they will assassinate—in all, when they will deserve being cashiered or put to death.

Give me leave to tell your excellency how I am adverse to court-martials. I know it is the English custom, and I believe it is a very bad one. It comes from their love of lawyers, speakers, and of that black apparatus of sentences and judgments; but such is not the American temper, and I think this new army must pick up the good institutions, and leave the bad ones wherever they may be. In France, an officer is arrested by his superior, who gives notice of it to the commanding officer, and then he is punished enough in being deprived of going out of his room in time of peace—of going his duty in time of war. Nobody knows of it but his comrades. When the fault is greater, he is confined in a common room for prisoner officers, and this is much more shameful. Notice of it is immediately given to the general officer, who commands there. That goes, too, to the king's minister, who is to be replaced here by the commander-in-chief; in time of war, it goes to the general-in-chief.

Soldiers are punished the same, or next day, by order of proper officers, and the right of punishing is proportionate to their ranks.

But when both officers and soldiers have done something which deserves a more severe punishment; when their honour, or their life, or their liberty for more than a very short time, is concerned, then a court-martial meets, and the sentence is known. How will you let an unhappy soldier be confined several weeks with men who are to be hanged, with spies, with the most horrid sort of people, and in the same time be lost for the duty, when they deserve only some lashes. There is no proportion in the punishments.

How is it possible to carry a gentleman before a parcel of dreadful judges, at the same place where an officer of the same rank has been just now cashiered, for a trifling neglect of his duty; for, I suppose, speaking to his next neighbour, in a manœuvre for going into a house to speak to a pretty girl, when the army is on its march, and a thousand other things? How is it possible to bring to the certainty of being cashiered or dishonoured, a young lad who has made a considerable fault because he had a light head, a too great vivacity, when that young man would be, perhaps, in some years, the best officer of the army, if he had been friendly reprimanded and arrested for some time, without any dishonour?

The law is always severe, and brings with it an eternal shameful mark. When the judges are partial, as on this occasion, it is much worse, because they have the same inconvenience as law itself.

In court-martial, men are judged by their inferiors. How it is averse to discipline, I don't want to say. The publication exposes men to be despised by the least soldier. When men have been before a court-martial, they should be or acquitted or dismissed. What do you think can be produced by the half condemnation of a general officer? What necessity for all the soldiers, all the officers, to know that *General Maxwell has been prevented from doing his duty by his being drunk?* Where is the man who will not laugh at him, if he is told by him, *you are a drunkard;* and is it right to ridiculize a man, respectable by his rank, because he drank two or three gills of rum?

These are my reasons against courts-martial, when there is not some considerable fault to punish. According to my affair, I am sorry in seeing the less guilty being *the only one punished.* However, I shall send to courts-martial but for such crimes that there will be for the judges no way of indulgence and partiality.

With the most tender respect, I am, &c.

TO MADAME DE LAFAYETTE.

York, February 3rd, 1778.

I SHALL never have any cause to reproach myself, my dearest love, with having allowed an opportunity to pass without writing to you, and I have found one by M. du Bouchet, who has the happiness of embarking for France. You must have already received several letters in which I speak of the birth of our new infant, and of the pleasure this joyful event has given me. If I thought that you could imagine the happiness I feel at this event had been at all diminished because our Anastasia is only a daughter, I should be so much displeased with you, that I should but love you a very little for a few moments. O, my love! what an enchanting pleasure it will be for me to embrace you all; what a consolation to be able to weep with my other friends for the dear friend whom I have lost!

I will not give you a long account of the proofs of confidence with which I have been honoured by America. Suffice it to say that Canada is oppressed by the English; the whole of that immense country is in the power of the enemy, who are there in possession of troops, forts, and a fleet. I am to repair thither with the title of General of the Northern Army, at the head of three thousand men, to see if no evil can be done to the English in that country. The idea of rendering the whole of New France free, and of delivering her from a heavy yoke, is too glorious for me to allow myself to dwell upon it. My army would, in that case, increase at an immense rate, and would be increased also by the French. I am undertaking a most difficult task, above all taking into account the few resources I possess. As to those my own merit offers, they are very trifling in comparison to the importance of the place; nor can a man of twenty be fit to command an army, charged with the numerous details to which a general must attend, and having under his direct orders a vast extent of country.

The number of the troops I shall command would appear, I own, trifling in Europe, but it is considerable for America. What gives me most pleasure in all this is, that, under any circumstances, I shall be now sooner able to inform you. How delightful it will be to hurry through my affairs with the English there above! I am just setting out for Albany, and from thence to another place, nearly an hundred and fifty leagues from hence, where my labours will commence. I shall go part of the way on sledges; having once reached that spot, I shall have only ice to tread upon.

I do not write to any of my friends by this opportunity. I have an immense deal of business to do; there is an infinite number of military and political affairs to arrange; there are so many things to repair, so many new obstacles to remove, that I should require, in truth, forty years' experience, and very superior talents, to be able to conquer all the difficulties I meet with. I will, at least, do the best I can, and if I only succeed in occupying the enemy's attention in the north, even if I do them no other injury, it would be rendering an important service, and my little army would not be wholly useless. Be so kind as to tell the prince* that his youthful captain, although now a general-in-chief, has not acquired more knowledge than he possessed at Polygone, and that he knows not how, unless chance or his good angel should direct him, to justify the confidence which has been placed in him. A thousand tender respects to Madame d'Ayen. A thousand assurances of my tender affection to the viscountess and all my sisters. Do not forget me to your father, Madame de Tessé, and the Marshal de Noailles. Adieu, adieu, my dearest love; em-

* The Prince de Poix, colonel of the regiment de Noailles, in which M. de Lafayette was captain.

brace our dear children; I embrace a million of times their beloved mother. When shall I find myself again within her arms?

TO GENERAL WASHINGTON.

(ORIGINAL.)

Hemingtown, the 9th February, 1778.

DEAR GENERAL,—I cannot let go my guide without taking this opportunity of writing to your excellency, though I have not yet public business to speak of. I go on very slowly; sometimes drenched by rain, sometimes covered by snow, and not entertaining many handsome thoughts about the projected incursion into Canada; if successes were to be had, it would surprise me in a most agreeable manner by that very reason that I don't expect any shining ones. Lake Champlain is too cold for producing the least bit of laurel, and if I am not starved I shall be as proud as if I had gained three battles.

Mr. Duer had given to me a rendezvous at a tavern, but nobody was to be found there. I fancy that he will be with Mr. Conway sooner than he has told me; they will perhaps conquer Canada before my arrival, and I expect to meet them at the governor's house in Quebec.

Could I believe, for one single instant, that this pompous command *of a northern army* will let your excellency forget a little us absent friends, then, I would send the project to the place it comes from. But I dare hope that you will remember me sometimes. I wish you, very heartily, the greatest public and private happiness and successes. It is a very melancholy idea for me that I cannot follow your fortunes as near your person as I could wish; but my heart will take, very sincerely, its part of everything which can happen to you, and I am already thinking of the agreeable moment when I may come down to assure your excellency of the most tender affection and highest respect. I have the honour to be, &c.

TO GENERAL WASHINGTON.

(ORIGINAL.)

Albany, the 19th February, 1778.

DEAR GENERAL,—Why am I so far from you and what business had the board of war to hurry me through the ice and snow without knowing what I should do, neither what they were doing themselves? You have thought, perhaps, that their project would be attended with some difficulty, that some means had been neglected, that I could not obtain all the success and the immensity of laurels which they had promised to me; but I defy your excellency to conceive any idea of what I have seen since I left the place where I was quiet and near my friends, to run myself through all the blunders of madness or treachery (God knows what). Let me begin the journal of my fine and glorious campaign.

According to Lord Stirling's advice, I went by Corich-ferry to Ringo's tavern, where Mr. Duer had given me a rendezvous; but there no Duer was to be found, and they did never hear from him.

From thence I proceeded by the State of New York, and had the pleasure of seeing the friends of America as warm in their love for the commander-in-chief as his best friend could wish. I spoke to Governor Clinton, and was much satisfied with that gentleman. At length I met Albany, the 17th, though I was not expected before the 25th. General Conway had been here only three days before me, and I must confess I found him very active and looking as if he had good intentions; but we know a great deal upon that subject. His first word has been that the expedition is quite impossible. I was at first very diffident of this report, but have found that he was right. Such is, at least, the idea I can form of this ill-concerted operation within these two days.

General Schuyler, General Lincoln, General Arnold, had written, before my arrival, to General Conway, in the most expressive terms, that, in our present circumstances, there was no possibility to begin, now, an enterprise into Canada. Hay, deputy quarter-master-general; Cuyler, deputy commissary-general; Mearsin, deputy clothier-general, in what they call the northern department, are entirely of the same opinion. Colonel Hazen, who has been appointed to a place which interferes with the three others above mentioned, was the most desirous of going there. The reasons of such an order I think I may attribute to other motives. The same Hazen confesses we are not strong enough to think of the expedition in this moment. As to the troops, they are disgusted, and (if you except some Hazen's Canadians) reluctant, to the utmost degree, to begin a winter incursion in a so cold country. I have consulted everybody, and everybody answers me that it would be madness to undertake this operation.

I have been deceived by the board of war; they have, by the strongest expressions, promised to me one thousand, and (what is more to be depended upon) they have assured to me in writing, *two thousand and five hundred combatants, at a low estimate.* Now, Sir, I do not believe I can find, *in all,* twelve hundred fit for duty, and most part of those very men are naked, even for a summer's campaign. I was to find General Stark with a large body, and indeed General Gates had told to me, *General Stark will have burnt the fleet before your arrival.* Well, the first letter I receive in Albany is from General Stark, who wishes to know *what number of men, from whence, for what time, for what rendezvous, I desire him to raise.* Colonel Biveld, who was to rise too, would have done something *had he received money.* One asks, what encouragement his people will have, the other has no clothes; not one of them has received a dollar of what was due to them. I have applied to every body, I have begged at every door I could these two days, and I see that I could do something were the expedition to be begun in five weeks. But you know we have not an hour to lose, and indeed it is now rather too late, had we every thing in readiness.

There is a spirit of dissatisfaction prevailing among the soldiers, and even the officers, which is owing to their not being paid for some time since. This department is much indebted, and as near as I can ascertain, for so short a time, I have already discovered near eight hundred thousand dollars due to the continental troops, some militia, the quartermaster's department, &c. &c. &c. It was with four hundred thousand dollars, only the half of which is arrived to day, that I was to undertake the operation, and satisfy the men under my commands. I send to congress the account of those debts. Some clothes, by Colonel Hazen's activity, are arrived from Boston, but not enough by far, and the greatest part is cut off.

We have had intelligence from a deserter, who makes the enemy stronger than I thought. There is no such thing *as straw on board the vessels to burn them.* I have sent to congress a full account of the matter; I hope it will open their eyes. What they will resolve upon I do not know, but I think I must wait here for their answer. I have inclosed to the president, copies of the most important letters I had received. It would be tedious for your excellency, were I to undertake the minutest detail of everything; it will be sufficient to say that the want of men, clothes, money, and the want of time, deprives me of all hopes as to this excursion. If it may begin again in the month of June, by the east, I cannot venture to assure; but for the present moment such is the idea I conceive of the famous incursion, as far as I may be informed, in a so short time.

Your excellency may judge that I am very distressed by this disappointment. My being appointed to the command of the expedition is known through the continent, it will be soon known in Europe, as I have been desired, by members of congress, to write to my friends; my being at the head of an army, people will be in great expectations, and what shall I answer?

I am afraid it will reflect on my reputation, and I shall be laughed at. My fears upon that subject are so strong, that I would choose to become again only a volunteer, unless congress offers the means of mending this ugly business by some glorious operation; but I am very far from giving to them the least notice upon that matter. General Arnold seems very fond of a diversion against New York, and he is too sick to take the field before four or five months. I should be happy if something was proposed to me in that way, but I will never ask, nor even seem desirous, of anything directly from congress; for you, dear general, I know very well, that you will do everything to procure me the only thing I am ambitious of—glory.

I think your excellency will approve of my staying here till further orders, and of my taking the liberty of sending my despatches to congress by a very quick occasion, without going through the hands of my general; but I was desirous to acquaint them early of my disagreeable and ridiculous situation.

With the greatest affection and respect, I have the honour to be, &c.

TO GENERAL WASHINGTON

(ORIGINAL.)

The 23rd February, 1778.

Dear General,—I have an opportunity of writing to your excellency which I will not miss by any means, even should I be afraid of becoming tedious and troublesome; but if they have sent me far from you, I don't know for what purpose, at least I must make some little use of my pen, to prevent all communication from being cut off between your excellency and myself. I have written lately to you my distressing, ridiculous, foolish, and, indeed, nameless situation. I am sent, with a great noise, at the head of an army for doing great things; the whole continent, France and Europe herself, and what is the worse, the British army, are in great expectations. How far they will be deceived, how far we shall be ridiculed, you may judge by the candid account you have got of the state of our affairs.

There are things, I dare say, in which I am deceived—a certain colonel is not here for nothing: one other gentleman became very popular before I went to this place; Arnold himself is very fond of him. Every part on which I turn to look I am sure a cloud is drawn before my eyes; however, there are points I cannot be deceived upon. The want of money, the dissatisfaction among the soldiers, the disinclination of every one (except the Canadians, who mean to stay at home) for this expedition, are as conspicuous as possible; however, I am sure I will become very ridiculous, and laughed at. *My expedition* will be as famous as the *secret expedition* against Rhode Island. I confess, my dear general, that I find myself of very quick feelings whenever my reputation and glory are concerned in anything. It is very hard indeed that such a part of my happiness, without which I cannot live, should depend upon schemes which I never knew of but when there was no time to put them into execution. I assure you, my most dear and respected friend, that I am more unhappy than I ever was.

My desire of doing something was such, that I have thought of doing it by surprise with a detachment, but it seems to me rash and quite impossible. I should be very happy if you were here to give me some advice; but I have nobody to consult with.

They have sent to me more than twenty French officers; I do not know what to do with them; I beg you will acquaint me the line of conduct you advise me to follow on every point. I am at a loss how to act, and indeed I do not know what I am here for myself. However, as being the eldest officer, (after General Arnold has desired me to take the command,) I think it is my duty to mind the business of this part of America as well as I can. General Gates holds yet the title and power of commander-in-chief of the Northern department; but, as two hundred thousand dollars are arrived, I have taken upon myself to pay the most necessary part of the debts we are involved in. I am about sending provisions to Fort Schuyller: I will go to see the fort. I will try to get some clothes for the troops, to buy some articles for the next campaign. I have directed some money to be borrowed upon my credit to satisfy the troops, who are much discontented. In all I endeavour to do for the best, though I have no particular authority or instructions; and I will come as near as I can to General Gates's intentions, but I want much to get an answer to my letters.

I fancy (between us) that the actual scheme is to have me out of this part of the continent, and General Conway in chief, under the immediate direction of General Gates. How they will bring it up I do not know, but you may be sure something of that kind will appear. You are nearer than myself, and every honest man in congress is your friend; therefore you may foresee and prevent, if possible, the evil a hundred times better than I can: I would only give that idea to your excellency.

After having written in Europe (by the desire of the members of congress) so many fine things about my commanding an army, I shall be ashamed if nothing can be done by me in that way. I am told General Putnam is recalled; but your excellency knows better than I do what would be convenient, therefore I don't want to mind these things myself.

Will you be so good as to present my respects to your lady. With the most tender affection and highest respect, I have the honour to be,

LAFAYETTE.

FROM GENERAL WASHINGTON TO THE MARQUIS DE LAFAYETTE.

(ORIGINAL.)

Head Quarters, 10th March, 1778.

MY DEAR MARQUIS,—I have had the pleasure of receiving your two favours of the 19th and 23rd of February, and hasten to dispel those fears respecting your reputation, which are excited only by an uncommon degree of sensibility. You seem to apprehend that censure, proportioned to the disappointed expectations of the world, will fall on you in consequence of the failure of the Canadian expedition. But, in the first place, it will be no disadvantage to you to have it known in Europe that you had received so manifest a proof of the good opinion and confidence of congress as an important detached command; and I am persuaded that every one will applaud your prudence in renouncing a project, in pursuing which you would vainly have attempted physical impossibilities; indeed, unless you can be chargeable with the invariable effects of natural causes, and be arraigned for not suspending the course of the seasons, to accommodate your march over the lake, the most prompt to slander can have nothing to found blame upon.

However sensibly your ardour for glory may make you feel this disappointment, you may be assured that your character stands as fair as ever it did, and that no new enterprise is necessary to wipe off this imaginary stain. The expedition which you hint at I think unadvisable in our present circumstances. Anything in the way of a formal attack, which would necessarily be announced to the enemy by preparatory measures, would not be likely to succeed. If a stroke is meditated in that quarter, it must be effected by troops stationed at a proper distance for availing themselves of the first favourable opportunity offered by the enemy, and success would principally depend upon the suddenness of the attempt. This, therefore, must rather be the effect of time and chance than premeditation. You undoubtedly have determined judiciously in waiting the further orders of congress. Whether they allow me the pleasure of seeing you shortly, or destine you to a longer absence, you may assure yourself of the sincere good wishes of,

Dear Sir, &c.

P. S. Your directing payment of such debts as appear to be most pressing is certainly right. There is not money enough to answer every demand; and I wish your supplies of clothing had been better. Your ordering a large supply of provisions into Fort Schuyler was a very judicious measure, and I thank you for it.

TO BARON DE STEUBEN.

(ORIGINAL—A FRAGMENT.)

Albany, March 12th.

PERMIT me to express my satisfaction at your having seen General Washington. No enemies to that great man can be found except among the enemies to his country; nor is it possible for any man of a noble spirit to refrain from loving the excellent qualities of his heart. I think I know him as well as any person, and such is the idea which I have formed of him; his honesty, his frankness, his sensibility, his virtue, to the full extent in which this word can be understood, are above all praise. It is not for me to judge of his military talents; but, according to my imperfect knowledge of these matters, his advice in council has always appeared to me the best, although his modesty prevents him sometimes from sustaining it; and his predictions have generally been fulfilled. I am the more happy in giving you this opinion of my friend with all the sincerity which I feel, because some persons may perhaps attempt to deceive you on this point.

FRAGMENT OF A LETTER TO THE PRESIDENT OF CONGRESS.

(ORIGINAL.)

Albany, 20th March, 1778.

. . . . HIS Excellency General Washington will, I believe, mention to congress that, at the request of the commissioners of Indian affairs, I send Colonel

Gouvion, and have given proper directions for the building of a small fort, which they and myself have thought very necessary to be granted to the Oneydas. The love of the French blood, mixed with the love of some French *Louis d'or*, have engaged those Indians to promise they would come with me.*

As I am very certain the Congress of the United States will not propose anything to me but consistent with my feelings and the sentiment I flatter myself to have obtained from them, I can assure them, by advance, that any post they will give, any disposition they will make, with such manners, will be cheerfully received and complied to by me with acknowledgment. However, I will beg leave to say, that any command, whatever honourable it may be, where I would not be so near the danger or occasions of doing something, I shall always look upon as not suited to me.

I never mentioned to congress a long letter I have written, four months ago, to France, about a project for the East Indies, to which I expect the answer. Was I to succeed in my expectation, it would bring, soon, that so much desired French war, in spite of some peaceful men, and be of some use to the noble cause of freedom, without bringing the continent in any expense.

With the greatest respect, I have the honour to be, &c.

* M. de Lafayette, during this journey, some curious relations with the Indian, in a letter of the 27th of February, to General Washington, which, being void of interest in other respects, has been suppressed. It appears that he was solicited by General Schuyler to be present at a numerous meeting of Indians, convoked for a treaty. The traces of those communications will be found further.

TO GENERAL WASHINGTON.

(ORIGINAL.)

Albany, 25th March, 1778.

DEAR GENERAL,—How happy I have been in receiving your excellency's favour of the tenth present; I hope you will be convinced by the knowledge of my tender affection for you. I am very sensible of that goodness which tries to dissipate my fears about that ridiculous Canadian expedition. At the present time we know which was the aim of the honourable board, and for which project three or four men have rushed the country into a great expense, and risked the reputation of our arms, and the life of many hundred men, had the general, your deceived friend, been as rash and foolish as they seem to have expected. O, American freedom, what shall become of you if you are in such hands?

I have received a letter from the board and a resolve of congress,* by which you are directed to recall me and the Baron de Kalb, whose presence is deemed absolutely necessary to your army. I believe this of General Conway is *absolutely necessary* to Albany, and he has received orders to stay there, which I have no objection to, as nothing, perhaps, will be done in this quarter but some disputes of Indians and tories. However, you know I have wrote to congress, and as soon as their leave will

* That congress entertain a high sense of his prudence, activity, and zeal, and that they are fully persuaded nothing has or would have been wanting on his part, or on the part of his officers who accompanied him, to give the expedition the utmost possible effect.—(Secret Journal, March 2.)

come, I shall let Conway have the command of these few regiments, and I shall immediately join my respectable friend; but till I have received instructions for leaving that place from yourself, I shall stay, as powerful commander-in-chief, as if congress had never resolved my presence absolutely necessary for the great army.

Since your last letter, I have given up the idea of New York, and my only desire is to join you. The only favour I have asked of your commissioners in France, has been, not to be under any orders but those of General Washington. I seem to have had an anticipation of our future friendship, and what I have done out of esteem and respect for your excellency's name and reputation, I should do now out of mere love for General Washington himself. I am glad to hear General Greene is quarter-master-general; it is very interesting to have there an honest man and a friend of yours. But I feel the greatest pain not to hear anything about reinforcements. What can you do with a handful of men,—and my poor division, whom I was so desirous of instructing, clothing, managing myself in the winter, whom, I was told, I should find six thousand strong at the opening of the campaign? Don't your excellency think that I could recruit a little in General Greene's division now that he is quarter-master-general? By that promotion I find myself very proud to be the third officer of your army.

With the utmost respect and affection, I have the honour to be, &c.

TO MADAME DE LAFAYETTE.

Valley Forge Camp, in Pennsylvania, April 14th, 1778.

If thirty opportunities were to present themselves at once, my dearest love, you may rest assured that I would write thirty letters; and that, if you do not receive any news from me, I have nothing, at least, to reproach myself with. This letter will be accompanied by others, saying nearly the same things, and having nearly the same date; but accidents are unfortunately very common, and by this means, some letters may reach you safely. Respecting your own, my love, I prefer accusing fate, the waves, Lord Howe, and the devil, to suspecting you for one moment of negligence. I am convinced that you will not allow a single opportunity to escape of writing to me; but I should feel, if possible, still more so, if I could only hope that you knew the degree of happiness your letters give me. I love you more ardently than ever, and repeated assurances of your affection are absolutely necessary to my repose, and to that species of felicity which I can enjoy whilst separated from all I love most fondly—if, however, the word *felicity* can be applied to my melancholy, exiled state. Endeavour to afford me some consolation, and neglect no opportunity of writing to me. Millions of ages have elapsed since I have received a line from any one. This complete ignorance of the situation of all those who are most dear to me, is, indeed, a dreadful calamity: I have, however, some reason to believe that it cannot last for ever; the scene will soon become interesting; France must take some decisive part, and vessels will then arrive with letters. I can give you no news at present; we are all in a state of repose, and are waiting with impatience for the opening campaign to awaken us from our stupor. In my other letters, I mentioned my journey to Albany, and my visit to an assembly of savages. I am expecting some good Iroquois who have promised to rejoin me here. Either after, or before receiving this letter, Madame d'Ayen, the viscountess, and my grandfather,* will receive letters by an opportunity which, I believe, is more secure than the one I am now writing by; I have written a longer letter to you also at the same time. I write an immense number of epistles; God grant that they may arrive! Present my affectionate respects to your mother, and my grandfather; embrace a thousand times the viscountess and my sisters; recall me to the remembrance of the Countess Auguste, Madame de Fronsac, and all your and my friends. Embrace a thousand times our dearest family. When shall I be able to assure you, my dearest life, that I love you better than any other person in the world, and that I shall love you as long as I live? Adieu; I only look upon this letter as a note.

Present my respects to the Marshal de Noailles, and tell him that I have sent him some trees from Albany; but I will send him others also at various times, that I may feel certain of his receiving a few of them. When you present my compliments to my acquaintance, do not forget the Chevalier de Chastellux.

* The Count de la Rivière, (Charles-Ives-Thibault), lieutenant-captain of the black musketeers, was grandfather of the mother of M. de Lafayette of whom he had been appointed guardian.

TO MADAME DE LAFAYETTE.

Germantown, April 28th, 1778.

I WRITE to you, my dearest love, by a very strange opportunity, since it is an English officer who has taken charge of my letter. But your wonder will cease, when you hear that that officer is my friend Fitz-Patrick.* He is returning to England, and I could not resist my wish of embracing him before his departure. It was the first time we had met unarmed in America, and that manner of meeting suits us both much better than the hostile appearance which we had, until now, thought proper to affect. It is long since I have received any news from France, and I am very impatiently expecting letters. Write frequently, my love, I need the consolation of hearing often from you during this painful separation. There is no important news ; neither would it be proper for Mr. Fitz-Patrick to carry political news from a hand at present engaged in fighting with his army. I am in perfect health ; my wound is completely healed, but my heart is far from being tranquil, for I am far from all those I love ; and my anxiety about them, as well as my impatience to behold them, increase every hour. Say a thousand things for me to all my friends ; present my respects to Madame d'Ayen, and to the Marshal de Noailles. Embrace, above all, our children, my dearest love, and be convinced yourself that every moment that separates me from you and

† M. de Lafayette had become very intimate with him in England : he is the same General Fitz-Patrick, who made two famous motions in the House of Commons ; the one March 17th, 1794, for the prisoners of Magdebourg, and the other, December 16th, 1796, for the prisoners of Olmütz.

them appears to me an age. Adieu; I must quit you, for the hour is far advanced, and to-morrow will not be an idle day. Adieu, Adieu!

TO GENERAL WASHINGTON.

(ORIGINAL.)

Valley Forge Camp, the 19th May, 1778.

MY DEAR GENERAL,—Agreeable to your excellency's orders, I have taken the oath of the gentlemen officers in General Woodford's brigade, and their certificates have been sent to the adjutant-general's office. Give me leave, now, to present you with some observations delivered to me by many officers in that brigade, who desire me to submit them to your perusal. I know, sir, (besides I am not of their opinion in the fact itself,) that I should not accept for you the objections those gentlemen could have had, as a body, to any order from congress; but I confess the desire of being agreeable to them, of giving them any mark of friendship and affection which is in my power, and acknowledging the kind sentiments they honour me with, have been my first and dearest considerations. Besides that, be pleased to consider that they began by obeying orders, and want only to let their beloved general know which were the reasons of their being rather reluctant (as far as reluctance may comply with their duty and honour) to an oath, the meaning and spirit of which was, I believe, misunderstood by them. I may add, sir, with a perfect conviction, that there is not one among them but would be thrice happy were occasions offered to them of distinguishing yet, by new exertions, their love for their country, their zeal for their duty as officers, their consideration for the civil superior power, and their love for your excellency.

With the greatest respect and most tender affection,—I have the honour to be, &c.

FROM GENERAL WASHINGTON TO THE MARQUIS DE LAFAYETTE.

(ORIGINAL.)

Camp, 17th May, 1778.

DEAR SIR,—I received yesterday your favour of the 15th instant, enclosing a paper subscribed by sundry officers of General Woodford's brigade, setting forth the reasons for not taking the oath of abjuration, allegiance, and office; and I thank you much for the cautious delicacy used in communicating the matter to me. As every oath should be a free act of the mind, founded on the conviction of its propriety, I would not wish, in any instance, that there should be the least degree of compulsion exercised; nor to interpose my opinion, in order to induce any to make it of whom it is required. The gentlemen, therefore, who signed the paper, will use their own discretion in the matter, and swear, or not swear, as their conscience and feelings dictate.

At the same time, I cannot but consider it as a circumstance of some singularity, that the scruples against the oath should be peculiar to the officers of one brigade, and so very extensive. The oath in itself is not new. It is substantially the same with that required in all governments, and, therefore, does not imply any indignity; and it is perfectly consistent with the professions, actions, and implied engagements of every officer. The objection founded on the supposed unsettled rank of the officers, is of no validity, rank being only mentioned as a further designation of the party swearing; nor can it be seriously thought that the oath is either intended to prevent, or can prevent, their being promoted, or their resignation.

The fourth objection, stated by the gentlemen, serves as a key to their scruples; and I would willingly persuade myself, that their own reflections will point out to them the impropriety of the whole proceeding, and not suffer them to be betrayed in future into a similar conduct. I have a regard for them all, and cannot but regret that they were ever engaged in the measure. I am certain they will regret it themselves;—sure I am that they ought. I am, my dear marquis, your affectionate friend and servant.

TO THE MARQUIS DE LAFAYETTE.

(ORIGINAL—INSTRUCTION.*)

Sir,—The detachment under your command, with which you will immediately march towards the enemy's lines, is designed to answer the following

* This instruction has been inserted as the one which M. de Lafayette received to repair, as a detached body, betwixt the Delaware and Schuylkill. It was after this movement that he made the retreat of Barren Hill, which was praised by General Washington. (See the Memoirs, in Mr. Spark's collection, the letter of Washington, May 24th, 1778.)

purposes; namely, to be a security to this camp, and a cover to the country, between the Delaware and the Schuylkill, to interrupt the communication with Philadelphia, to obstruct the incursions of the enemy's parties, and to obtain intelligence of their motions and designs. This last is a matter of very interesting moment, and ought to claim your particular attention. You will endeavour to procure trusty and intelligent spies, who will advise you faithfully of whatever may be passing in the city, and you will, without delay, communicate to me every piece of material information you obtain. A variety of concurring accounts make it probable that the enemy are preparing to evacuate Philadelphia; this is a point of the utmost importance to ascertain, and, if possible, the place of their future destination. Should you be able to gain certain intelligence of the time of their intended embarkation, so that you may be able to take advantage of it, and fall upon the rear of the enemy in the act of withdrawing, it will be a very desirable event; but this will be a matter of no small difficulty, and will require the greatest caution and prudence in the execution. Any deception or precipitation may be attended with the most disastrous consequences.

You will remember that your detachment is a very valuable one, and that any accident happening to it would be a severe blow to this army; you will, therefore, use every possible precaution for its security, and to guard against a surprise. No attempt should be made, nor anything risked, without the greatest prospect of success, and with every reasonable advantage on your side. I shall not point out any precise position to you, but shall leave it to your discretion to take such posts occasionally, as shall appear to you best adapted to the purposes of your detachment. In general, I would observe, that a stationary post is unadvisable, as it gives the enemy an opportunity of knowing your situation, and concerting plans successfully against you. In case of any offensive movement against this army, you will keep yourself in such a state as to have an easy communication with it, and, at the same time, harass the enemy's advance.

Our parties of horse and foot, between the rivers, are to be under your command, and to form part of your detachment. As great complaints have been made of the disorderly conduct of the parties which have been sent towards the enemy's lines, it is expected that you will be very attentive in preventing abuses of the like nature, and will inquire how far complaints already made are founded in justice.

Given under my hand, at head quarters, this 18th May, 1778.

TO MADAME DE LAFAYETTE.

Valley Forge Camp, June 16, 1778.

Chance has furnished me, my dearest love, with a very uncertain opportunity of writing to you, but, such as it is, I shall take advantage of it, for I cannot resist the wish of saying a few words to you. You must have received many letters from me lately, if my writing unceasingly, at least, may justify this hope. Several vessels have sailed, all laden with my letters. My expressions of heartfelt grief must even have added to your distress. What a dreadful thing is absence! I never experienced before all the horrors of separation. My own deep sorrow is aggravated by the feeling that I am not able to share and sympathize in your anguish. The length of time that elapsed before I heard of this event had also increased my misery. Consider, my love, how dreadful it must be to weep for what I have lost, and tremble for what remains. The distance between Europe and America appears to me more enormous than ever. The loss of our poor child is almost constantly in my thoughts : this sad news followed immediately that of the treaty; and whilst my heart was torn by grief, I was obliged to receive and take part in expressions of public joy. I learnt, at the same time, the loss of our little Adrien, for I always considered that child as my own, and I regretted him as I should have done a son. I have written twice to the viscount and viscountess, to express to them my deep regret, and I hope my letters will reach them safely. I am writing only to you at present, because I neither know when the vessel sails, nor when she will arrive, and I am told that a packet will soon set out which will probably reach Europe first.

I received letters from M. de Cambrai and M. Carmichael. The first one will be employed, I hope, in an advantageous and agreeable manner; the second, whom I am expecting with great impatience, has not yet arrived at the army: how delighted I shall be to see him, and talk to him about you!—he will come to the camp as soon as possible. We are expecting every day news from Europe; they will be deeply interesting, especially to me, who offer up such earnest prayers for the success and glory of my country. The King of Prussia, it is said, has entered into Bohemia, and has forgotten to declare war. If a conflict were to take place between France and England, I should prefer our being left completely to ourselves, and that the rest of Europe should content herself with looking on; we should, in that case, have a glorious war, and our successes would be of a kind to please and gratify the nation.

If the unfortunate news had reached me sooner, I should have set out immediately to rejoin you; but the account of the treaty, which we received the first of May, prevented my leaving this country. The opening campaign does not allow me to retire. I have always been perfectly convinced that by serving the cause of humanity, and that of America, I serve also the interest of France. Another motive for remaining longer is, that the commissioners have arrived, and that I am well pleased to be within reach of the negotiations. To be useful in any way to my country will always be agreeable to me. I do not understand why a minister plenipotentiary, or something of that kind, has not been already sent to America; I am most anxious to see one, provided always it may not be myself, for I am but little disposed to quit the military career to enter into the diplomatic corps.

There is no news here; the only topic of conversation is the news from Europe, and to that many idle tales are always prefixed: there has been little action on either side; the only important affair was the one which fell to my share the 20th of last month, and there was not any blood shed even there.

General Washington had entrusted me to conduct a detachment of two thousand four hundred chosen men to the vicinity of Philadelphia. It would be too long to explain to you the cause, but it will suffice to tell you, that, in spite of all my precautions, I could not prevent the hostile army from making a nocturnal march, and I found myself the next morning with part of the army in front, and seven thousand men in my rear. These gentlemen were so obliging as to take measures for sending to New York those who should not be killed; but they were so kind, also, as to permit us to retire quietly, without doing us any injury. We had about six or seven killed or wounded, and they twenty-five or thirty, which did not make them amends for a march, in which one part of the army had been obliged to make forty miles.

Some days afterwards, our situation having altered, I returned to the camp, and no events of importance have occurred since. We are expecting the evacuation of Philadelphia, which must, we fancy, soon take place. I have been told that on the 10th of April they were thinking of negotiating rather than of fighting, and that England was becoming each day more humble.

If this letter ever reaches you, my dearest love, present my respects to the Duke d'Ayen, the Marshal de Noailles, and Madame de Tessé, to whom I have written by every vessel, although she accuses me of having neglected her, which my heart is incapable of doing. I have also written to Madame d'Ayen by the two last ships, and by several previous ones. Embrace a thousand times the dear viscountess, and tell her how well I love her. A thousand tender regards to my sisters; a thousand affectionate ones to the viscount, M. de Poix, to Coigny,* Segur, his brother, Etienne,† and all my other friends. Embrace, a million of times, our little Anastasia;—alas! she alone remains to us! I feel that she has engrossed the affection that was

* Probably the Marquis de Coigny.

† The Count Etienne de Durfort, now peer of France.

once divided between my two children: take great care of her. Adieu; I know not when this may reach you, and I even doubt its ever reaching you.

TO THE MARQUIS DE LAFAYETTE.

(ORIGINAL—INSTRUCTIONS.)

Sir,—You are immediately to proceed with the detachment commanded by General Poor, and form a junction, as expeditiously as possible, with that under the command of General Scott. You are to use the most effectual means for gaining the enemy's left flank and rear, and giving them every degree of annoyance. All continental parties that are already on the lines, will be under your command, and you will take such measures, in concert with General Dickinson, as will cause the enemy the greatest impediment and loss in their march. For these purposes you will attack them, as occasion may require, by detachment, and if a proper opening could be given, by operating against them with the whole force of your command. You will naturally take such precautions as will secure you against surprise, and maintain your communications with this army.

Given at Kingston, this 25th day of June, 1778.

TO GENERAL WASHINGTON

(ORIGINAL.)

Ice Town, 26th June, 1778, at a quarter after seven.

Dear General,—I hope you have received my letter from Cranberry, where I acquaint you that I am going to Ice Town, though we are short of provisions. When I got there, I was sorry to hear that Mr. Hamilton, who had been riding all the night, had not been able to find anybody who could give him certain intelligence; but by a party who came back, I hear the enemy are in motion, and their rear about one mile off the place they had occupied last night, which is seven or eight miles from here. I immediately put Generals Maxwell and Wayne's brigades in motion, and I will fall lower down, with General Scott's, with Jackson's regiment, and some militia. I should be very happy if we could attack them before they halt, for I have no notion of taking one other moment but this of the march. If I cannot overtake them, we could lay at some distance, and attack to-morrow morning, provided they don't escape in the night, which I much fear, as our intelligences are not the best ones. I have sent some parties out, and I will get some more light by them.

I fancy your excellency will move down with the army, and if we are at a convenient distance from you, I have nothing to fear in striking a blow if opportunity is offered. I believe that, in our present strength, *provided they do not escape*, we may do something.

General Forman says that, on account of the nature of the country, it is impossible for me to be turned by the right or left, but that I shall not quite depend upon.

An officer just from the lines confirms the account of the enemy moving. An intelligence from General Dickinson says that they hear a very heavy fire in the front of the enemy's column. I apprehend it is Morgan, who had not received my letter, but it will have the good effect of stopping them, and if we attack, he may begin again.

Sir, I want to repeat you in writing what I have told to you, which is, that if you believe it, or if it is believed necessary or useful to the good of the service and the honour of General Lee, to send him down with a couple of thousand men, or any greater force; I will cheerfully obey and serve him, not only out of duty, but out of what I owe to that gentleman's character.

I hope to receive, soon, your orders as to what I am to do this day or to-morrow, to know where you are and what you intend, and would be very happy to furnish you with the opportunity of completing some little advantage of ours.

LAFAYETTE.

The road I understand the enemy are moving by, is the straight road to Monmouth.

FROM GENERAL WASHINGTON TO THE MARQUIS DE LAFAYETTE.

(ORIGINAL.)

Cranberry, 26th June, 1778.

MY DEAR MARQUIS,—General Lee's uneasiness, on account of yesterday's transaction, rather increasing than abating, and your politeness in wishing to ease him of it, have induced me to detach him from this army with a part of it, to reinforce, or at least cover, the several detachments at present under your command. At the same time, that I felt for General Lee's distress of mind, I have had an eye to your wishes and the delicacy of your situation; and have, therefore, obtained a promise from him, that when he gives you notice of his approach and command, he will request you to prosecute any plan you may have already concerted for the purpose of attacking, or otherwise annoying the enemy; this is the only expedient I could think of to answer the views of both. General Lee seems satisfied with the measure, and I wish it may prove agreeable to you, as I am, with the warmest wishes for your honour and glory, and with the sincerest esteem and affection, yours, &c.*

FROM GENERAL WASHINGTON TO THE MARQUIS DE LAFAYETTE.†

(ORIGINAL.)

White Plains, 22nd July, 1778.

SIR,—You are to have the immediate command of that detachment from this army, which consists of Glover's and Varnum's brigades, and the detachment under the command of Colonel Henry Jackson. You are to march them, with all convenient expedition, and by the best routes, to Providence, in the state of Rhode Island. When there, you are to subject yourself to the orders of Major-General Sul-

* The combination offered by M. de Lafayette, and desired by General Washington, did not prove successful. In spite of the happy issue of the battle of Monmouth, the results were not such as might have been expected, on account of the conduct of General Lee, who was summoned before a court martial, and condemned to be suspended for one year. (See on this subject the Memoirs of the Life of Washington, by Marshall, and the Appendix No. 8, of the 5th vol. of the Letters of Washington.)

† Order for the expedition of Rhode Island.

livan, who will have the command of the expedition against Newport, and the British and other troops in their pay, on that and the Islands adjacent.

If, on your march, you should receive certain intelligence of the evacuation of Rhode Island, by the enemy, you are immediately to counter-march for this place, giving me the earliest advice thereof. Having the most perfect reliance on your activity and zeal, and wishing you all the success, honour, and glory, that your heart can wish, I am, with the most perfect regard, yours, &c.

FROM GENERAL WASHINGTON TO THE MARQUIS DE LAFAYETTE

(ORIGINAL.)

Head Quarters, White Plains, 27th July, 1778.

DEAR MARQUIS,—This will be delivered to you by Major-General Greene, whose thorough knowledge of Rhode Island, of which he is a native, and the influence he will have with the people, put it in his power to be particularly useful in the expedition against that place, as well in providing necessaries for carrying it on, as in assisting to form and execute a plan of operations proper for the occasion. The honour and interest of the common cause are so deeply concerned in the success of this enterprise, that it appears to me of the greatest importance to omit no step which may conduce to it; and General Greene, on several accounts, will be able to render very essential service.

These considerations have determined me to send him on the expedition, in which, as he could not with propriety act, nor be equally useful merely in his official capacity as quartermaster-general, I have concluded to give him a command in the troops to be employed in the descent. I have, therefore, directed General Sullivan to throw all the American troops, both continental, state, and militia, into two divisions, making an equal distribution of each, to be under the immediate command of General Greene and yourself. The continental troops being divided in this manner, with the militia, will serve to give them confidence, and probably make them act better than they would alone. Though this arrangement will diminish the number of continental troops under you, yet this diminution will be more than compensated by the addition of militia; and I persuade myself your command will not be less agreeable, or less honourable, from this change in the disposition. I am, with great esteem and affection, dear marquis, your most obedient servant.

TO GENERAL WASHINGTON.

(ORIGINAL.)

Providence, 6th August, 1778.

DEAR GENERAL,—I have received your excellency's favour by General Greene, and have been much pleased with the arrival of a gentleman who, not only on account of his merit, and the justness of his views, but also by his knowledge of the country, and his popularity in this state, may be very serviceable to the expedition. I willingly part with the half of my detachment, though I had a great dependence upon them, as you find it convenient to the good of the service. Any thing, my dear General, you will order, or even wish, shall always be infinitely agreeable to me, and I will always feel happy in doing any thing which may please you, or forward the public good. I am of the same opinion as your excellency, that dividing our continental troops among the militia, will have a better effect than if we were to keep them together in one wing.

You will receive, by General Sullivan, an account of his dispositions, preparations, &c.; I, therefore, have nothing to add, but that I have been on board of the Admiral* the day before yesterday. I saw among the fleet an ardour and a desire of doing something, which would soon turn into impatience, if we don't give them a speedy occasion of fighting. The officers cannot contain their soldiers and sailors, who are complaining that they have been these four months running after the British, without getting at them; but I hope they will be soon satisfied.

The Count d'Estaing was very glad of my arrival, as he could open freely his mind to me. He expressed the greatest anxiety on account of his wants of every kind, provisions, water, &c.; he hopes the taking of Rhode Island will enable him to get some of the two abovementioned articles. The admiral wants me to join the French troops to these I command, as soon as possible. I confess I feel very happy to think of my co-operating with them, and, had I contrived in my mind an agreeable dream, I could not have wished a more pleasing event than my joining my countrymen with my brothers of America, under my command, and the same

* Admiral d'Estaing. It was the 8th July that the French fleet appeared at the entrance of the Delaware. It was at this period stationed before Newport, below the passage, betwixt Rhode Island and Long Island.

standards. When I left Europe, I was very far from hoping such an agreeable turn of our business in the American glorious revolution.

Though I have no account, neither observations, to give to your excellency, as I am here *a man of war of the third rate*, I will, after the expedition, scribble some lines to you, and join to the account of General Sullivan, the assurance that I have all my limbs, and that I am, with the most tender affection, and entire confidence, yours, with high respect.

FROM GENERAL WASHINGTON TO THE MARQUIS DE LAFAYETTE.

(ORIGINAL.)

White Plains, 10th August, 1778.

My dear Marquis,—Your favour of the 6th instant, which came to my hands yesterday, afforded a fresh proof of the noble principles on which you act, and has a just claim to my sincere and hearty thanks. The common cause, of which you have been a zealous supporter, would, I knew, be benefitted by General Greene's presence at Rhode Island, as he is a native of that state, has an interest with the people, and a thorough knowledge of the country, and, therefore, I accepted his proffered services; but I was a little uneasy, lest you should conceive that it was intended to lessen your command. General Greene did not incline to act in a detached part of the army, merely as quartermaster-general; nor was it to be expected. It became necessary, therefore, to give him a detached command, and consequently to divide the continental troops. Your cheerful acquiescence in the measure, after being appointed to the command of the brigades which marched from this army, obviated every difficulty, and gave me singular pleasure.

I am very happy to find that the standards of France and America are likely to be united under your command, at Rhode Island. I am persuaded, that the supporters of each will be emulous to acquire honour, and promote your glory upon this occasion. The courier to Count d'Estaing is waiting. I have only time, therefore, to assure you, that, with most perfect esteem, and exalted regard, I have the honour to be, my dear marquis, your obedient and affectionate servant.

TO GENERAL WASHINGTON.*

(ORIGINAL.)

Camp before Newport, 25th August, 1778.

MY DEAR GENERAL,—I had expected in answering your first letter that something interesting would have happened that I might communicate to your excellency. Every day was going to termi-

* The circumstances which gave rise to this letter are mentioned in the memoirs. The following details will still further explain them :—

When the storm had dispersed his fleet, M. de Estaing wrote a very remarkable letter to General Sullivan, in which he explained to him the impossibility of remaining in sight of Rhode Island without danger, and without disobeying the precise orders of the king. He expressed his regret that the landing of the Americans in the island, which had been effected one day before the day agreed upon, should not have been protected by the vessels; and he rejected strongly the imputation of having blamed him under these circumstances for having operated so early, and with only two thousand men. To his great regret, his situation obliged him to answer the proposal of a combined nate our uncertainties; nay, every day was going to bring the hope of a success which I did promise myself to acquaint you of. Such was the reason of my deferring what my duty and inclination did urge me to do much sooner. I am now indebted for two favours of yours, which I beg leave to offer here my thanks for. The first letter reached me in the time we expected to hear again from the French fleet; the second I have just received. My reason for not writing the same day the French fleet went to Boston was, that I did not choose to trouble your friendship with the sentiments of an afflicted, injured heart, and injured by that very people I came from so far to love and support. Don't be surprised, my dear general; the generosity of your honest mind would be offended at the shocking sight I have under my eyes.

So far am I from a critical disposition that I will not give you the journal of our operations, neither of several instances during our staying here, which, however, might occupy some room in this letter. I

attack, by a refusal. This answer excited much dissatisfaction amongst the Americans. Their officers signed a protestation, which appears to have been considered by some of them as the means of seconding the secret inclination of the admiral by forcing him to fight. The report was spread, in truth, that a cabal in the naval force alone obliged him to make a retreat, from a feeling of jealousy of the glory which he might have acquired, as he had belonged formerly to the land forces. This protestation was carried to him by Colonel Laurens; after a recapitulation of all the arguments which might be used against the departure of the fleet, it terminated by the solemn declartion that that measure was *derogatory to the honour of France*, contrary to the intentions of his V. C. Majesty, and to the interests of the American nation, &c. When this protestation was submitted to congress, they immediately ordered that it will not even say to you, how contracted was the French fleet when they wanted to come in at their arrival; which, according to the report of the advertors, would have had the greatest effect. How surprised was the admiral, when, after a formal and agreed convention, one hour after the American general had given a new written assurance, our troops made the landing a day before it was expected. How mortified the French officers were to find out that there was not a gun left in these very forts to whose protection they were recommended. All these things, and many others, I would not take notice of, if they were not at this moment the supposed ground upon which, it is said, that the Count d'Estaing is gone on to Boston. Believe me, my dear sir, upon my honour, the admirals, though a little astonished by some instances of conduct on our part, did consider them in the same light as you

should be kept secret, and that M. Gérard should be informed of this order, which General Washington was charged with executing by every means in his power.

General Sullivan issued the following order at the same time:—

"It having been supposed, by some persons, that by the orders of the 21st instant, the commander-in-chief meant to insinuate that the departure of the French fleet was owing to a fixed determination not to assist in the present enterprise, and that, as the general did not wish to give the least colour to ungenerous and illiberal minds to make such an unfair interpretation, he thinks it necessary to say, that as he could not possibly be acquainted with the orders of the French admiral, he could not determine whether the removal of the fleet was absolutely necessary or not; and, therefore, did not mean to censure an act which those orders might render absolutely necessary." These details, borrowed from the edition of the writings of Washington, will explain some passages of this letter, and the sense of the following letters.

and myself would have done, and if he is gone off, it is because he thought himself obliged by necessity.

Let us consider, my dear general, the motions of that fleet since it was proposed by the Count d'Estaing himself, and granted by the king in behalf of the United States. I will not go so far up as to remember other instances of the affection the French nation have for the Americans. The news of that fleet have occasioned the evacuation of Philadelphia. Its arrival has opened all the harbours, secured all the coasts, obliged the British navy to be together. Six of those frigates, two of them I have seen, sufficient for terrifying all the trading people of the two Carolinas, are taken or burnt. The Count d'Estaing went to offer battle, and act as a check to the British navy for a long time. At New York, it was agreed he should go to Rhode Island, and there he went. They prevented him from going in at first; afterwards, he was desired to come in, and so he did. The same day we landed without his knowledge; an English fleet appears in sight. His being divided into three parts by *our directions*, for, though he is a *lieutenant-general*, he never availed himself of that title, made him uneasy about his situation. But finding the next morning that the wind was northerly, being also convinced that it was his duty to prevent any reinforcement at Newport, he goes out under the hottest fire of the British land batteries, he puts the British navy to flight, and pursues them, and they were all in his hands when that horrid storm arrives to ruin all our hopes. Both fleets are divided, scattered; the Cæsar, a 74 gun ship, is lost; the Marseillais, of the same size, loses her masts, and after that accident is obliged to send back an enemy's ship of 64; the Languedoç having lost her masts, unable to be governed and make any motions, separated from the others, is attacked by a ship of the line against which she could only bring six guns.

When the storm was over, they met again in a shattered condition, and the Cæsar was not to be found. All the captains represented to their general that, after a so long navigation, in such a want of victuals, water, &c., which they had not been yet supplied with, after the intelligence given by General Sullivan that there was a British fleet coming, they should go to Boston; but the Count d'Estaing had promised to come here again, and so he did at all events. The news of his arrival and situation came by the *Senegal*, a frigate taken from the enemy. General Greene and myself went on board. The count expressed to me not so much as to the envoy from General Sullivan, than as to his friend, the unhappy circumstances he was in. Bound by express orders from the King to go to Boston in case of an accident or a superior fleet, engaged by the common sentiment of all the officers, *even of some American pilots*, that he would ruin all his squadron in deferring his going to Boston, he called a new council of war, and finding every body of the same opinion, he did not think himself justifiable in staying here any longer, and took leave of me with true affliction not being able to assist America for some days, which has been rewarded with the most horrid ungratefulness; but no matter. I am only speaking of facts. The count said to me these last words: after many months of sufferings, my men will rest some days; I will man my ships, and, if I am assisted in getting masts, &c., three weeks after my arrival I shall go out again, and then we shall fight for the glory of the French name, and the interests of America.

The day *the count* went off, the general American officers drew a protestation, which, as *I had been very strangely called there*, I refused to sign, but I wrote a letter to the admiral. The protestation and the letter did not arrive in time.

Now, my dear general, I am going to hurt your generous feelings by an imperfect picture of what I am forced to see. Forgive me for it; it is not to the commander-in-chief, it is to my most dearest friend, General Washington, that I am speaking. I want to lament with him the ungenerous sentiments I have been forced to see in many American breasts.

Could you believe, that forgetting any national obligation, forgetting what they were owing to that same fleet, what they were yet to expect from them, and instead of resenting their accidents as these, of allies and brothers, the people turned mad at their departure, and wishing them all the evils in the world, did treat them as a generous one would be ashamed to treat the most inveterate enemies. You cannot have any idea of the horrors which were to be heard in that occasion. Many leaders themselves finding they were disappointed, abandoned their minds to illiberality and ungratefulness. Frenchmen of the highest character have been exposed to the most disagreeable circumstances, and yet, myself, the friend of America—the friend of General Washington. I am more upon a warlike footing in the American lines, than when I come near the British lines at Newport.

Such is, my dear general, the true state of matters. I am sure it will infinitely displease and hurt your feelings. I am also sure you will approve the part I have taken in it, which was to stay much at home with all the French gentlemen who are here, and declare, at the same time, that anything thrown before me against my nation I would take as the most particular affront.

Inclosed I send you the general orders of the 24th, upon which I thought I was obliged to pay a visit to General Sullivan, who has agreed to alter them in the following manner. Remember, my dear general, that I don't speak to the commander-in-chief, but to my friend, that I am far from complaining of anybody. I have no complaints at all to make you against any one; but I lament with you that I have had an occasion of seeing so ungenerous sentiments in American hearts.

I will tell you the true reason. The leaders of the expedition are, most of them, ashamed to return after having spoken of their Rhode Island success in proud terms before their family, their friends, their internal enemies. The others, regardless of the expense France has been put to by that fleet, of the tedious, tiresome voyage, which so many men have had for their service, though they are angry that the fleet takes three weeks, upon the whole campaign, to refit themselves, they cannot bear the idea of being brought to a small expense, to the loss of a little time, to the fatigue of staying some few days more in a camp at some few miles off their houses; for I am very far from looking upon the expedition as having miscarried, and there I see even a certainty of success.

If, as soon as the fleet is repaired, which (in case they are treated as one is in a country one is not at war with,) would be done in three weeks from this time, the Count d'Estaing was to come around, the expedition seems to offer a very good prospect. If the enemy evacuates New York, we have the whole continental army, if not, we might perhaps have some more men, what number, however, I cannot pretend to judge. All that I know is, that I shall be very happy to see the fleet co-operating with General Washington himself.

I think I shall be forced, by the board of general officers, to go soon to Boston. That I will do as soon as required, though with reluctance, for I do not believe that *our position on this part of the island is without danger*; but my principle is to do everything which is thought good for the service. I have very often rode express to the fleet, to the frigates, and that, I assure you, with the greatest pleasure; on the other hand, I may perhaps be useful to the fleet. Perhaps, too, it will be in the power of the count to do something which might satisfy them. I wish, my dear general, you could know as well as myself, how desirous the Count d'Estaing is to forward the public good, to help your success, and to serve the cause of America.

I earnestly beg you will recommend to the several chief persons of Boston to do everything they can to put the French fleet in a situation for sailing soon. Give me leave to add, that I wish many people, by the declaration of your sentiments in that affair, could learn how to regulate theirs, and blush at the sight of your generosity.

You will find my letter immense. I began it one day and finished it the next, as my time was swallowed up by those eternal councils of war. I shall have the pleasure of writing you from Boston. I am afraid the Count d'Estaing will have felt to the quick the behaviour of the people on this occasion. You cannot conceive how distressed he was to be prevented from serving this country for some time. I do assure you his circumstances were very critical and distressing.

For my part, my sentiments are known to the world. My tender affection for General Washington is added to them; therefore I want no apologies for writing upon what has afflicted me both as an American and as a Frenchman.

I am much obliged to you for the care you are so kind as to take of that poor horse of mine; had he not found such a good stable as this at head-quarters, he would have cut a pitiful figure at the end of his travels, and I should have been too happy if there had remained so much of the horse as the bones, the skin, and the four shoes.

Farewell, my dear general; whenever I quit you, I meet with some disappointment and misfortune. I did not need it to desire seeing you as much as possible. With the most tender affection and high regard, I have the honour to be, &c.

Dear General,—I must add to my letter, that I have received one from General Greene, very different, from the expressions I have to complain of, he seems there very sensible of what I feel. I am very happy when placed in a situation to do justice to any one.

FROM GENERAL WASHINGTON TO THE MARQUIS DE LAFAYETTE.

(ORIGINAL.)

White Plains, September 1778.

My dear Marquis,—I have been honoured with your favour of the 25th ultimo by Monsieur Pontgibaud, and I wish my time, which at present is taken up by a committee at congress, would permit me to go fully into the contents of it; this, however, it is not in my power to do; but in one word let me say, I feel everything that hurts the sensibility of a gentleman, and consequently, upon the present occasion, I feel for you and for our good and great allies the French. I feel myself hurt, also, at every illiberal and unthinking reflection which may have been cast upon the Count d'Estaing, or the conduct of the fleet under his command; and, lastly, I feel for my country. Let me entreat you, therefore, my dear marquis, to take no exception at unmeaning expressions, uttered, perhaps, without consideration, and in the first transport of disappointed hope. Every body, sir, who reasons, will acknowledge the advantages which we have derived from the French fleet, and the zeal of the commander of it; but, in a free and republican government, you cannot restrain the voice of the multitude; every man will speak as he thinks, or, more properly, without thinking, and consequently will judge at effects without attending to the causes. The censures which have been levelled at the officers of the French fleet would, more than probably, have fallen in a much higher degree upon a fleet of our own if we had one in the same situation. It is the nature of man to be displeased with everything that disappoints a favourite hope or flattering project; and it is the folly of too many of them to condemn without investigating circumstances.

Let me beseech you, therefore, my good sir, to afford a healing hand to the wound that, unintentionally, has been made. America esteems your virtues and your services, and admires the principles upon which you act; your countrymen, in our army, look up to you as their patron; the count and his officers consider you as a man high in rank, and high in estimation here and also in France; and I, your friend, have no doubt but you will use your utmost endeavours to restore harmony, that the honour, the glory, and mutual interest of the two nations maybe promoted and cemented in the firmest manner. I would say more on the subject, but am restrained for the want of time, and therefore shall only add, that with every sentiment of esteem and regard, I am, my dear marquis, &c.

FROM GENERAL WASHINGTON TO MAJOR-GENERAL SULLIVAN.

(ORIGINAL.)

Head Quarters, White Plains, 1st September, 1778.

DEAR SIR,—The disagreement between the army under your command and the fleet, has given me very singular uneasiness: the continent at large is concerned in our cordiality, and it should be kept up, by all possible means, consistent with our honour and policy. First impressions, you know, are generally longest remembered, and will serve to fix, in a great degree, our national character among the French. In our conduct towards them we should remember that they are people old in war, very strict in military etiquette, and apt to take fire, where others scarcely seem warmed. Permit me to recommend, in the most particular manner, the cultivation of harmony and good agreement, and your endeavours to destroy that ill-humour which may have got into the officers. It is of the greatest importance, also, that the soldiers and the people should know nothing of the misunderstanding, or, if it has reached them, that ways may be used to stop its progress and prevent its effects.

I have received from congress the enclosed, by which you will perceive their opinion with regard to keeping secret the protest of the general officers: I need add nothing on this head. I have one thing, however, more to say: I make no doubt but you will do all in your power to forward the repair of the count's fleet, and render it fit for service, by your recommendations for that purpose to those who can be immediately instrumental.

I am, dear Sir, &c.

FROM GENERAL WASHINGTON TO MAJOR-GENERAL GREENE.

(ORIGINAL.)

Head-quarters, White Plains, 1st September, 1778.

DEAR SIR,—I have had the pleasure of receiving your several letters, the last of which was of the 22nd of August. I have not now time to take notice of the arguments that were made use of for and against the count's quitting the harbour of Newport and sailing for Boston: right or wrong, it will probably disappoint our sanguine expectations of success; and, what I esteem a still worse consequence, I fear it will sow the seeds of dissension and distrust between us and our new allies, unless the most prudent measures are taken to suppress the feuds and jealousies that have already arisen. I depend much upon your aid and influence to conciliate that animosity which I plainly perceive, by a letter from the marquis, subsists between the American officers and the French in our service; this, you may depend, will extend itself to the count, and to the officers and men of his whole fleet, should they return to Rhode Island, unless, upon their arrival there, they find a reconciliation has taken place. The marquis speaks kindly of a letter from you to him on the subject; he will therefore take any advice coming from you in a friendly light; and, if he can be pacified, the other French gentlemen will of course be satisfied, as they look up to him as their head. The marquis grounds his complaint upon a general order of the 24th of August, the latter part of which is certainly very impolitic, especially considering the universal clamour that prevailed against the French nation.

I beg you will take every measure to keep the protest entered into by the general officers from being made public. The congress, sensible of the ill consequences that will flow from the world's knowing our differences, have passed a resolve to that purpose. Upon the whole, my dear sir, you can conceive my meaning better than I can express it; and I therefore fully depend upon your exerting yourself to heal all private animosities between our principal officers and the French, and to prevent all illiberal expressions and reflections that may fall from the army at large.

I have this moment received a letter from General Sullivan of the 29th of August, in which he barely informs me of an action upon that day, in which he says we had the better, but does not mention particulars.

I am, &c.

TO GENERAL WASHINGTON.

(ORIGINAL.)

Tyvertown, 1st September, 1778.

My dear General,—That there has been an action fought where I could have been, and where I was not, is a thing which will seem as extraordinary to you as it seems so to myself. After a long journey and a longer stay from home, (I mean from head-quarters,) the only satisfactory day I have, finds me in the middle of a town. There I had been sent, pushed, hurried, by the board of general officers, and principally by Generals Sullivan and Greene, who thought I should be of great use to the common cause, and to whom I foretold the disagreeable event which would happen to me; I felt, on that occasion, the impression of that bad star which, some days ago, has influenced the French undertakings, and which, I hope, will soon be removed. People say that I don't want an action; but if it is not necessary to my reputation as a tolerable private soldier, it would at least add to my satisfaction and pleasure. However, I was happy enough to arrive before the second retreat: it was not attended with such trouble and danger as it would have been had not the enemy been so sleepy, I was thus once more deprived of my fighting expectations.

From what I have heard from sensible and *candid* French gentlemen, the action does great honour to General Sullivan: he retreated in good order; he opposed, very properly, every effort of the enemy; he never sent troops but well supported, and displayed great coolness during the whole day. The evacuation I have seen extremely well performed, and *my private opinion* is, that if both events are satisfactory to us, they are very shameful to the British generals and troops; they had, indeed, so many fine chances to cut us to pieces; but they are very good people.

Now, my dear general, I must give you an account of that journey for which I have paid so dear. The Count d'Estaing arrived the day before in Boston. I found him much displeased at a protest of which you have heard, and many other circumstances which I have reported to you: I did what I could on the occasion; but I must do the admiral the justice to say that it has not at all diminished his warm desire of serving America. We waited together on the council, General Heath, General Hancock, and were very well satisfied with them; the last one distinguished himself very much by his zeal on the occasion. Some people in Boston were rather dissatisfied; but when they saw the behaviour of the council, Generals Heath and Hancock, they, I hope, will do the same; I, therefore, fear nothing but delays. The marts are very far off, provisions difficult to be provided. The Count d'Estaing was ready to come with his land forces and put himself under General Sullivan's orders, though dissatisfied with the latter; but our new circumstances will alter that design.

I beg you will pardon me once more, my dear general, for having troubled and afflicted you with the account of what I had seen after the departure of the French fleet. My confidence in you is such, that I could not feel so warmly upon this point without communicating it to your excellency. I have now the pleasure to inform you that the discontent does not appear so great. The French hospital is arrived at Boston, though under difficulties, which, however, I think I have diminished a good deal by sending part of my family, with orders to some persons, and entreaties to others, to give them all the assistance in their power. Now, everything will be right provided the Count d'Estaing is enabled to sail soon. Every exertion, I think, ought to be employed for that purpose in all the several parts of the continent: marts, biscuit, water, and provisions are his wants. I long to see that we have again the command, or at least an equal force, upon the American seas.

By your letters to General Sullivan, I apprehend that there is some general move in the British army, and that your excellency is going to send us reinforcements. God grant you may send us as many as with the militia will make a larger army, that you might command them yourself. I long, my dear general, to be again with you, and to have the pleasure of co-operating with the French fleet, under your immediate orders, this will be the greatest I can feel; I am sure everything will then be right. The Count d'Estaing (if Rhode Island is again to be taken, which I ardently wish,) would be extremely happy to take it in conjunction with General Washington, and it would remove the other inconveniences. I am now entrusted, by General Sullivan, with the care of Warren, Bristol, and the eastern shore. I am to defend a country with very few troops who are not able to defend more than a single point. I cannot answer that the enemy won't go and do what they please, for I am not able to prevent them, only with a part of their army, and yet this part must not land far from me; but I answer, that if they come with equal or not very superior forces to those I may collect, we shall flog them pretty well; at least, I hope so. My situation seems to be uncertain, for we expect to hear soon from your excellency. You know Mr. Touzard, a gentleman of my family—he met with a terrible accident in the last action; running before all the others, to take a piece of cannon in the midst of the enemy, with the greatest excess of bravery, he was immediately covered with their shots, had his horse killed, and his right arm shattered to pieces. He was happy enough not to fall into their hands: his life is not despaired of. Congress was going to send him a commission of major.

Give me joy, my dear general, I intend to have your picture, and Mr. Hancock has promised me a copy of that he has in Boston. He gave one to Count d'Estaing, and I never saw a man so glad at possessing his sweetheart's picture, as the admiral was to receive yours.

In expecting, with the greatest impatience, to hear from your excellency as to what are to be the general plans, and your private movements, I have the honour to be, with the highest respect, the warmest and most endless affection, dear general, &c.

TO GENERAL WASHINGTON.

(ORIGINAL.)

Camp, near Bristol, the 7th September, 1778.

My Dear General,—I cannot let M. de la Neuville go to head-quarters without recalling to your excellency's memory an inhabitant of the eastern Rhode Island, those who long much to be again reunited to you, and conceive now great hopes, from Sir Henry Clinton's movement to New York, that you will come to oppose him in person. I think if we meet to oppose the enemy in this quarter, that more troops are absolutely necessary, for we are not able to do anything in our scattered situation. I confess I am myself very uneasy in this quarter, and fear that these people will put it in their heads to take some of our batteries, &c., which, if properly attacked, it will be difficult to prevent. I am upon a little advance of land, where, in case of an alarm, a long stay might be very dangerous; but we will do the best.

I am told that the enemy is going to evacuate New York. My policy leads me to believe that some troops will be sent to Halifax, to the West Indies, and to Canada; that Canada, I apprehend, will be your occupation next winter and spring. This idea, my dear general, alters a plan I had to make a voyage home some months hence, however, as long as you fight I want to fight along with you, and I much desire to see your excellency in Quebec next summer.

With the most tender affection and highest respect, I have the honour to be, &c.

TO THE DUKE D'AYEN.

Bristol, near Rhode Island, September 11th, 1778.

I HAVE already endeavoured to describe to you some part of the pleasure your last letter gave me; but I cannot write again without repeating my assurance of the delight I derived from its perusal. I have blessed, a thousand times, the vessel that brought that letter, and the favourable winds that blew it, to the American shore. The kindness and affection you express have sunk deeply into a heart which is fully sensible of all their value. Your partiality has far over-rated my slight merit; but your approbation is so precious to me, my desire of obtaining it is so very strong, that I experience the same pleasure as if I were conscious of meriting your good opinion. I love you too well not to be enchanted and overjoyed when I receive any proof of your affection. You may find many persons more worthy of it, but I may take the liberty of challenging you to find one human being who either values it more highly, or is more desirous of obtaining it. I place full reliance on your kindness, and even if I were unhappy enough to fall under your displeasure, I hope I should not forfeit your affection. I think I may promise that that last misfortune shall never occur through any fault of mine, and I wish I could feel as certain of never erring from my head as from my heart. The goodness of my friends imposes a weight of obligation upon me. My greatest pleasure will be to hear you say, whilst I embrace you, that you do not disapprove of my conduct, and that you retain for me that friendship which renders me so happy. It is impossible for me to describe to you the joy your letter, and the kind feeling which dictated it, have inspired me with. How delighted I shall be to thank you for it, and to find myself again in your society! If you should ever amuse yourself by looking at the American campaigns, or following them on your maps, I shall ask permission to insert a small river or a mountain: this would give me an opportunity of describing to you the little I have seen, of confiding to you my own trifling ideas, and of endeavouring so to combine them as to render them more military: for there is so great a difference between what I behold here, and those large, fine, well-organised armies of Germany, that, in truth, when I recur from them to our American armies, I scarcely dare say that we are making war. If the French war should terminate before that of the rest of Europe, and you were disposed to see how things were going on, and permitted me to accompany you, I should feel perfectly happy; in the meantime, I have great pleasure in thinking that I shall pass some mornings with you at your own house, and I promise myself as much improvement as amusement from conversing with you, if you are so kind as to grant me some portion of your time.

I received, with heartfelt gratitude, the advice you gave me to remain here during this campaign; it was inspired by true friendship and a thorough knowledge of my interest: such is the species of advice we give to those we really love, and this idea has rendered it still dearer to me. I will be guided by it in proportion as events may follow the direction you appear to have expected. A change of circumstances renders a change of conduct sometimes necessary. I had intended, as soon as war was declared, to range myself under the French banner: I was induced to take this resolution from the fear that the ambition of obtaining higher rank, or the wish of retaining the one I actually enjoy, should appear to be my only motives for remaining here. Such unworthy sentiments have never found entrance into my heart. But your letter, advising me to remain, and assuring me there would be no land campaign, induced me to change my determination, and I now rejoice that I have done so. The arrival of the French fleet upon this coast, has offered me the agreeable prospect of acting in concert with it, and of being a happy spectator of the glory of the French banner. Although the elements, until now, have declared themselves against us, I have not lost the sanguine hopes of the future, which the great talents of M. d'Estaing have inspired us with. You will be astonished to hear that the English still retain all their posts, and have contented themselves with merely evacuating Philadelphia. I expected, and General Washington also expected, to see them abandon everything for Canada, Halifax, and their islands; but these gentlemen are apparently in no great haste. The fleet, it is true, may hitherto have rendered such a division of their troops rather difficult; but now that it is removed to Boston, they might easily begin to make a move: they appear to me, instead of moving off, to intend fighting a little in this part of the country. I thought I ought to consult M. d'Estaing, and even M. Gérard on this subject. Both agreed that I was right to remain, and even said, that my presence here would not prove wholly useless to my own country. That I might have nothing to reproach myself with, I wrote to M. de Montbarrey a short letter, which apprised him of my being still in existence, and of the resolution I had taken not to return to France in the midst of this campaign.

The kind manner in which you received the gazette which John Adams conveyed to you, induced me to send you a second, which must have made you acquainted with the few events that have taken place during this campaign. The visit that the English army designed to pay to a detachment which I commanded the 28th of May, and which escaped their hands owing to their own dilatory movements; the arrival of the treaty, subsequently that of the commissioners, the letter they addressed to congress, the firm answer they received, the evacuation of Philadelphia, and the retreat of General Clinton through Jersey, are the only articles worthy of attention. I have also described to you in what manner we followed the English army, and how General Lee, after my detachment had joined him, allowed himself to be beaten. The arrival of General Washington arrested the disorder, and determined the victory on our side. It is the battle, or rather affair, of Monmouth. General Lee has since been suspended for a year by a council of war, for his conduct on this occasion.

I must now relate to you what has occurred since the arrival of the fleet, which has experienced contrary winds ever since it sailed; after a voyage of three months it reached the Delaware, which the English had then quitted; from thence it proceeded to Sandyhook, the same place General Clinton sailed from after the check he encountered at Monmouth. Our army repaired to White Plains, that former battle-field of the Americans. M. d'Estaing blockaded New York, and we were thus neighbours of the English both by land and sea. Lord Howe, enclosed in the harbour, and separated from our fleet only by the Sandy-hook bar, did not accept the combat which the French admiral ardently desired, and offered him for several days. A noble project was conceived—that of entering into the harbour; but our ships drew too much water, and the English seventy-fours could not enter with their guns. Some pilots gave no hopes on this subject; but, when we examined the case more narrowly, all agreed as to its impossibility, and soundings proved the truth of the latter opinion; we were therefore obliged to have recourse to other measures.

General Washington, wishing to make a diversion on Rhode Island, ordered General Sullivan, who commanded in that state, to assemble his troops. The fleet stationed itself in the channel which leads to Newport, and I was ordered to conduct a detachment of the great army to General Sullivan, who is my senior in command. After many delays, which were very annoying to the fleet, and many circumstances, which it would be too long to relate, all our preparations were made, and we landed on the island with twelve thousand men, many of them militia, of whom I commanded one half upon the left side. M. d'Estaing had entered the channel the day before, in spite of the English batteries. General Pigot had enclosed himself in the respectable fortifications of Newport. The evening of our arrival, the English fleet appeared before the channel with all the vessels that Lord Howe had been able to collect, and a reinforcement of four thousand men for the enemy, who had already from five to six thousand men.

A north wind blew most fortunately for us the next day, and the French fleet passing gallantly under a sharp fire from the batteries, to which they replied with broadside shot, prepared themselves to accept the conflict which Lord Howe was apparently proposing to them. The English admiral suddenly cut his cables, and fled at full sail, warmly pursued by all our vessels, with the admiral at their head. This spectacle was given during the finest weather possible, and within sight of the English and American armies. I never felt so proud as on that day.

The next day, when the victory was on the point of being completed, and the guns of the *Languedoc* were directed towards the English fleet, at the most glorious moment for the French navy, a sudden gale, followed by a dreadful storm, separated and dispersed the French vessels, Howe's vessels, and those of Biron, which, by a singular accident, had just arrived there. The *Languedoc* and the *Marseillais* were dismasted, and the *Cesar* was afterwards unheard of for some time. To find the English fleet was impossible. M. d'Estaing returned to Rhode Island, remained there two days, to ascertain whether General Sullivan wished to retire, and then entered the Boston harbour. During these various cruises, the fleet took or burnt six English frigates, and a large number of vessels, of which several were armed; they also cleared the coast and opened the harbours. Their commander appeared to me to have been formed for great exploits; his talents, which all men must acknowledge, the qualities of his heart, his love of discipline and of the honour of his country, and his indefatigable activity, excite my admiration, and make me consider him as a man created for great actions.

As to ourselves, we remained some time at Rhode Island, and spent several days firing cannon shot at each other, which produced no great result on either side; but General Clinton having led himself a reinforcement of five thousand men, and a part of our militia having returned to their own homes, we thought of retiring; the harbour was no longer blockaded, and the English were resuming their naval advantage. Our retreat at that period was preceded by a trifling skirmish, at which I was not present, having repaired to Boston respecting an affair which I dare not write for fear of accidents. I returned in great haste, as you may imagine, and, after my arrival, we completed the evacuation of the Island. As the English were gone out, we were such near neighbours, that our picquets touched each other; they allowed us, however, to re-embark without perceiving it, and this want of activity appeared to me more fortunate, as they would have incommoded me exceedingly had they attacked the rear.

I am at present on the continent, and have the command of the troops stationed nearest Rhode Island; General Sullivan is at Providence; M. d'Estaing is taking in, at Providence, masts and provisions; General Washington is at White Plains, with three brigades, stationed some miles in advance on that side, in case of need. As to the English, they occupy New York and the adjacent Islands, and are better defended by their vessels than by their troops. They possess the same number of troops at Rhode Island that they did formerly, and General Grey, at the head of about five thousand men, marches along the coast, with the intention of burning the towns and ransoming the small Islands. It is thought, however, that the scene will soon become more animated; there are great movements in New York; Lord Howe has gone out with all his fleet, strengthened with the greatest part of Biron's squadron; M. d'Estaing has taken possession of the harbour, and has established some formidable batteries. On the other side, Mr. Grey may form and execute more serious projects; he is at present in my neighbourhood, and I am obliged to keep myself still more on the alert, because the stations which I occupy extend from Seconnet Point, which you may see on the map, to Bristol. I hope all this will soon end, for we are now in a very tiresome state of inaction.

I am becoming extremely prolix, but I perceive that I have forgotten dates, and two lines more or less will not add much to your fatigue. The evacuation of Philadelphia took place the 18th June; the affair of Monmouth the 28th; we arrived on Rhode Island, I think, the 10th August, and evacuated it the 30th of the same month: my gazette is now completed.

An accident has occurred on this Island which has affected me deeply. Several French officers, in the service of America, have the kindness to pass much of their time with me, especially when I am engaged firing musket balls. M. Touzard, an artillery officer in the regiment of *La Fère*, has been, during the last months, one of my constant associates. Finding a good opportunity on the Island of snatching a piece of cannon from the enemy, he threw himself in the midst of them, with the greatest gallantry and courage; but his temerity drew upon himself a hot fire from the enemy, which killed his horse, and carried away his right arm. His action has been admired, even by the English; it would be indeed unfortunate if distance should prevent its being known in France; I could not refrain from giving an account of it to M. de Montbarrey, although I have not any right to do so; but I am very anxious to be of use to this brave officer. If any opportunity offers of serving him, I recommend him earnestly to your love of noble actions. I confide my letters to M. d'Estaing, who will send them to France. If you should have the kindness to write to me, and any packet ships be sent out to the fleet, I beg you to take advantage of them. The admiration I feel for him who commands it, and my firm conviction that he will not let an opportunity escape of performing glorious deeds, will always make me desirous of being employed in unison with him; and the friendship of General Washington gives me the assurance that I need not even make such a request; I often also receive letters from M. d'Estaing, and he will send me yours as soon as he receives them. You must feel how impossible it is for me to ascertain when I can return to you. I shall be guided entirely by circumstances. My great object in wishing to return was the idea of a descent upon England. I should consider myself as almost dishonoured if I were not present at such a moment. I should feel so much regret and shame, that I should be tempted to drown or hang myself, according to the English mode. My greatest happiness would be to drive them from this country, and then to repair to England, serving under your command. This is a very delightful project; God grant it may be realized! It is the one which would be most peculiarly agreeable to me. I entreat you to send me your advice as soon as possible; if I but receive it in time, it shall regulate my conduct. Adieu, I dare not begin another page; I beg you to accept the assurance of my tender respect, and of all the sentiments that I shall ever feel for you during the remainder of my life.

I shall add this soiled bit of paper, which might have suited Harpagon himself, to my long epistle, to tell you that I am become very reasonable as relates to expenses. Now that I have my own establishment, I shall spend still less, and I really act very prudently, when you consider the exorbitant price of every thing, principally with paper money.

I shall write by another opportunity, perhaps a more speedy one, to Madame de Tessé. I entreat you to present her with my tender respects. If M. de Tessé, M. de Mun, M. de Neuilly, M. Senac,* retain a kind remembrance of me, deign to present my compliments to them. If M. de Comte le Broglie does not receive news from this country, as he has always expressed great interest in me, be so good as to give him an account of our proceedings when you see him.

May I flatter my*self* that I still possess your good opinion? I should not doubt it, if I could but convince you how much I value it; I will do everything in my power to deserve it, and I should be miserable if you doubted for an instant how very deeply this feeling is engraven in my breast. If I have ever erred in the path I am pursuing, forgive the illusions of my head in favour of the good intentions and rectitude of my heart, which is filled with feel-

* M. de Tessé, first squire to the Queen, had married Mademoiselle de Noailles, daughter of the Marshal, and aunt to Madame de Lafayette; M. de Neuilly was attached, under the Marshal's orders, to the stables of the Queen; M. de Mun, father to M. de Mun, peer of France, was intimate with the whole family; M. Sénac de Meilhan has been named comptroller general.

ings of the deepest gratitude, affection, and respect for you; and these it will ever retain, in all countries, and under all circumstances, until my latest breath. LAFAYETTE.

TO MADAME DE LAFAYETTE.

Bristol, near Rhode Island, Sept. 13th, 1778.

IF any thing could lessen my pleasure in writing to you, my dearest love, it would be the painful idea that I am writing to you from a corner of America, and that all I love is two thousand leagues from me. But I have reason to hope that the actual state of things cannot subsist for any length of time, and that the moment appointed for our meeting is not very far removed. War, which so often causes separation, must reunite us; it even secures my return by bringing French vessels here, and the fear of being taken will soon completely vanish; we shall be at least two to play at the game, and if the English attempt to interrupt my course, we shall be able to answer them. How delightful it would be for me to congratulate myself upon having heard from you; but that happiness has not been granted me. Your last letter arrived at the same time as the fleet; since that very distant day, since two months, I have been expecting letters, and none have reached me. It is true that the admiral, and the King's minister, have not been better treated by fortune; it is true that several vessels are expected, one in particular, every day: this gives me hope; and it is upon hope, that void and meagre food, that I must even subsist. Do not leave me in such a painful state of uncertainty, and although I do not expect to be here to receive an answer to the letter I am now writing, yet I entreat you to send me a very long one immediately, as if I were only waiting for your letter to depart; when you read this, therefore, call instantly for pen and ink, and write to me by every opportunity that you love me, and that you will be glad to see me again, not but that I am well convinced of this; my affection does not permit me to make use of any compliments with you, and there would be more vanity in telling you that I doubt your love, than in assuring you that I depend fully upon it, and for the remainder of my life. But every repetition of this truth always gives me pleasure. The feeling itself is so dear to me, and is so very necessary to my happiness, that I cannot but rejoice in your sweet expressions of it. It is not my reason (for I do not doubt your love) but my heart that you delight by repeating a thousand times what gives me more pleasure, if possible, each time you utter it. O, when shall I be with you, my love; when shall I embrace you a hundred times?

I flattered myself that the declaration of war would recall me immediately to France: independent of the ties which draw my heart towards those most dear to me, the love of my country, and my wish to serve her, are powerful motives for my return. I feared even that people, who did not know me, might imagine that ambition, a taste for the command I am entrusted with, and the confidence with which I am honoured, would induce me to remain here some time longer. I own that I felt some satisfaction in making these sacrifices to my country, and in quitting everything to fly to her assistance, without saying one word about the service

I was giving up. This would have been a source of the purest gratification to me, and I had resolved to set out the moment the news of war arrived. You shall now learn what has delayed me, and I may venture to say you will approve of my conduct.

The news was brought by a French fleet, who came to co-operate with the American troops; new operations were just commencing; it was in the midst of a campaign; this was not a moment to quit the army. I was also assured, from good authority, that nothing would take place this year in France, and that I lost, therefore, nothing by remaining here. I ran the risk, on the contrary, of passing the whole autumn in a vessel, and with a strong desire to fight everywhere, to fight in truth nowhere. I was flattered in this country with the hope of undertaking some enterprise in concert with M. d'Estaing; and persons like himself, charged with the affairs of France, told me my quitting America would be prejudicial, and my remaining in it useful, to my country. I was forced to sacrifice my delightful hopes, and delay the execution of my most agreeable projects. But at length the happy moment of rejoining you will arrive, and next winter will see me united to all I love best in the world.

You will hear so much said about war, naval combats, projected expeditions, and military operations, made and to be made, in America, that I will spare you the ennui of a gazette. I have, besides, related to you the few events that have taken place since the commencement of the campaign. I have been so fortunate as to be constantly employed, and I have never made an unlucky encounter with balls or bullets, to arrest me in my path. It is now more than a year since I dragged about, at Brandywine, a leg that had been somewhat rudely handled, but since that time it has quite recovered, and my left leg is now almost as strong as the other one. This is the only scratch I have received, or ever shall receive, I can safely promise you, my love. I had a presentiment that I should be wounded at the first affair, and I have now a presentiment that I shall not be wounded again. I wrote to you after our success at Monmouth, and I scrawled my letter almost on the field of battle, and still surrounded with slashed faces. Since that period, the only events that have taken place, are the arrival and operations of the French fleet, joined to our enterprise on Rhode Island. I have sent a full detail of them to your father. Half the Americans say that I am passionately fond of my country, and the other half say that since the arrival of the French ships, I have become mad, and that I neither eat, nor drink, nor sleep, but according to the winds that blow. Betwixt ourselves, they are a little in the right; I never felt so strongly what may be called national pride. Conceive the joy I experienced on beholding the whole English fleet flying full sail before ours, in presence of the English and American armies, stationed upon Rhode Island. M. d'Estaing having unfortunately lost some masts, has been obliged to put into the Boston harbour. He is a man whose talents, genius, and great qualities of the heart, I admire as much as I love his virtues, patriotism, and agreeable manners. He has experienced every possible difficulty; he has not been able to do all he wished to do; but he appears to me a man formed to advance the interests of such a nation as ours. Whatever may be the private feeling of friendship that unites me to him, I separate all partiality from the high opinion I entertain of our admiral. The Americans place great confidence in him, and the English fear him. As to the Rhode Island expedition, I shall content myself with saying that General Washington was not there, and that he sent me to conduct a reinforcement to the commanding officer, my senior in service. We exchanged, for several days, some cannon balls, which did no great harm on either side, and General Clinton having brought succours to his party, we evacuated the island, not without danger, but without any accident. We are all in a state of inaction, from which we shall soon awaken.

Whilst we were on the Island, an officer, who has passed the winter with me, named Touzard, of the regiment of *La Fère*, seeing an opportunity of snatching a piece of cannon from the enemy, threw himself amongst them with the utmost bravery. This action attracted the fire of his antagonists, which killed his horse, and carried off part of his right arm, which has since been amputated. If he were in France, such an action, followed by such an accident, would have been the means of his receiving the cross of St. Louis and a pension. I should feel the greatest pleasure if, through you and my friends, I could obtain for him any recompence.

I entreat you to present my respectful and affectionate compliments to the Marshal de Noailles; he must have received the trees I sent him. I will take advantage of the month of September, the most favourable time, to send him a still larger quantity. Do not forget me to Madame la Maréchale de Noailles; embrace my sisters a thousand and a thousand times. If you see the Chevalier de Chastellux, present to: him my compliments and assurances of affection.

But what shall I say to you, my love? What expressions can my tenderness find sufficiently strong for our dear Anastasia? You will find them but in your own heart, and in mine, which is equally open to you. Cover her with kisses; teach her to love me by loving you. We are so completely united, that it is impossible to love one without loving also the other. That poor little child must supply all we have lost; she has two places to occupy in my heart, and this heavy task our misfortune has imposed on her. I love her most fondly, and the misery of trembling for her life does not prevent my feeling for her the warmest affection. Adieu; when shall I be permitted to see thee, to part from thee no more; to make thy happiness as thou makest mine, and kneel before thee to implore thy pardon. Adieu, adieu; we shall not be very long divided.

PRESIDENT LAURENS TO THE MARQUIS DE LAFAYETTE.*

Philadelphia, 13th September, 1777.

Sir,—I am sensible of a particular degree of pleasure in executing the order of congress, signified in their act of the 9th instant, which will be enclosed with this, expressing the sentiments of the representatives of the United States of America, of your high merit on the late expedition against Rhode Island. You will do congress justice, Sir, in receiving the present acknowledgment as a tribute of the respect and gratitude of a free people. I have the honour to be, with very great respect and esteem, Sir, your obedient and most humble servant,

Henry Laurens, President.

* This letter, as well as all those that follow to that of the 11th of January, 1779, with the exception of the letter to Lord Carlisle, was written originally in English.

RESOLUTION OF CONGRESS.

Resolved :—The president is charged with writing to the Marquis de Lafayette; that congress conceives that the sacrifice he made of his personal feelings, when, for the interest of the United States, he repaired to Boston, at the moment when the opportunity of acquiring glory on the field of battle could present itself; his military zeal in returning to Rhode Island, when the greatest part of the army had quitted it, and his measures to secure a retreat, have a right to this present expression of the approbation of congress.

September 9th, 1778.

MARQUIS DE LAFAYETTE TO PRESIDENT LAURENS.

Camp, 23rd September, 1778.

Sir,—I have just received your favour of the 13th instant, acquainting me with the honour congress have been pleased to confer on me by their most gracious resolve. Whatever pride such an approbation may justly give me, I am not less affected by the feelings of gratefulness, and the satisfaction of thinking my endeavours were ever looked on as useful to a cause, in which my heart is so deeply interested. Be so good, Sir, as to present to congress my plain and hearty thanks, with a frank assurance of a candid attachment, the only one worth being offered to the representatives of a free people. The moment I heard of America, I loved her; the moment I knew she was fighting for freedom, I burnt with a desire of bleeding for her; and the moment I shall be able to serve her at any time, or in any part of the world, will be the happiest one of my life. I never so much wished for occasions of deserving those obliging sentiments with which I am honoured by these states and their representatives, and that flattering confidence they have been pleased to put in me, has filled my heart with the warmest acknowledgments and eternal affection. I am, &c., LAFAYETTE.

TO GENERAL WASHINGTON.

(ORIGINAL.)

Warren, 24th September, 1778.

MY DEAR GENERAL,—I am to acknowledge the reception of your late favour. Your excellency's sentiments were already known to me, and my heart had anticipated your answer. I, however, confess it gave me a new pleasure when I received it. My love for you is such, my dear general, that I should enjoy it better, if possible, in a private sentimental light than in a political one. Nothing makes me happier than to see a conformity of sentiments between you and me, upon any matter whatsoever; and the opinion of your heart is so precious to me, that I will ever expect it to fix mine. I don't know how to make out a fine expression of my sentiments, my most respected friend; but you know, I hope, my heart, and I beg you will read in it.

Agreeably to your advices and my own feelings, I made every effort that I could for preventing any bad measures being taken on either side; which conduct I also closely kept in the late affair of Boston concerning M. de St. Sauveur. I wished to have been of some use on both occasions, and I hope we have pretty well succeeded. The Count d'Estaing is entirely ours; so, at least, I apprehend by his confidential letters to me; and it affords me great pleasure. I have found by him an occasion of writing to

France; and you will better conceive than I may describe, how I have acted on the occasion. I thought the best way of speaking of those internal affairs was not to speak of them, or at least very indifferently, so as to give any such report which might arrive as groundless and insignificant. I daresay my scheme will have the desired effect, and nothing will be thought of it in France. I thought it would be well to let the admiral know that you do not lay any blame upon him, and that you entertained the sentiments any honest Frenchman might wish upon this matter.

Agreeably to a very useful article of a letter to General Sullivan, I have removed my station from Bristol, and am in a safer place, behind Warren. The few spies I have been able to procure upon the island seem rather to think of an evacuation than of any enterprise; but, you know, New York is the fountain-head. I long much, my dear general, to be again with you; our separation has been long enough, and I am here as inactive as anywhere else. My wish, and that you will easily conceive, had been to co-operate with the French fleet; I don't know now what they will do. The admiral has written to me upon many plans, and does not seem well fixed on any scheme: he burns with the desire of striking a blow, and is not yet determined how to accomplish it. He wrote me that he wanted to see me, but I cannot leave my post, lest something might happen: it has already cost dear enough to me. However, if you give me leave, I'll ask this of General Sullivan, and will do what I think best for both countries.

I have heard of a *pistolade* between two gentlemen, which lasted very long without much effect: it looks like our too much spoken of *cannonade* at

Newport, while *the siege* was continued. I have not yet been able to find out what your excellency desires me to inquire into, on account of the French queen :* but the people of the navy are too remote from Versailles to have any knowledge of it, and the Count d'Estaing himself has not any intimacy with her. I'll get that intelligence from a better source, and *more agreeable to your feelings on the matter*, in order that you may do what you think fit to be done if the report is true.

I beg, my dear general, when you write to your lady, that you would present my respects to her; and I beg also the liberty to make here a thousand compliments to your family. With the highest respect and most tender friendship, I have the honour to be, dear general.

FROM GENERAL WASHINGTON TO THE MARQUIS DE LAFAYETTE.

(ORIGINAL.)

Fredericksburg, 25th September, 1778.

MY DEAR MARQUIS,—The sentiments of affection and attachment, which breathe so conspicuously in all your letters to me, are at once pleasing and

* Several ladies had lately come out from New York, who reported that a vessel had been captured and brought to that city, in which was contained a present from the Queen of France to Mrs. Washington, as "an elegant testimonial of her approbation of the general's conduct," and that it had been sold at auction for the benefit of the captors. This intelligence was so confidently affirmed from such a respectable source, that General Washington had requested the Marquis de Lafayette to make inquiry as to the truth of it through the medium of Madame de Lafayette.—*Writings of Washington*, vol. vi p. 74.

honourable, and afford me abundant cause to rejoice at the happiness of my acquaintance with you. Your love of liberty, the just sense you entertain of this valuable blessing, and your noble and disinterested exertions in the cause of it, added to the innate goodness of your heart, conspire to render you dear to me; and I think myself happy in being linked with you in bonds of the strictest friendship.

The ardent zeal which you have displayed during the whole course of the campaign to the eastward, and your endeavours to cherish harmony among the officers of the allied powers, and to dispel those unfavourable impressions which had begun to take place in the minds of the unthinking, from misfortunes, which the utmost stretch of human foresight could not avert, deserved, and now receives, my particular and warmest thanks. I am sorry for Monsieur Touzard's loss of an arm in the action on Rhode Island; and offer my thanks to him, through you, for his gallant behaviour on that day.

Could I have conceived that my picture had been an object of your wishes, or in the smallest degree worthy of your attention, I should, while M. Peale was in the camp at Valley Forge, have got him to take the best portrait of me he could, and presented it to you; but I really had not so good an opinion of my own worth, as to suppose that such a compliment would not have been considered as a greater instance of my vanity, than means of your gratification; and therefore, when you requested me to sit to Monsieur Lanfang, I thought it was only to obtain the outlines and a few shades of my features, to have some prints struck from.

If you have entertained thoughts, my dear marquis, of paying a visit to your court, to your lady, and to your friends this winter, but waver on account of an expedition into Canada, friendship induces me to tell you, that I do not conceive that the prospect of such an operation is so favourable at this time, as to cause you to change your views. Many circumstances and events must conspire to render an enterprise of this kind practicable and advisable. The enemy, in the first place, must either withdraw wholly, or in part, from their present posts, to leave us at liberty to detach largely from this army. In the next place, if considerable reinforcements should be thrown into that country, a winter's expedition would become impracticable, on account of the difficulties which would attend the march of a large body of men, with the necessary apparatus, provisions, forage, and stores, at that inclement season. In a word, the chances are so much against the undertaking, that they ought not to induce you to lay aside your other purpose, in the prosecution of which you shall have every aid, and carry with you every honourable testimony of my regard and entire approbation of your conduct, that you can wish. But it is a compliment, which is due, so am I persuaded you would not wish to dispense with the form of signifying your desires to congress on the subject of your voyage and absence.

I come now, in a more especial manner, to acknowledge the receipt of your obliging favour of the 21st, by Major Dubois, and to thank you for the important intelligence therein contained.

I do most cordially congratulate you on the glorious defeat of the British squadron under Admiral Keppel, an event which reflects the highest honour on the good conduct and bravery of Monsieur d'Orrilliers and the officers of the fleet under his command; at the same time that it is to be considered, I hope, as the happy presage of a fortunate and glorious war to his most Christian Majesty. A confirmation of the account I shall impatiently wait and devoutly wish for. If the Spaniards, under this favourable beginning, would unite their fleet to that of France, together they would soon humble the pride of haughty Britain, and no long suffer her to reign sovereign of the seas, and claim the privilege of giving laws to the main.

You have my free consent to make the Count d'Estaing a visit, and may signify my entire approbation of it to General Sullivan, who, I am glad to find, has moved you out of a *cul de sac*. It was my advice to him long ago, to have no detachments in that situation, let particular places be ever so much unguarded and exposed from the want of troops. Immediately upon my removal from White Plains to this ground, the enemy threw a body of troops into the Jerseys; but for what purpose, unless to make a grand forage, I have not been able yet to learn. They advanced some troops at the same time from their lines at Kingsbridge towards our old encampment at the plains, stripping the inhabitants not only of their provisions and forage, but even the clothes on their backs, and without discrimination.

The information, my dear marquis, which I begged the favour of you to obtain, was not, I am persuaded, to be had through the channel of the officers of the French fleet, but by application to your fair lady, to whom I should be happy in an opportunity of paying my homage in Virginia, when the war is ended, if she could be prevailed upon to quit, for a few months, the gaieties and splendour of a court, for the rural amusements of a humble cottage.

I shall not fail to inform Mrs. Washington of your polite attention to her. The gentlemen of my family are sensible of the honour you do them by your kind inquiries, and join with me in a tender of best regards; and none can offer them with more sincerity and affection than I do. With every sentiment you can wish, I am, my dear marquis, &c.

TO GENERAL WASHINGTON.*

(ORIGINAL.)

Camp, near Warren, 24th September, 1778.

My Dear General,—I am going to consult your excellency upon a point in which I not only want your leave and opinion, as the commander-in-chief, but also your candid advice, as the man whom I have the happiness to call my friend. In an address

* In the preceding session, the English parliament had passed bills called conciliatory, and in the month of June, conciliatory commissioners had presented themselves to negotiate an arrangement. These were, Lord Carlisle, Governor George Johnstone, and William Eden. Dr. Adam Ferguson, professor of moral philosophy at the University of Edinburgh, was secretary of the commission. They addressed a letter to Mr. Laurens which was to be communicated to congress. To that letter were joined private letters from Mr. Johnstone to several members of the assembly, whom he endeavoured to seduce by exciting interested hopes. The letters were given up to the congress, who declared "*that it was incompatible with their own honour to hold any sort of correspondence or relation with the said George Johnstone.*"—(See the Letters of General Washington, vol. v., p. 397, and vol. vi., p. 31; and the *History of the American Revolution,* by David Ramsay, vol. ii., chap. 16.)

from the British commissaries to congress, the first after *Johnstone* was excluded, they speak in the most disrespectful terms of my nation and country. The whole is undersigned by them, and more particularly by the president, Lord Carlisle. I am the first French officer, in rank, of the American army; I am not unknown to the British, and if somebody must take notice of such expressions, that advantage does, I believe, belong to me. Don't you think, my dear general, that I should do well to write a letter on the subject to Lord Carlisle, wherein I should notice his expressions conveyed in an unfriendly manner? I have mentioned something of this design to the Count d'Estaing, but wish entirely to fix my opinion by yours, which I instantly beg, as soon as you may find it convenient.

As everything is perfectly quiet, and General Sullivan is persuaded that I may, with all safety, go to Boston, I am going to undertake a short journey towards that place. The admiral has several times expressed a desire of conversing with me; he has also thrown out some wishes that something might be done towards securing Boston, but it seems he always refers to a conversation for further explanation. My stay will be short, as I don't like towns in time of war, when I may be about a camp. If your excellency answers me immediately, I may soon receive your letter.

I want much to see you, my dear general, and consult you about many points, part of them are respecting myself. If you approve of my writing to Lord Carlisle, it would be a reason for coming near you for a short time, in case the gentleman is displeased with my mission.

With the most perfect respect, confidence, and affection, I have the honour to be, &c.

TO LORD CARLISLE.*

I EXPECTED, until the present moment, my lord, to have only affairs to settle with your generals, and I hoped to see them at the head only of the armies which are respectively confided to us; your letter to the Congress of the United States, the insulting phrase to my country, which you yourself have signed, could alone bring me into direct communication with you. I do not, my lord, deign to refute your assertion, but I do wish to punish it. It is to you, as chief of the commission, that I now appeal, to give me a reparation as public as has been the offence, and as shall be the denial which arises from it; nor would that denial have been so long delayed if the letters had reached me sooner. As I am obliged to absent myself for some days, I hope to find your answer on my return. M. de Gimat, a French officer, will make all the arrangements for me which may be agreeable to you; I doubt not but that General Clinton, for the honour of his countryman, will consent to the measure I propose. As to myself, my lord, I shall consider all measures good, if, to the glory of being a Frenchman, I can add that of proving to one of your nation that my nation can never be attacked with impunity.

LAFAYETTE.

* This letter was written in French.

TO GENERAL WASHINGTON.

(ORIGINAL.)

Boston, 28th September, 1778.

Dear General,—The news I have got from France, the reflections I have made by myself, and those which have been suggested to me by many people, particularly by the admiral, increases more than ever the desire I had of seeing again your excellency. I want to communicate to you my sentiments, and take your opinion upon my present circumstances—I look upon this as of high moment to my private interests. On the other hand, I have some ideas, and some intelligence in reference to public interests, which I am very desirous of disclosing to your excellency. I am sure, my dear general, that your sentiments upon my private concerns are such, that you will have no objection to my spending some hours with you.*

The moment at which the fleet will be ready is not very far, and I think it of importance to have settled my affair with you before that time. I am going to write to General Sullivan on the subject,

* In spite of the obstacles which had arrested M. de Lafayette at the commencement of the projected northern campaign, he had embraced with ardour the idea of a diversion which was to be operated in Canada, with the combined forces of France and America; and it was partly to converse on this plan with Washington, and later with the cabinet of Versailles, that he insisted upon having a conference with the general-in-chief, and returning to France before the winter. He was even summoned to explain himself on this subject with a committee from the congress, who adopted the plan in principle, but decided that General Washington should be first consulted. The latter expressed his objections in a public letter addressed to the congress, and in a private letter addressed to Laurens, (14th November, 1778.)

and if he has no objection, I'll go immediately to head-quarters; but should he make difficulties, I beg you will send me that leave. I intend to ride express, in order that I may have time enough. You may think, my dear general, that I don't ask, what I never asked in my life—a leave to quit the post I am sent to—without strong reasons for it; but the letters I have received from home make me very anxious to see you.

With the most tender affection and highest respect, &c.

FROM GENERAL WASHINGTON TO THE MARQUIS DE LAFAYETTE.

(ORIGINAL.)

Fishkill, 4th October, 1778.

MY DEAR MARQUIS,—I have had the pleasure of receiving, by the hands of Monsieur de la Colombe, your favour of the 28th ultimo, accompanied by one of the 24th, which he overtook somewhere on the road. The leave requested in the former, I am as much interested to grant, as to refuse my appro-

It was long before the final decision of congress became known. M. de Lafayette was still ignorant of it when he embarked for Europe. The 29th December, only, a letter was addressed to him from President John Jay, who was charged by congress to express to him that the difficulties of execution—the want of men and materials, and, above all, the exhausted state of the finances, did not permit the accomplishment of this project; that if, however, France would first enter into it, the United States would make every effort to second her. But France, from various motives, did not shew herself disposed to snatch Canada from the English. (See the Correspondence of Washington, vol. vi., and his Life by Marshal, vol. iii.)

bation of the challenge proposed in the latter. The generous spirit of chivalry, exploded by the rest of the world, finds a refuge, my dear friend, in the sensibility of your nation only. But it is in vain to cherish it, unless you can find antagonists to support it; and, however well adapted it might have been to the times in which it existed, in our days, it is to be feared, that your opponent, sheltering himself behind modern opinions, and under his present public character of commissioner, would turn a virtue of such ancient date into ridicule. Besides, supposing his lordship accepted your terms, experience has proved that chance is often as much concerned in deciding these matters as bravery, and always more than the justice of the cause. I would not, therefore, have your life, by the remotest possibility, exposed, when it may be reserved for so many greater occasions. His excellency, the admiral, I flatter myself, will be in sentiment with me; and, as soon as he can spare you, will send you to head-quarters, where I anticipate the pleasure of seeing you.

Having written very fully to you a few days ago, and put the letter under cover to General Sullivan, I have nothing to add at this time, but to assure you that, with the most perfect regard—I am, dear sir, &c.

MARQUIS DE LAFAYETTE TO PRESIDENT LAURENS.

(ORIGINAL.)

Philadelphia, 13th October, 1778.

SIR,—Whatever care I should take not to employ the precious time at congress in private considerations, I beg leave to lay before them my present circumstances, with that confidence which naturally springs from affection and gratitude. The sentiments which bind me to my country, can never be more properly spoken of than in the presence of men who have done so much for their own. As long as I thought I could dispose of myself, I made it my pride and pleasure to fight under American colours, in defence of a cause, which I dare more particularly call ours, because I had the good fortune to bleed for it. Now, sir, that France is involved in a war, I am urged by a sense of duty, as well as by patriotic love, to present myself before the king, to know in what manner he may judge proper to employ my services. The most agreeable of all will be such as may enable me always to serve the common cause among those whose friendship I have the happiness to obtain, and whose fortune I have had the honour to follow in less smiling times. That reason, and others, which I leave to the feelings of congress, engage me to beg from them the liberty of going home for the next winter.

As long as there were any hopes of an active campaign, I did not think of leaving the field. Now that I see a very peaceable and undisturbed moment, I take this opportunity of waiting on congress. In case my request is granted, I shall so manage my departure as to be certain before going off that the campaign is really over. Inclosed you will find a letter from his excellency General Washington, where he expresses his assent to my getting leave of absence. I dare flatter myself, that I shall be looked upon as a soldier on furlough, who most heartily wants to join again his colours, and his most esteemed and beloved fellow-soldiers. In case it is thought that I can be in any way useful to the service of America, when I shall find myself among my countrymen, and in case any exertion of mine is deemed serviceable, I hope, sir, I shall always be considered as a man who is deeply interested in the welfare of the United States, and who has the most perfect affection, regard, and confidence for representatives: With the highest regard, I have the honour to be, &c.

LAFAYETTE.

PRESIDENT LAURENS TO THE MARQUIS DE LAFAYETTE.

(ORIGINAL.)

Philadelphia, 24th October, 1778.

SIR,—I had the honour of presenting to congress your letter, soliciting leave of absence, and I am directed by the house to express their thanks for your zeal in promoting that just cause in which they are engaged, and for the disinterested services you have rendered to the United States of America. In testimony of the high esteem and affection in which you are held by the good people of these states, as well as in acknowledgment of your gallantry and military talents, displayed on many signal occasions, their representatives in congress assembled have ordered an elegant sword to be presented to you by the American minister at the court of Versailles.

Enclosed within the present cover will be found an act of congress, of the 21st instant, authorizing these declarations, and granting a furlough for your return to France, to be extended at your own pleasure. I pray God to bless and protect you, Sir; to conduct you in safety to the presence of your prince, and to the re-enjoyment of your noble family and friends. I have the honour to be, with the highest respect, and with the most sincere affection, Sir, your most obedient and most humble servant,

HENRY LAURENS, President.

1778. In Congress, October 21st.—Resolved, That the Marquis de Lafayette, major-general in the service of the United States, have leave to go to France, and that he return at such time as shall be most convenient to him.

Resolved, That the president write a letter to the Marquis de Lafayette, returning him the thanks of congress for that disinterested zeal which led him to America, and for the services he has rendered to the United States by the exertion of his courage and abilities on many signal occasions.

Resolved, That the minister plenipotentiary of the United States of America at the court of Versailles be directed to cause an elegant sword, with proper devices, to be made, and presented in the name of the United States to the Marquis de Lafayette.

October 22nd.—Resolved, That the following letter of recommendation of the Marquis de Lafayette be written to the King of France:—

To our great, faithful, and beloved friend and ally, Louis the Sixteenth, king of France and Navarre:—

The Marquis de Lafayette having obtained our leave to return to his native country, we could not suffer him to depart without testifying our deep sense of his zeal, courage, and attachment. We have advanced him to the rank of major-general in our armies, which, as well by his prudent as spirited conduct, he has manifestly merited. We recommend this young nobleman to your majesty's notice, as one whom we know to be wise in council, gallant in the field, and patient under the hardships of war. His devotion to his sovereign has led him in all things to demean himself as an American, acquiring thereby the confidence of these United States, your good and faithful friends and allies, and the affection of their citizens. We pray God to keep your majesty in his holy protection.

Done at Philadelphia, the 22nd day of October, 1778, by the congress of the United States of North America, your good friends and allies.

HENRY LAURENS, President.

TO GENERAL WASHINGTON.

(ORIGINAL.)

Philadelphia, the 24th of October, 1778.

MY DEAR GENERAL,—You will be surprised to hear that I am yet in this city, and that I could never get out this time. My own business was immediately done, and I received from congress all possible marks of kindness and affection; but public affairs do not go on quite so fast, and I am detained for the expedition of projects, instructions, and many papers which I am to carry with me. The zeal for the common cause prevents my leaving this place before I am dismissed. However, I will certainly set out to-morrow afternoon at farthest.

Congress have been pleased to grant me an undetermined furlough by the most polite and honourable resolves, to which they have added a letter for the king in my behalf. I will shew the whole to your excellency as soon as I have the pleasure to see you; and as I hope to arrive two days after this letter, I think it is useless to trouble you with copies.

I have received an answer from Lord Carlisle, in which he conceals himself behind his dignity, and, by a prudent foresight, he objects to entering into any explanation in any change of situation.

There is a plan going on which I think you will approve. The idea was not suggested by me, and I acted in the affair a passive part. I will speak to your excellency of it more at length, and with more freedom, at our first interview. May I hope, my dear general, that you will order the enclosed letters to be sent immediately to Boston, as some of them contain orders for a frigate to put herself in readiness.

With the highest respect and most tender affection, I have the honour to be.

LORD CARLISLE TO M. DE LAFAYETTE.

Sir,—I have received your letter by M. de Gimat; I own it appears to me difficult to make a serious answer to it; the only one that can be expected from me in my capacity of commissioner of the king, and which is one you should have foreseen, is, that I look upon myself, and shall always look upon myself, as not obliged to be responsible to any individual for my public conduct and mode of expression. I am only responsible to my king and country. In respect to the opinions or expressions contained in one of the public documents published by the authority of the commission to which I have the honour of belonging, unless they should be publicly retracted, you may feel certain that, whatever change may take place in my situation, I shall never be disposed to give any account of them, still less to disown them privately. I must recal to you that the insult you allude to as occurring in the correspondence between the king's commissioners and the congress is not of a private nature. I think, therefore, that all national disputes will be best decided when Admiral Biron and Count d'Estaing shall have met.

MARQUIS DE LAFAYETTE TO PRESIDENT LAURENS.

(ORIGINAL.)

Philadelphia, 26th October, 1778.

SIR,—I have received your excellency's obliging letter, enclosing the several resolutions congress have honoured me with, and the leave of absence they have been pleased to grant. Nothing can make me happier than the reflection that my services have met with their approbation; the glorious testimonial of confidence and satisfaction repeatedly bestowed on me by the representatives of America, though superior to my merit, cannot exceed the grateful sentiments they have excited. I consider the noble present offered to me in the name of the United States as the most flattering honour; it is my most fervent desire soon to employ that sword in their service against the common enemy of my country, and of their faithful and beloved allies.

That liberty, safety, wealth, and concord may ever extend to the United States, is the ardent wish of a heart glowing with a devoted zeal and unbounded love, and the highest regard and the most sincere affection for their representatives. Be pleased, Sir, to present my thanks to them, and to accept, yourself, the assurance of my respectful attachment. I have the honour to be, with profound veneration, your excellency's most obedient servant,

LAFAYETTE.

FRAGMENT OF A LETTER FROM THE FRENCH MINISTER, M. GERARD, TO COUNT DE VERGENNES.

October, 1778.

———I ought not to terminate this long despatch, without rendering to the wisdom and dexterity of the Marquis de Lafayette, in the part he has taken in these discussions, the justice which is due to his merits. He has given most salutary counsels, authorized by his friendship and experience. The Americans have strongly solicited his return with the troops which the king may send. He has replied with a due sensibility, but with an entire resignation to the will of the king. I cannot forbear saying, that the conduct, equally prudent, courageous, and amiable, of the Marquis de Lafayette, has made him the idol of the congress, the army, and the people of America. A high opinion is entertained of his military talents. You know how little I am inclined to adulation; but I should be wanting in justice, if I did not transmit to you these testimonials, which are here in the mouth of the whole world.

FROM GENERAL WASHINGTON TO THE MARQUIS DE LAFAYETTE.

(ORIGINAL.)

Philadelphia, 29th December, 1778.

My Dear Marquis,—This will be accompanied by a letter from congress, which will inform you, that a certain expedition, after a full consideration of all circumstances, has been laid aside. I am sorry, however, for the delay it has occasioned you, by remaining so long undecided.

I am persuaded, my dear marquis, that there is no need of fresh proofs to convince you either of my affection for you personally, or of the high opinion I entertain of your military talents and merits. Yet, as you are on the point of returning to your native country, I cannot forbear indulging my friendship, by adding to the honourable testimonies you have received from congress, the enclosed letter from myself to our minister at your court. I have therein endeavoured to give him an idea of the value this country sets upon you; and the interest I take in your happiness cannot but make me desire you may be equally dear to your own. Adieu, my dear marquis; my best wishes will ever attend you. May you have a safe and agreeable passage, and a happy meeting with your lady and friends. I am, &c.

FROM GENERAL WASHINGTON TO BENJAMIN FRANKLIN, AMERICAN MINISTER IN FRANCE.

(ORIGINAL.)

Philadelphia, 28th December, 1778.

SIR,—The Marquis de Lafayette, having served with distinction as major-general in the army of the United States for two campaigns, has been determined, by the prospect of an European war, to return to his native country. It is with pleasure that I embrace the opportunity of introducing to your personal acquaintance a gentleman, whose merit cannot have left him unknown to you by reputation. The generous motives which first induced him to cross the Atlantic; the tribute which he paid to gallantry at the Brandywine; his success in Jersey, before he had recovered from his wound, in an affair where he commanded militia against British grenadiers; the brilliant retreat, by which he eluded a combined manœuvre of the British forces in the last campaign; his services in the enterprise against Rhode Island; are such proofs of his zeal, military order, and talents, as have endeared him to America, and must greatly recommend him to his prince.

Coming with so many titles to claim your esteem, it were needless, for any other purpose than to indulge my own feelings, to add, that I have a very particular friendship for him; and that, whatever services you may have it in your power to render him, will confer an obligation on one who has the honour to be—with the greatest esteem, regard, and respect, sir, &c.

TO GENERAL WASHINGTON.

(ORIGINAL.)

Boston, 5th January, 1779.

DEAR GENERAL,—In my difficult situation, at such a distance from you, I am obliged to take a determination by myself, which, I hope, will meet with your approbation. You remember, that in making full allowance for deliberations, the answer from congress was to reach me before the 15th of last month, and I have long since waited without even hearing from them. Nay, many gentlemen from Philadelphia assure me, congress believe that I am gone long ago. Though my affairs call me home, private interests would, however, induce me to wait for your excellency's letters, for the decision of congress about an exchange in case I should be taken, and for the last determinations concerning the plans of the next campaign.

But I think the importance of the despatches I am the bearer of; the uncertainty and improbability of receiving any others here; my giving intelligence at Versailles may be for the advantage of both nations; the inconvenience of detaining the fine frigate, on board which I return, and the danger of losing all the men, who desert very fast, are reasons so important as oblige me not to delay any longer. I am the more of that opinion from congress having resolved to send about this time three fast sailing vessels to France, and the marine committee having promised me to give the despatches to such officers as I would recommend; it is a very good way of forwarding their letters, and sending such as your excellency may be pleased to write me. I beg you will send copies of them by the several vessels.

To hear from you, my most respected friend, will be the greatest happiness I can feel. The longer the letters you write, the more blessed with satisfaction I shall think myself. I hope you will not refuse me that pleasure as often as you can. I hope you will ever preserve that affection which I return by the tenderest sentiments.

How happy, my dear general, I should be to come next spring, principally, as it might yet be proposed, I need not to say. Your first letter will let me know what I am to depend upon on that head, and, I flatter myself, the first from me will confirm to you that I am at liberty, and that most certainly I intend to come next campaign.

My health is now in the best condition, and I would not remember I ever was sick, were it not for the marks of friendship you gave me on that occasion. My good doctor has attended me with his usual care and tenderness. He will see me on board and then return to head-quarters; but the charge of your friend was intrusted to him till I was on board the frigate. I have met with the most kind hospitality in this city, and, drinking water excepted, the doctor has done everything he could to live happy; he dances and sings at the assemblies most charmingly.

The gentlemen who, I hope, will go to France, have orders to go to head-quarters; and I flatter myself, my dear general, that you will write me by them. I beg you will let the bearer of this, Captain la Colombe, know that I recommend him to your excellency for the commission of major.

Be so kind, my dear general, as to present my best respects to your lady and the gentlemen of your family. I hope you will quietly enjoy the pleasure of being with Mrs. Washington, without any disturbance from the enemy, till I join you again; I also hope you will approve of my sailing, which, indeed, was urged by necessity, after waiting so long.

Farewell, my most beloved general; it is not without emotion I bid you this last adieu, before so long a separation. Don't forget an absent friend, and believe me for ever and ever, with the highest respect and tenderest affection.

On board the *Alliance*, 10th January, 1779.

I open again my letter, my dear general, to let you know that I am not yet gone, but if the wind proves fair, I shall sail to-morrow. Nothing from Philadelphia; nothing from head-quarters. So that everybody, as well as myself, is of opinion that I should be wrong to wait any longer. I hope I am right, and I hope to hear soon from you. Adieu, my dear, and for ever beloved friend,—adieu!

TO GENERAL WASHINGTON.

(ORIGINAL.)

On board the *Alliance*, off Boston, 11th Jan., 1779

THE sails are just going to be hoisted, my dear general, and I have but time to take my last leave of you. I may now be certain that congress did not intend to send anything more by me. The navy board and Mr. Nevil write me this very morning from Boston, that the North River is passable; that a gentleman from camp says, he did not hear of anything like an express for me. All agree for certain that congress think I am gone, and that the sooner I go the better.

Farewell, my dear general; I hope your French friend will ever be dear to you; I hope I shall soon see you again, and tell you myself with what emotion I now leave the coast you inhabit, and with what affection and respect I am for ever, my dear general, your respectful and sincere friend.

SECOND VOYAGE TO AMERICA,

AND

CAMPAIGNS OF 1780 & 1781.

HISTORICAL MEMOIRS

OF

1779, 1780, & 1781.*

LAFAYETTE, who quitted France as a rebel and fugitive, returned there triumphant and in favour. He was scarcely punished by a week's arrest for his disobedience to the King, and that was only after he had had a conversation with the first minister, Maurepas. Lafayette found himself the tie between the United States and France; he enjoyed the confidence of both countries and both governments. His favour at court and in society was employed in serving the cause of the Americans, in destroying the false impressions that were endeavoured to be raised against them, and in obtaining for them succours of every kind. He experienced, however, many difficulties; the friends of the Austrian alliance saw, with displeasure, that that war would

* These Memoirs are extracted from the American Biography of M. de Lafayette, written by himself, which we have designated under the name of Manuscript, No. 1. We have completed them by extracts of Manuscript, No. 2, which contains observations on the historians of America.

cause the refusal of the forty thousand auxiliaries stipulated by the treaty of Vienna; the French ministry already feared the too great aggrandisement of the United States, and decidedly refused the conquest of Canada, on pretence that before a fourteenth state was added to those that had already declared themselves independent, it was necessary first to deliver the thirteen from the yoke of the English. M. Neckar feared everything that could either increase the expense of the war or prolong it. Maurepas himself, who had been reluctantly led into it, was completely weary of it; he hoped to obtain peace by making an attempt on England. Lafayette, taking advantage of this idea, had organized an expedition, in which the celebrated Paul Jones was to command the marines, and of which the object was to transport a body of troops, bearing the American banner, upon the coast of England, and levy contributions to supply the Americans with the money that could not be drawn from the treasury of France. Liverpool and some other towns would have been justly punished for the part they had taken in the vexations exercised against the colonies, to whom they were indebted for their prosperity; but the economy and timidity of the French ministers made this undertaking fail. Lafayette, despairing of the success of the Canada expedition, took a step that was undoubtedly a bold one, but which was quite justified by the issue. He had been enjoined not to ask for French auxiliary troops for the United States, because the popular feeling of jealousy against foreigners, and especially against Frenchmen, not only rendered the congress itself averse to this project, but made them believe it would excite general anxiety and discontent. Lafayette foresaw that before the succour could be ready, the United

States would feel its necessity, and that it might arrive, as did actually occur, in a decisive moment for the safety of the cause. He took, therefore, upon himself, not being able to obtain troops for Canada, to solicit, in the name of the congress, what he had been positively forbidden to ask, a succour of auxiliary troops sent to a port of the United States, and he made choice of that of Rhode Island which, having been evacuated by the English, and being in an Island suitable for defence, was more likely than any other to obviate all kinds of difficulties. He obtained the promise of six thousand men, but four thousand only were afterwards sent, under Count Rochambeau: however trifling that number might appear, Lafayette knew that, by employing young officers of the court, and drawing the attention of the French upon that little corps, the ministers would sooner or later be obliged to render it of use by obtaining a decided naval superiority upon the American coast, which was Lafayette's principal object, and which it was very difficult to obtain, owing to other plans of operation; in fact, that naval superiority was never established until 1781, and then lasted but for a few weeks: events have since proved how right Lafayette was to speak every day of its necessity. The corps which had been granted were not in readiness to sail until the beginning of the year 1780. Lafayette in the meantime was employed in the staff of the army which was preparing for a descent on England, under the orders of the Marshal de Vaux. It was then that Dr. Franklin's grandson presented him officially with the sword that congress had decreed to him. Upon that sword were represented Monmouth, Barren Hill, Gloucester, and Rhode Island;

America, delivered from her chains, was offering a branch of laurel to a youthful warrior; the same warrior was represented inflicting a mortal wound upon the British lion. Franklin had placed in another part an ingenious device for America; it was a crescent, with these words: *Crescam ut prosim;* on the other side was the device, *Cur non?* which the youth himself had adopted when he first set out for America.

Lafayette, at the end of the campaign, renewed his efforts to obtain the fulfilment of the hopes which had been given him; he succeeded in gaining pecuniary succours, which were placed at the disposal of General Washington, for it was upon that general that reposed the whole confidence of the government, and the hopes of the French nation. Clothing for the army had been promised also, but that remained behind with the two thousand men which were to have completed the corps of Rochambeau; and Admiral Ternay, instead of bringing, as he ought to have done, a stronger naval force than the enemy had brought, set sail for Rhode Island with seven vessels. This expedition was kept very secret;* Lafayette had preceded it on board the

* It was settled that that corps of six thousand men, commanded by Lieutenant-General Rochambeau, was to be completely under the orders of the American commander-in-chief, and was only to form a division of his army. The order of service was regulated in such a manner that the French were only to be looked upon as auxiliaries, keeping the left of the American troops, and the command belonging, when there was equality of rank and age, to the American officers. In a word, the advantages to be derived by the government, the general, and the American soldiers, were stipulated beforehand in such a manner as to prevent all future discussions. (Manuscript, No. 2.)

French frigate the *Hermione;* he arrived at Boston before the Americans and English had the least knowledge of that auxiliary reinforcement.

(1780.) The arrival of Lafayette at Boston produced the liveliest sensation, which was entirely owing to his own popularity, for no one yet knew what he had obtained for the United States. Every person ran to the shore; he was received with the loudest acclamations, and carried in triumph to the house of Governor Hancock, from whence he set out for head-quarters. Washington learnt, with great emotion, of the arrival of his young friend. It was observed that on receiving the despatch which announced to him this event, his eyes filled with tears of joy, and those who are acquainted with the disposition of Washington, will consider this as a certain proof of a truly paternal love. Lafayette was welcomed with the greatest joy by the army; he was beloved both by officers and soldiers, and felt the sincerest affection for them in return. After the first pleasure of their meeting was over, General Washington and he retired into a private room to talk over the present state of affairs. The situation of the army was a very bad one; it was in want of money, and it was become almost impossible to raise recruits; in short, some event was necessary to restore the energy of the different states, and give the army an opportunity of displaying its vigour. It was then that Lafayette announced to the commander-in-chief what had been done, and the succours which might soon be expected to arrive. General Washington felt the importance of this good news, and considered it as deciding the successful issue of their affairs. All the necessary preparations were made: the secret was well kept, although steps were obliged to be taken for the arrival of the troops, who landed safely at Rhode Island, and who, in spite of their long inaction, formed a necessary and powerful force to oppose to the English army.

During the campaign of 1780, the French corps remained at Rhode Island. After the defeat of Gates, Greene went to command in Carolina; Arnold was placed at West Point; the principal army, under the immediate orders of Washington, had for its front guard the light infantry of Lafayette, to which was joined the corps of the excellent partisan, Colonel Lee. This is the proper time to speak of that light infantry. The American troops had no grenadiers; their *chasseurs*, or riflemen, formed a distinct regiment, under the orders of the colonel, since Brigadier-General Morgan, and had been taken, not from different corps, but from parts of the country on the frontiers of the savage tribes, and from amongst men whose mode of life, and skill in firing their long carabines, rendered them peculiarly useful in that service. But the regiments of the line supplied some chosen men, whose officers were also all picked men, and who formed a select band of about two thousand, under the orders of Lafayette. The mutual attachment of that corps and its head had become even a proverb in America. As a traveller brings from distant countries presents to his family and friends, he had brought from France the value of a large sum of money in ornaments for the soldiers, swords for the officers and under officers, and banners* for the battalions. This troop of

* Upon one of these banners a cannon was painted, with this device: *Ultima ratio*, suppressing the word *regum*, which is used in Europe; upon another, a crown of laurel united to a civic crown, with the device—*No other*. And thus with the other emblems.—(Note de M. de Lafayette.)

chosen men, well exercised and disciplined, although badly clothed, were easily recognised by their red and black plumes, and had an excellent and a very pleasing appearance. But, except the few things which M. de Lafayette himself supplied, none of the things France had promised to send arrived: the money she lent proved, however, of essential service to the army.

During that year, a conference took place at Hartford, in Connecticut, between the French generals and General Washington, accompanied by General Lafayette and General Knox; they resolved to send the American Colonel Laurens, charged to solicit new succours, and above all, a superiority of force in the navy. On their return from this conference, the conspiracy of Arnold was discovered. General Washington would still have found that general in his quarters, if chance, or rather the desire of showing Lafayette the fort of West Point, constructed during his absence, had not induced him to repair thither before proceeding to Robinson's house, in which General Arnold then resided.*

* West Point, a fort on a tongue of land which advances upon the Hudson, and governs its whole navigation, is such an important position that it is called by an historian the Gibraltar of America. Arnold had been entrusted with its command, and his treachery, if it had proved successful, and been even attended with no other result but that of yielding up this fort to the enemy, would have inflicted a deadly wound upon the cause of the United States. He had entered, during eighteen months, into a secret relation with Sir Henry Clinton, who confided the whole charge of that affair to an aide-de-camp, Major André. Arnold failed at an appointment for the first interview with André the 11th September, at Dobb's Ferry. A second one was proposed on board the sloop of war the *Vulture*, which Clinton sent for that purpose, on the 16th, to Teller's Point, about fifteen or twenty miles below West Point. General Washington, who was repairing, with M. de Lafayette, to the Hartford conference,

Historians have rendered a detailed account of the treachery of Arnold. When, at his own request, the command of West Point was confided to him, he urged General Washington to inform him what means of information he possessed at new York. He made the same request to Lafayette, who accidentally had several upon his own account, and to the other officers who commanded near the enemy's lines. All these generals fortunately considered themselves bound by the promise of secrecy they had made, especially as several of the correspondents acted from a feeling of patriotism only. If Arnold had succeeded in discovering them, those unfortunate persons would have been ruined, and all means of communication cut off.

Arnold was very near receiving the letter of Lieutenant-Colonel Jameson in the presence of the commander-in-chief: he had turned aside, with Lafayette and Knox, to look at a redoubt; Hamilton

crossed the Hudson the 18th, and saw Arnold, who shewed him a letter from Colonel Robinson, on board the *Vulture*, which stated that that officer requested a rendezvous with him to converse upon some private affairs. Washington told him to refuse the rendezvous. Arnold then made arrangements for a private interview. Major André quitted New York, came on board the sloop, and from thence proceeded, with a false passport, to Long Clove, where he saw Arnold, the night of the 21st. They separated the next morning. André, on his return to New York, was taken at Tarry Town, by three of the militia, and conducted to the post of North Castle, commanded by Lieutenant-Colonel Jameson, who gave notice of this event, on the 23d, to his superior officer, General Arnold. The latter received the letter on the 25th, the same day on which he expected General Washington on his return from Hartford. He fled immediately; a few minutes after the general-in-chief arrived, and he received, only four hours later, the despatches which apprised him of the plot.—(Washington's Writings, vol. vii. Appendix No. 7.)

and Mac-Henry, lieutenant-colonels, the one aid-de-camp to Washington, the other to Lafayette, had gone on before to request Mrs. Arnold not to wait breakfast for them. They were still there, and Arnold with them, when he received the note: he turned pale, retired to his own room, and sent for his wife, who fainted. In that state he left her, without any one perceiving it: he did not return into the drawing room, but got upon his aide-de-camp's horse, which was ready saddled at the door, and desiring him to inform the general that he would wait for him at West Point, hurried to the bank of the river, got into his canoe, and was rowed to the *Vulture*. The general, when he learnt on his arrival that Arnold was at West Point, fancied that he had gone to prepare for his reception there, and without entering into the house, stepped into a boat with the two generals who accompanied him. When they arrived at the opposite shore, they were astonished at finding they were not expected: the mystery was only explained on their return, because the despatches of Lieutenant-Colonel Jameson had arrived in the interim.

An historian has spoken of the generosity with which Mrs. Arnold was treated. It is, in truth, highly honourable to the American character that, during the first effervescence of indignation against her husband, she was able to go to Philadelphia, take her effects, and proceed with a flag of truce to New York, without meeting with the slightest insult. The same historian (Mr. Marshall) might have added that, the very evening of Arnold's evasion, the general, having received from him a very insolent letter, dated on board the *Vulture*, ordered one of his aides-de-camp to tell Mrs. Arnold, who was in an agony of terror, that he had done everything he could to seize her husband, but that, not having been able to do so, he felt pleasure in informing her that her husband was safe.*

It is impossible to express too much respect or too deep regret for Major André. The fourteen general officers who had the painful task of pronouncing his sentence, the commander-in-chief, and the whole American army, were filled with sentiments of admiration and compassion for him. The conduct of the English in a preceding circumstance had been far from being similar. Captain Hale, of Connecticut, a distinguished young man, beloved by his family and friends, had been taken on Long Island, under circumstances of the same kind as those that occcasioned the death of Major André; but, instead of being treated with the like respect, to which Major André himself bore testimony, Captain Hale was insulted to the last moment of his life. "This is a fine death for a soldier!" said one of the English officers who were surrounding the cart of execution. "Sir," replied Hale, lifting up his cap, "there is no death which would not be rendered noble in such a

* General Arnold is the only American officer who ever thought of making use of his command to increase his fortune. The disinterestedness of those soldiers, during a period of revolution, which facilitates abuses, forms a singular contrast with the reproach of avidity that other governments, who have not shown the same moderation themselves, have thought proper to make against the citizens of the United States. The generals and American officers have almost all of them fought at their own expense; the affairs of many of them have been ruined by their absence. Those who had professions lost the power of exercising them. It has been proved, by accounts exacted in France during times of terror and proscription, that Lafayette had spent in the service of the American revolution, independent of his income, more than seven hundred thousand francs of his capital. The conduct of Washington was even more simple, and, according to our opinion, more praiseworthy: he would neither accept

glorious cause." He calmly replaced his cap, and the fatal cart moving on, he died with the most perfect composure.

During the winter, there was a revolt in the Pennsylvanian line. Lafayette was at Philadelphia; the congress, and the executive power of the state, knowing his influence over the troops, induced him to proceed thither with General Saint Clair. They were received by the troops with marked respect, and they listened to their complaints, which were but too well grounded. General Wayne was in the midst of them, and had undertaken a negotiation in concert with the state of Pennsylvania. Lafayette had only, therefore, to repair to head quarters. The discontent of the Pennsylvanians was appeased by the measures of conciliation which had been already begun; but the same kind of revolt in a Jersey brigade was suppressed with more vigour by the general-in-chief, who, setting out with some battalions of Lafayette's light infantry, brought the mutineers to reason, and the generals, no longer restrained by the interference of the civil authority,

the profit of emolument, nor the pride of sacrifice; he was paid for all necessary expenses, and, without increasing his fortune, only lessened it, from the injury it unavoidably received from his absence. Whilst all the American officers conducted themselves with the most patriotic disinterestedness, and all the pretensions of the army were satisfied with the compensation of seven years pay, we can only quote the single example of the traitor Arnold, who endeavoured, from circumstances the slightest, to draw pecuniary advantage. Some grants of lands have been made by the southern states to Generals Greene and Wayne, and Colonel Washington, but only since the revolution. The shares of the Potomac, given also since the revolution to General Washington, were left by him in his will for the foundation of a college: in a word, we may affirm, that delicacy and disinterestedness have been universal in the American army. (Note of M. de Lafayette.)

re-established immediately that military discipline which was on the point of being lost.*

(1781.) General Arnold was at Portsmouth, in Virginia; Washington formed the project of combining with the French to attack him, and take the garrison. Lafayette set out from the head quarters with twelve hundred of the light infantry; he pretended to make an attack on Staten Island, and marching rapidly by Philadelphia to Head-of-Elk, he embarked with his men in some small boats, and arrived safely at Annapolis. He set out from thence in a canoe, with some officers, and, in spite of the English frigates that were stationed in the bay, he repaired to Williamsburg, to assemble the militia, whilst his detachment was still waiting for the escort which the French were to send him. Lafayette had already blockaded Portsmouth, and driven back the enemy's picquets, when the issue of the combat between Admiral Arbuthnot and M.

* The writings of that period give an account of the revolt of the soldiers of Pennsylvania; the complaints of most of them were well founded. When General Saint Clair, Lafayette, and Laurens, repairing from Philadelphia to head quarters, stopped at Princetown, as they had been desired to do by the council of state of Pennsylvania, they found a negotiation begun by General Wayne, and Colonels Stewart and Butler, who were all three much beloved by the Pennsylvanian soldiers; committees arrived from the congress and state, to arrange the affair, not in a military, but in a civil manner: they remained but a few hours at Princetown, and the business was soon settled in the same manner in which it was commenced. But when the soldiers of the Jersey line wished to imitate the revolt of the Pennsylvanians, General Washington stifled it in its birth by vigorous measures. But it should be added that the sufferings and disappointments of that brave and virtuous army were sufficient to weary the patience of any human being: the conduct of the continental troops, during the revolution, has been, in truth, most admirable.

Destouches, the commander of the French squadron, left the English complete masters of the Chesapeake. Lafayette could only then return to Annapolis, to re-conduct his detachment to the camp. He found himself blockaded by small English frigates, which were much too considerable in point of force for his boats; but having placed cannon on some merchant ships, and embarked troops in them, he, by that manœuvre, made the English frigates retreat, and taking advantage of a favourable wind, he reached with his men the Head-of-Elk, where he received some very important despatches from General Washington. The enemy's plan of campaign was just at that time become known: Virginia was to be its object. General Phillips had left New York with a corps of troops to reinforce Arnold. The general wrote to Lafayette to go to the succour of Virginia. The task was not an easy one; the men whom he commanded had engaged themselves for a short expedition: they belonged to the northern states, which still retained strong prejudices as to the unhealthiness of the southern states; they had neither shirts nor shoes. Some Baltimore merchants lent Lafayette, on his bill, two thousand guineas, which sufficed to buy some linen. The ladies of Baltimore, whom he met with at a ball given in his honour when he passed through the town, undertook to make the shirts themselves. The young men of the same city formed themselves into a company of volunteer dragoons. His corps were beginning to desert. Lafayette issued an order, declaring that he was setting out for a difficult and dangerous expedition; that he hoped that the soldiers would not abandon him, but that whoever wished to go away might do so instantly; and he sent away two soldiers who had just been punished for some serious offences. From that hour all desertions ceased, and not one man would leave him: this feeling was so strong, that an under officer, who was prevented by a diseased leg from following the detachment, hired, at his own expense, a cart, rather than separate from it. This anecdote is honourable to the American troops, and deserves to become publicly known.

Lafayette had conceived that the capital of Virginia would be the principal object of the enemy's attack. Richmond was filled with magazines; its pillage would have proved fatal to the cause. Lafayette marched thither with such rapidity, that when General Phillips, arriving before Richmond, learnt that Lafayette had arrived there the night before, he would not believe it. Having ascertained, however, the truth of the report, he dared not attack the heights of Richmond. Lafayette had a convoy to send to the southern states; he reconnoitred Petersburg carefully. This threatened attack assembled the English, and whilst the removing of cannon, and other preparations for an assault, amused them, the convoy was sent off rapidly with the munition and clothes which General Greene required. After the death of General Phillips, who died that same day, Arnold wrote, by a flag of truce, to Lafayette, who refused to receive his letter. He sent for the English officer, and, with many expressions of respect for the British army, told him that he could not consent to hold any correspondence with its present general. This refusal gave great pleasure to General Washington and the public, and placed Arnold in an awkward situation with his own army.

Lord Cornwallis, on entering Virginia by Carolina, got rid of all his equipage, and did the same also respecting the heavy baggage of the army under his orders. Lafayette placed himself under the same regimen, and, during the whole of that campaign, the two armies slept without any shelter, and only carried absolute necessaries with them. Upon that active and decisive conflict the issue of the war was to depend; for if the English, who bore all the force of the campaign on that point, became masters of Virginia, not only the army of Lafayette, but also that of Greene, who drew from thence all his resources,—and not only Virginia, but all the states south of the Chesapeake, would inevitably be lost. Thus the letters of the commander-in-chief, whilst telling Lafayette that he did not deceive himself as to the difficulties of the undertaking, merely requested him to prolong as much as possible the defence of the state. The result was far more successful than any person had dared to hope, at a period when all eyes and all thoughts were directed towards that one decisive point.

The military scene in Virginia was soon to become more interesting. General Greene had marched to the right, to attack the posts of South Carolina, whilst Lord Cornwallis was in North Carolina. Cornwallis allowed him to depart, and, marching also to the right, burnt his own equipage and tents, to be enabled to remove more easily; he then advanced rapidly towards Petersburg, and made Virginia the principal seat of war. General Washington wrote to Lafayette that he could send him no other reinforcement than eight hundred of the mutinous Pennsylvanians, who had been formed again into a corps on the side of Lancaster. Lord Cornwallis had obtained, and generally by the aid of negroes, the best horses in Virginia. His Tarleton front guard, mounted on race horses, stopped, like birds of prey, all they met with. The active corps of Cornwallis was composed of more than four thousand men, of which eight hundred were supplied with horses. The command was divided in the following manner: General Rochambeau remained at Rhode Island with his French corps; Washington commanded in person the American troops before New York; he summoned, some time after, the corps of Rochambeau to join him. That French lieutenant-general was under his orders the same as the American major-generals, for when Lafayette asked for the succour of troops, he took care to stipulate, in the most positive manner, that it was to be placed entirely under Washington's orders. The Americans were to have the right side; the American officer, when rank and age were equal, was to command the French officer. Lafayette had wished to give the rising republic all the advantages and all the consequence of the greatest and longest established powers. Washington had sent, the preceding year, General Greene to command in the southern states; Virginia was nominally comprised in that command, and had not yet become the theatre of war, but the distance between the operations of Carolina and those of Virginia was so great, and the communications were so difficult, that it was impossible for Greene to direct what was passing in Virginia. Lafayette took, therefore, the chief command, corresponding in a direct manner with General Washington, and occasionally with the congress. But he wished that Greene should retain his title of supremacy, and he only sent to the head quarters copies of General Greene's letters, who was his intimate friend, in the same way that both he and Greene had always been on the most intimate footing with General Washington. During the whole of this campaign the most perfect harmony always subsisted between the generals, and contributed much to the success of the enterprise.

Lafayette, after having saved the magazines of Richmond, hastened to have them evacuated; he had taken his station at Osborn, and wrote to General Washington that he would remain there, as long as his weakest point, which was the left, should not be threatened with an attack. Lord Cornwallis did not fail soon to perceive the weakness of that point, and Lafayette retreated with his little corps, who, including recruits and the militia, did not exceed two thousand five hundred men. The richest young men of Virginia and Maryland had come to join him as volunteer dragoons, and from their intelligence, as well as from the superiority of their horses, they had been of essential service to him. The Americans retreated in such a manner that the front guard of the enemy arrived on the spot just as they had quitted it, and, without running any risk themselves, they retarded as much as possible its progress. Wayne was advancing with the reinforcement of Pennsylvanians. Lafayette made all his calculations so as to be able to effect a junction with that corps, without being prevented from covering the military magazines of the southern states, which were at the foot of the mountains on the height of Fluvana. But the Pennsylvanians had delayed their movements, and Lafayette was thus obliged to make a choice. He went to rejoin his reinforcement at Raccoon-Ford, and hastened, by forced marches, to come into contact with Lord Cornwallis, who had had time to make one detachment at Charlottesville, and another at the James River Fork. The first had dispersed the Virginian assembly; the second had done no material injury; but the principal blow was to be struck: Lord Cornwallis was established in a good position, within one march of the magazines, when Lafayette arrived close to him on a road leading towards those magazines. It was necessary for him to pass before the English army, presenting them his flank, and exposing himself to a certain defeat: he fortunately found out a shorter road which had remained for a long time undiscovered, which he repaired during the night; and the next day, to the great surprise of the English general, he was established in an impregnable station, between the English and the magazines, whose loss must have occasioned that of the whole southern army, of whom they were the sole resource; for there was a road behind the mountains that the English never intercepted, and by which the wants of General Greene's army were supplied. Lord Cornwallis, when he commenced the pursuit of Lafayette, had written a letter, which was intercepted, in which he made use of this expression: *The boy cannot escape me.* He flattered himself with terminating, by that one blow, the war in the whole southern part of the United States, for it would have been easy for him afterwards to take possession of Baltimore, and march towards Philadelphia. He beheld in this manner the failure of the principal part of his plan, and retreated towards Richmond, whilst Lafayette, who had been joined in his new station by a corps of riflemen, as well as by some militia, received notice beforehand to proceed forward on a certain day, and followed, step by step, the English general, without, however, risking an engagement with a force so superior to his own. His corps gradually increased. Lord Cornwallis thought proper to evacuate Richmond; Lafayette followed him, and ordered Colonel Butler to attack his rear guard near Williamsburg. Some manœuvre took place on that side, of which the principal object on Lafayette's part was, to convince Lord Cornwallis that his force was more considerable than it was in reality. The English evacuated Williamsburg, and passed over James River to James Island. A warm action took place between the English army and the advance guard, whom Lafayette had ordered to the attack whilst they were crossing the river. Lord Cornwallis had stationed the first troops on the other side, to give the appearance as if the greatest number of the troops had already passed over the river. Although every person was unanimous in asserting that this was the case, Lafayette himself suspected the deception, and quitted his detachment to make observations upon a tongue of land, from whence he could more easily view the passage of the enemy. During that time, a piece of cannon, exposed, doubtless, intentionally, tempted General Wayne, a brave and very enterprising officer.

Lafayette found, on his return, the advance guard engaged in action with a very superior force; he withdrew it, however (after a short but extremely warm conflict), in good order, and without receiving a check. The report was spread that he had had a horse killed under him, but it was merely the one that was led by his side.* The English army pur-

* Mr. Marshall relates the affair of Jamestown. There were no militia present, except the riflemen, who were placed in advance in the wood. They threw down successively three commandants of the advance post, placed there by Cornwallis, that what was passing behind might not be seen. This obstinacy in covering the position excited the suspicion of Lafayette, in spite of the unanimous opinion that a rear guard was alone remaining there. As soon as he saw, from the projecting tongue of land, that those who had crossed over were placed in

sued its route to Portsmouth; it then returned by water to take its station at Yorktown and Gloucester, upon the York River. A garrison still remained at Portsmouth. Lafayette made some demonstrations of attack, and that garrison united itself to the body of the army at Yorktown.

Lafayette was extremely desirous that the English army should unite at that very spot. Such had been the aim of all his movements, ever since a slight increase of force had permitted him to think of any other thing than of retiring without being destroyed and of saving the magazines. He knew that a French fleet was to arrive from the islands upon the American coast. His principal object had been to force Lord Cornwallis to withdraw towards the sea-shore, and then entangle him in such a manner in the rivers, that there should remain no possibility of a retreat. The English, on the contrary, fancied themselves in a very good position, as they were possessors of a sea-port by which they could receive succours from New York, and communicate with the different parts of the coast. An accidental, but a very fortunate circumstance, increased their security. Whilst Lafayette, full of hope, was writing to General Washington that he foresaw he could push Lord Cornwallis into a situation in which it

such a manner as to appear numerous, he returned with all possible haste; but General Wayne had yielded to the temptation. He fortunately perceived his error, and being a good and brave officer, came forward with much gallantry; fortunately, also, Lafayette had only placed the Pennsylvanians in advance, and had left the light infantry in a situation to offer them some assistance. The first half of his continental troops retired upon the other half, and the whole were placed in such a manner that Lord Cornwallis feared an ambuscade, and the more so, observes Mr. Marshall, as he had always been deceived as to the real force of Lafayette's army.—(Manuscript, No. 2.)

would be easy for him, with some assistance from the navy, to cut off his retreat, the general, who had always thought that Lafayette would be very fortunate if he could save Virginia without being cut up himself, spoke to him of his project of attack against New York, granting him permission to come and take part in it, if he wished it, but representing how useful it was to the Virginian army that he should remain at its head. The two letters passed each other; the one written by Lafayette arrived safely, and Washington prepared beforehand to take advantage of the situation of Lord Cornwallis. Gen. Washington's letter was intercepted, and the English, upon seeing that confidential communication, never doubted for a moment but the real intention of the Americans was to attack New York: their own security at Yorktown was therefore complete.*

The Count de Grasse, however, arrived with a naval force, and three thousand troops † for the

* James Moody rendered an ill service to those who employed him, by seizing the letter-bag in the Jerseys. Among the letters, those in which General Washington informed Lafayette of the project respecting New York, contained friendly and confidential communications, written in the General's own hand, which could not leave the slightest doubt in any person's mind: they may be found in the publications of the Generals Clinton and Cornwallis, which contain also Lafayette's intercepted letters. But the enemy did not take those in which General Lafayette gave an account to General Washington of his manœuvres, of his hopes, and of all that determined the commander-in-chief to adopt the project on Virginia, nor Washington's answers to that effect; so that when the combined troops made their first march towards the south, General Clinton still remained deceived, owing to the singular chance of the capture of the letter-bag by Moody.—(Manuscript, No. 2.)

† The entreaties of Count de Rochambeau contributed much towards persuading the Count de Grasse to bring his whole fleet, to land there the three thousand two hundred men, who joined, on

land service. He was met at the landing place of Cape Henry by Colonel Gimat, a Frenchman by birth, commander of the American battalion, who was charged with despatches from Lafayette; which explained fully to the admiral his own military position, and that of the enemy, and conjured him to sail immediately into the Chesapeake; to drive the frigates into the James River, that the passage might be kept clear; to blockade the York River; to send two vessels above the position of Lord Cornwallis, before the batteries on the water-side, at Yorktown and Gloucester could be put in a proper state. The Count de Grasse adhered to these proposals, with the exception of not forcing the batteries with two vessels, which manœuvre would have made the blockade of Cornwallis by the land troops still more easy of achievement. The Marquis de St. Simon landed with three thousand men at James Island. Lafayette assembled a small corps in the county of Gloucester, led, himself, the American forces on Williamsburg, where he was met by the corps of the Marquis de St. Simon, who came to range themselves under his orders, so that Lord Cornwallis found himself suddenly, as if by enchantment, blockaded both by sea and land. The combined army, under the orders of Lafayette, was placed in an excellent situation at Williamsburg. It was impossible to arrive there except by two dif-

their arrival, the army of Lafayette, and to repair immediately to Cape Henry, in Virginia. This is one more obligation which the common cause of the allies owes to General Rochambeau, who, from his talents, experience, moderation, and his subordination to the general-in-chief, respect for the civil power, and maintenance of discipline, proved that the King of France had made an excellent choice for the command of the auxiliary corps sent to the United States. (Note of M. de Lafayette.)

ficult and well-defended passages. Lord Cornwallis presented himself before them in the hope of escaping, by making a forcible attack; but having ascertained the impossibility of forcing them, he only occupied himself with finishing speedily the fortifications of Yorktown; his hopes, however, declined, when the Count de Grasse, having only left the ships necessary for the blockade, and having gone out of the harbour to attack Admiral Graves, forced the English to retire; and returned to his former station in the bay. The French admiral was, however, impatient to return to the islands; he wished that Yorktown should be taken by force of arms. The Marquis de St. Simon was of the same opinion: they both represented strongly to Lafayette that it was just, after such a long, fatiguing, and fortunate campaign, that the glory of making Cornwallis lay down his arms should belong to him who had reduced him to that situation. The admiral offered to send to the attack not only the garrisons from the ships, but all the sailors he should ask for. Lafayette was deaf to this proposal, and answered, that General Washington and the corps of General Rochambeau would soon arrive, and that it was far better to hasten their movements than act without them; and, by making a murderous attack, shed a great deal of blood from a feeling of vanity and a selfish love of glory; that they were certain, after the arrival of the succours, of taking the hostile army by a regular attack, and thus spare the lives of the soldiers; which a good general ought always to respect as much as possible, especially in a country where it was so difficult to obtain others to replace those who fell. General Washington and Count Rochambeau were the first to arrive: they were soon followed by their troops; but, at the same moment, the Admiral de Grasse wrote word that he was obliged to return to the islands. The whole expedition seemed on the point of failing, and General Washington begged Lafayette to go on board the admiral's ship in the bay, and endeavour to persuade him to change his mind: he succeeded, and the siege of Yorktown was begun. The Count de Rochambeau commanded the French, including the corps of St Simon; the Americans were divided in two parts; one, under Major-general Lincoln, who had come from the north with some troops; the other, under General Lafayette, who had been joined by two more battalions of light infantry, under the orders of Colonel Hamilton. It became necessary to attack two redoubts. One of these attacks was confided to the Baron de Viomenil, the other to General Lafayette. The former had expressed, in a somewhat boasting manner, the idea he had of the superiority of the French in an attack of that kind: Lafayette, a little offended, answered, "We are but young soldiers, and we have but one sort of tactic on such occasions, which is, to discharge our muskets, and push on straight with our bayonets." He led on the American troops, of whom he gave the command to Colonel Hamilton, with the Colonels Laurens and Gimat under him. The American troops took the redoubt with the bayonet. As the firing was still continued on the French side, Lafayette sent an aide-de-camp to the Baron de Viomenil, to ask whether he did not require some succour from the Americans;* but the French were

* The French were much struck on this occasion by the extreme coolness of one of the officers whom Lafayette sent to the Baron de Viomenil, from a secret feeling of pleasure, perhaps, in marking how much the present comparison stood in

not long in taking possession also of the other redoubt, and that success decided soon after the capitulation of Lord Cornwallis, (19th October, 1781.) Nor must the mention of an action be omitted here which was honourable to the humanity of the Americans. The English had disgraced themselves several times, and again recently at New London, by the murder of some imprisoned garrisons. The detachment of Colonel Hamilton did not for an instant make an ill use of their victory; as soon as the enemy deposed their arms, they no longer received the slightest injury. Colonel Hamilton distinguished himself very much in that attack.*

favour of the American troops. However this might be, Major Barber received a contusion in his side, but would not allow his wound to be dressed until he had executed his commission. —(Manuscript, No. 2.)

* The humanity of the American soldiers in that assault has been attested by all historians. The following letter must be quoted :—

TO THE EDITOR OF THE EVENING POST.

New York, August 10, 1802.

Sir,—Finding that a story, long since propagated, under circumstances which it was expected would soon consign it to oblivion, (and by which I have been complimented at the expense of Generals Washington and Lafayette,) has of late been revived, and has acquired a degree of importance by being repeated in different publications, as well in Europe as America, it becomes a duty to counteract its currency and influence by an explicit disavowal.

The story imports, in substance, that General Lafayette, with the approbation or connivance of General Washington, ordered me, as the officer who was to command the attack on a British redoubt, in the course of the siege of Yorktown, to put to death all those of the enemy who should happen to be taken in the redoubt, and that, through motives of humanity, I forbore to execute the order.

Positively, and unequivocally, I declare, that no such or

Lord Cornwallis had demanded, in the capitulation, the permission of marching out with drums beating and colours flying; the Count de Rochambeau and the French officers were of opinion that this request ought to be granted; the American generals did not oppose this idea; Lafayette, recollecting that the same enemy had required General Lincoln, at the capitulation of Charlestown, to furl the American colours and not to play an English march, insisted strongly on using the same measures with them in retaliation, and obtained that these two precise conditions should be inserted in the capitulation. Lord Cornwallis did not himself file out with the detachment. The Generals, Washington, Rochambeau, and Lafayette, sent to present him their compliments by their aides-de-camp. He retained Lafayette's aide-de-camp, young George Washington,

similar order, was ever by me received, or understood to have been given, nor any intimation or hint resembling it.

It is needless to enter into an explanation of some occurrences on the occasion alluded to, which may be conjectured to have given rise to the calumny. It is enough to say, that they were entirely disconnected with any act of either of the generals who have been accused.

With esteem, I am, sir, your most obedient servant,

A. Hamilton.

The circumstance alluded to in this letter has been related in the Life of Hamilton, published by his son. A short time before the taking of Yorktown, a Colonel Scammell, surprised by the English whilst reconnoitring, had been taken prisoner and dangerously wounded. When the redoubt was taken, and Colonel Campbell, who commanded, advanced to give himself up, a captain, who had served under Scammell, seized a bayonet, and was on the point of striking him; Hamilton turned aside the blow, and Campbell exclaimed, "I place myself under your protection," and was made prisoner by Laurens. (The Life of A. Hamilton, vol. i., chap. 14.)

and told him that having made this long campaign against General Lafayette, he wished, from the value he annexed to that general's esteem, to give him a private account of the motives which had obliged him to surrender. He told him several things which have since been found in his discussion with General Clinton. Lafayette went the next day to see him. "I know," said Lord Cornwallis, "your humanity towards prisoners, and I recommend my poor army to you." This recommendation was made in a tone which implied that in Lafayette alone he felt real confidence, and placed but little in the Americans. Lafayette therefore replied, "You know, my lord, that the Americans have always been humane towards imprisoned armies;" in allusion to the taking of General Burgoyne at Saratoga.* The English army was in fact treated with every possible mark of attention.

Although the French troops held in every respect the place of auxiliary troops, yet the Americans always yielded them every preference in their power relating to food or any other comfort. It is a singular circumstance that when the troops of the

* Lord Cornwallis affected being indisposed, in order that he might not march out at the head of his troops: they passed between two rows of the American and French army, commanded by General O'Hara, and surrendered their arms at the order of General Lincoln. Each of the generals, Washington, Rochambeau, and Lafayette, sent an aide-de-camp to offer their compliments to Lord Cornwallis. He retained Lafayette's aide-de-camp, Major Washington, the nephew of General Washington, to tell him how anxious he was that the general against whom he had made this campaign should be convinced that he only surrendered from the impossibility of defending himself any longer. The American, French, and English generals visited each other, and everything passed with every possible mark of attention,

Marquis de St. Simon joined those of Lafayette, the young general, although a Frenchman, took upon himself to order that no flour should be delivered to the American troops until the French had received their full provision for three days. The Americans had therefore seldom any thing but the flour of Indian corn. He gave the horses of the gentlemen of that country to the French hussars, and the superior officers themselves were obliged to give up theirs: yet not one murmur escaped as to that preference, which the Americans felt ought to be shewn to foreigners who came from such a distance to fight in their cause.*

The news of the capture of Yorktown was carried to France by a French frigate, who made the voyage in eighteen days. The English were thrown into consternation at that news, which occasioned the downfall of the ministry of Lord North. It was felt in London, as in the rest of all Europe, that the decisive check the English had received, had completely settled the final issue of the conflict, and from that period nothing was thought of but to acknowledge the independence of the United States on favourable terms for Great Britain.

especially towards Lord Cornwallis, one of the most estimable men of England, who was considered their best general. O'Hara having said one day, at table, to the French generals, affecting not to wish to be overheard by Lafayette, that he considered it as fortunate not to have been taken by the Americans alone, "General O'Hara, probably," replied Lafayette, "does not like repetitions." He had, in fact, been taken with Burgoyne, and has since been taken for the third time at Toulon.—(Manuscript, No. 2.)

* See at the end of the volume a precise account of this whole campaign in Virginia, edited by M. de Lafayette.—(Part, No. 1.)

Generals Washington and Lafayette wished to take advantage of the superiority of the Count de Grasse in order to attack Charlestown, and the English who remained in the southern states. Lafayette was to take his light infantry, as well as the corps of St. Simon, and land on the Charlestown side, to co-operate with General Greene, who still commanded in Carolina. It is evident that this project would have been successful. It has since become known that Lord Cornwallis, when he saw Lafayette enter into a canoe to go on board the fleet of the Count de Grasse, said to some English officers, "He is going to decide the loss of Charlestown." But the admiral refused obstinately to make any operation upon the coast of North America.*

General Lafayette afterwards repaired to congress. To him, who was then but four-and-twenty, the happy issue of that campaign was as flattering a

* General Lafayette was to have taken two thousand Americans and St. Simon's corps, who, landing near Charlestown, on the sea side, and co-operating with the troops of General Greene, would have secured the capture of the capital of Carolina, and of all the English who were remaining south of New York. Lowering their demands, they then requested that Lafayette should take the five thousand men who were at Wilmington, and who were so much struck by the dangers they had encountered, that they did not retain that post. At length, they contented themselves with asking the admiral to conduct General Wayne and his detachment, which were sent to reinforce Greene's army. He would not do so. It has also since become known, that when Lafayette, returning from his last visit to the admiral, landed at Yorktown, Lord Cornwallis, who was still there, said to his officers, "I lay a bet that he has been making arrangements for our ruin at Charlestown." The English acknowledged that the expedition could not fail; but the Count de Grasse did not think he ought to lose more time upon the North American coast, before returning to the defence of the West Indies.—(Manuscript, No. 2.)

success as it had been decisive to the American cause. He received the instructions of congress, in relation to the affairs of the United States in Europe; and embarked at Boston in the frigate *the Alliance.* He reached France in twenty-three days. The reception he met with, and the credit he enjoyed both at court and in society were constantly and usefully employed in the service of the cause he had embraced.

CORRESPONDENCE.

1779—1781.

TO COUNT DE VERGENNES.*

Paris, 24th February, 1779.

Sir,—A desire to render an exact obedience to the orders of the king, impels me to take the liberty of importuning you to let me know what is my duty. The prohibition which the Marshal de Noailles has put upon me, makes no exception as to one, whom I do not think, nevertheless, I should be forbidden to visit. Dr. Franklin was to have met me at Versailles this morning, if I had been there, to communicate to me some affairs of importance, as he said. I have informed him of the cause that detained me at Paris; but I did not think I ought to refuse an interview, which might not be wholly useless to the king's interests. He is coming to-morrow morning, and I trust you will add to your kindnesses that of directing me how to conduct myself in this matter.

Suffer me, sir, to inform you that I have heard

* During this period of three years, we do not find, as in the preceding years, a great number of family letters and those of friendship. We have inserted all those we have been able to discover. In amends, more than two hundred political, diplomatic, or military letters, are in our hands. We do not publish a third of them, although there are few that would not be interesting to the historian of the American revolution. We again repeat, that all the letters to Americans, or from Americans, were written originally in English.

many persons speak of an expedition, somewhat resembling the one proposed by congress. I flatter myself I am too well known by you to have it suspected of me, that any tie of kindred or friendship could make me forget the profound secrecy which is due to affairs of state. I have added to nature some acquired skill in this particular. My sole reason for mentioning the subject, therefore, is to add, that the indiscretion of some of the members of congress, and the number of officers returning from America, will always spread rumours, which it will be impossible to suppress. Truth cannot remain hidden but by being buried in a mass of false reports. Hence, caution is necessary in order to preserve our secrets from all the inconveniences to which they are subject in America, both from the form of the government and from the character of some of those at the head of affairs. I have the honour to be, with profound respect, &c.

FROM GENERAL WASHINGTON TO THE MARQUIS DE LAFAYETTE.*

(ORIGINAL.)

Camp, at Middlebrook, 8th March, 1779.

My Dear Marquis,—I am mortified exceedingly, that my letter from Philadelphia, with the several enclosures, did not reach Boston before your departure from that port. It was written as soon as congress had come to a decision upon the several matters, which became the subject of the president's letter to you, and was committed for conveyance to

* We believe this letter never reached M. de Lafayette.

the messenger, who was charged with his despatches to that place.

Monsieur la Colombe did me the honour of delivering to me your favours, and will probably be the bearer of my thanks for the affectionate manner in which you have expressed your sentiments in your last adieu, than which nothing can be more flattering and pleasing; nor is there anything more wished for by me, than opportunities of giving substantial proofs of the sincerity of my attachment and affection.

Nothing of importance has happened since you left us, except the enemy's invasion at Georgia, and possession of its capital; which, though it may add something to their supplies, on the score of provisions, will contribute very little to the brilliancy of their arms, for, like the defenceless island of St. Lucia, it only required the appearance of force to effect the conquest of it, as the whole militia of the state did not exceed twelve hundred men, and many of them disaffected. General Lincoln is assembling a force to dispossess them, and my only fear is, that he will precipitate the attempt before he is fully prepared for the execution. In New York and at Rhode Island, the enemy continued quiet till the 25th ultimo, when an attempt was made by them to surprise the post at Elizabethtown; but failing therein, and finding themselves closely pressed, and in danger from detachments advancing towards them from this army, they retreated precipitately through a marsh, waist-deep in mud, after abandoning all their plunder; but not before they had, according to their wonted custom, set fire to two or three houses. The regiment of Anspach, and some other troops, are brought from Rhode Island to New York.

We are happy in the repeated assurances and proofs of the friendship of our great and good ally, whom we hope and trust, ere this, may be congratulated on the birth of a prince, and on the joy which the nation must derive from an instance of royal felicity. We also flatter ourselves, that before this period the kings of Spain and the two Sicilies may be greeted as allies of the United States; and we are not a little pleased to find, from good authority, that the solicitations and offers of the Court of Great Britain to the Empress of Russia have been rejected; nor are we to be displeased, that overtures from the city of Amsterdam, for entering into a commercial connexion with us, have been made in such open and pointed terms. Such favourable sentiments, in so many powerful princes and states, cannot but be considered in a very honourable, interesting, and pleasing point of view, by all those who have struggled with difficulties and misfortunes to maintain the rights, and secure the liberties, of their country. But, notwithstanding these flattering appearances, the British king and his ministers continue to threaten us with war and desolation. A few months, however, must decide whether these or peace is to take place. For both we will prepare; and, should the former be continued, I shall not despair of sharing fresh toils and dangers with you in America; but if the latter succeeds, I can entertain little hopes, that the rural amusements of an infant world, or the contracted stage of an American theatre, can withdraw your attention and services from the gaieties of a court, and the active part you will more than probably be called upon to share in the administration of your government. The soldier will then be transformed into the statesman, and your employment in this new walk of life will afford you no time to revisit this continent, or think of friends who lament your absence.

The American troops are again in huts; but in a more agreeable and fertile country, than they were in last winter at Valley Forge; and they are better clad and more healthy, than they have ever been since the formation of the army. Mrs. Washington is now with me, and makes a cordial tender of her regards to you; and if those of strangers can be offered with propriety, and will be acceptable, we respectively wish to have them conveyed to your amiable lady. We hope and trust, that your passage has been short, agreeable, and safe, and that you are as happy as the smiles of a gracious Prince, beloved wife, warm friends, and high expectations, can make you. I have now complied with your request in writing you a long letter, and I shall only add, that, with the purest sentiments of attachment, and the warmest friendship and regard, I am, my dear Marquis, your most affectionate and obliged, &c.

P.S. Harrison and Meade are in Virginia. All the other officers of my staff unite most cordially in offering you their sincere compliments.

10th March, 1779.—I have this moment received the letters which were in the hands of Major Nevill, accompanying yours of the 7th and 11th of January. The Major himself has not yet arrived at head quarters, being, as I am told, very sick. I must again thank you, my dear friend, for the numerous sentiments of affection which breathe so conspicuously in your last farewell, and to assure you that I shall always retain a warm and grateful remembrance of it. Major Nevill shall have my consent to repair to France, if his health permits it, and if the sanction of congress can be obtained, to whom all applications of officers for leave to go out of the United States are referred.

TO M. DE VERGENNES.

Paris, April 1st, 1779.

Sir,—From what M. de Sartine said to me, I requested M. de Chaumont yesterday to send for Captain Jones, and although the place of his present residence be unknown, our messenger will do all that can be done to bring him immediately to us. I gave him an urgent letter for Jones, and as Dr. Franklin was not at home, I left one also for him, in which I expressed our desire to see the captain, rather as if to consult him, than as if we had formed any definite project. The time I passed with M. de Chaumont enabled me to discover what I shall now have the honour of relating to you.*

* In the previous recital a few words have been said relating to this armament. Two frigates, bearing the American colours, were to have been placed under the orders of Paul Jones, and M. de Lafayette was to command the small army intended to descend unexpectedly upon the western coast of England, and to ransack Bristol, Liverpool, and other commercial towns, for the advantage of the American finances. But this expedition was soon considered below the position in which M. de Lafayette was placed, and was abandoned for the plan of a descent on England, which was to be executed by the combined forces of France and Spain. The slowness of the latter power occasioned, at a later period, the failure of the project; and the only result it produced was Paul Jones's expedition, and the conflict between the *Bonhomme Richard* and *the Serapis*. See farther on the first letters to congress and to Washington. In a collection of Franklin's private letters, there is also found a letter relating to this affair, and the note written by M. de Lafayette to Paul Jones when the expedition was aban-

The armament of the *Bonhomme Richard* (the vessel of fifty guns) goes on as slowly as possible. The refusal to supply what is wanted, especially guns, from the king's magazines, will retard the expedition for a whole month, because it will be the same for all the other ships. The only way to obviate this delay, would be to charge one man with the whole armament, and to send him to the ports with orders to get all that was necessary.

I have discovered that Jones had a little plan for an enterprise formed under the direction of M. Garnier, and in which M. de Chaumont has taken part. The manner in which M. de Sartine brought him to us, was by making M. de Chaumont a half confidant, (the most dangerous of all things, because it gives information without binding to secrecy,) and I think it would be now better to communicate the secret of the armament without betraying that of the expedition, and desire him to employ all his activity in completing it. The other person need not, in that case, take any part in it, and according to the orders received from M. de Sartine, it appeared to me, from what M. de Chaumont said, that the *Bonhomme Richard*, and other vessels, if required, might be in readiness before the expiration of three weeks.

I intend to have the honour of paying my respects to you after dinner on Saturday. If you approve of my idea, M. de Chaumont, or any other person you may prefer, might be summoned at the same time; for by the ordinary method this business will never be achieved. I hope that, in consequence of my aversion to delays in military affairs, you will

doned. (*A Collection of the Familiar Letters and Miscellaneous Papers* of B. Franklin, Boston, 1833. Washington's writings, Vol. vi., Appendix viii.)

pardon the importunity which my confidence in you has inspired, in favour of a project of which you feel the importance.

I have the honour to be, with the most sincere respect and affection, &c.

Permit me to confide to you, also, under the same secrecy, my fears that orders have not yet been sent to all the ports.

TO M. DE VERGENNES.

Paris, April 26th, 1779.

Sir,—Allow me the honour of proposing to you a plan, the success of which, uncertain as it now is, will depend perhaps upon your approbation. As your means of attack or defence depend on our maritime force, would it not be doing a service to the common cause to increase for a time that of our allies? To purchase vessels would be too expensive for a nation so destitute of money; it would answer all purposes to hire them, and would enable us to make such diversions, or to undertake such operations, as might be deemed necessary.

Do you not think, sir, if the King of Sweden would lend to America four ships of the line, with the half of their crews, and the United States would engage to return them within a year upon certain conditions, that the step would be advantageous for us? The vessels might come to us under the Swedish flag. France need not be implicated at all. We could supply them in part, provide them with officers in blue, and send them out under the American flag. It would only be necessary to know, whether France would engage to be responsible for the sum requisite for the hire, and would help to complete the equipment. Even if the first part should meet with obstacles, the government might pledge itself only in case it should exceed my fortune.

I have not as yet spoken to Dr. Franklin about the scheme, but I have sounded the Swedish ambassador on the subject, much to my satisfaction; he asked me for a letter, directed to him, which might be sent to his king; and since I saw that this important project might result in something advantageous, I was constrained to confide it to you, and ask your opinion. The Swedish ambassador states that the vessels may be here in two months and a half; consequently, including the rest of the fleet, the whole might be at sea in the month of August, and arrive at Rhode Island, Bermuda, or somewhere else in America, in the month of October, which would be a good season.

It will be necessary for Dr. Franklin to send a trustworthy man, or, what would be better, for you to send one, upon whom he might depend. The proposed engagement requires some promise, and especially some hopes, of commerce, that would diminish the expense which must be incurred. Inform me, sir, I pray you, whether this little romantic scheme has any difficulties, and whether I am to prosecute or resign my proposition.

I am, &c.

If, whilst we are arranging the negotiation with Sweden, the contributions of England should yield us anything, I might then recal to your attention a favourite project of mine.

TO THE PRESIDENT OF CONGRESS.

(ORIGINAL.)

St. Jean d'Angely, near Rochfort, June 12, 1779.

SIR,—How happy I shall think myself whenever a safe opportunity of writing to congress is offered, I cannot in any way better express than in reminding them of that unbounded affection and gratitude which I shall ever feel for them. So deeply are those sentiments engraven on my heart, that I every day lament the distance which separates me from them, and that nothing was ever so warmly and passionately wished for, as to return again to that country of which I shall ever consider myself as a citizen; there is no pleasure to be enjoyed which could equal this, of finding myself among that free and liberal nation, by whose affection and confidence I am so highly honoured; to fight again with those brother soldiers of mine to whom I am so much indebted. But congress knows that former plans have been altered by themselves, that others have been thought impossible, as they were asked too late in the year.* I will therefore make use of the leave of absence they were pleased to grant me, and serve the common cause among my countrymen, their allies, until happy circumstances may conduct me to the American shores, in such a way as would make that return more useful to the United States. The affairs of America I shall ever look upon as my first business whilst I am in Europe. Any confidence from the king and ministers, any popularity I may have among my own

* This relates to the project of an expedition to Canada, and other plans of the same kind.

countrymen, any means in my power, shall be, to the best of my skill, and till the end of my life, exerted in behalf of an interest I have so much at heart. What I have hitherto done or said relating to America, I think needless to mention, as my ardent zeal for her is, I hope, well known to congress; but I wish to let them know that if, in my proposals, and in my repeated urgent representation for getting ships, money, and support of any kind, I have not always found the ministry so much in earnest as I was myself, they only opposed to me *natural fears* of inconveniences which might arise to both countries, or the conviction that such a thing was impossible for the present; but I never could question their good will towards America. If congress believe that my influence may serve them, in any way, I beg they will direct such orders to me, that I may the more certainly and properly employ the knowledge I have of this court and country for obtaining a success in which my heart is so much interested.

His excellency, Doctor Franklin, will, no doubt, inform you, sir, of the situation of Europe, and the respective state of our affairs. The Chevalier de la Luzerne will also add thereto the intelligence which will be intrusted to him at the time of his departure. By the doctor you will learn what has been said or thought on account of finances. Germany, Prussia, Turkey, and Russia, have made such a peace as the French have desired. All the northern kingdoms, the Dutch themselves, seem rather disgusted with English pride and vexations; they put themselves in a situation to protect their trade of every kind with France. Irish intelligence you will be fully and particularly acquainted of. What concerns Spain will also be laid before you; so that I have nothing to add but to tell you that our affairs seem going very fast towards a speedy and honourable end. England is now making her last effort, and I hope that a great stroke will, before long, abate their fantastic, swollen appearance, and shew the narrow bounds of their actual power.

Since we have taken Senegal I don't know of any military event which I can mention. There has been a privateering expedition against Jersey Island, which has been stopped by the difficulty of getting ashore. That little attempt, made by some few private volunteers, England honoured with the name of a public French expedition, and very unwisely employed there Admiral Arbuthnot, which will interpose a great delay to his reported departure. Congress will hear of an expedition against our friends of Liverpool and other parts of the English coast; to show there French troops under American colours, which on account of raising contributions, my concern for American finances had at length brought into my head. But the plan was afterwards reduced to so small a scale that they thought the command would not suit me, and the expedition itself has been delayed until more important operations take place. There I hope to be employed, and if anything important should be the matter, I shall, as a faithful American officer, give an accurate account thereof to congress and General Washington.

The so flattering affection which congress and the American nation are pleased to honour me with, makes me very desirous of letting them know, if I dare speak so friendly, how I enjoyed my private situation. Happy, in the sight of my friends and family, after I was, by your attentive goodness, safely brought again to my native shore, I met there with such an honourable reception, with such kind sentiments, as by far exceeded any wishes I durst have conceived ; I am indebted for that inexpressible satisfaction which the good will of my countrymen towards me affords to my heart, to their ardent love for America, to the cause of freedom and its defenders, their new allies, and to the idea they entertain that I have had the happiness to serve the United States. To these motives, sir, and to the letter congress was pleased to write on my account, I owe the many favours the king has conferred upon me ; there was no time lost in appointing me to the command of his own regiment of dragoons, and every thing he could have done, every thing I could have wished, I have received on account of your kind recommendations.

I have been some days in this small town, near Rochefort harbour, where I have joined the king's regiment, and where other troops are stationed which I for the moment command ; but I hope to leave this place before long, in order to play a more active part and come nearer the common enemy. Before my departure from Paris I sent to the minister of foreign affairs, (who, by the bye, is one of our best friends,) intelligence concerning a loan in Holland, which I want France to make or answer for in behalf of America ; but I have not yet heard any thing on that head. M. le Chevalier de la Luzerne will give you more explicit and fresher news, as he is particularly ordered to do so, and he sets out directly from Versailles. That new minister plenipotentiary I beg leave to recommend most earnestly to congress, not only as a public man, but also as a private gentleman. From the acquaintance I have made with him, I conceive he is a sensible, modest, well-meaning man ; a man truly worthy of enjoying the spectacle of American freedom. I hope that by his good qualities and his talents, he will obtain both public confidence and private friendship.

Wherever the interests of beloved friends are seriously concerned, candid and warm affection knows not how to calculate, and throws away all considerations. I will frankly tell you, sir, that nothing can more effectually hurt our interests, consequence, and reputation, in Europe, than to hear of disputes or divisions between the whigs. Nothing could urge my touching upon this delicate matter but the unhappy experience of every day on that head, since I can hear, myself, what is said on this side of the Atlantic, and the arguments I have to combat with.

Let me, sir, finish this long letter, by begging you will present once more to the congress of the United States, the tribute of an unbounded zeal and affection, of the highest respect and most sincere gratitude, with which I shall be animated, till the last moment of my life.

With the most, &c.

TO GENERAL WASHINGTON.

(ORIGINAL.)

St. Jean d'Angély, near Rochefort harbour, June 12, 1779.

My dear General,—Here is at length a safe opportunity of writing to you, and I may tell you what sincere concern I feel at our separation. There never was a friend, my dear general, so much, so tenderly beloved, as I love and respect you: happy in our union, in the pleasure of living near to you, in the pleasing satisfaction of partaking every sentiment of your heart, every event of your life, I have taken such a habit of being inseparable from you, that I cannot now accustom myself to your absence, and I am more and more afflicted at that enormous distance which keeps me so far from my dearest friend. I am the more concerned at this particular time, my dear general, as I think the campaign is opened, you are in the field, and I ardently wish I might be near you; and, if possible, contribute to your success and glory. Forgive me for what I am going to say, but I cannot help reminding you that a commander-in-chief should never expose himself too much; that in case General Washington was killed, nay, even seriously wounded, there is no officer in the army who could fill his place, every battle would most certainly be lost, and the American army, the American cause itself, would, perhaps, be entirely ruined.

Inclosed I send your excellency a copy of my letter to congress, in which you will find such intelligence as I was able to give them. The Chevalier de la Luzerne intends going to congress by passing through head quarters. I promised I would introduce him to your excellency, and I have requested him to let you know of any news he may have been entrusted with. Such a conversation will better acquaint you than the longest letter. The ministry told me they would let him know the true state of affairs before his departure. By what you will hear, my dear general, you will see that our affairs take a good turn, and I hope England will receive a good stroke before the end of the campaign. Besides the good dispositions of Spain, Ireland is a good deal tired of English tyranny. I, *in confidence*, tell you that the scheme of my heart would be to make her as free and independent as

America. I have formed some private relations there. God grant that we may succeed, and the era of freedom at length arrive for the happiness of mankind. I shall know more about Ireland in a few weeks, and then I will immediately communicate with your excellency. As to congress, my dear general, it is too numerous a body for one safely to unbosom oneself, as with one's best friend.

In referring you to M. le Chevalier de la Luzerne, for what concerns the public news of this time, the present situation of affairs, and the designs of our ministry, I will only speak to your excellency about that great article, money. It gave me much trouble, and I insisted upon it so much, that the director of finances looks upon me as a devil. France has met great expenses lately; those Spaniards will not give their dollars easily. However, Dr. Franklin has got some money to pay the bills of congress, and I hope I shall determine them to greater sacrifices. Serving America, my dear general, is to my heart an inexpressible happiness.

There is another point for which you should employ all your influence and popularity. For God's sake prevent their loudly disputing together. Nothing hurts so much the interest and reputation of America, as to hear of their intestine quarrels. On the other hand there are two parties in France: MM. Adams and Lee on one part, Doctor Franklin and his friends on the other. So great is the concern which these divisions give me, that I cannot wait on these gentlemen as much as I could wish, for fear of occasioning disputes and bringing them to a greater collision. That, my dear general, I intrust to your friendship, but I could not help touching upon that string in my letter to congress.

Since I left America, my dear General, not a single line has arrived from you ;* this I attribute to winds, accidents, and deficiency of opportunities; for I dare flatter myself General Washington would not lose that of making his friend happy. In the name of that very friendship, my dear general, never miss any opportunity of letting me know how you do. I cannot express to you how uneasy I feel on account of your health, and the dangers you are, perhaps at this moment, exposing yourself to. These you may possibly laugh at, and call womanlike considerations; but so, my dear friend, I feel, and I never could conceal the sentiments of my heart.

I don't know what has become of Colonel Nevill and the Chevalier de la Colombe. I beg you will make some inquiries respecting them, and do every thing in your power for their speedy exchange, in case they have been taken. Inclosed I send you a small note for Mr. Nevill. Give me leave to recommend to your excellency our new plenipotentiary minister, who seems to me extremely well calculated for deserving general esteem and affection.

I know, my dear general, you wish to hear something about my private affairs: these I give an account of to congress, and shall only add that I am here as happy as possible. My family, my friends, my countrymen, made me such a reception, and shewed me every day such an affection, as I should not have dared to hope. I have been for some days in this place,

* This conjecture was a just one: by the correspondence of General Washington, who kept copies of all his letters, we perceive that he often wrote to M. de Lafayette, whose letters, on the contrary, during this voyage, consist but of two, because we have been able to find only those that arrived in America.

where there is the king's own regiment of dragoons, which I command, and some regiments of infantry, which are, for the present, under my orders; but I hope soon to begin a more active life, and in consequence thereof my return to Paris is, I believe, very near at hand; from thence I shall get employed in whatever may be done against the common enemy. What I wish, my dear general, what would make me the happiest of men, is to join again American colours, or to put under your orders a division of four or five thousand countrymen of mine. In case any such co-operation or private expedition should be desired, I think (if peace is not settled this winter) that an *early* demand might be complied with for the next campaign.

Our ministry is rather slow in their operations, and have a great propensity for peace, provided it be an honourable one, so that I think America must shew herself in good earnest for war till such conditions are obtained. American independence is a certain, undoubted point, but I wish to see that independence acknowledged with advantageous conditions. This, my dear general, is between us; as for what concerns the good will of the king, of the ministers, of the public, towards America, I, an American citizen, am fully satisfied with it; and I am sure the alliance and friendship between both nations will be established in such a way as will last for ever.

Be so kind, my dear general, as to present my best respects to your lady, and tell her how happy I should feel to present them myself to her at her own house. I have a wife, my dear general, who is in love with you, and her affection for you seems to me to be so well justified that I cannot oppose myself to that sentiment of hers. She begs you will receive her compliments and make them acceptable to Mrs.

Washington. I hope, my dear general, you will come to see us in Europe, and most certainly I give you my word that if I am not happy enough to be sent to America before the peace, I shall by all means go there as soon as I can escape. I must not forget to tell you, my dear friend, that I have the hope of being soon once more a father.

All Europe wants to see you so much, my dear general, that you cannot refuse them that pleasure. I have boldly affirmed that you will pay me a visit after the peace is settled, so that if you deny me, you will hurt your friend's reputation throughout the world.

I beg you will present my best compliments to your family, and remind them of my tender affection for them all. Be so kind, also, to present my compliments to the general officers, to all the officers of the army, to every one, from the first major-general to the last soldier.

I most earnestly entreat you, my dear general, to let me hear from you. Write me how you do, how things are going on. The minutest detail will be infinitely interesting to me. Don't forget anything concerning yourself, and be certain that any little event or observation concerning you, however trifling it may appear, will have my warmest attention and interest. Adieu, my dear general, I cannot lay down the pen, and I enjoy the greatest pleasure in scribbling you this long letter. Don't forget me, my dear general; be ever as affectionate to me as you have been; these sentiments I deserve from the ardent ones which fill my heart. With the highest respect, with the most sincere and tender friendship that ever human heart has felt, I have the honour to be, &c.

For God's sake write me frequent and long letters, and speak chiefly about yourself and your private circumstances.

St. Jean, d'Angély, 13th June, 1779.

I HAVE just received, my dear general, an express from court, with orders to repair immediately to Versailles. There I am to meet M. le Comte de Vaux, Lieutenant-General, who is appointed to the command of the troops intended for an expedition. In that army I shall be employed in the capacity of aide-maréchal-général des logis, which is, in our service, a very important and agreeable place; so that I shall serve in the most pleasing manner, and shall be in a situation to know everything and to render services. The necessity of setting off immediately prevents my writing to General Greene, to the gentlemen of your family, and other friends of mine in the army, whom I beg to accept my excuses on account of this order, which I did not expect so soon. Everything that happens you shall most certainly be acquainted of by me, and I will for the moment finish my letter in assuring your excellency again of my profound respect and tenderest friendship. Farewell, my dear general, and let our mutual affection last for ever.

TO THE COUNT DE VERGENNES.

Havre, 30th July, 1779.

SIR,—I have received the letter which you have had the goodness to write to me, and in which you promise me another after having read to M. de

Maurepas the paper which I addressed to you.* It is shewing me a great favour to employ, in answering me, a part of your time, which is so precious; and I remain in eager expectation of your second letter. Being convinced that there is no time to lose in adopting the measures which I propose, my love for my country makes me feel an impatience, which I fear may pass for importunity; but you will excuse a fault arising from a feeling which is dear to every good citizen.

The Prince de Montbarrey will give you, with regard to Havre, all the information you may desire. You are certainly right in saying that my blood is in fermentation. We hear nothing of M. d'Orvilliers. Some say that he has gone to the Azores, to intercept the West Indian fleet, and to join M. d'Estaing, who was to return here, as I was informed by yourself and M. de Sartine; others affirm that he has gone to America.

The latter reasoning does not bring me to their opinion; and it is very probable that if our fleet had been sent, as they suppose, I should not now be in Normandy. Be that as it may, you know, I hope that any arrangement, and any station, will satisfy me, and that I do not claim promotion, or assistance, or any mark of favour whatsoever. If M. d'Orvilliers, or a detachment, is now in the independent states of America, and my presence there can be in any way more serviceable than here, I shall be very willing to go over in an American frigate, which I will take on my own authority; and with the very natural pretext of rejoining the army in which I served, I

* This letter, in the form of a memorial, and containing the plan of an expedition to America, has been placed at the end of the volume.—(See Appendix 2.)

will go and endeavour to use my influence for the advantage of my country. Several persons say, also, that Spanish dollars have been sent to the Americans; I earnestly hope it is so, as my last advices shew the necessity for them.

If the project, for want of sufficient means, should not be adopted this year, I deem it my duty to submit to you a proposition which would in a great measure accomplish the same object.

While waiting until next year to commence combined operations with a squadron, why might you not send to Boston three thousand, or even two thousand men, with three hundred dragoons, who should be joined in the spring by ships of war and a reinforcement of troops? This detachment could be sent by two fifty gun ships, using one of the India Company's ships for a transport, or Spanish vessels, if you prefer them. To avoid expense, let them sail in company with the ships destined for the West Indies, with the escort of the merchantmen, with the *Bonhomme Richard*, and all the frigates at Lorient. These troops will be left in America until the next campaign, and I will now mention what would be the result of such a measure; it being well understood that the convoy would proceed to the West Indies, or to any other destination, after having landed the detachment. First, we should raise by our presence the value of their paper money, an important point for French commerce; secondly, we should be at hand to obtain information, and might take such preliminary steps as would conduce, eventually, to our obtaining possession of Halifax; thirdly, such a detachment would inspire the American army with new vigour, would powerfully support an attack for retaking the forts on the north river, and would lead the

Americans to such undertakings as circumstances might render advisable.

You have told me to give you all my ideas. It is my duty to submit to you this last one, which, as it seems to me, is not liable to any objection. At first, I was afraid of expressing my opinion so strongly as I was inclined to do, lest I should be suspected of peculiar motives and predilections; but, now that people must know me better, and that you have my entire confidence, I speak more freely, and I solemnly affirm, upon my honour, that if half my fortune was spent in sending succours of troops to the Americans, I should believe that, in so doing, I rendered to my country a service more important than this sacrifice.

You will say, perhaps, that it will be difficult to find subsistence for the troops during the winter; but in paying in specie, we should obtain provisions very cheap, and the additional number of mouths would be very small in comparison to the population of the country.

Permit me, sir, to offer you the assurance of my attachment.

TO M. DE VERGENNES.

Paris, Monday morning, August, 1779.

It is not, sir, to the king's minister that I am now writing, but my confidence in your kindness makes me hope that I am addressing a man whom I may safely call my friend, to whom I am merely giving an account of all that is most interesting to me. You may confer a great obligation upon me, (and render one perhaps to the public,) by employing in a less useless manner the few talents a soldier may possess, who has been hitherto rather fortunate in war, and who supplies his want of knowledge by the purest ardour in the cause.

I have seen the Comte de Maurepas, and I told him what I have the honour of communicating to you; he would not agree to the projects in question, and was doubtless right, although my own opinion remains unchanged; but he thinks that I, who was one of the first to speak of the expedition with fifteen hundred or two thousand men, must now command six hundred hussars, and that this change would be injurious to me. He, perhaps, imagined, as some others have done, from kindness towards me, that such a command would be beneath me. I ought not, besides, he added, to exchange a certainty for an uncertainty.

To this I answer, in the first place, that from the extreme kindness of the public towards me, nothing (I mean in relation to what passes in my own heart) can ever be injurious to me; that my setting out with only six hundred men would have been attributed to its real motive, and therefore pardoned. In the second place, to suspect me of entering into a calculation with my country, and of despising any means whatever of serving her, would either prove a want of discernment or of memory; and to the last objection, I reply, that the expedition of which I spoke to you yesterday, is quite as certain as my own.

If the troops had remained in a state of inactivity, it would have been very natural if my ardour had induced me to adopt the trade of a corsair; nay, it would have been natural if I had set out in an armed boat; but when an opportunity offers for employing on a grander scale the talents of a man who has never exercised a soldier's trade but on a wide field, it would be unfortunate for him to lose the power of distinguishing himself, and rendering, perhaps, some important services to his own country; and it would be injudicious in the government not to put to the test that reputation which has been gained in foreign service.

May I, sir, speak to you with frankness? What is most proper for me, would be an advance guard of grenadiers and *chusseurs*, and a detachment of the king's dragoons, making in all, from fifteen hundred to two thousand men, to raise me above the line, and give me the power of action. There are not many lieutenants-general, still fewer field-marshals, and no brigadiers, who have had such important commands confided to them as chance has given me. I also know the English, and they know me—two important considerations during a war. The command I wished for has even been given to a colonel.

It is said that M. de Maillebois, M. de Voyer, and M. de Melfort, will be employed; I know the first and last of these gentlemen; M. de Melfort is a field-marshal, and although I have exercised that trade myself, I should be well pleased to be under his orders. I wish to be chosen in the report of the army, not of the court; I do not belong to the court, still less am I a courtier; and I beg the king's ministers to look upon me as having belonged to a corps of the guards.

The Count de Maurepas only replied to me, perhaps, to divert my attention from some projects which are known unto me; I shall see him again on Wednesday morning, and my fate will then be decided. You would give me, sir, a great proof of friendship, by paying him a visit either to-night or to-morrow morning, and communicating to him the same sentiments you expressed to me yesterday.

It is more important that you should see him at that time, because, if I hear from Lorient that the vessels are in readiness, I know not how to dissemble, and I must demand my farewell audience. The little expedition will then be given to some lieutenant-colonel, who may never have looked with the eye of a general, who may not possess great talents, but who, if he be brave and prudent, will lead the six hundred men as well as M. de Turenne could do if he were to return to life. The detachment of dragoons might then be kept back, the more so, as when reduced to fifty it would only become ridiculous; and the major, who takes charge of the detail, would likewise attend to the detail of my advance guard, in which I place great dependence.

I acknowledge to you, that I feel no dependence on M. de Montbarry, and I even wish, that my affairs could be arranged by you and M. de Maurepas. I know, sir, that I am asking for a proof of friendship which must give you some trouble, but I request it because I depend fully upon that friendship.

Pardon this scrawl, sir; pardon my importunity; and pardon the liberty I take in assuring you so simply of my attachment and respect.

DR. FRANKLIN TO THE MARQUIS DE LAFAYETTE.

(ORIGINAL.)

Passy, 24th August, 1779.

Sir,—The congress, sensible of your merit towards the United States, but unable adequately to reward it, determined to present you with a sword, as a small mark of their grateful acknowledgment: they directed it to be ornamented with suitable devices. Some of the principal actions of the war, in which you distinguished yourself by your bravery and conduct, are therefore represented upon it. These, with a few emblematic figures, all admirably well executed, make its principal value. By the help of the exquisite artists of France, I find it easy to express everything but the sense we have of your worth, and our obligations to you for this, figures, and even words, are found insufficient. I, therefore, only add that, with the most perfect esteem, I have the honour to be, B. Franklin.

P.S. My grandson goes to Havre with the sword, and will have the honour of presenting it to you.

TO DR. FRANKLIN.

(ORIGINAL.)

Havre, 29th August, 1779.

Sir,—Whatever expectations might have been raised from the sense of past favours, the goodness of the United States to me has ever been such, that on every occasion it far surpasses any idea I could have conceived. A new proof of that flattering truth I find in the noble present, which congress has been pleased to honour me with, and which is offered in such a manner by your excellency as will exceed everything, but the feelings of an unbounded gratitude.

In some of the devices I cannot help finding too honourable a reward for those slight services which, in concert with my fellow soldiers, and under the god-like American hero's orders, I had the good fortune to render. The sight of those actions, where I was a witness of American bravery and patriotic spirit, I shall ever enjoy with that pleasure which becomes a heart glowing with love for the nation, and the most ardent zeal for its glory and happiness. Assurances of gratitude, which I beg leave to present to your excellency, are much too inadequate to my feelings, and nothing but such sentiments can properly acknowledge your kindness towards me. The polite manner in which Mr. Franklin was pleased to deliver that inestimable sword, lays me under great obligations to him, and demands my particular thanks.

With the most perfect respect, I have the honour to be, &c.

FROM GENERAL WASHINGTON TO THE MARQUIS DE LAFAYETTE.

(ORIGINAL.)

West Point, 30th Sept., 1779.

MY DEAR MARQUIS,—A few days ago, I wrote a letter in much haste; since that, I have been honoured with the company of Chevalier de la Luzerne, and by him was favoured with your obliging letter of the 12th of June, which filled me with equal pleasure and surprise; the latter at hearing that you had not received one of the many letters I had written to you since you left the American shore. It gave me infinite pleasure to hear from your sovereign, and of the joy which your safe arrival in France had diffused among your friends. I had no doubt that this would be the case; to hear it from yourself adds pleasure to the account; and here, my dear friend, let me congratulate you on your new, honourable, and pleasing appointment in the army commanded by the Count de Vaux, which I shall accompany with an assurance that none can do it with more warmth of affection, or sincere joy, than myself. Your forward zeal in the cause of liberty; your singular attachment to this infant world; your ardent and persevering efforts, not only in America, but since your return to France, to serve the United States; your polite attention to Americans, and your strict and uniform friendship for me, have ripened the first impressions of esteem and attachment which I imbibed for you into such perfect love and gratitude, as neither time nor absence can impair. This will warrant my assuring you that, whether in the character of an officer at the head of a corps of gallant Frenchmen, if circumstances should require this; whether as a major-general, commanding a division of the American army; or whether, after our swords and spears have given place to the ploughshare and pruning-hook, I see you as a private gentleman, a friend and companion, I shall welcome you with all the warmth of friendship to Columbia's shores; and, in the latter case, to my rural cottage, where homely fare and a cordial reception shall be substituted for delicacies and costly living. This, from past experience, I know you can submit to; and if the lovely partner of your happiness will consent to participate with us in such rural entertainment and amusements, I can undertake, in behalf of Mrs. Washington, that she will do everything in her power to make Virginia agreeable to the Marchioness. My inclination and endeavours to do this cannot be doubted, when I assure you that I love everybody that is dear to you, and, consequently, participate in the pleasure you feel in the prospect of again becoming a parent; and do most sincerely congratulate you and your lady on this fresh pledge she is about to give you of her love.

I thank you for the trouble you have taken, and your polite attention, in favouring me with a copy of your letter to congress; and feel, as I am persuaded they must do, the force of such ardent zeal as you therein express for the interest of this country. The propriety of the hint you have given them must carry conviction, and, I trust, will have a salutary effect; though there is not, I believe, the same occasion for the admonition now that there was several months ago. Many late changes have taken place in that honourable body, which have removed, in a very great degree, if not wholly, the discordant spirit which, it is said, prevailed in the winter, and I hope measures will also be taken to remove those unhappy and improper differences which have extended themselves elsewhere, to the prejudice of our affairs in Europe.

I have a great pleasure in the visit which the Chevalier de la Luzerne and Monsieur Marbois did me the honour to make at this camp; concerning both of whom I have imbibed the most favourable impressions, and I thank you for the honourable mention you made of me to them. The chevalier, till he had announced himself to congress, did not choose to be received in his public character; if he had, except paying him military honours, it was not my intention to depart from that plain and simple manner of living which accords with the real interest and policy of men struggling under every difficulty for the attainment of the most inestimable blessing of life, *liberty*. The chevalier was polite enough to approve my principle, and condescended to appear pleased with our Spartan living. In a word, he made us all exceedingly happy by his affability and good humour, while he remained in camp.

You are pleased, my dear marquis, to express an earnest desire of seeing me in France, after the establishment of our independency, and do me the honour to add, that you are not singular in your request. Let me entreat you to be persuaded, that, to meet you anywhere, after the final accomplishment of so glorious an event, would contribute to my happiness; and that to visit a country to whose generous aid we stand so much indebted, would be an additional pleasure; but remember, my good friend, that I am unacquainted with your language, that I am too far advanced in years to acquire a knowledge of it, and that, to converse through the medium of an interpreter, upon common occasions, especially with the ladies, must appear so extremely awkward, insipid, and uncouth, that I can scarcely bear it in idea. I will, therefore, hold myself disengaged for the present; but when I see you in Virginia, we will talk of this matter, and fix our plans.

The declaration of Spain in favour of France has given universal joy to every Whig; while the poor Tory droops like a withering flower under a declining sun. We are anxiously expecting to hear of great and important events on your side of the Atlantic;

at present, the imagination is left in the wide field of conjecture, our eyes one moment are turned to an invasion of England, then of Ireland, Minorca, Gibraltar; in a word, we hope everything, but know not what to expect, or where to fix. The glorious success of Count d'Estaing in the West Indies, at the same time that it adds dominion to France, and fresh lustre to her arms, is a source of new and unexpected misfortune to our *tender and generous parent*, and must serve to convince her of the folly of quitting the substance in pursuit of a shadow; and, as there is no experience equal to that which is bought, I trust she will have a superabundance of this kind of knowledge, and be convinced, as I hope all the world and every tyrant in it will be, that the best and only safe road to honour, glory, and true dignity, is *justice*.

We have such repeated advice of Count d'Estaing's being in these seas, that, though I have no official information of the event, I cannot help giving entire credit to the report, and looking for his arrival every moment, and I am preparing accordingly; the enemy at New York also expect it; and, to guard against the consequences, as much as it is in their power to do, are repairing and strengthening all the old fortifications, and adding new ones in the vicinity of the city. Their fears, however, do not retard an embarkation which was making, and generally believed to be for the West Indies or Charlestown: it still goes forward; and, by my intelligence, it will consist of a pretty large detachment. About fourteen days ago, one British regiment (the forty-fourth completed) and three Hessian regiments were embarked, and are gone, as is supposed, to Halifax. The operations of the enemy this campaign have been confined to the establishment of works of defence, taking a post at King's Ferry, and burning the defenceless towns of New Haven, Fairfield, and Norwalk, on the Sound, within reach of their shipping, where little else was, or could be, opposed to them, than the cries of distressed women and helpless children; but these were offered in vain. Since these notable exploits, they have never stepped out of their works or beyond their lines. How a conduct of this kind is to effect the conquest of America, the wisdom of a North, a Germain, or a Sandwich can best decide, it is too deep and refined for the comprehension of common understandings and the general run of politicians.

Mrs. Washington, who set out for Virginia when we took the field in June, has often, in her letters to me, inquired if I had heard from you, and will be much pleased at hearing that you are well and happy. In her name, as she is not here, I thank you for your polite attention to her, and shall speak her sense of the honour conferred on her by the Marchioness. When I look back to the length of this letter, I have not the courage to give it a careful reading for the purpose of correction: you must, therefore, receive it with all its imperfections, accompanied with this assurance, that, though there may be many inaccuracies in the letter, there is not a single defect in the friendship of, my dear Marquis, yours, &c.

TO GENERAL WASHINGTON.*

(ORIGINAL.)

Havre, 7th October, 1779.

My Dear General,—From those happy ties of friendship by which you were pleased to unite yourself with me, from the promises you so tenderly made me when we parted at Fishkill, gave me such expectations of hearing often from you, that complaints ought to be permitted to my affectionate heart. Not a line from you, my dear general, has yet arrived into my hands, and though several ships from America, several despatches from congress or the French minister, are safely brought to France, my ardent hopes of getting at length a letter from General Washington have ever been unhappily disappointed: I cannot in any way account for that bad luck, and when I remember that in those little separations where I was but some days from you, the most friendly letters, the most minute account of your circumstances, were kindly written to me, I am convinced you have not neglected and almost forgotten me for so long a time. I have, therefore, to complain of fortune, of some mistake or neglect in acquainting you that there was an opportunity, of anything, indeed, but what could injure the sense I have of your affection for me. Let me beseech you, my dear general, by that mutual, tender, and experienced friendship in which I have put an immense portion of my happiness, to be very exact in inquiring for occasions, and never to miss those

* To this letter was joined a long letter to the president of congress, which contained nearly the same things, expressed in a different manner.

which may convey to me letters that I shall be so much pleased to receive.

Inclosed I send to your excellency the copy of my letters to congress, which, in concert with Mr. Franklin's longer despatches, will give you a sketch of European intelligence. Contrary winds have much delayed an expedition which I think should have been undertaken much sooner: the kings of France and Spain seem desirous of carrying it on before the winter; it may be, however, deferred till next spring, and the siege of Gibraltar would be the only land expedition for the present campaign. In a few weeks time, when West India successes may be compared to those in Europe, my gazettes and predictions will have a greater degree of certainty, but one must not be a conjuror to see that England is in such a way that one may defy her to get up again, and that a happy peace, blessed with American independence, will, in this or the ensuing campaign, be the certain effect of the present war.

As my private circumstances are somewhat interesting to your friendship, I will tell you, my dear general, that since my last letter I have hardly quitted this place, where head-quarters had been fixed. I was to disembark with the grenadiers forming the vanguard, and am, therefore, one of the first who will land on the English shore. The king's own regiment of dragoons, which he gave me on my return, was to embark at Brest, and join us a few days after the landing. From Count d'Estaing's expedition on the American coasts, the nation raises great expectations, and very impatiently waits for intelligence. How unhappy I am to find myself so far from you on such an occasion you will easily conceive. The impression of sorrow such a thought gives me cannot be alleviated but by the sense I have that the general opinion of the turn warlike operations will take this campaign, the ties of my duty towards my own country, where my services had been employed for the expedition against England, and the hope I entertained of being here more useful to the United States, had not left me the choice of the part I should take for this campaign. I hope, my dear sir, you will agree in opinion with me.

Whatever may be Count d'Estaing's success in America, it will bring on new projects and operations. My ideas I laid before your excellency at Fishkills; but permit me to tell you again how earnestly I wish to join you. Nothing could make me so delighted as the happiness of finishing the war under your orders. That, I think, if asked by you, will be granted to congress and your excellency. But be certain, my dear general, that in any situation, in any case, let me act as a French or as an American officer, my first wish, my first pleasure, will be to serve again with you. However happy I am in France, however well treated by my country and king, I have taken such a habit of being with you, I am tied to you, to America, to my fellow soldiers by such an affection, that the moment when I shall sail for your country will be one of the most wished for and the happiest in my life.

From an American newspaper I find that a certain English intelligence had been propagated through the United States, that, at the head of fifteen hundred officers or non-commissioned officers, I was going to embark for America, and that, with soldiers of your army embodied under them, I wanted to teach military discipline throughout the *American army*. However remote I am from thinking of teaching my own masters, and however distant from such views was that command in France, whose end you very well know, I could not help taking it as a reflection on the *American army*. The English troops may remember that on some particular occasions I have not had to lament the want of discipline and spirit in the troops which I had the honour to command. Whilst we have but the same British army to fight with, we need not be looking out for any other improvement than the same qualities which have often enabled my fellow American soldiers to give, instead of receiving, pretty good lessons to an enemy, whose justly-reputed courage added a new reputation to American bravery and military conduct.

The above article, my dear general, I beg you will have *printed in the several newspapers*.

As there is but a little time to write before the sailing of the vessel, I cannot call to mind all the friends I have in the army, unless your excellency is pleased to make them a thousand compliments from one who heartily loves them, and whose first wish is to be again in their company.

I congratulate you, my dear general, on the spirited expedition of Stony Point,* and am glad it has added a new lustre to our arms.

Be so kind, my dear friend, as to present my best respects to your lady. Mine begs leave to be kindly remembered to you and to her. Thousand assurances of friendship wait from me on your family.

Oh! my dear general, how happy I should be to embrace you again!

* A brilliant exploit of General Wayne, who, on the 15th of July, took by assault the fort of Stony Point, and forced five hundred and fifty-four English to capitulate.

With such affection as is above all expressions any language may furnish, I have the honour to be, very respectfully, &c.

TO M. DE VERGENNES.

Versailles, February 2d, 1780.

You approved, sir, of my putting down in writing, before conversing with you upon the subject of the expedition, some of the measures necessary to be taken in either of the following cases: first, if I should command the French detachment; and secondly, if I should resume an American division.*

I must begin by observing that this commission is not only a military and political, but also a social affair; and from the circumstances under which I am now placed, I assure you, on my honour, that I believe the first measure would be most favourable to the public service, and the interest of France as regards her allies.

As I must immediately begin my preparations, I should wish to be informed of the decision in sufficient time to select some officers of proper age, experience, and talents, with whom I can become acquainted before I take charge of the corps; and on this account it is necessary to arrange matters

* This letter contains the basis of the plan which was finally adopted. We have been obliged to retrench several letters which relate to projects analogous to those presented at various periods by M. de Lafayette. It was at length determined to send an auxiliary corps even stronger than he had hoped to obtain. As to himself, he was to precede it to America, whither he repaired with political instructions from the French cabinet, and to resume a command in the army of the United States. His instructions are dated the 5th of March; his departure took place the 19th.

immediately with the Prince de Montbarrey. Two old experienced lieutenant-colonels should command the infantry under me: in distant expeditions, it is necessary that officers should suit each other, and I am particularly fond of old officers.

In regard to myself, sir, I ask for nothing,—and as during the course of a war I may hope to acquire rank, you might either give me one of those commissions of M. de Sartine, which are only of use in America, or one that would not prevent my seniors from resuming afterwards their rank, or else letters of service, to enable me simply to command in the capacity of an American general officer.

There are three methods of concealing the real aim of the expedition: 1st, to set out together for Lorient, under pretence of taking an island, and operating in Carolina in the autumn;—2nd, to pretend to send troops to M. de Bouillé; there need be no commander, and I should have the title of *maréchal-des-logis*;—3d, for me to set out immediately with the grenadiers and dragoons for America, and that the four battalions, commanded by the two ancient officers, should join me at Rhode Island.

If I should have the command, you may act with perfect security, because the Americans know me too well to feel the slightest anxiety. I will bind myself, if it be desired, to ask for neither rank nor titles, and, to put the ministry quite at their ease, I will even promise to refuse them should they be offered me.

In the second case, sir, it would be necessary to prevent, beforehand, in America, the bad effects that the arrival of another commander would excite: that I am not to lead that detachment is the last idea that could ever occur in that country; I will say, therefore, that for myself I prefer having an American division.

I must be in the secret to prepare the various measures, and inform General Washington of the transaction. A secret with which I was not acquainted would appear very suspicious at Philadelphia.

Three merchant frigates and a transport ship would be procured at Lorient. We have, it is said, an American crew; the fifteen thousand suits of clothes, and fifteen thousand guns, &c. might be embarked; at the end of the month it would be necessary to set out for the continent.

On arriving at a port, I should endeavour to commence my operations with General Washington; I should take a division in the army, and, with M. de la Luzerne's aid, prepare everything for the arrival of the French. To increase the number of my division,—to serve as an example to them,—to change the ideas entertained respecting us,—and to shew in what perfect good intelligence French and Americans may live together,—I should request to take with me, at once, a battalion of six hundred grenadiers, three hundred dragoons, and one hundred hussars.

Two or three officers, whom I should bring back with me, must obtain the same rank in France which they had in America, and I should say that I have refused that rank myself from motives which are purely social. This attention is necessary to flatter the self-love of the Americans. We may stop at Bermuda on our way, and establish there the party for liberty.

I shall set out on Wednesday for Nantes, where the clothes are making; I shall also attend to the selection of the arms; I shall see the king's regiment at Angers, to form a detachment from it; I shall repair to Lorient to hasten the arrangement of the frigates, and to see the battalion of grenadiers; I shall only be here the 20th, and as my departure must be public, I shall take leave the 25th, in an American uniform, and if the wind be favourable, I shall sail the 1st of March.

As it is physically impossible that a detachment commanded by a foreigner should amalgamate together well, I believe it would be necessary to increase it by a battalion, which would raise the number to about three thousand six hundred, and the grenadiers would remain more particularly attached to me during the campaign.

If that little corps be given to an old field-marshal, we should certainly displease all the American chiefs. Gates, Sullivan, and Saint Clair, would not like to be under the orders of others, and their opinion in the council would be opposed to combined expeditions. I think it necessary, very necessary, to select a brigadier, and name him field-marshal, which he would look upon as a promotion. The corps must consider itself as a division of our army; its commander must abjure all pretensions, think himself an American major-general, and execute, in all respects, the orders of General Washington. The naval commander may have more power placed in his hands.

Conclusion. 1st, I think it would be best to give me the corps.—2d, If it be not given to me, I must instantly set out with the powers I demand. In either case, it is, unfortunately, necessary to reveal to me the secret, and set me immediately to work.

I shall have the honour, sir, of paying my respects to you during the procession.

TO HIS EXCELLENCY GENERAL WASHINGTON.*

(ORIGINAL.)

At the entrance of Boston harbour, April 27, 1780.

HERE I am, my dear general, and, in the midst of the joy I feel in finding myself again one of your loving soldiers, I take but the time to tell you that I came from France on board a frigate which the king gave me for my passage. I have affairs of the utmost importance which I should at first communicate to you alone. In case my letter finds you anywhere this side of Philadelphia, I beg you will wait for me, and do assure you a great public good may be derived from it. To-morrow we go up to the town, and the day after I shall set off in my usual way to joined my beloved and respected friend and general.

Adieu, my dear general; you will easily know the hand of your young soldier.

My compliments to the family.

TO M. DE VERGENNES.

Waterburg, on the Boston road,
From the Camp, May 6th, 1780.

I HAVE already had the honour of writing to you, sir, and of announcing to you the news of my arrival; but I place so much confidence in the kindness you express for me, that I do not hesitate to repeat the contents of my former letter. It was the

* The second of the measures discussed in the preceding letter was the one preferred, and M. de Lafayette embarked alone at the island of Aix.

28th of April, after a voyage of thirty-eight days, and after having experienced both calms and contrary winds, that the *Hermione* entered the Boston harbour. I cannot sufficiently express my admiration of the frigate herself, and my gratitude to her commanding officers.

I can neither give you any certain information, sir, nor promise you any degree of accuracy respecting numbers and dates. General Washington can alone inform me of the truth; but this does appear to me certain :—

Our army is not numerous; the eastern states are occupied in recruiting it. Paper has been regulated by congress at forty for one : these are very high taxes, and they hope to be able to raise the finances a little, which are in a very low state ; but, at present, I cannot give you any settled ideas upon this point.

The scarcity of horses, their price, and the want of provisions, have very much increased during my absence; but I assure you, sir, that, in a moral point of view, I continue to see a most favourable prospect for my American friends.

General Clinton has besieged Charlestown, and as he has eight or ten thousand men, and the report is spread that his vessels have crossed the bar, it is impossible not to fear for that place, unless Spanish or French vessels should come from the islands to its succour. Some troops from the army of General Washington have proceeded thither.

New York has only six or seven thousand garrisoned men ; such is, at least, the public report, and I do not believe that the hostile forces are much more numerous at present. They say, at Boston, that there are only four thousand men ; but I repeat, sir, that my gazettes cannot be at all accurate at present.

The English have but few vessels at Charlestown; at most they have only, I think, one or two at New York. It is said here, and every one seems to believe it, that if some French forces were to arrive at this moment, they might strike some decisive blows.

Be pleased, sir, to accept the assurance of the warm and respectful affection with which I have the honour to be, &c.

P.S. Some American officers, just come from New York, assure me that a frigate has arrived with important despatches from the English government. Don Juan de Miralles, who has been long established at Philadelphia, and who knows M. d'Aranda, died at Morristown; he was buried with much honour.

FROM GENERAL WASHINGTON.

(ORIGINAL.)

Morristown, May, 1783.

MY DEAR MARQUIS,—Your welcome favour of the 27th of April came to my hands yesterday. I received it with all the joy that the sincerest friendship would dictate, and with that impatience which an ardent desire to see you could not fail to inspire. I am sorry I do not know your route through the State of New York, that I might with certainty send a small party of horse, all I have at this place, to meet and escort you safely through the Tory settlements, between this place and the North River. At all events, Major Gibbs will go as far as Compton, where the roads unite, to meet you and will proceed from thence, as circumstances may direct, either towards King's Ferry or New Windsor. I most sincerely congratulate you on your safe arrival in America, and shall embrace you with all the warmth of an affectionate friend, when you come to head-quarters, where a bed is prepared for you. Adieu till we meet. Yours, &c.*

TO THE COUNT DE ROCHAMBEAU.

Philadelphia, 19th May, 1780.

Sir,—This letter will be handed to you by M. de Galvan, a French officer in the service of the United States, and you may receive with confidence the various accounts which he will have the honour to give you. I have appointed him to await your arrival at Cape Henry, and you will see that my instructions to this officer are in conformity with

* General Washington expressed, in several letters, the pleasure he felt at M. de Lafayette's return. (See his letters of the 13th and 14th of May.) The 16th of May, the congress declared, by a public resolution, that "they consider his return as a fresh proof of the disinterested zeal and persevering attachment which have justly recommended him to the public confidence and applause, and that they receive with pleasure a tender of the further services of so gallant and meritorious an officer."—(Journal of Congress, May 20th.).

It was afterwards resolved that the commander-in-chief, after having received the communications M. de Lafayette had to make to him, was to take the proper measures which were most likely to forward the success of the plan they had in view. The communications related to the expected arrival of a French squadron and land forces. The plan in contemplation was to make some attacks, especially on New York.

those which I have received from the Count de Vergennes.*

I reached Boston on the 26th of April. On the morning of the 10th of May, I was at head-quarters, and after passing four days with General Washington, I went to meet the Chevalier de la Luzerne. The military preparations and the political measures which it was necessary for us to attend to, have delayed M. de Galvan up to the present moment. I now hasten to despatch him to his destination, and shall keep him informed of whatever news may be interesting to you, continuing to add the ideas of the general, with regard to the best means of improving present circumstances.

Immediately upon my arrival, confidential persons were sent out to procure plans and details upon the different points which become interesting for the operations of this campaign. As to other matters, the Chevalier de la Luzerne has had the goodness to enable me, as far as possible, to fulfil my instructions, and he has taken the first measures requisite to procure a supply of food and other

* The instructions given to M. de Lafayette by the minister of foreign affairs, (5th March, 1780,) were, that, to prevent any mistake or delay, he was to place, both on Rhode Island and on Cape Henry (the mouth of the Chesapeake), a French officer, to await the arrival of the French squadron, which was to land at one of those two points, and to give it all the information it might require on its arrival. This letter was consequently given to M. de Galvan, and he repaired to Cape Henry, but vainly expected those frigates: they landed at Rhode Island. They left Brest the 2nd of May, under the orders of the Chevalier de Ternay, and appeared before Newport the 10th of July. This letter was delivered afterwards to M. de Rochambeau, as well as several others, which want of space and interest do not allow us to insert.

necessaries for the land and naval forces. Although the scarcity of all things is infinitely greater than when I left America, the precautions taken beforehand by the Chevalier de la Luzerne, and the measures we are now taking here, render it certain that the French will not be in want, either of flour or of fresh meat. . . . . .

I will now give you a summary of the present situation of the enemy on the continent. I shall say nothing of Canada, or Halifax, or the Penobscot, from whence we are expecting news, and which, for the moment, are not of essential importance. Rhode Island is in our possession ; you can enter there in full security ; letters, signals, and pilots will await you there, agreeably to my instructions. Your magazines, your sick, and all your unnecessary baggage, can go up the Providence by water ; I shall soon send to Rhode Island more particular information on this point.

The enemy have, at the present moment, seven thousand men of their best troops employed at the siege of Charlestown ; they have also some ships of the line without the harbour ; one vessel of fifty guns, two frigates of forty-four, and several smaller vessels. According to news from New York, Charlestown still held out on the 3rd of this month. On the Islands of New York, Long Island, and Staten Island, the forces of the enemy consisted of eight thousand regular troops, a few militia, upon which they place no dependence, and a small number of royalists, very contemptible in all respects. They have only one ship of seventy-four guns, and some frigates. The American army is in three divisions ; one guards the fort of West Point and keeps open the North River ; another is in South Carolina ; and the third, which is the largest, is in the Jerseys, under the immediate command of General Washington. This last division, not very numerous at present, will be increased in a few days; and for that reason, I shall defer till another letter giving you a more exact account of its situation.

Your voyage is known at New York. Advices were immediately sent on to Charlestown, recalling either the troops, or at least the ships of war. They are erecting fortifications on the Island, and preparing vessels loaded with stones to obstruct the passage; in a word, if it be true that the present divided state of the English forces seems to insure their destruction, and to promise us the conquest of New York, it is equally true that, at the moment of your arrival, if by good fortune things remain in their present state, we shall have no time to lose in taking advantage of those favourable circumstances.

At the same time that I here execute the orders of my general, and communicate to you the sentiments of my friend, permit me to assure you of the strong desire of our army to do whatever may please you, and how much we shall all endeavour to merit the friendship and the esteem of troops, whose assistance at the present moment is so essential to us. You will find amongst us a great deal of good will, a great deal of sincerity, and above all, a great desire to be agreeable to you.

I send a duplicate of this letter to the Chevalier de Ternay, and I shall send the same to Point Judith and Seaconnet; so that in case you should make land at Rhode Island, you may at once sail for Sandy Hook. The next letter which I shall have the honour to write to you, will be dated at head-quarters. The confidence of General Washington, which M. de Galvan has deserved, and the means which he has of fulfilling his instructions, all assure me that you will be satisfied with our choice. I have the honour to be, &c.

TO GENERAL WASHINGTON.

(ORIGINAL.)

Camp at Preakness, July 4th, 1780.

You know, my dear general, that I am very anxious to see the army well clothed for this campaign; the importance of such a measure is on every account obvious, and from the knowledge I have of the auxiliary troops that are coming, I can so well demonstrate its necessity that I shall for the present but attend to the means of executing it.

In the space of six months (we know from experience) the coats of our soldiers begin to be worn out, so that there is no great inconvenience in giving some new clothes to the draftsmen, and after they shall be discharged, the number of the remaining soldiers will not much exceed six or seven thousand men; as those very men will have been completely clothed by the middle of July, I think I make full allowance for them by keeping in store the seven thousand unmade suits that have been shipped by Mr. Ross.

If more are wanted in the course of next summer, I engage to go over to France and bring back ten thousand complete suits properly conveyed.

Excluding wagoners, servants, and all such people who do not want to be uniformly clothed, we may calculate the continental army to consist of fourteen thousand men in the field.

There may be found in the army four thousand coats and waistcoats which are not absolutely bad, four thousand stocks or cravats, and one thousand pretty good hats.

We may get from the stores fifteen thousand overalls, ten thousand pairs of shoes, three thousand round hats, and some few shirts.

There are also six or seven hundred coats of every colour, to which may be added about three or four hundred of the same kind, and some indifferent hats found in the army, &c.

A small quantity of buff and red cloth to be bought for the facings of the Pennsylvanian and Jersey lines.

The four thousand good hats in the stores or in the army to be cut round, or cocked in the form of caps, but to be in an uniform manner.

All the articles now in the possession of the clothier-general, to be immediately ordered to North River, and, if necessary, wagons should be pressed for their speedy transportation.

I will write a letter to the Chevalier de Ternay, wherein I will desire him to send to the most convenient place the clothing which has been put under his convoy.

We shall then have ten thousand new coats and waistcoats, and four thousand old ones, the whole of an uniform ground, ten thousand new hats and stocks, and four thousand old ones, five and twenty thousand overalls, more than twenty thousand shirts, and thirty thousand pairs of shoes.

Each soldier enlisted for the war, let them even be ten thousand, shall have, if you choose, a new complete suit, one hat, one stock, two shirts, two pairs of overalls, and two pairs of shoes.

Each draftsman, if he has not the same, will at

least receive a decent uniform coat, one stock, one hat, one pair of overalls, and two pairs of shoes; he will not certainly come out but well provided with shirts.

By the above mentioned arrangement, there remain about a thousand coats of every colour, a thousand hats, which are not absolutely bad, and two thousand pairs of shoes; these I propose to give to such men as will not appear under arms in the field, and, if necessary, some hunting-shirts may be added to the said clothing.

The dragoons are generally better clothed than the infantry, and we might very easily complete their coats or stable-jackets, as each different regiment could adopt a different colour.

As soon as the French clothing comes, I wish the whole army to be clothed at once, in observing to give the round hats to some particular brigades, for the sake of uniformity, and to turn up the facings according to the plan agreed.

There will be then no excuse for the officers who, out of neglect, should suffer their men to lose a single article, and the most strict orders may be given for that purpose.

The French arms that are coming might be put in the hands of soldiers enlisted for the war.

I wish that there was a distinction of one woollen epaulette for the corporal, and two for the serjeant.

As to the feathers, (become a distinction of ranks,) I wish such as have been pointed out might be forbidden to other officers, and for the light division I shall beg the leave of wearing a black and red feather, which I have imported for the purpose.

These ideas, my dear general, are not given to you as a great stroke of genius, but I heartily wish something of the kind may be thought proper.

TO MM. LE COMTE DE ROCHAMBEAU, AND LE CHEVALIER DE TERNAY.*

Camp, before Dobb's Ferry, Aug. 9, 1780.

GENTLEMEN,—I arrived two days ago at head quarters, and in consequence of the mission I was charged with, my first care was to render an account of our conversations; but the most minute details of them are so important, and the fate of America, and the glory of France, depend so completely upon the result of our combinations here, that, in order to feel more certain of having perfectly understood your meaning, I will submit to you a summary of our conversations, and entreat you to write me word

* General Heath, who commanded the militia in the state of Rhode Island, announced, on the 13th of July, the arrival of the French squadron to Washington, who was then stationed with his staff at Bergen. M. de Lafayette set out instantly, bearing instructions from the general-in-chief dated the 15th, to meet the French Generals and to concert with them. Washington had long formed a plan of offensive operations, for the reduction of the town and garrison of New York (letter to General Greene the 14th of July); this plan was to take effect on condition, first, that the French and American troops should form a junction; second, that the French should have a decided naval superiority over the united forces of Admiral Graves and Admiral Arbuthnot. In nine letters, written between the 20th of July and the 1st of August, which would not perhaps have offered much interest to the reader, M. de Lafayette rendered an account of his mission, of which a short analysis will give the principal details.

The first letters relate to the multiplied difficulties he encountered in the states of Connecticut and Rhode Island, in collecting provisions, clothing, arms, and, above all, powder, in sufficient quantities for the projected expedition. These difficulties were much increased by the insufficiency of every kind of munition brought by the French squadron, which but half realized the promises of the French cabinet. M. de Lafayette repaired to Newport the 25th, and found the army, which had been disemimmediately whether I have rightly understood your meaning. Before quitting Rhode Island, gentlemen, I should have taken this precaution, if General Washington's march against New York had not obliged me to join my division, at the very moment when, from our further arrangements, you most required some information.

1st. I have described to you the actual situation of America, the exhausted state in which I found her, and the momentary efforts she had made, which could only have been produced by the hope of being delivered, by one decisive blow, from the tyranny of the English.

I told you those efforts were so enormous, when we consider the state of our finances, and the failure

barked, encamped in Rhode Island, and M. de Rochambeau much occupied by the news of an important attack, and, in fact, four of the enemy's ships appeared on the 19th, and nine or ten more two days after, before Block Island. Sir Henry Clinton had on his side left New York. By a combination of his land and sea forces, he intended to surprise the French army. But he experienced some delay; his soldiers could only embark in the transports the 27th; there was a wrong understanding between him and Admiral Arbuthnot. He learnt that the French had fortified themselves at Newport, and that the neighbouring militia had joined them; and at length that General Washington was making a rapid movement upon New York. He hastened to pass over the Sound, and landed his troops on the 31st.

M. de Lafayette, who had always felt doubtful, himself, of Clinton's making the attack, had then the opportunity of discussing with the allies the project for an offensive operation. He was extremely anxious to put it into execution, and General Washington was desirous also of doing the same.

The thing was, however, difficult. Although the capture of New York had always been one of the objects of the French ministry, the instructions of M. de Rochambeau prescribed to him to attach great importance to the station of Rhode Island, and to endeavour to make it the basis for his other operations. He was therefore reluctant to quit it in order to march upon New York. M. de Ternay, at the same time, considered it as impossible to of all our resources, that I do not expect to see them renewed during another campaign. I added that on the 1st of November we should no longer have any militia, that the 1st of January one half of our continental army would be disbanded, and I took the liberty of saying, in my own name, that I thought it necessary, as a political measure, to enter into action this campaign; and this I had ascertained also to be the case, by sounding, on my journey, the wishes of the people.

2nd. I confirmed what I have already had the honour of writing to you respecting the continental troops, and the militia whom we are to have with us. I told you that by counting the enemies in New York at fourteen thousand men, of which ten thousand are regulars, and four thousand very bad militia, I thought their numbers were somewhat exaggerated,

enter with his ships of war into the harbour of that town, and contented himself with promising a blockade; he did not, besides, possess that naval superiority which could only be obtained by the arrival of the second division, which was so vainly expected from France, or by the junction of the squadron of M. de Guichen, then in the West Indies, to whom M. de Lafayette had written to promote that object. M. de Rochambeau's own opinion was, however, in favour of offensive measures, and he promised to conform, according to his instructions, to the orders of the general-in-chief. Everything was discussed and regulated in two or three conferences, which took place from the end of July to the commencement of August, between MM. de Rochambeau, de Ternay, and de Lafayette. The result of these conferences is resumed in a letter, to which is annexed this note—

In the suppressed letters it is also seen that the French troops evinced the greatest ardour, and that the good intelligence that reigned between the two allies completely justified the expectations of M. de Lafayette, and the measures he had proposed. He wrote, in a letter of the 31st, to General Washington:—

"The French army hate the idea of staying here, and want to join you. They swear at those that speak of waiting the second and that it was necessary to begin by deducting the sailors employed by Admiral Arbuthnot. As to the fortifications, I said that the American troops would take charge of New York, and that the fort of Brooklyn (upon which you might operate in concert with a division of our troops) is merely an earthen work of four bastions, with a ditch and a shed, containing from a thousand to fifteen hundred men, and having in front another smaller work, which cannot contain more than a hundred men. I added that nothing could prevent a regular approach upon Brooklyn, and that that post is the key of New York.

3rd. I explained to you General Washington's plan, and told you that the moment you began your march, he would repair to Morrisania, where, I again repeat, he would establish batteries that would close the passage of Hell's Gate, and secure the one

division: they are enraged to be blockaded in this harbour. As to their dispositions towards the inhabitants and our troops, and the dispositions of the inhabitants and the militia for them, they are such as I may wish. You would have been glad the other day to see two hundred and fifty of our drafts that came on from Connanicut, without provisions and tents, and who were mixed in such a way with the French troops, that every French soldier and officer took an American with him, and divided his bed and his supper in the most friendly manner. The patience and sobriety of our militia are so much admired by the French officers, that, two days ago, a French colonel called all his officers together, to take the good examples which were given to the French soldiers by the American troops. So far are they gone in their admiration, that they find a great deal to say in favour of General Varnum, and his escort of militia dragoons, who fill up all the streets of Newport. On the other hand, the French discipline is such, that chickens and pigs walk between the tents without being disturbed, and that there is in the camp a corn-field, of which not one leaf has been touched. The Tories dont know what to say to it."—(ORIGINAL.)—(*Letters of Washington from the* 14*th of July to the* 5*th of August*, 1780, *and Appendix*, *Nos*. 1 *and* 3, VOL. VII.)

from the continent to Long Island, so as to have nothing to fear from the enemy's ships. Whilst awaiting your arrival, gentlemen, our army would entrench itself at Morrisania, or, if possible, on the Island of New York, and would place itself in a situation to detach a corps of troops, as soon as you shall have approached us, either by coming by land to Westchester, and passing afterwards under favour of our batteries, or by repairing by sea to Wistown, or any other bay in that neighbourhood. General Washington would furnish a sufficient corps of Americans, and fifteen large cannon, to co-operate with your troops, and he believes that with these forces, and united with artillery, the point of Brooklyn might soon be taken, and consequently the town of New York.

4th. I represented to you that Long Island was a rich country, which, even after the destruction effected by the English, still possesses some resources; that we might feel certain of being joined there by the militia of the island; and, in short, that with the assistance of our Morrisanian under-batteries, and still more with a battery on the Island of New York, we should assure the communication between Long Island and the continent. From these various circumstances, my own private opinion would decidedly be to commence our action, if the fleet could be placed in security, before we possessed any superiority of naval force.

5th. I strongly insisted upon the necessity of taking possession, as soon as possible, of the New York harbour. I requested M. de Ternay to examine that point with the pilots I gave him, and by the immense advantages of that measure I hoped that, either with the aid of land forces on the side of Sandy Hook, or merely by the superiority of his own naval force, he would be enabled to accomplish the object we had feared his attempting when we expected him with Admiral Graves.

6th. When proposing to you to send your magazines to Providence, I told you that Rhode Island was completely useless to the Americans, but very important for the succours arriving from France, in case, however, no army should be necessary to preserve it; that if the English were to commit the fault of taking it, a superior fleet, aided by forces from the continent, would always have the power of retaking it.

7th. I ended by having the honour of telling you, gentlemen, that in order to operate upon New York it would be necessary not to commence later than the first days of September; and, after this explanation, I said that General Washington, feeling the most perfect confidence in you, was very desirous of having your opinion upon the subject, and would only undertake what might appear to you most advantageous.

This, gentlemen, is what I had the honour of saying to you, and this is what you did me the honour to reply to:—

1st. That the succour sent to the United States was anything rather than trifling; that the second division was to set out a short time after you, and that it might justly be expected every instant; that it would consist at least of two thousand five hundred, and, in all probability, of a still greater number of troops; that it was to be sent by three ships, but that, according to all appearances, a larger number of vessels would be granted; that the only reason which could prevent its arriving before the 1st of September, would be the impossibility of a junction between the French and Spanish fleets, and that, in the latter case, it would arrive, at farthest, by the end of autumn, and would then be a great deal stronger; that M. de Guichen has been apprised of our projects, and has received the order to facilitate them; that, consequently, the Chevalier de Ternay has written to him for the five promised vessels; and that, from all these circumstances, you hoped to be able to act before the end of the campaign, but did not doubt, at least, having the power of furnishing us with very superior forces for this winter, and for the next campaign.

2nd. The project of attacking Brooklyn was extremely agreeable to you, and appeared to you the most proper measure for the reduction of New York; but you think that we ought to have upon that Island a force at least equal to that which the enemy may offer us, and you added that by leaving a counterfeit at New York, they may fall on the corps of Long Island, with nearly their whole army, which contingency, you will perceive, had been already provided for by Washington's arrangements.

3rd. You appeared to me doubtful whether it would be possible to stop the enemy at the passage of Morrisania, but on this point I can give you no decisive information. The idea of repairing by land to Westchester appeared less agreeable to you than that of going by sea into a bay of Long Island. As to the landing, the Count de Rochambeau looks upon it as a very long operation, and, from his own experience on the subject, he believes that it would require nearly three weeks to land an army, with all its accoutrements, for a campaign and siege. You desired to have every possible information concerning Brooklyn, in order to be able to make calculations accordingly for the artillery and engineer service.

You appeared to me to consider a naval superiority as necessary, even at the commencement of the campaign; but it is true that this idea may partly proceed from your doubts relating to the communication concerning Morrisania.

5th. The Chevalier de Ternay conceives it would be difficult to take possession of New York harbour, and hopes to accomplish the same object by the situation in which he has placed his cruisers. He does not think that his seventy-fours can enter, but from the difference of opinion which I ventured to express, as to the importance at least of occupying the harbour, he told me he would again attend to this project. As to his manner of protecting the disembarkation, it would be to cruise in the Sound, and his frigates, and one or two vessels, would enter into the bay at the place where the troops should land.

6th. Rhode Island appears to you a very important point to preserve; but if M. de Ternay should have the superiority, you think, as we do, that it would be unnecessary to leave a garrison there during the attack of New York. The Count de Rochambeau desired me to assure General Washington that, in every case, upon receiving an order, he would instantly repair to that spot which the commander-in-chief should appoint. I told him, also, that the French generals wished that it were possible to have an interview with him.

At the termination of our conversation, we decided upon the following measures, of which I consequently gave an account to General Washington.

1st. You have written to France to urge the speedy arrival and augmentation of the promised succours. You have already asked for the five vessels of M. de Guichen, and I have also taken charge of another letter, which repeats the same request, and which will pass through the hands of the Chevalier de la Luzerne.

2d. As soon as you receive news of the arrival either of the second division or of the ships from the West Indies, you will immediately despatch a messenger to General Washington; and, whilst our army is marching towards Westchester, and your own making preparation for embarkation, M. de Ternay will endeavour to effect his junction.

3d. If the French fleet should be equal to that of the enemy, it will immediately enter into a contest for superiority; if it should be superior, it will take the French troops instantly on board, and carry them towards the bay intended for their landing.

4th. A spot shall be chosen from whence the ships may protect the operation, and which will also afford to the troops first landed a position well sheltered by the fire from the ships, and behind which the remainder of the troops may join them; or by advancing with all the landed troops, the right and left wings may be so placed as to cover the last of the disembarkation. The spot selected shall be situated in such a manner that the corps of the American army intended for this particular expedition, may arrive and land at the very moment of the landing of the Count de Rochambeau, and that their general may be able to co-operate instantly with the French general.

5th. According to the number of French troops in a state to operate, General Washington will either conduct himself, or send to Long Island, a sufficient number of troops to obtain a force nearly equal to that of the enemy, and he will also have a corps of troops of nearly the same strength as the one opposed to him, either at Westchester or in the Island of New York.

6th. The Chevalier de Ternay will examine, attentively, the possibility of forcing the passage of Sandy Hook, and if it be deemed practicable, will attain that important end.

7th. As soon as the arms, clothes, and ammunition, belonging to the United States, shall arrive, the Chevalier de Ternay will have the goodness, without giving them time to enter the harbour, to send them with a convoy of frigates, or, if the batteries be not yet erected, by a ship of the line, to that point in the Sound which General Washington may judge proper to select.

8th. The French fleet will take charge of the boats we shall require, which will be delivered up to them at Providence; they will also land us all the powder that they can do without themselves; this does not amount, at present, to more than thirty thousand pounds.

9th. I shall send to the French generals all the correct information I may obtain respecting the passage of the Sound by Hell Gate; I shall communicate to them, likewise, all the details relating to Brooklyn, and they will send us the calculations which have been made in consequence by the artillery and engineers,—from thence we shall decide what must be sent with the American Long Island corps for these two companies. Some doubts are entertained by the French generals concerning the two points of this last article; I shall send them from home some information respecting that subject, of which I had before the honour of speaking to them.

10th. The invalids, magazines, &c., shall be sent

to Providence, and the batteries of that river are to be placed by us in proper order. It is clearly specified that the instant the expected naval superiority of force arrives, the French are not to lose a single day in commencing their co-operative measures.

Such is, gentlemen, the abridgment of the account rendered to General Washington; and it will serve as the basis for his preparations, as well as a rule for the future elucidations you may receive. From the confidence with which he has honoured me, I was obliged to settle finally all that it was possible for me to arrange with you,—the fate of America, in short, appears to be dependent upon your activity or repose during the remainder of this summer. I attach the greatest importance to all your ideas being clearly rendered, and I entreat you to lose no time in writing a few words to say whether I have understood your meaning.

A short time after my departure, gentlemen, you must have learnt that General Clinton, fearing for New York, had been obliged, by a sudden movement of our army, to enclose himself in that island. The army is at present near Dobb's Ferry, ten miles above King's Bridge, on the right side of the North River, and our advance guard is nearly three miles before it.

If General Clinton, with a force and position equal to our own, should judge proper to fight, we shall give him a favourable opportunity of doing so, and he may take advantage of that kind of challenge to make the most impartial trial of the English and Hessian against the American troops.

I shall wait here, most impatiently, gentlemen, your answer to this letter. I shall have the honour of communicating to you the various advices General

Washington may find it expedient to send you. The first intelligence of the arrival of the ships is very necessary to our peace of mind, and from an intimate knowledge of our situation, I assure you, gentlemen, in my own private name and person, that it is important to act during this campaign, that all the troops you may hope to obtain from France next year, as well as all the projects of which you may flatter yourselves, will never repair the fatal consequences of our present inactivity. Without resources in America, all foreign succours would prove of no avail; and although, in every case, you may rely wholly upon us, I think it important to take advantage of the moment when you may find here a co-operation, without which you will not be able to achieve anything for the American cause.

I have the honour to be, &c.

P.S. Such, gentlemen, is the long official letter which I have the honour of writing to you, but I cannot send it without thanking you for the kindness you expressed for me at Rhode Island, and presenting you the assurance of my sincere and respectful attachment.

FROM THE COUNT DE ROCHAMBEAU TO M. DE LAFAYETTE.

Newport, August 12th, 1780.

I RECEIVED, my dear marquis, the letter you did me the honour of writing the 9th of August; permit me to send you, in reply, the one I had the honour of addressing to our general on the 10th of this month, to express to him the opinion you asked for by his desire. I am only now, therefore, waiting for his last orders, and I have earnestly requested him to grant me the favour of an interview, that the admiral and I may receive from his own lips the last plan he has decided upon; we should do more in a quarter of an hour's conversation than we could do by multiplied despatches. I am as thoroughly convinced as any person can be of the truth of what your letters mentioned, that it was his marching which had detained Clinton, who intended to come and attack us; but I must observe to you also, at the same time, that there was much reason to hope that he would have been well beaten here, and during that time our general would have taken New York. As to your observation, my dear marquis, that the position of the French at Rhode Island is of no use to the Americans, I reply:—

First, That I never heard it had been injurious to any one of them.

Second, That it would be well to reflect that the position of the French corps may have had something to do with Clinton's evacuation of the continent, when he has been obliged to confine himself to Long Island and New York; that, in short, while the French fleet is guarded here by an assembled and a superior naval force, your American shores are undisturbed, your privateers are making considerable prizes, and your maritime commerce enjoys perfect liberty. It appears to me, that, in so comfortable a situation, it is easy to wait patiently the naval and land forces that the king assured me should be sent; that, in short, as I have received no letter from France since my departure, I can only flatter myself that the second division is already on the road, and is bringing me despatches, since, if it had been blockaded by superior forces, some sort of advice would have been sent me from the shores of France. I fear those savannahs and other events of the kind, of which I have seen so many during the course of my life. There exists a principle in war, as in geometry, *vis unita fortior.* I am, however, awaiting orders from our generalissimo, and I entreat him to grant the admiral and myself an interview. I will join the latter's despatch to this packet as soon as I receive it.

I beg you to accept, my dear marquis, the assurance of my sincerest affection.

TO MM. DE ROCHAMBEAU AND DE TERNAY.

Camp, August 18th, 1780.

Gentlemen,—As I wish to submit the same observations to you both, permit me to address this letter to you in common, and permit me also (without pretending to complain of the interpretation you have given to my last letter) to accuse myself of having explained my own meaning in a very awkward manner.

On my return here, gentlemen, General Washington asked me for an account of our conversations. You know that he had given me full powers to explain to you our situation, and to settle finally the plan of the campaign. When he knew that you wished to confer with him, he again wrote me word that I was to arrange everything in his name, as if he were himself present. It was natural that he should wish to know what I said to you, what you replied, and what we had finally decided upon. He thought that the best manner of collecting our ideas was to write them down ; and I, fearing to say a single word that was not precisely according to your intentions, thought it more polite, more respectful towards you, to submit to your examination the written account which my general had requested. I may add, at this place, gentlemen, that the general, thinking that you were only acquainted with our position from what I had the honour of saying to you, did not consider the previous letters he had received as answers to what I had undertaken to explain to you. All that I said to you, gentlemen, concerning Rhode Island, the passage of Hell Gate, the harbour of New York, and the disembarkation, was from the reiterated orders of General Washington ; and as to the political opinions, which I will dispense myself with expressing in future, because they must come from the Chevalier de la Luzerne, I assure you that if, as your own countryman, it was more delicate for me to give them in my own name, they are not less conformable to the ideas of General Washington. The only time when I took the liberty of speaking for myself was, when, wearied by the questions that have been made to me by a thousand American individuals upon the second division, and the superiority of the English at this present period, I yielded to my ardent wish of entering at once on action, and to the hope of commencing our operations immediately. If I have been to blame, I think it can only be in this one instance.

I believe that the march towards New York has recalled Clinton from the bay of Huntington, but I believe that if he had been guilty of the folly of attacking you, he would have both lost at Rhode Island a portion of his army, owing to our French troops, and the Island of New York by our attack.

This was my opinion, and the one I found most prevalent here, and I also think that it is very unfortunate for the common cause that General Clinton did not pursue his enterprise. Is it I who could imagine the contrary?—I who have always been laughed at for thinking it impossible that the French could ever be beaten!

When, after having received three letters from General Washington, and held twenty conversations with him on the subject, I thought it proper to tell you in what point of view we looked upon Rhode Island, I do not think it ever occurred to me to say you had injured any person by staying there, and as to the advantage America derives from having a French squadron and French troops, allow me to mention, gentlemen, that M. d'Estaing found me formerly well disposed to acknowledge this truth; that for more than eighteen months, and especially since the commencement of last summer, I held a regular correspondence with the French government, to represent to it the utility of such a measure; and, although the gratitude of the Americans does not by any means require being excited, few hours pass without my employing a part of my time in pointing out to them the advantages that you may procure for them even when inferior to the hostile forces, and in which I do not take the measures most proper to publish this truth from the extremity of Canada to that of Florida, as I may prove to you by the few copies of letters which I have preserved.

As to the political opinions with which I took the liberty of closing my letter, although I acknowledge having committed the fault of expressing them to you, I am certain beforehand that, from an intimate acquaintance with the American character and resources, the Chevalier de la Luzerne and General Washington are both of my opinion.

I will do all that depends upon me, gentlemen, to prevail upon the general to meet you half way; but, from his proximity to the enemy, and from the present situation of the army, which he has never quitted since the commencement of the war, I fear it will appear to him very difficult to absent himself. Whenever you have any orders to give me, look upon me as a man who, you must well know, idolizes his own country with a peculiar degree of enthusiasm, and who unites to that feeling (the strongest one of his heart) the respectful affection with which he has the honour of being, &c.

TO M. DE ROCHAMBEAU.

Camp, August 18th, 1780.

HAVING written, sir, one letter to you in common with the Chevalier de Ternay, permit me to address myself to you with the frankness authorised by the warm affection I have felt, and endeavoured to prove to you, from my earliest youth. Although your letter expresses your usual kindness for me, I observed a few sentences in it which, without being individually applied to me, prove to me that my last epistle displeased you. After having been engaged night and day for four months, in preparing the minds of the people to receive, respect, and love you; after all I have said to make them sensible of the advantages they derived from your residence at Rhode Island, and after having made use of my own popularity to propagate this truth; in short, sir, after all that my patriotism and affection for you have dictated to me, my feelings were unavoidably hurt by your giving such an unfavourable turn to my letter, and one which had never for a moment occurred to myself. If in that letter I have offended or displeased you; if, for example, you disapprove of that written account which General Washington asked for, and which I thought I ought to submit to you, I give you my word of honour that I thought I was doing a very simple thing; so simple, indeed, that I should have considered I was wronging you by not doing it.

If you had heard that second division spoken of, sir, as I have done; if you knew how strongly the English and the Tories endeavour to persuade the Americans that France only wishes to kindle, without extinguishing the flame, you would readily conceive that my desire of silencing those reports might have inspired me, perhaps, with too much warmth. I will confide to you that, thus placed in a foreign country, my self-love is wounded by seeing the French blockaded at Rhode Island, and the pain I feel induces me to wish the operations to commence. As to what you write to me, sir, respecting Rhode Island, if I were to give you an account of all I have said, written, and inserted in the public papers; if you had heard me, frequently in the midst of a group of American peasants, relating the conduct of the French at Newport; if you were only to pass three days here with me, you would see the injustice of your reproach.

If I have offended you, I ask your pardon, for two reasons; first, because I am sincerely attached to you; and secondly, because it is my earnest wish to do everything I can to please you here. As a private individual, in all places your commands will ever be laws to me, and for the meanest Frenchman here I would make every possible sacrifice rather than not contribute to their glory, comfort, and union with the Americans. Such, sir, are my feelings, and although you have imagined some which are very foreign to my heart, I forget that injustice to think only of my sincere attachment to you.

P. S. I am far from thinking, sir, that I am in any degree the cause of the sentiments that are experienced in this country for yourself and the officers of your army. I am not so vain as to have entertained such an idea; but I have had the advantage of knowing you, and I was, therefore, able to foresee what would occur on your arrival, and to circulate the opinions adopted by all those who have personally known you. I am convinced, and no one here can deny it, that but for your arrival, American affairs would have gone on badly this campaign; but, in our present situation, this alone is not sufficient, and it is important to gain advantages over the enemy. Believe, that when I wrote in *my own name*, that opinion did not belong to myself alone; my only fault was writing with warmth, in an official manner, that which you would have forgiven on account of my youth, if I had addressed it as a friend to yourself alone; but my intentions were so pure, that I was as much surprised as pained by your letter, and that is saying a great deal.

FROM M. DE ROCHAMBEAU.

Newport, August 27th, 1780.

PERMIT an aged father, my dear marquis, to reply to you as he would do to a son whom he tenderly loves and esteems. You know me well enough to feel convinced that I do not require being excited, that when I, at my age, formed a resolution founded upon military and state reasons, and supported by circumstances, no possible instigation can induce me to change my mind without a positive order from my general. I am happy to say that his despatches, on the contrary, inform me that my ideas correspond substantially with his own, as to all those points which would allow us to turn this into an offensive operation, and that we only differ in relation to some small details, on which a slight explanation, or his commands, would suffice to remove all difficulties in an instant. As a Frenchman, you feel humiliated, my dear friend, at seeing an English squadron blockading in this country, with a decided superiority of frigates and ships, the Chevalier de Ternay's squadron; but console yourself, my dear marquis, the port of Brest has been blockaded for two months by an English fleet, and this is what prevents the second division from setting out under the escort of M. de Bougainville. If you had made the two last wars, you would have heard nothing spoken of but these same blockades; I hope that M. de Guichen, on one side, and M. de Gaston, on the other, will revenge us for these momentary mortifications.

It is always right, my dear marquis, to believe that Frenchmen are invincible; but I, after an experience of forty years, am going to confide a great secret to you: there are no men more easily beaten when they have lost confidence in their chiefs, and they lose it instantly when their lives have been compromised, owing to any private or personal ambition. If I have been so fortunate as to have retained their confidence until the present moment, I may declare, upon the most scrupulous examination of my own conscience, that I owe it entirely to this fact, that, of about fifteen thousand men who have been killed or wounded under my command, of various ranks, and in the most bloody actions, I have not to reproach myself with having caused the death of a single man for my own personal advantage.

You wrote to the Chevalier de Chastellux, my dear marquis, that the interview I requested of our general has embarrassed him, because it only becomes necessary after the arrival of the second division, when there will be quite time enough to act. But you must surely have forgotten that I have unceasingly requested that interview immediately, and that it is absolutely necessary that he, the admiral, and I, should concert together all our projects and details, that in case one of the three chances should occur and enable us to act offensively, our movements may be prompt and decisive. In either of these three cases, my dear marquis, you will find in your old prudent father some remnants of vigour and activity. Be ever convinced of my sincere affection, and that if I pointed out to you very gently what displeased me in your last despatch, I felt at the time convinced that the warmth of your heart had somewhat impaired the coolness of your judgment. Retain that latter quality in the council-room, and reserve all the former for the hour of action. It is always the aged father, Rochambeau, who is addressing his dear son Lafayette, whom he loves, and will ever love and esteem until his latest breath.

TO THE CHEVALIER DE LA LUZERNE.

Robinson House, opposite W. Point, Sept. 26, 1780.

When I parted from you yesterday, sir, to come and breakfast here with General Arnold, we were far from foreseeing the event which I am now going to relate to you.* You will shudder at the danger to which we have been exposed; you will admire the miraculous chain of unexpected events and singular chances that have saved us; but you will be

* The project of an expedition against New York had not been abandoned: it was still canvassed by letter. General Washington agreed with the French generals as to the necessity of waiting for a naval reinforcement. The latter insisted upon having a conference with the General and M. de Lafayette. (See especially Washington's Letter of the 21st August, vol. vii. p. 169.) That long deferred conference was at length granted, and it was fixed that it should take place at Hartford (Connecticut). Washington left his army the 18th of September. It will be recollected that it was his interview with Arnold at the passage of the Hudson, that induced the latter to take the steps which led to the discovery of the conspiracy. (See above.) Some days after, M. de Rochambeau wrote thus to M. de Lafayette:—

"Providence has declared itself for us, my dear marquis,—and that important interview, which I have so long wished for, and which has given me so much pleasure, has been crowned by a peculiar mark of the favour of Heaven. The Chevalier de la Luzerne has not yet arrived; I took the liberty of opening your letter to him, in which I found all the details of that horrible conspiracy, and I am penetrated with mingled feelings, of grief at the event itself, and joy at its discovery.

still more astonished when you learn by what instruments this conspiracy has been formed. West Point was sold—and sold by Arnold: the same man who formerly acquired glory by rendering such immense services to his country. He had lately entered into a horrible compact with the enemy, and but for the accident that brought us here at a certain hour, but for the combination of chances that threw the adjutant-general of the English army in the hands of some peasants, beyond the limits of our stations, West Point and the North River, we should both at present, in all probability, be in possession of the enemy.

When we set out yesterday for Fishkill, we were preceded by one of my aides-de-camp, and one of General Knox's, who found General Arnold and his wife at breakfast, and sat down at table with them. Whilst they were together, two letters were given to Arnold, which apprised him of the arrestration of the spy. He ordered a horse to be saddled, went into his wife's room to tell her he was ruined, and desired his aide-de-camp to inform General Washington that he was going to West Point and would return in the course of an hour.

On our arrival here, we crossed the river and went to examine the works. You may conceive our astonishment when we learnt, on our return, that the arrested spy was Major André, adjutant-general of the English army; and when amongst his papers were discovered the copy of an important council of war, the state of the garrison and works, and observations upon various means of attack and defence, the whole in Arnold's own hand writing.

The adjutant-general wrote also to the general, avowing his name and situation. Orders were sent to arrest Arnold; but he escaped in a boat, got on board the English frigate the *Vulture*, and as no person suspected his flight, he was not stopped at any post. Colonel Hamilton, who had gone in pursuit of him, received soon after, by a flag of truce, a letter from Arnold to the general, in which he entered into no details to justify his treachery, and a letter from the English commander, Robertson, who, in a very insolent manner, demanded that the adjutant-general should be delivered up to them, as he had only acted with the permission of General Arnold.

The first care of the general has been to assemble, at West Point, the troops that, under various pretences, Arnold had dispersed. We remain here to watch over the safety of a fort, that the English may respect less as they become better acquainted with it. Continental troops have been summoned here, and as Arnold's advice may determine Clinton to make a sudden movement, the army has received orders to be prepared to march at a moment's warning.

TO MADAME DE SESSE.

Camp, on the right side of the North River, near the Island of New York, October 4th, 1780.

A French frigate arriving from America,—the son of M. de Rochambeau on board! Good God, what a commotion all that will excite, and how much trouble inquisitive people will take to discover the secrets of the ministers. But I, my dear cousin, will confide to you our secret. The French army has arrived at Rhode Island, and has not quitted that spot. M. de Ternay's seven vessels have been blockaded the whole time, and the English have nineteen vessels here under that lucky commander, Rodney. We Americans, without money, without pay, and without provisions, by holding out fair promises, have succeeded in forming an army, which has been offering to fight a battle with the English for the last three months, but which cannot without vessels reach the island of New York. Gates, who was no favourite of mine, has become still less so since he has allowed himself to be beaten in the south. But all this is quite as monstrous as an European war, and catastrophes are necessary to excite and sustain the interest of men.

You must know, then, my cousin, that a certain General Arnold, of some reputation in the world, was our commander at West Point, a fort on the North River, whose importance the Duke d'Ayen will explain to you. General Washington and I, returning from Hartford, where we had held a conference with the French generals, discovered a conspiracy of the highest importance. We owe that discovery to an almost incredible combination of accidents. West Point was sold by Arnold, and we were consequently lost. The traitor has fled to join the enemy.

I received letters from you by the fleet, and by the *Alliance*, and I am impatiently expecting more recent ones. The nation will not be pleased with the state of tranquillity in which we remain. But as we have no ships, we can only wait for the enemy's blows, and General Clinton does not appear in any haste to attack us. As to ourselves, we republicans preach lectures to our sovereign master, the people, to induce him to recommence his exertions. In the mean while we practise so much frugality, and are in such a state of poverty and nudity, that I trust an account will be kept in the next world, whilst we remain in purgatory, of all we have suffered here.

Poircy* is here, and although he does not find a St. Germain in this part of the world, he accustoms himself extremely well, I assure you, to a soldier's life. I thank you from the bottom of my heart for all the news you gave me. Although they afforded me the greatest pleasure, I scarcely dare reply to them, from the fear that my answers may appear to come from another world. I saw in the paper that the King of Spain was dead: has God, then, punished him for having conferred the title of grandee upon M. de Montbarrey?

I need not tell you that I am in good health, for that is, you know, my usual custom. My situation here is as agreeable as possible. I am in high favour, I believe, with the French army: the American army shew me every possible kindness and attention. I have the command of a flying corps, composed of the élite of the troops. My friend General Washington continues to be everything to me that I before described to you.

Adieu, my dear cousin. When shall I again see you? I pray that God may grant us an honourable peace, and that I may embrace my friends, and I willingly, for my own part, will give up my share of the glory in the hope eventually to win.

Present my affectionate regards to M. de Tessé, M. de Mun, M. Ténai, and the baron;† I was on the point of saying, embrace his daughter for me.

* Secretary. The Marshal de Noailles had a house at Saint Germain.

† The Baron de Tott.

TO MADAME DE LAFAYETTE.

Near Fort Lee, opposite Fort Washington, on the North River, Oct. 7th, 1780.

You must have already learnt, my dearest love, all that can interest you relating to myself, from my arrival at Boston until my voyage to Rhode Island, which place public affairs, and the desire of seeing my friends, induced me to visit soon after my landing. I have been since to Hartford in Connecticut, to be present at an interview between the French generals and General Washington: of all my young friends, Damas* was the only one who accompanied us. The viscount† and I often write to each other, but we do not meet, and the poor man remains shut up in Rhode Island; the French squadron detains the army there, and is itself detained by nineteen ships of the line and sundry other ships of war, upon which M. Rodney proudly exhibits the British colours. So long as our naval inferiority lasts, you need feel no anxiety about the health of your friends in America.

I must speak to you, however, about my health; it continues excellent, and has not been interrupted for a single moment; a soldier's mode of living is extremely frugal, and the general officers of the rebel army fare very differently from the French army at Newport. You have probably heard that, on my arrival in America, I found the army of General Washington very weak in numbers, and still more so in resources. Our prospects were not brilliant, and the loss of Charleston was for us a most heavy

* The Count Charles de Damas, died a peer of France under the restoration.

† The Viscount de Noailles.

blow, but the desire of co-operating with their allies gave new vigour to the states. General Washington's army increased more than half in number, and more than ten thousand militia were added to it, who would have come forward if we had acted offensively. Associations of merchants and patriotic banks were formed to supply the army with subsistence. The ladies made, and are still making, subscriptions, to afford succour to the soldiers. When that idea was first proposed, I made myself your ambassador to the ladies of Philadelphia, and you are inscribed on the list for a hundred guineas. General Gates had in the south an army quite sufficient for defence; but he has been completely beaten in Carolina. The fruit of all these labours has been, to prove to the French that the Americans desire nothing better than to second their views upon England, to prove to the English that the flame of liberty was not wholly extinguished in America, and to keep us, during the whole campaign, in daily expectation of a battle, which General Clinton, although equal to us in number, has never thought proper to accept. If we had only had ships, we should have been enabled to do a great deal more.

As I know that all that interests me deeply is also interesting to you, I will tell you that we are much occupied by an important system, which would secure to us a considerable army during the whole war, and would bring into action all the resources which America is capable of making. God grant that the nation may understand its true interests, and our affairs will go on without difficulty!

M. de Rochambeau and M. de Ternay, as well as all the other French officers, conduct themselves extremely well here. A little ebullition of frankness gave rise to a slight altercation between those generals and myself. As I perceived I could not convince them, and that it was important for the public good that we should remain friends, I declared, with due humility, that I had been mistaken, that I had committed an error, and, in short, in proper terms, I asked their pardon, which produced such an excellent effect that we are now on a more amicable footing than ever.

I command a flying corps, which always forms an advance guard, and is quite independent of the great army; this is far too grand for our pacific situation.

On the Hackensack River, Oct. 8th, 1780.

You will learn, my dearest love, an important event, which has exposed America to the greatest danger. A frightful conspiracy has been planned by the celebrated Arnold: he sold to the English the fort of West Point, which was under his command, and, consequently, the whole navigation of the river: the plot was within an ace of succeeding, and quite as many chances combined together to discover it as in that affair of the *Alliance*, which I have so often described to you.* After our journey to Hartford, General Washington passed by West Point, which was not on his road; but he was desirous of shewing me the works that had been constructed since my departure for France. Detained by various accidents upon the road, we arrived at the traitor's house just as he received the letters which announced that he had been discovered. He had not time to intercept those proofs of infamy, and consequently

* The conspiracy discovered on board the frigate, which brought home M. de Lafayette, in September, 1779.

he could only make his escape towards New York half an hour before our arrival.

The adjutant-general of the English army has been arrested under a feigned name and dress. He was an important person, the friend and confidant of General Clinton. He behaved with so much frankness, courage, and delicacy, that I could not help lamenting his unhappy fate.

I received, with great delight, the letters of my dear sisters; I shall write to them to-morrow; but I shall send this scrawl, as I fear the frigate may depart. I finish my letter in this place, having begun it rather more close to the enemy: we had approached them to protect a small enterprise, in which a detachment of my advance-guard has been engaged, and which only ended by capturing two officers, and fifteen men and horses. We are now marching towards a place you will find marked upon the map Sotawa, whither the grand army is also to repair. I shall write to Madame d'Ayen and to my sisters.

Sotawa Bridge, October 10th, 1780.

I AM closing my letter, but before sealing it, I must again speak to you for a moment of my affection. General Washington was much pleased by the kind messages which I delivered from you; he desires me to present to you his tender regards; he is affectionately attached to George, and is much gratified by the name we have given him. We often speak of you and of the little family. Adieu, adieu.

TO GENERAL WASHINGTON.

(ORIGINAL.)

Light Camp, October 30th, 1780.

My dear General,—In our conversations upon military operations you have often told me that, since the beginning of the campaign, your eyes were turned towards a project upon which I generally agree in opinion with you, and beg leave to offer some observations.

Far from lessening my desire of finishing the campaign by some brilliant stroke,* the project of Staten Island, though it miscarried, has strengthened my opinions, as I have clearly seen, by the details of this operation, that we should, in all human probability, have succeeded, and that our men were fully equal to any enterprise of that kind.*

My reasons for wishing to undertake something are these :—1st. Any enterprise will please the

* M. de Lafayette had taken, since the 7th of August, command of the corps of light infantry, consisting of six companies of men, selected in different lines of the army. Those battalions were divided into two brigades; one under the command of General Hand, the other of General Poor. The inactivity of the army was very opposite to the character and policy of M. de Lafayette; he endeavoured incessantly to find means of putting an end to it, at least as far as regarded himself. The 14th of August he had written to General Washington to ask his permission to attempt a nocturnal surprise on the two camps of Hessians established at New York Island. At the beginning of October, he attempted an expedition on Italian Island, which could not be accomplished, owing to a mistake made by the administration of the materality of the army. This letter, and the letters of the 13th of November, allude to this circumstance. We have been obliged to retrench ten letters, which relate solely to the unimportant incidents of a war of observation.

people of this country, and shew them that when we have men we do not lie still; and even a defeat (provided it was not fatal) would have its good consequences. 2ndly. The French court have often complained to me of the inactivity of the American army, who, before the alliance, had distinguished themselves by their spirit of enterprise. They have often told me, your friends leave us now to fight their battles, and do no more risk themselves: it is, moreover, of the greatest political importance to let them know, that, on our side, we were ready to co-operate. Be sure, my dear general, that many people's interest will be to let it be believed that we *were not ready*, and if anything may engage the ministry to give us the asked for support, it will be our proving to the nation that, on our side, *we had been ready*. So far was the Chevalier de la Luzerne convinced of this (and on this point the minister's interest is the same as ours) that he was made happy by my mentioning to him the Staten Island affair. I well know the court of Versailles, and were I to go to it, I should think it very impolitic to go there unless we had done something. 3rdly. It is more than probable that mediators will interfere this winter by a negotiation. Then England will say, how can we give up people whom we consider as half conquered; their best city has been taken by an army not much superior to the people that were to defend it; their southern army was routed almost as soon as looked at by the British troops: New York is so much ours, that they dare not approach it, and General Washington's army does not exceed five thousand men. What shall France answer? Principally now that from the letters I have received I find the Charleston affair has brought our arms into contempt. But what difference, if France might say, the American army has taken, sword in hand, your best works; they have offered to you the battle upon your own island, and, perhaps they may add (for news increases in travelling), they are now in possession of New York.

Upon these considerations, my dear general, what I want is this, to find an expedition which may wear a brilliant aspect, and afford probable advantages, also an immense, though very remote one, which, if unsuccessful, may not turn fatal to us, for the loss of two or three hundred men, half of them being enlisted for two months, I do not consider as a ruinous adventure.

The basis of the plan will be, that Fort Washington, being in our possession, may, with the Fort *Lee* batteries, protect our crossing North River, and be a security for our retreat, principally if some works are added on the point of embarkation. The taking of Fort Washington we may demonstrate to be very probable, and upon that point you are of my opinion.

The enemy have, on the upper part of the Island from fifteen hundred to two thousand men, who would immediately occupy all the other upper posts. Their army on Long Island would repair to New York, and there would also retire the troops posted at Harlem.

As soon as Fort Washington should be ours, the army would cross over to the island, and those of West Point arrive in the same time (which calculation may be easily done) so that we should effectually possess all the upper posts, or cut them off from their main army. Some militia would come to our assistance, and as these posts are not well furnished with provisions we should take them, at least, by famine.

The enemy's army consists of nine thousand men: they must certainly leave one thousand men in their several posts; fifteen hundred of them, at least, will be either killed at Fort Washington or blocked up at Laurel Hill, and they will then have between six and seven thousand men to attack ten. The two thousand militia (in supposing that they durst take them out) I do not mention, because we may have four thousand militia for them: under such circumstances it is, probable that Sir Henry Clinton will venture a battle. If he does, and by chance beat us, we retire under Fort Washington; but, if we beat him, his works will be at such a distance, that he will be ruined in the retreat. If, on the contrary, he knows that the French army is coming, and if we spread the report of a second division, or of Count de Guichen being upon the coasts, he will keep in his works, and we will, some way or other, carry the upper posts. When we are upon the spot we may reconnoitre New York, and see if something is to be done. If Clinton was making a forage into the Jerseys, I should be clear for pushing to the city.

If we undertake, the circumstances of the weather make it necessary that we undertake immediately. I would move the army, as soon as possible, to our position near the new bridge. This movement may invite Clinton in the Jerseys, and bring us nearer to the point of execution.

Though my private glory and yours, my dear general, both of which are very dear to my heart, are greatly interested, not so much for the opinions of America, as for those of Europe, in our doing something this campaign, I hope you know me too well to think I should insist upon steps of this nature unless I knew that they were politically necessary, and had a sufficient military probability.

I have the honour to be, &c.

The six hundred men of Luzerné's legion might be got in twelve days. If our movements had no other effect but to make a diversion in favour of the south, it would, on that footing, meet with the approbation of the world, and perhaps impeach the operations of General Leslie.

FROM GENERAL WASHINGTON TO THE MARQUIS DE LAFAYETTE.

(ORIGINAL.)

Head-quarters, 30th October, 1780.

It is impossible, my dear marquis, to desire more ardently than I do, to terminate the campaign by some happy stroke; but we must consult our means rather than our wishes, and not endeavour to better our affairs by attempting things which, for want of success, may make them worse. We are to lament that there has been a misapprehension of our circumstances in Europe; but to endeavour to recover our reputation, we should take care that we do not injure it more. Ever since it became evident that the allied arms could not co-operate this campaign, I have had an eye to the point you mention, determined, if a favourable opening should offer, to embrace it; but, so far as my information goes, the enterprise would not be warranted; it would, in my opinion, be imprudent to throw an army of ten thousand men upon an island against nine thousand, exclusive of seamen and militia. This, from the accounts we have, appears to be the enemy's force. All we can do at present, therefore, is to endeavour to gain a more certain knowledge of their situation, and act accordingly. This I have been some time employed in doing, but hitherto with little success. I shall thank you for any aids you can afford. Arnold's flight seems to have frightened all my intelligencers out of their senses. I am sincerely and affectionately yours.

TO GENERAL WASHINGTON.

(ORIGINAL.)

Light Camp, November 13th, 1780.

MY DEAR GENERAL,—In revolving in my mind the chances of discovery by moonlight, and, on the other hand, the inconveniences of staying longer than you wish under our tents, I have thought if there was any position which might enable us to take advantage of the first hours of the night. How far the sending of the Pennsylvanians towards Aquakanac, and going ourselves to the Hukinsac* position, may awaken the enemy, I cannot pretend to say. The most difficult affair in this would be the article of the boats. Colonel Smith will go to-morrow morning to West Point, unless any intelligence received at head-quarters had made it useful

* The general-in-chief projected an attack on the posts of the northern part of New York. While General Heath was to attract, by a feint, the attention of the enemy, Washington was to march in advance, and M. de Lafayette to attack Fort Washington. This expedition, for which great preparations had been made, terminated in a few reconnoitring parties. The campaign closed without an engagement.

that the enterprise be attempted soon, in which case he would go and reconnoitre the place. Suppose he was to bring from West Point Colonel Gouvion, who has often examined the place with the eye of an engineer. These ideas, my dear general, have rather started into my mind, than become fixed, and I thought I would communicate them.

Most affectionately and respectfully yours,

LAFAYETTE.

The Marquis de Laval Montmorency, one of the most illustrious families in France, is on his way to the camp. The Chevalier de Chastellux, a relation and friend of mine, major-general in the French army, is also coming. I every day expect my brother-in-law, and his friend, Count de Charlus, only son to the Marquis de Castries, who enjoys a great consideration in France, and has won the battle of Closter Camp. The Duke of Lauzun has also written to me that he would come soon.* These five gentlemen may, by their existence at home, be considered as the first people in the French army. This little history I give you before their arrival, in consequence of what you have desired from me at the beginning.

I write some letters to the commanding officers at Fishkill, West Point, and King's Ferry, so that the gentlemen may be directed to come by the best road to my quarters, from which I will present them

* The Marquis de Laval, is the Duke de Laval, who died under the restoration. The Chevalier de Chastellux is well known by his works. The Count de Charlus is at present the Duke de Castries, member of the chamber of peers. M. de Lauzun has been general in the service of the French republic.

to you. . . I think the letters ought to be sent as soon as possible.

P. S. As General Heath commands in all these parts, I think, upon recollection, that I had better write to him alone. You might also send him a line on the subject.

TO GENERAL WASHINGTON

(ORIGINAL.)

Paramus, November the 28th, 1780.

MY DEAR GENERAL,—We arrived last night at this place, and were much favoured by the weather in our recognising of the Island, where, I confess, my feelings were different from what I had experienced when looking at these forts with a hopeful eye. I saw the fatal sentry alluded to, Colonel Gouvion, on an upper battery of Jeffery's Hook. I also saw a small vessel playing off this Hook, but quite a trifling thing, without guns, and but two men on board. Nothing else on the river but the usual guards of spiting devil.

As you have been pleased to consult me on the choice of an adjutant-general, I will repeat here, my dear general, that though I have a claim upon General Hand, in every other point of view, his zeal, obedience, and love of discipline, have given me a very good opinion of him.

Colonel Smith has been by me wholly employed in that line, and I can assure you that he will perfectly answer your purpose.

Unless, however, you were to cast your eye on a man who, I think, would suit better than any other in the world. Hamilton is, I confess, the officer whom I should like to see in that station. With equal advantages, his services deserve from you the preference to any other. His knowledge of your opinions and intentions on military arrangements, his love of discipline, the superiority he would have over all the others, principally when both armies shall operate together, and his uncommon abilities, are calculated to render him perfectly agreeable to you. His utility would be increased by this preferment; and on other points he could render important services. An adjutant-general ought always to be with the commander-in-chief. Hamilton should, therefore, remain in your family, and his great industry in business would render him perfectly serviceable in all circumstances. On every public or private account, my dear general, I would advise you to take him.

I shall, on my arrival at Philadelphia, write you how those matters are going, upon which I build my private schemes. But I heartily wish that some account or other from Europe may enable you to act this winter on maritime operations. I hate the idea of being from you for so long a time; but I think I ought not to stay idle. At all events, I must return when your army takes the field.

I flatter myself with the hope of meeting Mrs. Washington on the road. Adieu, my dear general, most affectionately and respectfully yours.

TO HIS EXCELLENCY GENERAL WASHINGTON.*

(ORIGINAL.)

Philadelphia, December 5th, 1780.

My dear General,—By my letter of yesterday I have mentioned to you that a Spanish expedition was intended against St. Augustine. They mean to set out at the end of December, which will certainly delay them till the middle of January. It consists of twelve ships of the line, some frigates, bomb ketches, and a large number of troops. I have advised the minister to communicate officially to you this intelligence, and also to Count de Rochambeau, that proper means, if convenient, may be taken to improve it.

For my part, my dear general, I have conducted myself agreeably to what you said to me in our last conversations, that if, in the course of the winter, a naval superiority was obtained, our business should be to push for the southward, and that you would take for that purpose four thousand French and two thousand Americans. Nothing against New York can be undertaken before the end of May. Any thing, therefore, that could employ us during February, March, and April, is worthy of our attention.

* The winter, according to custom, causing the dispersion of the army, M. de Lafayette repaired to Philadelphia to be nearer arrivals and intelligence from Europe. It was there he first conceived the project of going to serve in the south under General Greene, who was to make a winter campaign. As regards the project of making a division in Florida, with the co-operation of the Spaniards, he seconded it with ardour, and to General Washington, M. de la Luzerne, and the Spanish commanders, he wrote long letters on the subject, which have but little interest, owing to the project not having been attended with any important result: those letters have been omitted.

The confederacy was going to sail for some clothing which we have in the West Indies. No time was left to wait for an answer from you. I knew perfectly your sense of this affair. I therefore, with the advice of Chevalier de la Luzerne, wrote him a letter dated from Camp, wherein I explained to him that something might be done in conjunction for the public good. My opinion is strengthened by your sentiments on this matter, without, however, bringing myself, and still less yourself, to make any formal application to the Spanish generals.

Inclosed you will find a copy of this letter, the first part of which mentions that if, after having landed their troops in Florida, they would send their ships of the line for us, we might, at three weeks notice before the departure of the squadron, have in readiness six thousand men for a powerful diversion in Carolina. Their own interest is the only thing I seem to consider in this business, and I endeavour to invite Spanish caution in this measure; but, unless a more particular application is made, I do not believe that this part of my letter will have any effect.

The second part will, I hope, be productive of some good for America. I urge the necessity immediately to open a correspondence with General Greene that he may, by his manœuvres, facilitate the operation of Spain. I tell them, that unless they land a corps of troops on the boundaries of Georgia, with a view at least to threaten Augusta and Savannah, their expedition will run a great risk. I advise the measure of cruizing off Charleston Harbour, the whole under the idea of their own interest.

I have also written to the naval French commander in the West Indies, advising him to succour Chevalier de Ternay, which I know he will not do.

But I take this opportunity of condemning their foolish neglect, in not appearing on our coasts when they return to Europe ; and I do also advise that, in their cruizes from St. Domingo, they may sometimes appear off Savannah and Charlestown Harbour. Inclosed you will find a copy of this letter.

Though I always speak of the beginning of February, it is, however, certain, that any time in February would be convenient to go to the southward. March and April are more than sufficient for the taking of Charlestown ; and in all cases, I know, from our last conversations, that you wish for a naval superiority this winter, in order to succour the southern states.

I had this morning, my dear general, a long conversation with the Chevalier de la Luzerne, relating to a southern operation. He is, as well as myself, clearly of opinion, that unless a formal application and a plan of campaign be proposed to them, they will not send their ships to us. In this last case their coming ought still to be questioned. But if you thought it better to try, you might propose to the French generals to send a frigate there, and see, with them, what might be done in conjunction. Suppose they were to take four thousand men, leaving some, and the militia, at Rhode Island. We could on our part muster two thousand Americans. However, the Spaniards are so positive and strict in following literally their instructions, that I do not believe anything will engage them to come. But my letter, which I look upon as a mere cipher on the first proposition, will, I hope, engage them to impart their projects to General Greene, and of course this diversion will become useful to us.

Suppose Count de Rochambeau and Chevalier de Ternay were to send to Havanna a copy of your letter, I think they ought to intrust it to Viscount de Noailles, who will soon return to Rhode Island, and whose name is highly respected by the court of Spain for many particular reasons, too long to be mentioned here.

I have seen Mr. Ross, and find that very little clothing is to be for the present expected. They have some arms on board the *Alliance*, and, I think, a hundred bales of cloth on board a vessel under Jones's convoy. The remainder will come with the *Serapis*. Unless the storm has forced Jones to put in some French harbour, he may be expected every minute.

The assembly of Pennsylvania have before them the affair of the recruits; but proper arrangements are not properly supported. They are fond of voluntary enlistments. I have an appointment for to-morrow with General Mifflin, where I will debate this matter with him.

To-morrow, my dear general, I will go to Brandywine with Chevalier de Chastellux, and also to Red Bank, Fort Mifflin, &c. On my return I hope to find news from France, and I will write you my determination about my going to the southward.

Inclosed you will find a newspaper, wherein congress have printed a letter from General Gates, relating to a new success of Sumpter.

Congress have lately received letters from Mr. Jay and Mr. Adams, but nothing very particular. They have more fully written by other opportunities that are expected. Portugal has entered into the convention of neutrality, and with such conditions as to shew their partiality to our side of the question.

Adieu, my dear general, most respectfully and affectionately.

FROM GENERAL WASHINGTON TO THE MARQUIS DE LAFAYETTE.

(ORIGINAL.)

New Windsor, 14th December, 1780.

MY DEAR MARQUIS,—Soon after despatching my last letter to you, your favour dated at Paramus was put into my hands by Colonel Gouvion. The Chevalier de la Luzerne's despatches came in time for the post, which is the only means left me for the conveyance of letters; there not being so much money in the hands of the quartermaster-general (I believe I might go further, and say in those of the whole army,) as would bear the expense of an express to Rhode Island. I could not get one the other day to ride so far as Compton.

I am now writing to the Count de Rochambeau and the Chevalier de Ternay, on the subject of your several letters. When their answer arrives, I will communicate the contents to you. You must be convinced, from what passed at the interview at Hartford, that my command of the French troops at Rhode Island stands upon a very limited scale, and that it would be impolitic and fruitless in me to propose any measures of co-operation to a third power, without their concurrence; consequently an application from you, antecedently to an official proposition from the minister of France, the gentlemen at the head of the French armament at Rhode Island, congress, or myself, could only be considered as coming from a private gentleman; it is, therefore, my advice to you to postpone your correspondence with the Spanish generals, and let your influence come in hereafter, as auxiliary to something more formal and official. I do not hesitate to give it clearly as my opinion to you, (but this opinion and this business should be concealed behind a curtain,) that the favourable moment of the Spanish operations in the Floridas ought to be improved to the utmost extent of our means, provided the Spaniards, by a junction of their maritime force with that of his most Christian Majesty, under the command of the Chevalier de Ternay, will give us a secure convoy, and engage not to leave us until the operations shall be at an end, or it can be done by consent of parties.

I am very thankful to the minister for permitting, and to you for communicating to General Greene, intelligence of the Spanish movements towards the Floridas. It may have a happy influence on his measures, and it may be equally advantageous to the Spaniards. Your expressions of personal attachment and affection to me are flattering and pleasing, and fill me with gratitude. It is unnecessary, I trust, on my part, to give you assurances of mutual regard, because I hope you are convinced of it; and as I have already put it absolutely in your own choice to go to the southern army or to stay with this, circumstances and inclination alone must govern you. It would add to my pleasure if I could encourage your hope of Colonel Nevill's exchange. I refused to interest myself in the exchange of my own aide. General Lincoln's were exchanged with himself; and upon that occasion, for I know of no other, congress passed a resolution, prohibiting exchanges out of the order of captivity.

Under one general head, I shall express my concern for your disappointment of letters, our disappointment of clothes, and disappointment in the mode of raising men ; but I shall congratulate you on the late change of the administration of France,* as it seems to be consonant to your wishes, and to encourage hope. I am much pleased at the friendly disposition of Portugal. Much good, I hope, will result from the combination of the maritime powers. I am in very confined quarters ; little better than those at Valley Forge, but such as they are I shall welcome into them your friends on their return to Rhode Island. I am, &c.

TO M. DE VERGENNES.†

New Windsor, on the North River, Jan. 30th, 1781.

The letters which I had the honour of writing to you, sir, and which were dated the 20th May, 19th July, 4th and 16th December, have, I hope, reached you safely. Since the arrival of the squadron, your despatch of the 3rd of June is the only one I have received. The Chevalier de la Luzerne has only received one letter of the same month, and none have yet reached the officers of the army and squadron.

The first copy of this letter will be delivered to

* The Marquis de Castries had succeeded, as minister of the navy, to M. de Sartine. This change gave rise to the hope that France would send the promised succours, and that expectation induced M. de Lafayette to renounce his journey to the south.

† This letter was written in ciphers. It is inserted here exactly as it was first deciphered at the archives of foreign affairs. To avoid repetitions, we have not inserted the answers of the minister ; these were written in a tone of confidence and friendship, and accord almost on every point with the ideas of M. de Lafayette, which were, in a measure, adopted by the cabinet of Versailles for the approaching campaign.

you by Lieutenant-Colonel Laurens, aide-de-camp to General Washington, who is charged by congress with a private mission. Permit me to recommend to you this officer as a man who, by his integrity, frankness, and patriotism, must be extremely acceptable to government.

According to the instructions of congress, he will place before you the actual state of our affairs, which demand, I think more than ever, the most serious attention. As to the opinions which I may allow myself to express, sir, they entirely correspond with those I have hitherto expressed, and the very slight alterations observable in them have been occasioned by a change of time, prejudices, and circumstances.

With a naval inferiority, it is impossible to make war in America. It is that which prevents us from attacking any point that might be carried with two or three thousand men. It is that which reduces us to defensive operations, as dangerous as they are humiliating. The English are conscious of this truth, and all their movements prove how much they desire to retain the empire of the sea. The harbours, the country, and all the resources it offers, appear to invite us to send thither a naval force. If we had possessed but a maritime superiority this spring, much might have been achieved with the army that M. de Rochambeau brought with him, and it would not have been necessary to have awaited the division he announced to us. If M. de Guichen had stopped at Rhode Island, on his way to France, Arbuthnot would have been ruined, and not all Rodney's efforts could have prevented our gaining victories. Since the hour of the arrival of the French, their inferiority has never for one moment ceased, and the English and the Tories have dared to say that France wished to kindle, without extinguishing the flame. This calumny becomes more dangerous at a period when the English detachments are wasting the south; when, under the protection of some frigates, corps of fifteen hundred men are repairing to Virginia, without our being able to get to them. On the whole continent, with the exception of the Islands of Newport, it is physically impossible that we should carry on an offensive war without ships, and even on those Islands the difficulty of transportation, the scarcity of provisions, and many other inconveniences, render all attempts too precarious to enable us to form any settled plan of campaign.

The result, sir, of all this is, that the advantage of the United States being the object of the war, and the progress of the enemy on that continent being the true means of prolonging it, and of rendering it, perhaps, even injurious to us, it becomes, in a political and military point of view, necessary to give us, both by vessels sent from France, and by a great movement in the fleet in the Islands, a decided naval superiority for the next campaign; and also, sir, to give us money enough to place the American forces in a state of activity; fifteen thousand of the regular army, and ten thousand, or, if we choose it, a still greater number of militia in this part of the country; a southern army, of which I cannot tell precisely the extent, but which will be formed by the five southern states, with all means of supporting in this country such a considerable force. Such, sir, are the resources that you may employ against the common enemy; immense sums of money could not transport resources of equal value from Europe to America, but these, without a succour of money, although established on the very theatre of war, will become useless; and that succour, which was always very important, is now absolutely necessary.

The last campaign took place without a shilling having been spent; all that credit, persuasion, and force could achieve, has been done,—but that can hold out no longer: that miracle, of which I believe no similar example can be found, cannot be renewed, and our exertions having been made to obtain an army for the war, we must depend on you to enable us to make use of it.

From my peculiar situation, sir, and from what it has enabled me to know and see, I think it is my duty to call your attention to the American soldiers, and on the part they must take in the operations of the next campaign. The continental troops have as much courage and real discipline as those that are opposed to them. They are more inured to privation, more patient than Europeans, who, on these two points, cannot be compared to them. They have several officers of great merit, without mentioning those who have served during the last wars, and from their own talents have acquired knowledge intuitively; they have been formed by the daily experience of several campaigns, in which, the armies being small, and the country a rugged one, all the battalions of the line were obliged to serve as advance-guards and light troops. The recruits whom we are expecting, and who only bear, in truth, the name of recruits, have frequently fought battles in the same regiments which they are now re-entering, and have seen more gun-shots than three-fourths of the European soldiers. As to the militia, they are only armed peasants, who have occasionally fought, and who are not deficient in ardour and discipline, but whose services would be most useful in the labours of a siege. This, sir, is the faithful picture that I think myself obliged to send you, and which it is not my interest to paint in glowing colours, because it would be more glorious to succeed with slighter means. The Chevalier de la Luzerne, who, having himself seen our soldiers, will give you a detailed and disinterested account of them, will doubtless tell you, as I do, that you may depend upon our regular troops. The result of this digression, sir, is, to insist still more earnestly on the necessity of sending money to put the American troops in movement, and to repeat that well-known truth, that a pecuniary succour and a naval superiority must be the two principal objects of the next campaign.

It would take us too long to examine the faults that have been committed, and the efforts that the states may still endeavour to make: we must return to the former point, that, under present circumstances, money is requisite to derive any advantage from the American resources; that the means which have been substituted for funds are almost completely worn out; that those to which we are at present reduced, do not fulfil the proposed end, and are opposed to the ideas which induced the nation to commence the revolution; that, consequently, we require money to restore to the army that degree of activity without which it cannot operate in an efficacious manner. Clothes, arms, ammunition, are comprised in the same article, and Colonel Laurens carries with him a copy of the former list, from which some deductions have been made. I will content myself with saying, that nothing of any importance has been sent us, that it is necessary to clothe the American army, that it requires arms, and, to be enabled to besiege places, a great augmentation of powder. As these expenses relate to the pecuniary succours, and are those which will strike most forcibly individuals, both of the army and nation, I think it important that the government should prepare them with promptness, and send them in a secure manner.

If it should appear strange, sir, to call that completion of the army a great effort, I would beg to observe, that hunger, cold, nudity, and labour, the certainty of receiving neither pay, clothes, nor necessary food, being the prospects held out to the American soldier, they must be but little inviting to citizens who are, generally speaking, accustomed to live at home with some degree of comfort; and the English having had sufficient time to think of all the naval points, the attacks of next year will be anything rather than surprises, and our forces must increase in proportion to their precautions. I could have wished that there had been some French troops, and my confidence in the decrease of prejudice has been even greater than that of congress, General Washington, or your minister at that time. The advance-guard of the Count de Rochambeau, although inactive itself from want of ships, by its presence alone has rendered an essential service to America: if it had not arrived, the campaign would have been a ruinous one. When I consider the present state of feeling, my notion, as I have had the honour of telling you before, would be to send hither, for the expedition of New York, a division of about ten thousand Frenchmen.

In our conference at Hartford, sir, the calculations were of course made, not according to the fortifications actually existing, but according to those they might intend erecting. The answers General

Washington thought proper to make to the questions put by the Count de Rochambeau, have been long since carried to you by the *Amazon*. A proposal to ask for a corps of fifteen thousand Frenchmen could only be acceptable to the commander-in-chief. But if that surplus were to lessen the sum of money by means of which fifteen thousand regular troops, ten thousand militia, and a southern army should be put into motion; if it were to lessen the number of ships that would enable us to act in all places, and with a decided superiority;—I must again repeat, that pecuniary succours and a naval superiority are the two most essential points; that the same quantity of money would, put into action here, double that number of American soldiers; and that, without ships, a few thousand men more would be but of little use to us.

The admirable discipline of the French corps, in addition to the honour it confers on M. de Rochambeau and the soldiers under his command, fulfils a still more important aim, by impressing on the minds of the Americans the highest idea of our nation.

The wisdom of the government, in placing that corps under the orders of General Washington, allows me only to repeat how essential it is that his authority should be complete, and without any sort of restriction. The talents, prudence, delicacy, and knowledge of country, which are all united in him in the greatest degree of perfection, are qualities of which one only would suffice to ensure the rigid observance of the instructions which I bear; and the longer I remain here, the more fully am I convinced that each of them is equally necessary to the harmony and success of the whole affair.

We have had, lately, sir, an important mutiny,

of which Colonel Laurens will give you the details.* A corps of Pennsylvanian troops, almost wholly composed of strangers, and stationed at Morristown (Jersey), unanimously rose against their officers, and, under the direction of one of their sergeants, marched on to Princetown. The civil authorities repaired thither, to afford them the justice they demanded. To be in want of food and clothes, to serve for more than a year without pay, some of them, indeed, having been forced to serve a whole year beyond their engagement, are evils to which no army would submit. It is singular enough that those mutineers should have hung up the envoys of General Clinton. The greatest part of the soldiers are disbanded, but they are to re-enter the service, and to join the recruits in different regiments of the state. I am not less positive as to the number of men we shall have in our continental army. Some troops belonging to the Jerseys, seduced by example, and being those next to the Pennsylvanians, which were composed of the greatest number of foreigners, wished to take the same method of obtaining justice; but General Washington, having taken the management of this affair in his own hands, sent forward a detachment; the mutineers submitted, and their chiefs were punished. It is impossible to pass too high encomiums upon the New England troops, almost all national ones, whose cause was at bottom the same, and who, in spite of their nudity, crossed heavy snows to march against the mutineers. This proves, sir, that human patience may have some

* The revolt of the Pennsylvanian line is of the 2nd of January. It was appeased ten days afterwards, and imitated, the 20th of the same month, by the New Jersey troops.—(See the Letters of Washington at that period, and the Appendix, No. x. vol. vii.)

limits, but that soldier citizens will endure far more than strangers. These events furnish another argument for the necessity of obtaining money.

I flatter myself, sir, that the government, conscious that the ensuing campaign may be a decisive one, will occupy itself seriously of rendering it favourable to us. The taking of New York would destroy the power of the English on this continent, and a short continuation of naval superiority would secure to us the easy conquest of all the other parts of the United States. As to the taking of New York, which it would be rash to consider easy, but absurd to respect the town as if it were a fortified one, it is, I believe, well authenticated, and General Washington has no doubt upon the subject, that with the means proposed in my letter, we should obtain possession of it in the course of the summer.

It is, I believe, important to turn, as far as possible, the enemy's attention towards Canada.

When General Washington gave Colonel Laurens his opinion respecting military affairs and the operations of the campaign, he also put down in writing some ideas on our present situation, and communicated to me that letter, which contains the substance of several of his conversations with me. I take the liberty of requesting the king's minister, to ask to see that letter. Our situation is not painted in flattering colours; but the general speaks from the sad experience of our embarrassments, and I agree with him, sir, that it is indispensable for us to obtain some pecuniary succours, and a decided naval superiority.

You must certainly have learnt, sir, that the defeat of Ferguson, and some other successes of ours, having disarranged the plans of Lord Cornwallis, General Leslie re-embarked to form the junction by water, and that he has since arrived at Charlestown. Arnold, become an English general, and honoured by the confidence of that nation, is at this moment at the head of a British detachment. Having landed in Virginia, he took possession of Richmond for some hours, and destroyed some public and private property: he must now have retired into a safe harbour, or has, perhaps, joined some other expedition. At the very moment when the English fancied that we were in the most awkward situation from the mutiny of some troops, General Washington sent a detachment on the left side of the Hudson, commanded by Lieutenant-Colonel Hull, supported by General Parsons, which surprised, at Westchester, a corps of three hundred men under Colonel Delancey, wounded several, killed thirty, took sixty prisoners, burnt all the barracks and provisions, and retired, after having destroyed a bridge of communication with the Island of New York.

The general is soon to pass some days with the French troops at Rhode Island, and I shall accompany him on that journey.

I have the honour to be, sir, with equal affection and respect, &c. &c.

New Windsor, February 4th, 1781.

By a letter from M. de Rochambeau, sir, we learn that the English squadron in Gardiner's Bay has suffered severely from a gale of wind. A seventy-four, it is said, has run on shore; the *London*, of ninety guns, is dismasted, and M. Destouches* was preparing to take advantage of this event. But you will receive more circumstantial, and perhaps more

* M. Destouches had replaced in the command of the frigates M. de Ternay, deceased the 15th December, after a short illness.

certain details, by letters from Rhode Island, and we are also ourselves expecting some, to fix more positively our own ideas and hopes. General Knox, commander of our artillery, a man of great merit and extreme probity, has just reported to the general the result of a mission which had been given him in the New England States. The spirit of patriotism and the zeal he found,—the exertions they are making to levy troops, either for the whole duration of the war, or for (what amounts, I trust, to the same thing) the period of three years, surpass our most sanguine hopes; and as they have twenty regiments in the continental service, I can only urge, in a still more positive manner, what I have already had the honour in writing to you.

TO MADAME DE LAFAYETTE.

New Windsor, in the North River, February 2nd, 1781.

The person who will deliver this to you, my dearest love, is a man I am much attached to, and whom I wish you to become intimate with. He is the son of president Laurens, who has been lately established in the Tower of London*; he is lieutenant-colonel in our service, and aide-de-camp to General Washington; he has been sent by congress on a private mission to the court of France. I knew him well during the two first campaigns, and his probity, frankness, and patriotism, have attached me extremely to him. General Washington is very fond of him; and of

* He was detained both as a prisoner of war and a rebel. The 18th of October, Madame de Lafayette had herself written in his favour to M. de Vergennes, a letter which is still preserved in the archives of foreign affairs.

all the Americans whom you have hitherto seen, he is the one I most particularly wish you to receive with kindness. If I were in France, he should live entirely at my house, and I would introduce him to all my friends (I have even introduced him to some by letter); and give him every opportunity in my power of making acquaintance, and of passing his time agreeably at Versailles; and in my absence, I entreat you to replace me. Introduce him to Madame d'Ayen, the Marshal dc Mouchy, the Marshal de Noailles, and treat him in every respect as a friend of the family: he will tell you all that has occurred during our campaign, the situation in which we are at present placed, and give you all details relating to myself.

Since my arrival here, my health has not for a moment failed. The air of this country agrees with me extremely well, and exercise is very beneficial to me. My exertions during the last campaign did not lead me into much danger, and in that respect we have not, in truth, much to boast. The French squadron has remained constantly blockaded in Rhode Island, and I imagine that the Chevalier Ternay died of grief in consequence of this event. However this may be, he is positively dead. He was a very rough and obstinate man, but firm, and clear in all his views, and, taking all things into consideration, we have sustained a great loss. The French army has remained at Newport, and although its presence has been very useful to us, although it has disconcerted some plans of the enemy which would have been very injurious to us, it might have done still more good if it had not been thus blockaded.

Several Frenchmen have passed by head quarters. They have all been delighted with General Washington, and I perceive with pleasure that he will be much beloved by the auxiliary troops. Laval and Custine disputed together during the whole journey, and at each station would have done much better than the American and English generals, but never both in the same manner. The viscount and Damas have taken a long journey on the continent; we have also had the Count des Deux-Ponts, whom I like very much; M. de Charlus is at present in Philadelphia. I intend setting out about the 15th, for Rhode Island, and I shall accompany General Washington during his visit to the French army. When you recollect how *those poor rebels* were looked upon in France, when I come to be hung with them, and when you reflect upon my warm affection for General Washington, you will conceive how delightful it will be for me to witness his reception there as generalissimo of the combined armies of the two nations.

The Americans continue to testify for me the greatest kindness: there is no proof of affection and confidence which I do not receive each day from the army and nation. I am serving here in the most agreeable manner possible. At every campaign I command a separate flying corps, composed of chosen troops; I experience for the American officers and soldiers that friendship which arises from having shared with them, for a length of time, dangers, sufferings, and both good and evil fortune. We began by struggling together; our affairs have often been at the lowest possible ebb. It is gratifying to me to crown this work with them, by giving the European troops a high idea of the soldiers who have been formed with us. To all these various motives of interest for the cause and army, are joined my sentiments of regard for General Washington: amongst his aides-de-camp there is one man I like very much, and of whom I have often spoken to you; this is Colonel Hamilton.

I depend on Colonel Laurens to give you the details of our campaign. We remained sufficiently near the English to merit the accusation of boldness; but they would not take advantage of any of the opportunities we offered them. We are all in winter quarters in this part of the country. There is some activity in the south, and I was preparing to go there; but the wishes of General Washington, and the hope of being useful to my countrymen, have detained me here. The corps I command having returned to the regiments, I have established myself at head-quarters. America made great efforts last summer, and has renewed them this winter, but in a more durable manner, by only making engagements for the war, and I trust that none will have cause to be dissatisfied with us.

Arnold, who has now become an English general, landed in Virginia, with a corps, which appears well pleased to serve under his orders. There is no accounting for taste; but I do not feel sorry, I own, to see our enemies rather degrade themselves, by employing one of our generals, whose talents, even before we knew his treachery, we held in light estimation: abilities must, in truth, be rare in New York. But whilst speaking of baseness, Colonel Laurens will tell you of the fine embassy sent by General Clinton to some mutinous soldiers. He will describe to you also the details of that mutiny; the means employed to arrest it with the Pennsylvanians, and also those we employed with the Jersey troops. This only proves, however, that human patience has its limits, as no European army would endure the tenth part of such sufferings, that *citizens* alone can support nudity, hunger, cold, labour, and the absolute want of that pay which is necessary to soldiers, who are more hardy and more patient, I believe, than any others in existence.

Embrace our children a thousand and a thousand times for me; their father, although a wanderer, is not less tender, not less constantly occupied with them, and not less happy at receiving news from them. My heart dwells with peculiar delight on the moment when those dear children will be presented to me by you, and when we may embrace and caress them together. Do you think that Anastasia will recollect me? Embrace tenderly for me my dear and amiable viscountess, Madame du Roure, my two sisters, de Noailles and d'Ayen, &c. &c.

TO GENERAL WASHINGTON.

(ORIGINAL.)

Elk, March the 8th, 1781.

My dear General,—Your letter of the 1st inst. did not come to hand until last evening, and I hasted to answer to its contents, though I should, in a few hours, be better able to inform you of my movements.* From what I hear of the difficulties to convoy us down the bay, I very much apprehend

* An instruction of the 20th of February, enjoined to General Lafayette to take the command of a detachment assembled at Peekskill, to act in conjunction with the militia, and some vessels of M. Destouches. He was to proceed by a rapid march to Hampton, on the Chesapeak bay, to surprise Arnold at Portsmouth: he had orders to return back immediately if he learnt that the latter had quitted Virginia, or that the French com-

that the winds will not permit any frigate to come up. Count de Rochambeau thinks his troops equal to the business, and wishes that they alone may display their zeal and shed their blood for an expedition which all America has so much at heart. The measures he is taking may be influenced by laudable motives, but I suspect they are not entirely free from selfish considerations. God grant this may not be productive of bad consequences. Baron de Viomenil will also want to do everything alone. As to the French troops, their zeal is laudable, and I wish their chiefs would reserve it for the time when we may co-operate with an assurance of success.

I heartily feel, my dear general, for the honour of our arms, and think it would be derogatory to them had not this detachment some share in the enterprise. This consideration induces me to embark immediately, and our soldiers will gladly put up with the inconveniences that attend the scarcity of vessels. We shall have those armed ones (though the largest has only twelve guns) and with this

mander had lost his naval superiority. M. de Lafayette reached Pompton the 23rd, (from whence he wrote to the general-in-chief,) Philadelphia the 2nd, and Head-of-Elk the 3rd of March. Washington, however, had himself repaired to Newport to urge the departure of M. Destouches, which event he announced in a letter of the 11th. The result of his encounter on the 16th with Admiral Arbuthnot was to oblige the squadron to return to Newport, and M. de Lafayette to begin his retreat on the 24th. He spoke himself in the following terms of the expedition of which this letter treats: —

"Dr. Ramsay and Mr. Marshall speak of the expedition attempted against Arnold, and the circumstances which caused its failure. Lafayette's detachment was composed of twelve hundred of those soldiers of light infantry which had formed, the preceding year, the advance guard of the army: these were drawn from regiments of the four states of New England and Jersey: Gordon has truly related that, after conducting them by water from every body assures us that we may go without any danger to Annapolis. For my part I am not yet determined what to do; but if I see no danger to our small fleet in going to Annapolis, and if I can get Commodore Nicholson to take the command of it, I shall perhaps proceed in a small boat to Hampton, where my presence can alone enable me to procure a frigate, and where I will try to cool the impetuosity or correct the political mistakes of both barons.*

Whichever determination I take, a great deal must be personally risked, but I hope to manage things so as to commit no imprudence with the excellent detachment whose glory is as dear, and whose safety is much dearer, to me than my own. I have written to General Greene, and will write to the governors, either to get intelligence or to prepare means to operate; but (General Greene excepted) I do not give them any hint of our intentions further than the expedition against Portsmouth.

When a man has delicate games to play, and when chance may influence so much his success or miscarriage, he must submit to blame in case

Head-of-Elk to Annapolis, he went himself in an open canoe to Elizabethtown to accelerate the preparations. The expedition having failed, he was obliged to return to Annapolis, where his continental troops had remained, vainly expecting that the French frigates would come to escort them. It was a bold and skilful stroke in him to take advantage of a favourable moment to convoy the American flotilla from Annapolis to Head-of-Elk, and the detachment had scarcely arrived when General Washington, announcing to him that General Phillips, with more than two thousand chosen men, had gone to reinforce Arnold, and take the command in Virginia, which was to become the centre of active operations, desired him to defend the state as well and as long as the weakness of his means allowed.—(Manuscript, No. 2.)

* Viomenil and Steuben.

›f misfortune. But your esteem, my dear general, nd your affection, will not depend upon events. Vith the highest respect and most tender friend-hip, &c.

TO GENERAL WASHINGTON.

(ORIGINAL.)

On board the *Dolphin*, March 9th, 1781.

My dear General,—Here I am at the mouth of Elk River, and the fleet under my command will proceed to Annapolis, where I am assured they can go without danger. .They are protected by the *Nesbitt*, of twelve guns, some field-pieces on board the vessel that carries Colonel Stevens, and we are going to meet an eight-gun and a six-gun-vessel from Baltimore. With this escort, we may go as far as Annapolis. No vessel of the enemy ever ventured so far up, and if by chance they should, our force is superior to any cruizer they have in the bay. At Annapolis we shall meet Commodore Nicholson, whom I have requested, by a letter, to take the general command of our fleet, and if there was the least danger, to proceed farther down. They are to remain at Annapolis until I send them new orders.

As to myself, my dear general, I have taken a small boat armed with swivels, and on board of which I have put thirty soldiers. I will precede the fleet to Annapolis, where I am to be met by intelligence, and conformable to the state of things below, will determine my personal movements and those of the fleet.

With a full conviction that (unless you arrived in

time at Rhode Island) no frigate will be sent to us I think it my duty to the troops I command, and the country I serve, to overlook some little personal danger, that I may ask for a frigate myself; and in order to add weight to my application, I have clapped on board my boat the only son of the minister of the French Navy, whom I shall take out to speak if circumstances require it.

Our men were much crowded at first, but I unload the vessels as we go along, and take possession of every boat that comes in my way.

These are, my dear general, the measures I thought proper to take. The detachment is, I hope, free from danger, and my caution on this point has been so far as to be called timidity by every seaman I have consulted. Captain Martin, of the *Nesbitt*, who has been recommended by General Gist, makes himself answerable for the safe arrival of the fleet at Annapolis before to-morrow evening.

I have the honour to be, &c.

TO GENERAL WASHINGTON.

(ORIGINAL.)

Williamsburg, March the 23rd 1781.

MY DEAR GENERAL,—By former letters your excellency has been acquainted with my motions, from my arrival at the head of Elk to the time of my landing at this place. The march of the detachment to Elk had been very rapid and performed in the best order. Owing to the activity of Lieutenant-Colonel Stevens, a train of artillery had been provided at Philadelphia, and notwithstanding some disappointments, namely, that relating to the want of vessels, no delay should have been imputed to us in this co-operation. Having received your excellency's letter, by which the sailing of the French fleet became a matter of certainty, I determined to transport the detachment to Annapolis, and did it for many essential reasons. The navigation of the bay is such that the going in and the going out of Elk River requires a different wind from those which are fair to go up and down the bay. Our stopping at Annapolis, and making some preparations on the road to Carolina, might be of use to deceive the enemy. But above all, I thought, with your excellency, that it was important, both to the success of the operation and the honour of our arms, that the detachment should be brought to co-operate, and from the time when the French were to sail and the winds that blew for some days, I had no doubt but that our allies were in the Chesapeak, before we could arrive at Annapolis.

Owing to the good disposition of Commodore Nicholson, whom I requested to take charge of our small fleet, the detachment was safely lodged in the harbour of Annapolis; and in the conviction that my presence here was necessary, not so much for preparations which Baron de Steuben provided, as for settling our plans with the French, and obtaining an immediate convoy for the detachment, I thought it better to run some risk than to neglect anything that could forward the success of the operation, and the glory of the troops under my command.

On my arrival at this place, I was surprised to hear that no French fleet had appeared, but attributed it to delays and chances so frequent in naval matters. My first object was to request that nothing be taken for this expedition which could have been intended for, or useful to, the southern army, whose welfare appeared to me more interesting than our success. My second object has been to examine what had been prepared, to gather and forward every requisite for a vigorous co-operation, besides a number of militia amounting to five thousand; I can assure your excellency that nothing has been wanting to ensure a complete success.

As the position of the enemy had not yet been reconnoitred, I went to General Muhlenberg's camp, near Suffolk, and after he had taken a position nearer to Portsmouth, we marched down with some troops to view the enemy's works. This brought on a trifling skirmish, during which we were able to see something; but the insufficiency of ammunition, which had been for many days expected, prevented my engaging far enough to push the enemy's outposts, and our reconnoitring was postponed to the 21st,—when, on the 20th, Major Mac Pherson, an officer for whom I have the highest confidence and esteem, sent me word from Hampton, where he was stationed, that a fleet had come to anchor within the Capes. So far it was probable that this fleet was that of M. Destouches, that Arnold himself appeared to be in great confusion, and his vessels, notwithstanding many signals, durst not, for a long time, venture down. An officer of the French navy bore down upon them from York, and nothing could equal my surprise in hearing from Major Mac Pherson, that the fleet announced by a former letter certainly belonged to the enemy.

Upon this intelligence, the militia were removed to their former position, and I requested Baron de Steuben (from whom, out of delicacy, I would not take the command until the co-operation was begun, or the continental troops arrived) to take such measures as would put out of the enemy's reach the several articles that had been prepared. On my return to this place, I could not hear more particular accounts of the fleet. Some people think they are coming from Europe; but I believe them to be the fleet from Gardiner's Bay. They are said to be twelve sail in all, frigates included. I have sent spies on board and shall forward their report to head-quarters.

Having certain accounts that the French had sailed on the 8th, with a favourable wind, I must think that they are coming to this place, or were beaten in an engagement, or are gone somewhere else. In these three cases, I think it my duty to stay here until I hear something more, which must be in a little time. But as your excellency will certainly recal a detachment composed of the flower of each regiment, whose loss would be immense to the army under your immediate command, and as my instructions are to march them back as soon as we lose the naval superiority in this quarter, I have sent them orders to move at the first notice which I will send to-morrow or the day after, or upon a letter from your excellency, which my aide-de-camp is empowered to open.

Had I not been here upon the spot, I am sure that I should have waited an immense time before I knew what to think of this fleet, and my presence at this place was the speediest means of forwarding the detachment either to Hampton or your excellency's immediate army. By private letters, we hear that General Greene had, on the 19th, an engagement with Lord Cornwallis. The honour of keeping the field was not on our side. The enemy lost more men than we did. General Greene displayed his usual prudence and abilities, both in making his dispositions and posting his troops at ten miles from the first field of battle, where they bid defiance to the enemy, and are in a situation to check his progress.

FROM GENERAL WASHINGTON TO THE MARQUIS DE LAFAYETTE.

(ORIGINAL.)

New Windsor, 6th April, 1781.

MY DEAR MARQUIS,—Since my letter to you of yesterday,* I have attentively considered of what vast importance it will be to reinforce General Greene as speedily as possible; more especially as there can be little doubt that the detachment under General Phillips, if not part of that now under the command of General Arnold, will ultimately join, or in some degree co-operate with Lord Cornwallis. I have communicated to the general officers at present with the army my sentiments on the subject; and they are unanimously of opinion that the detachment under your command should proceed and join the southern army. Your being already three hundred miles advanced, which is nearly half way, is the reason that operates against any which can be offered in favour of marching that detachment back. You will therefore, immediately at the receipt of this, turn the detachment to the southward. Inform

* This related merely to the expedition which had lately failed. Washington deplored its result, which had been occasioned by maritime events, but he approved and eulogised the conduct of M. de Lafayette.

General Greene that you are upon your march to join him, and take his directions as to your route, when you begin to approach him. Previously to that, you will be guided by your own judgment, and by the roads on which you will be most likely to find subsistence for the troops and horses. It will be well to advise Governor Jefferson of your intended march through the state of Virginia, or, perhaps, it will answer a good purpose were you to go forward to Richmond yourself, after putting the troops in motion, and having made some necessary arrangement for their progress.

You will take with you the light artillery and smallest mortars, with their stores and the musket cartridges. But let these follow, under a proper escort, rather than impede the march of the detachment, which ought to move as expeditiously as possible without injury to them. The heavy artillery and stores you will leave at some proper and safe place, if it cannot be conveniently transported to Christiana River, from whence it will be easily got to Philadelphia. You may leave to the option of Lieutenant-Colonel Stevens to proceed or not, as he may think proper ; his family is in peculiar circumstances, and he left it with the expectation of being absent for a short time. Should there be other officers under similar circumstances, you may make them the same offers, and they shall be relieved.

I am, my dear marquis, yours, &c.

TO GENERAL WASHINGTON.

(ORIGINAL.)

Elk, April 8th, 1781.

My dear General,—Your excellency's letters of the 5th and 6th instant are just come to hand, and before I answer their contents, I beg leave to give you a summary account of the measures I have lately taken. As to the part of my conduct you have been acquainted with, I am happy, my dear general, to find it has met with your approbation.

When the return of the British fleet put it out of doubt that nothing could be undertaken for the present against Portsmouth, I sent pressing orders to Annapolis, in order to have everything in readiness, and even to move the troops by land to the Head-of-Elk. I myself hastened back to Maryland, but confess I could not resist the ardent desire I had of seeing your relations, and, above all, your mother, at Fredericksburg. For that purpose I went some miles out of my way, and, in order to conciliate my private happiness to duties of a public nature, I recovered by riding in the night those few hours which I had consecrated to my satisfaction. I had also the pleasure of seeing Mount Vernon, and was very unhappy that my duty and my anxiety for the execution of your orders prevented my paying a visit to Mr. Curtis.*

On my arrival at Annapolis, I found that our preparations were far from promising a speedy departure. The difficulty of getting wagons and horses is immense. No boats sufficient to cross over the ferries. The state is very desirous of

* Son of Mrs. Washington by a former marriage.

keeping us as long as possible, as they were scared by the apparition of the *Hope*, twenty guns, and the *Monk*, eighteen guns, who blockaded the harbour, and who (as appeared by intercepted letters) were determined to oppose our movements.

In these circumstances, I thought it better to continue my preparations for a journey by land, which, I am told, would have lasted ten days, on account of ferries, and, in the meanwhile, had two eighteen-pounders put on board a small sloop, which appeared ridiculous to some, but proved to be of great service. In the morning of the 6th, Commodore Nicholson went out with the sloop and another vessel, full of men. Whether the sound of eighteen pounders, or the fear of being boarded, operated upon the enemy, I am not able to say; but, after some manœuvres, they retreated so far as to render it prudent for us to sail to this place. Every vessel with troops and stores was sent in the night by the commodore, to whom I am vastly obliged; and having brought the rear with the sloop and other vessels, I arrived this morning at Elk. It is reported that the ships have returned to their stations; if so, they must have been reinforced; their commander had already applied for an augmentation of force.

Before I left Annapolis, hearing that General Greene was in want of ammunition, I took the liberty of leaving for the southern army four six-pounders, with three hundred rounds each, nearly a hundred thousand cartridges, and some small matters, which I left to the care of the governor and General Smallwood, requesting them to have wagons and horses impressed, to send them to a place of safety, where they must be by this time. I also wrote to the governor of Virginia, to General

Greene, and the baron. These stores will set off in a few days, under the care of a detachment, for the Maryland line, commanded by Lieutenant-Colonel Stuart.

In consequence of previous orders, everything was in readiness for our movement. The troops were ordered to march the next morning, and I expect a sufficiency of vessels is now at Wilmington or Christiana Creek; so that I am in hopes to join your excellency in a very few days. Your letter of the 6th, ordering me to the southward, is just come to hand. Had I been still at Annapolis, or upon the road by land, and of course with the same means to return that I had to advance, your commands should have been immediately obeyed; but necessity keeps us here for some days, and as your letters arrived in two days, your answer to this must be here before we are in a situation to move.

When your excellency wrote to me, I was supposed to be at Annapolis, or very near that place, with the means of returning, which makes a great difference. Another circumstance, still more material, is, that, instead of joining either Arnold or Phillips (if Phillips be there), Lord Cornwallis is so disabled as to be forced to a retreat, as appears from General Greene's letter.

To these considerations I have added this one, which is decisive: that being fitted only to march twelve miles, part of it in the State of Delaware, and a part of our provisions being asked for from Philadelphia, it is impossible to have the necessary apparatus to march and subsist, or to cross ferries on our way to the southern army, so as to leave this place under four or five days. As to a transportation through the bay, we cannot expect the same good luck of frightening an enemy, who must know how despicable our preparations are ; and we must, at least, wait for the return of look-out boats which, if sent immediately, will not possibly return under five or six days.

In these circumstances, my dear general, I am going to make every preparation to march to Virginia, so as to be ready as soon as possible. I shall keep here the vessels, and will also keep those which have been ordered to Christiana Creek. This state of suspense will distract the enemy's conjectures, and put me in a situation to execute your excellency's orders, which will be here before I can be able to move with any degree of advantage towards the southward.

Had it been possible to obey to-morrow morning, I would have done it immediately ; but since I am obliged to make preparations, I beg leave to make these observations, which I should have been allowed to present, had I been at the meeting of general officers.

The troops I have with me being taken from every northern regiment, have often (though without mentioning it) been very uneasy at the idea of joining the southern army. They want clothes ; shoes particularly ; they expect to receive clothes and money from their states. This would be a great disappointment for both officers and men. Both thought at first they were sent out for a few days, and provided themselves accordingly ; both came cheerfully to this expedition, but both have had already their fears at the idea of going to the southward. They will certainly obey, but they will be unhappy, and some will desert.

Had this corps considered themselves as light infantry, destined for the campaign, to be separated from their regiments, it would be attended with less inconveniences ; and such a corps, in the course of the campaign, might be brought there without difficulty, particularly by water, as they would be prepared accordingly.

Supposing the Jersey line were to join the detachment of their troops at this place, it would hardly make any difference, as we have been but five days coming from Morristown to the Head-of-Elk.

These considerations, my dear general, I beg you to be convinced, are not influenced by personal motives. I should most certainly prefer to be in a situation to attack New York, nor should I like, in an operation against New-York, to see you deprived of the New England light infantry ; but I think with you, that these motives are not to influence our determination, if this be the best way to help General Greene.

By the letters I have received from my two friends, Marquis de Castries and Count de Vergennes, I am assured that we shall soon get an answer to our propositions against New York, and am strongly led to hope that, having a naval superiority, the army under your immediate command will not remain inactive.

At all events, my dear general, I will use my best endeavours to be ready to move either way as soon as possible ; and have the honour to be, with the highest respect and affection, &c.

TO COLONEL HAMILTON.

(ORIGINAL.)

Susquehannah Ferry, 18th April, 1781.

DEAR HAMILTON,*—You are so sensible a fellow, that you can certainly explain to me what is the matter that New York should be given up; that our letters to France go for nothing; that when the French are coming, I am going. This last matter gives great uneasiness to the minister of France. All this is not comprehensible to me, who, having been long from head-quarters, have lost the course of intelligence.

Have you left the family, my dear sir? I suppose so. But from love to the general, for whom you know my affection, I ardently wish it was not the case. Many, many reasons conspire to this desire of mine; but if you do leave it, and if I go to exile, come and partake it with me. Yours, &c.

* The 11th of April, Washington renewed, with more detail, his instructions upon the movement to the south, and General Greene, desiring to carry the theatre of war into South Carolina, urged General Lafayette to march upon the capital of Virginia. The latter made his preparations accordingly, and with great activity, in spite of the regret he experienced, and the difficulties he encountered. He deplored, in truth, that long-promised expedition on New York being abandoned; and he had to combat the repugnance of the troops, who threatened to become weakened by desertion. This was the subject of several long letters we have thought proper to suppress. He wrote, also, frequently, to Colonel Hamilton, and we may see some of those letters in the life of the latter. We have only inserted this one letter, which expresses all he felt. Hamilton, at that period, having had a coolness with Washington, wished to quit his staff; and it was in reality as an officer of the line that he took part in the siege of Yorktown.—(See his Life, vol. i., chap. xiii.)

TO GENERAL WASHINGTON.

(ORIGINAL.)

Baltimore, April 18th, 1781.

My dear General,—Every one of my letters were written in so lamentable a tone, that I am happy to give you a pleasanter prospect. The anxiety I feel to relieve your mind from a small part of those many solicitudes and cares which our circumstances conspire to gather upon you, is the reason of my sending this letter by the chain of communication, and with a particular recommendation. When I left Susquehannah Ferry, it was the general opinion that we could not have six hundred men by the time we should arrive at our destination. This, and the shocking situation of the men offered the more gloomy prospects, as the board of war have confessed their total inability to afford us relief. Under these circumstances, I have employed every personal exertion, and have the pleasure to inform you that desertion has, I hope, been put to an end.

On my arrival on this side of the Susquehannah, I made an order for the troops, wherein I endeavoured to throw a kind of infamy upon desertion, and to improve every particular affection of theirs. Since then, desertion has been lessened. Two deserters have been taken up; one of whom has been hanged to-day, and the other (being an excellent soldier) will be forgiven, but dismissed from the corps, as well as another soldier who behaved amiss. To these measures, I have added one which my feelings for the sufferings of the soldiers, and the peculiarity of their circumstances, have prompted me to adopt. The merchants of Baltimore lent me a sum of about 2,000*l.*, which will procure some shirts, linen, overalls, shoes, and a few hats. The ladies will make up the shirts, and the overalls will be made by the detachment, so that our soldiers have a chance of being a little more comfortable. The money is lent upon my credit, and I become security for the payment of it in two years' time, when, by the French laws, I may better dispose of my estate. But before that time, I shall use my influence with the French court, in order to have this sum of money added to any loan congress may have been able to obtain from them.

In case you are told, my dear general, that my whole baggage has been taken in the bay, I am sorry I cannot discountenance the report. But when the mention of papers and maps is made, do not apprehend anything bad for the papers or maps you have put in my possession. Nothing has been lost but writing paper and printed maps. The fact is this: when at York, I had some continental soldiers and my baggage to send up in a safe barge and an unsafe boat. I, of course, gave the barge to the soldiers, who easily went to Annapolis. The baggage was put into the boat, and has not been since heard of. But being aware of the danger, I took by land with me every article that was, on public accounts, in the least valuable. By a letter from Baron de Steuben, dated Chesterfield Court House the 10th of April, I find that General Phillips has at Portsmouth 1500 or 2000 men added to the force under Arnold. Proper allowance being made for exaggerations, I apprehend that his whole army amounts to 2800 men, which obliges me to hasten my march to Fredericksburg and Richmond, where I expect to receive orders from General Greene.

The importance of celerity, the desire of lengthening the way home, and immense delays that would stop me for an age, have determined me to leave our tents, artillery, &c., under a guard, and with orders to follow as fast as possible, while the rest of the detachment, by forced marches, and with impressed wagons and horses, will hasten to Fredericksburg or Richmond, and by this derange the calculations of the enemy. We set off to-morrow, and this rapid mode of travelling, added to my other precautions, will, I hope, keep up our spirits and good humour.*

I am, my dear general, &c.

P. S. The word *lessened* does not convey a sufficient idea of what experience has proved to be true, to the honour of our excellent soldiers. It had been announced in general orders, that the detachment was intended to fight an enemy far superior in number, under difficulties of every sort. That the general was, for his part, determined to en-

* This letter announces the real commencement of the Virginian campaign. M. de Lafayette marched upon Richmond, and thus wrote on the 4th of May:—

"The leaving of my artillery appears a strange whim, but had I waited for it, Richmond had been lost. It is not without trouble I have made this rapid march. General Phillips has expressed to a flag officer the astonishment he felt at our celerity; and when on the 30th, as he was going to give the signal to attack, he reconnoitred our position, Mr. Osburn, who was with him, says, that he flew into a violent passion, and swore vengeance against me and the corps I had brought with me."

The subsequent operations are given in detail, both in the Memoirs, and in a relation of the campaign; it was, therefore, thought proper to suppress the greatest part of the letters in which M. de Lafayette gave an account of them to General Washington. To each of those letters is usually annexed a copy of his official reports to General Greene.

counter them, but that such of the soldiers as had an inclination to abandon him, might dispense with the danger and crime of desertion, as every one of them who should apply to head-quarters for a pass to join their corps in the north might be sure to obtain it immediately.

TO GENERAL WASHINGTON.

(ORIGINAL.)

Alexandria, April 23rd, 1781.

MY DEAR GENERAL,—Great happiness is derived from friendship, and I experience it particularly in the attachment which unites me to you. But friendship has its duties, and the man who likes you best, will be the first to let you know everything in which you may be concerned.

When the enemy came to your house, many negroes deserted to them. This piece of news did not affect me much, as I little value these matters. But you cannot conceive how unhappy I have been to hear that Mr. Lund Washington went on board the enemy's vessels, and consented to give them provisions.

This being done by the gentleman who, in some measure, represents you at your house, will certainly have a bad effect, and contrasts with spirited answers from some neighbours that have had their houses burnt accordingly.

You will do what you think proper about it, my dear general; but, as your friend, it was my duty confidentially to mention the circumstances.

With the help of some wagons and horses, we got, in two days, from the camp, near Baltimore, to this place. We halted yesterday, and having made a small bargain for a few pair of shoes, are now marching to Fredericksburg. No official account from Phillips, but I am told they are removing stores from Richmond and Petersburg. I am surprised nobody writes to me, and hope soon to receive intelligence.

Our men are in high spirits. Their honour having been interested in this affair, they have made a point to come with us; and murmurs, as well as desertion, are entirely out of fashion. Requesting my best respects to Mrs. Washington, and my compliments to the family, I have the honour to be, with those sentiments which you know, &c.

FROM GENERAL WASHINGTON TO MARQUIS DE LAFAYETTE.

(ORIGINAL.)

New Windsor, May 4, 1781.

My dear Marquis,—The freedom of your communications is an evidence to me of the sincerity of your attachment, and every fresh instance of this gives pleasure and adds strength to the bond which unites us in friendship. In this light I view the intimation respecting the conduct of Mr. Lund Washington. Some days previous to the receipt of your letter, which only came to my hands yesterday, I received an account of this transaction from that gentleman himself, and immediately wrote and forwarded the answer, of which the enclosed is a copy. This letter, which was written in the moment of my obtaining the first intimation of the matter, may be considered as a testimony of my disapprobation of his conduct, and the transmission of it to you, as a proof of my friendship; because I wish you to be assured, that no man can condemn the measure more sincerely than I do.

A false idea, arising from the consideration of his being my steward, and in that character more the trustee and guardian of my property than the representative of my honour, has misled his judgment and plunged him into error, upon the appearance of desertion among my negroes, and danger to my buildings; for sure I am, that no man is more firmly opposed to the enemy than he is. From a thorough conviction of this, and of his integrity, I entrusted every species of my property to his care, without reservation or fear of his abusing it. The last paragraph of my letter to him was occasioned by an expression of his fear, that all the estates convenient to the river would be stripped of their negroes and moveable property.

I am very happy to find that desertion has ceased, and content has taken place, in the detachment you command. Before this letter can reach you, you must have taken your ultimate resolution upon the proposal contained in my letters of the 21st and 22nd ultimo, and have made the consequent arrangements. I shall be silent, therefore, on the subject of them, and only beg, in case you should not return to this army, and the papers were not lost with your other baggage (on which event give me leave to express my concern) that you would permit M. Capitaine to furnish me with copies of the drafts, and the remarks of the pilots (taken at Colonel Day's) on the entrance of the harbour of New York. It is possible they may be wanted, and I am not able to furnish them without your assistance.

Mrs. Washington and the rest of my small family,

which, at present, consists only of Tilghman and Humphreys, join me in cordial salutations, and, with sentiments of the purest esteem and most affectionate regard, I remain, my dear marquis, &c.

FROM GENERAL WASHINGTON TO LUND WASHINGTON.

(ORIGINAL.)

New Windsor, April 30, 1781.

Dear Lund,—I am very sorry to hear of your loss; I am a little sorry to hear of my own; but that which gives me most concern is, that you should go on board the enemy's vessels, and furnish them with refreshments. It would have been a less painful circumstance to me to have heard that, in consequence of your non-compliance with their request, they had burnt my house and laid the plantation in ruins. You ought to have considered yourself as my representative, and should have reflected on the bad example of communicating with the enemy, and making a voluntary offer of refreshments to them, with a view to prevent a conflagration.

It was not in your power, I acknowledge, to prevent them from sending a flag on shore, and you did right to meet it; but you should, in the same instant that the business of it was unfolded, have declared explicitly, that it was improper for you to yield to the request; after which, if they had proceeded to help themselves by force, you could but have submitted, and, being unprovided for defence, this was to be preferred to a feeble opposition, which only serves as a pretext to burn and destroy.

I am thoroughly persuaded that you acted from your best judgment, and believe that your desire to preserve my property, and rescue the buildings from impending danger, was your governing motive; but to go on board their vessels, carry them refreshments, commune with a parcel of plundering scoundrels, and request a favour by asking a surrender of my negroes, was exceedingly ill judged, and, it is to be feared, will be unhappy in its consequences, as it will be a precedent for others, and, may be, become a subject of animadversion.

I have no doubt of the enemy's intention to prosecute the plundering plan they have begun; and, unless a stop can be put to it by the arrival of a superior naval force, I have as little doubt of its ending in the loss of all my negroes, and in the destruction of my houses. But I am prepared for the event, under the prospect of which, if you could deposit in a place of safety the most valuable and less bulky articles, it might be consistent with policy and prudence, and a means of preserving them hereafter. Such and so many things as are necessary for common and present use must be retained, and must run their chance through the fiery trial of this summer. I am sincerely, yours.

TO GENERAL WASHINGTON.

(ORIGINAL.)

Camp Wilton, on James River, May 17, 1781.

DEAR GENERAL,—My correspondence with one of the British generals, and my refusal of a correspondence with the other, may be, perhaps, misrepresented, I shall therefore give an account of what has passed, and I hope your excellency and General Greene will approve of my conduct. On the arrival of our detachment at Richmond, three letters were brought by a flag, which I have the honour to inclose, and which, as commander of the troops in this state, it became my duty to answer. The enclosed letters were successively sent in pursuit of General Phillips, who received them both with a degree of politeness that seemed to apologize for his unbecoming style. General Phillips being dead of a fever, an officer was sent with a passport and letters from General Arnold. I requested the gentleman to come to my quarters, and having asked *if General Phillips was dead,** to which he answered

* Gordon places the death of General Phillips on the 13th of May: he was very ill in his bed, when a cannon ball traversed his bed-room.

General Phillips commanded at Minden the battery whose cannon killed the father of M. de Lafayette.

in the negative, I made it a pretence not to receive a letter from General Arnold, which, being dated head-quarters, and directed to the commanding officer of the American troops, ought to come from the British general chief in command. I did, however, observe, should any officers have written to me I should have been happy to receive their letters. The next day the officer returned with the same passport and letter, and informed me that he were now at liberty to declare that Phillips was dead, and Arnold was commander-in-chief of the British army in Virginia. The high station of General Arnold having obliged me to an explanation, the enclosed note was sent to the officer of the flag, and the American officer verbally assured him that were I requested to put in writing a minute account of my motives, my regard for the British army was such that I would cheerfully comply with the demand.

Last evening, a flag of ours returned from Petersburg, who had been sent by the commander of the advanced corps, and happened to be on his way while the British officer was at our picquets. Inclosed is the note written by General Arnold, in which he announces his determination of sending our officers and men to the West Indies.

The British general cannot but perfectly know that I am not to treat of partial exchanges, and that the fate of the continental prisoners must be regulated by a superior authority to that with which I am invested.

With the highest respect, I have the honour to be, &c.

FROM GENERAL PHILLIPS TO THE MARQUIS DE LAFAYETTE.

(ORIGINAL.)

British Camp, at Osborn, April 28, 1781.

SIR,—It is a principle of the British army engaged in the present war, which they esteem as an unfortunate one, to conduct it with every attention to humanity and the laws of war; and in the necessary destruction of public stores of every kind, to prevent, as far as possible, that of private property. I call upon the inhabitants of Yorktown, Williamsburg, Petersburg, and Chesterfield, for a proof of the mild treatment they have received from the king's troops; in particular at Petersburg, when the town was saved by the labour of the soldiers, which otherwise must have perished by the wilful inactivity of its inhabitants.

I have now a charge of the deepest nature to make against the American arms: that of having fired upon the king's troops by a flag of truce vessel; and, to render the conduct as discordant to the laws of arms, the flag was flying the whole time at the mast head, seeming to sport in the violation of the most sacred laws of war.

You are sensible, sir, that I am authorized to inflict the severest punishment in return for this bad conduct, and that towns and villages lay at the mercy of the king's troops, and it is to that mercy alone you can justly appeal for their not being reduced to ashes. The compassion, and benevolence of disposition, which has marked the British character in the present contest, still govern the conduct of the king's officers, and I shall willingly remit the infliction of any redress we have a right to claim, provided the persons who fired from the flag of truce vessel are delivered into my possession, and a public disavowal made by you of their conduct. Should you, sir, refuse this, I hereby make you answerable for any desolation which may follow in consequence.

Your ships of war, and all other vessels, not actually in our possession in James River, are, however, driven beyond a possibility of escaping, and are in the predicament and condition of a town blockaded by land, where it is contrary to the rules of war that any public stores should be destroyed. I shall therefore demand from you, sir, a full account of whatever may be destroyed on board vessels or otherwise, and need not mention to you what the rules of war are in these cases.

I am, sir, your most humble servant,

W. Phillips.

FROM GENERAL PHILLIPS TO THE MARQUIS DE LAFAYETTE.

(original.)

Camp at Osborn, April 29th, 1781.

Sir,—When I was at Williamsburg, and at Petersburg, I gave several inhabitants and country people protections for their persons and properties. I did this without asking, or even considering, whether these people were either friends or foes, actuated by no other motive than that of pure humanity. I understand, from almost undoubted authority, that several of these persons have been taken up by their malicious neighbours, and sent to your quarters, where preparations are making for their being ill treated; a report which I sincerely hope may be without foundation. I repeat to you, sir, that my protections were given generally from a wish that, in the destruction of public stores, as little damage as possible might be done to private property, and to the persons of individuals; but at any rate, I shall insist upon my signs manual being held sacred, and I am obliged to declare to you, sir, that if any persons, under the description I have given, receive ill treatment, I shall be under the necessity of sending to Petersburg, and giving that chastisement to the illiberal persecutors of innocent people, which their conduct shall deserve. And I further declare to you, sir, should any person be put to death, under the pretence of their being spies of, or friends to, the British government, I will make the shores of James River an example of terror to the rest of Virginia. It is from the violent measures, resolutions of the present house of delegates, council, and governor of Virginia, that I am impelled to use this language, which the common temper of my disposition is hurt at. I shall hope that you, sir, whom I have understood to be a gentleman of liberal principles, will not countenance, still less permit to be carried into execution, the barbarous spirit which seems to prevail in the council of the present civil power of this colony.

I do assure you, sir, I am extremely inclined to carry on this unfortunate contest with every degree of humanity, and I will believe you intend doing the same.

I am, sir, your most obedient humble servant,

W. PHILLIPS.

TO MAJOR GENERAL PHILLIPS.

(ORIGINAL.)

American camp, April 30th, 1781.

SIR,—Your letters of the 26th, 28th, and 29th, came yesterday to hand. The duplicate dated at Petersburg being rather of a private nature, it has been delivered to Major-General Baron de Steuben. I am sorry the mode of your request has delayed the civility that had been immediately intended.

From the beginning of this war, which you observe is an unfortunate one to Great Britain, the proceedings of the British troops have been hitherto so far from evincing benevolence of disposition, that your long absence* from the scene of action is the only way I have to account for your panegyrics. I give you my honour, sir, that the charge against a flag vessel shall be strictly inquired into, and in case the report made to you is better grounded than the contrary one I have received, you shall obtain every redress in my power, that you have any right to expect. This complaint I beg leave to consider as the only part in your letter that requires an answer. Such articles as the requiring that the persons of spies be held sacred, cannot certainly be serious.

The style of your letters, sir, obliges me to tell you, that should your future favours be wanting in that regard due to the civil and military authority in the United States, which cannot but be construed into a want of respect to the American nation, I shall not think it consistent with the dignity of an American officer to continue the correspondence.

I have the honour to be, your most obedient servant,

LAFAYETTE.

* General Phillips had been made prisoner at Saratoga.

TO MAJOR GENERAL PHILLIPS.

(ORIGINAL.)

May 3rd, 1781.

SIR,—Your assertion relating to the flag vessel was so positive, that it becomes necessary for me to set you right in this matter. Inclosed I have the honour to send you some depositions, by which it is clearly proved that there has been on our side no violation of flags.

I have the honour to be, sir, your humble servant,

LAFAYETTE

NOTE FOR CAPTAIN EMYNE.

May 15th, 1781.

THE Major-General Marquis de Lafayette has the honour to present his compliments to Captain Emyne, and begs him to recollect that, on the supposition of the death of General Phillips, he said, "that he should know in that case what to do." From regard to the English army, he had made use of the most polite pretence for declining all correspondence with the English general who is at this moment commander-in-chief. But he now finds himself obliged to give a positive denial. In case any other English officer should honour him with a letter, he would always be happy to give the officers every testimony of his esteem.

NOTE FROM GENERAL ARNOLD TO CAPTAIN RAGEDALE.

BRIGADIER-GENERAL ARNOLD presents his compliments to Captain Ragedale, and takes the liberty of informing him, that the flag of truce having been sent by Brigadier-General Nelson, who is not commander-in-chief of the American army, is an inadmissible act. The letters are accordingly sent back unopened. If Captain Ragedale thinks proper to leave them with the servants, a receipt must be given for them.

Brigadier-General Arnold has given orders that the officers lately taken in that place should be sent to New York; their baggage will follow soon after them, and all the officers and soldiers of the American army that shall be taken prisoners in future, shall be sent to the West Indies, unless a cartel be immediately granted for the exchange of prisoners, as General Arnold has repeatedly demanded.

Head-quarters, at Petersburg, 17th May, 1781.

TO GENERAL WASHINGTON.

(ORIGINAL.)

Richmond, May 24th, 1781.

MY DEAR GENERAL,—My official letter, a copy of which I send to congress, will let you know the situation of affairs in this quarter. I ardently wish my conduct may meet with your approbation. Had I followed the first impulsion of my temper, I should have risked something more; but I have been guarding against my own warmth; and this consideration, that a general defeat, which, with such a proportion of militia, must be expected, would involve this state and our affairs in ruin, has rendered me extremely cautious in my movements. Indeed, I am more embarrassed to move, more crippled in my projects, than we have been in the northern states.

As I am for the present fixed in the command of the troops in this state, I beg it as a great favour that you will send me Colonel Gouvion. Should a junction be made with General Greene, he will act as my aide-de-camp. Had the Pennsylvanians arrived before Lord Cornwallis, I was determined to attack the enemy, and have no doubt but what we should have been successful. Their unaccountable delay cannot be too much lamented, and will make an immense difference to the fate of this campaign. Should they have arrived time enough to support me in the reception of Lord Cornwallis's first stroke, I should still have thought it well enough; but from an answer of General Wayne, received this day, and dated the 19th, I am afraid that at this moment they have hardly left Yorktown.

Public stores and private property being removed from Richmond, this place is a less important object.

I don't believe it would be prudent to expose the troops for the sake of a few houses, most of which are empty; but I am wavering between two inconveniences. Were I to fight a battle, I should be cut to pieces, the militia dispersed, and the arms lost. Were I to decline fighting, the country would think itself given up. I am therefore determined to skirmish, but not to engage too far, and particularly to take care against their immense and excellent body of horse, whom the militia fear as they would so many wild beasts.

A letter from General Greene to General Sumner is dated 5th May, seven miles below Camden. The baron is going to him with some recruits, and will get more in North Carolina. When the Pennsylvanians come, I am only to keep them a few days, which I will improve as well as I can. Cavalry is very necessary to us. I wish Lauzun's legion could come. I am sure he will like to serve with me, and as General Greene gave me command of the troops in this state, Lauzun might remain with me in Virginia. If not, Shelden's dragoons might be sent. As to Moylan, I do not believe he will be ready for a long time.

Were I anyways equal to the enemy, I should be extremely happy in my present command; but I am not strong enough even to get beaten. Government in this state has no energy, and laws have no force. But I hope this assembly will put matters upon a better footing. I had a great deal of trouble to put the departments in a tolerable train; our expenses were enormous, and yet we can get nothing. Arrangements for the present seem to put on a better face, but for this superiority of the enemy, which will chase us wherever they please. They can overrun the country, and, until the Pennsylvanians arrive, we are next to nothing in point of opposition to so large a force. This country begins to be as familiar to me as Tappan and Bergen. Our soldiers are hitherto very healthy: I have turned doctor, and regulate their diet. Adieu, my dear general. Let me hear sometimes from you; your letters are a great happiness to your affectionate friend, &c.

TO GENERAL WASHINGTON.

(ORIGINAL.)

Camp, 28th June, 1781.

My dear General,—Inclosed, I have the honour to send you a copy of my letter to General Greene. The enemy have been so kind as to retire before us.* Twice I gave them a chance of fighting (taking care not to engage farther than I pleased), but they continued their retrograde motions. Our

* It was the 20th of May that Lord Cornwallis effected his junction with the troops of Arnold, whose unexpected opposition re-established the affairs of the English in Virginia. The war became from that moment extremely active, and the movements of the two armies very complicated. M. de Lafayette maintained his position, and experienced no other check than the loss of some magazines, at the forks of James River, which had been confided to the care of Baron Steuben. His position was, however, rather a defensive one, until the period at which that letter was written, when the English abandoned Richmond. Cornwallis obtained, and usually by the aid of negroes, the best horses of Virginia. He had mounted an advance-guard of Tarleton on race-hores, who, like birds of prey, seized all they met with, so that they had taken many couriers who were bearers of letters. Cornwallis stopped once during his retrograde march on Williamsburg; the Americans being close to him, it was thought an affair would take place, but he continued on his road. It was before he reached Williamsburg that his rear-guard was

numbers are, I think, exaggerated to them, and our seeming boldness confirms the opinion. . . .

I thought, at first, Lord Cornwallis wanted to get me as low down as possible, and use his cavalry to advantage. But it appears that he does not as yet come out, and our position will admit of a partial affair. His lordship had (exclusive of the reinforcement from Portsmouth, said to be six hundred) four thousand men, eight hundred of whom were dragoons, or mounted infantry. Our force is about equal to his, but only one thousand five hundred regulars and fifty dragoons. Our little action more particularly marks the retreat of the enemy. From the place whence he first began to retire to Williamsburg is upwards of one hundred miles. The old arms at the Point of Fork have been taken out of the water. The cannon was thrown into the river, undamaged, when they marched back to Richmond; so that his lordship did us no harm of any consequence, but lost

attacked by the advance corps of Lafayette under Colonel Butler. He evacuated Williamsburg the 4th; Lafayette had done all he could to convince him that his own forces were more considerable than they really were. Either the night of, or two nights before, the evacuation of Williamsburg, a double spy had taken a false order of the day to Lord Cornwallis,—found, he said, in the camp,—which ordered General Morgan's division to take a certain position in the line. The fact was, that General Morgan had arrived in person, but unaccompanied by troops. Dr. Gordon justly observes, that Lord Cornwallis, from Charlestown to Williamsburg, had made more than eleven hundred miles, without counting deviations, which amounts, reckoning those deviations, to five hundred leagues. The whole march through North Carolina and Virginia, and the campaign against Lafayette, were effected without tents or equipages, which confers honour on the activity of Lord Cornwallis, and justifies the reputation he had acquired, of being the best British general employed in that war.—(Extract of Manuscript, No. 2.)

an immense part of his former conquests, and did not make any in this state. General Greene only demanded of me to hold my ground in Virginia. But the movements of Lord Cornwallis may answer better purposes than that in the political line. Adieu, my dear general; I don't know but what we shall, in our turn, become the pursuing enemy; and in the meanwhile, have the honour to be, &c.

EXTRACTS OF SEVERAL LETTERS TO GENERAL WASHINGTON.*

(ORIGINAL.)

Ambler's Plantation, July 8th, 1781.

The inclosed copy, my dear general, will give you an account of our affairs in this quarter. Agreeably to your orders I have avoided a general action, and when Lord Cornwallis's movements indicated that it was against his interest to fight, I ventured partial engagements. His lordship seems to have given up the conquest of Virginia. It has been a great secret that our army was not superior, and was most

* From Williamsburg, the English retreated towards Portsmouth, near the mouth of James River, and consequently not far from Chesapeak Bay. The sea was open to them, and those repeated retrograde movements seemed to indicate the project of evacuating Virginia. M. de Lafayette, therefore, when he learnt that they were embarking on board their ships, never doubted but that their intention was to leave that part of the country, to repair, in all probability, to New York. But it became evident, at the same time, that if those naval forces appeared upon the coast, they would be blockaded without any means of escape. This is what occasioned their inexplicable and unhoped for retreat upon Yorktown and Gloucester.

generally inferior, to the enemy's numbers. Our returns were swelled up, as militia returns generally are; but we had very few under arms, particularly lately, and to conceal the lessening of our numbers, I was obliged to push on as one who had heartily wished a general engagement. Our regulars did not exceed one thousand five hundred, the enemy had four thousand regulars, eight hundred of whom were mounted: they thought we had eight thousand men. I never encamped in a line, and there was greater difficulty to come at our numbers.

Malvan Hill, July 20th.

When I went to the southward, you know I had some private objections; but I became sensible of the necessity there was for the detachment to go, and I knew that had I returned there was nobody that could lead them on against their inclination. My entering this state was happily marked by a service to the capital. Virginia became the grand object of the enemy, as it was the point to which the ministry tended. I had the honour to command an army and oppose Lord Cornwallis. When incomparably inferior to him, fortune was pleased to preserve us; when equal in numbers, though not in quality of troops, we have also been pretty lucky. Cornwallis had the disgrace of a retreat, and this state being recovered, government is properly re-established. The enemy are under the protection of their works at Portsmouth. It appears an embarkation is taking place, probably destined to New York. The war in this state would then become a plundering one, and great manœuvres be out of the question. A prudent officer would do our business here, and the baron is prudent to the utmost. Would it be possible, my dear general, in case a part of the British troops go to New York, I may be allowed to join the combined armies?

Malvan Hill, July 20th.

No accounts from the northward, no letter from head quarters. I am entirely a stranger to every thing that passes out of Virginia; and Virginian operations being for the present in a state of languor, I have more time to think of my solitude; in a word, my dear general, I am home sick, and if I cannot go to head quarters, wish at least to hear from thence. I am anxious to know your opinion concerning the Virginian campaign. That the subjugation of this state was the great object of the ministry is an indisputable fact. I think your diversion has been of more use to the state than my manœuvres; but the latter have been much directed by political views. So long as my lord wished for an action, not one gun has been fired; the moment he declined it, we have been skirmishing; but I took care never to commit the army. His naval superiority, his superiority of horse, of regulars, his thousand advantages over us, so that I am lucky to have come off safe. I had an eye upon European negotiations, and made it a point to give his lordship the disgrace of a retreat.

From every account it appears that a part of the army will embark. The light infantry, the guards, the 80th regiment, and the Queen's rangers, are, it is said, destined to New York. Lord Cornwallis, I am told, is much disappointed in his hopes of command. I cannot find out what he does with himself. Should he go to England, we are, I think, to rejoice for it; he is a cold and active man, two dangerous qualities in this southern war.

The clothing you have long ago sent to the light

infantry is not yet arrived. I have been obliged to send for it, and expect it in a few days. These three battalions are the best troops that ever took the field; my confidence in them is unbounded; they are far superior to any British troops, and none will ever venture to meet them in equal numbers. What a pity these men are not employed along with the French grenadiers; they would do eternal honour to our arms. But their presence here, I must confess, has saved this state, and, indeed, the southern part of the continent.

Malvan Hill, July 26th.

I HAD some days ago the honour to write to your excellency, and informed you that a detachment from the British army would probably embark at Portsmouth. The battalions of light infantry and the Queen's rangers were certainly, and the guards, with one or two British regiments, were likely to be, ordered upon that service. My conjectures have proved true, and forty-nine sail have fallen down in Hampton-road, the departure of which I expect to hear every minute. A British officer, a prisoner, lately mentioned that Lord Cornwallis himself was going.

It appears the enemy have some cavalry on board. The conquest of Virginia, and the establishment of the British power in this state, not having succeeded to the expectation of the British court, a lesser number might be sufficient for the present purpose, and two thousand men easily spared. So that I do not believe the present embarkation is under that number; so far as a land force can oppose naval operations and naval superiority, I think the position now occupied by the main body of our small army affords the best chance to support the several parts of Virginia.

Malvan Hill, July 30th.

Some expressions in your last favour will, if possible, augment my vigilance in keeping you well apprised of the enemy's movements.* There are in Hampton-road thirty transport ships full of troops, most of them red coats. There are eight or ten brigs which have cavalry on board, they had excellent winds and yet they are not gone. Some say they have received advices from New York in a row boat: the escort, as I mentioned before, is the *Charon*, and several frigates, the last account says seven. I cannot be positive, and do not even think Lord Cornwallis has been fully determined.

I have sent, by a safe hand, to call out some militia, mount some cannon at the passes, and take out of the way every boat which might serve the enemy to go to North Carolina. You know, my dear general, that, with a very trifling transportation,

* The 13th, Washington, who was then at Dobb's Ferry, while congratulating M. de Lafayette on his success, announced to him the junction of his army with that of Rochambeau, and that very important information would be carried to him by a confidential officer. He recommended to him to concentrate his forces, and obtain means of corresponding with him. The 15th, he apprised him that the Count de Grasse intended quitting St. Domingo on the 3rd, with his fleet, to proceed to the Chesapeak, and prescribed to him to shut out from Lord Cornwallis all retreat on North Carolina. He added, "You shall hear further from me." The 30th, he no longer concealed his intention of marching to the south. But he only announced on the 21st of August that his troops were actually on their march. While recurring to the necessity of inclosing the enemy on every side, he ended by saying, "The particular mode I shall not at this distance attempt to dictate; your own knowledge of the country, from your long continuance in it, and the various and extended movements you have made, have given you great opportunities for observation; of which I am persuaded your military genius and judgment will lead you to make the best improvement."—(Letters of Washington, vol. viii.)

they may go by water from Portsmouth to Wilmington. The only way to shut up that passage is, to have an army before Portsmouth, and possess the heads of these rivers, a movement which, unless I was certain of a naval superiority, might prove ruinous. But should a fleet come in Hampton-road, and should I get some days' notice, our situation would be very agreeable.

Malvan Hill, July 31.

A correspondent of mine, servant to Lord Cornwallis, writes on the 26th of July, at Portsmouth, and says his master, Tarleton, and Simcoe, are still in town, but expect to move. The greatest part of the army is embarked. My lord's baggage is yet in town. His lordship is so shy of his papers that my honest friend says he cannot get at them. There is a large quantity of negroes, but, it seems, no vessels to take them off. What garrison they leave I do not know: I shall take care at least to keep them within bounds. . . . Should a French fleet now come in Hampton Road, the British army would, I think, be ours.

Camp on Pamunkey, August 6.

The embarkation which I thought, and do still think, to have been destined for New York, was reported to have sailed up the bay, and to be bound for Baltimore; in consequence of which I wrote to your excellency, and as I had not indulged myself too near Portsmouth, I was able to cut across towards Fredericksburg. But, instead of continuing his voyage up the bay, my lord entered York River, and landed at York and Gloucester. To the former vessels were added a number of flat-bottomed boats.

Our movements have not been precipitate. We were in time to take our course down Pamunkey River, and shall move to some position where the several parts of the army will unite. I have some militia in Gloucester county, some about York. We shall act agreeably to circumstances, but avoid drawing ourselves into a false movement, which, if cavalry had command of the rivers, would give the enemy the advantage of us. His lordship plays so well, that no blunder can be hoped from him to recover a bad step of ours.

York is surrounded by the river and a morass; the entrance is but narrow. There is, however, a commanding hill, (at least, I am so informed,) which, if occupied by the enemy, would much extend their works. Gloucester is a neck of land projected into the river, and opposite to York. Their vessels, the biggest of whom is a forty-four, are between the two towns. Should a fleet come in at this moment, our affairs would take a very happy turn.

New Kent Mountain, August 11.

Be sure, my dear general, that the pleasure of being with you will make me happy in any command you may think proper to give me; but for the present I am of opinion, with you, I had better remain in Virginia, the more so, as Lord Cornwallis does not choose to leave us, and circumstances may happen that will furnish me agreeable opportunities in the command of the Virginian army. I have pretty well understood you, my dear general, but would be happy in a more minute detail, which, I am sensible, cannot be entrusted to letters. Would not Gouvion be a proper ambassador? indeed, at all events, I should be happy to have him with me;

but I think he would perfectly well answer your purpose; a gentleman in your family could with difficulty be spared. Should something be ascertained, Count Damas might come, under pretence to serve with me; it is known he is very much my friend. But, to return to operations in Virginia, I will tell you, my dear general, that Lord Cornwallis is entrenching at York and at Gloucester. The sooner we disturb him, the better; but unless our maritime friends give us help, we cannot much venture below. . . . . . .

Forks of York River, August 21.

The greater part of the enemy are at York, which they do not as yet fortify, but are very busy upon Gloucester neck, where they have a pretty large corps under Colonel Dundas. They have at York a forty-four gun ship; frigates and vessels are scattered lower down. There is still a small garrison at Portsmouth. Should they intend to evacuate, they at least are proceeding with amazing slowness. From the enemy's preparations, I should infer that they are working for the protection of one fleet, and for a defence against another; that in case they hold Portsmouth, the main body would be at York, and a detached corps upon Gloucester neck to protect the water battery. Their fortifications are much contracted. From the enemy's caution and partial movements, I should conclude their intelligence is not very good, and that they wish to come at an explanation of my intentions and prospects.

We have hitherto occupied the forks of York River, thereby looking both ways. Some militia have prevented the enemy's parties from remaining any time at or near Williamsburg, and false accounts have given them some alarms. Another body of militia, under Colonel Ennis, has kept them pretty close in Gloucester town, and foraged in their vicinity. Upon the receipt of your orders, I wrote to the governor, that intelligence of some plans of the enemy rendered it proper to have six hundred militia collected upon Blackwater. I wrote to General Gregory, near Portsmouth, that I had an account that the enemy intended to push a detachment to Carolina, which would greatly defeat a scheme we had there. I have requested General Wayne to move towards the southward, to be ready to cross James River at Westover. A battalion of light infantry, and our only hundred dragoons, being in Gloucester county, I call them my vanguard, and will take my quarters there for one or two days, while the troops are filing off towards James River. Our little army will consequently assemble again upon the waters of Chickahonimy; and should Jamestown Island be thought a good place for a junction, we shall be in a situation to form it, while we render it more difficult for the enemy to attempt a journey to Carolina.*

* After the arrival of Lord Cornwallis at York, General Lafayette asked Colonel Barber for a faithful and an intelligent soldier, whom he could send as a spy into the English camp. Morgan, of the New Jersey line, was pointed out to him. The general sent for him, and proposed to him the difficult task of going over to the enemy as a deserter, and enrolling himself in their army. Morgan answered, that he was ready to do everything for his country and his general, but that to act the part of a spy was repugnant to all his feelings; he did not fear for his life, but for his name, which might be blotted with an eternal stain. He ended, however, by yielding, but on condition, that in case of any misfortune, the general would make the truth known, and publish all the particulars of the case in the New Jersey papers. M. de Lafayette promised this should be done.

In the present state of affairs, my dear general, I hope you will come yourself to Virginia, and that, if the French army moves this way, I will have, at least, the satisfaction of beholding you myself at the head of the combined armies. In two days I will write again to your excellency, and keep you particularly and constantly informed, unless something is done the very moment (and it will probably be difficult). Lord Cornwallis must be attacked with pretty great apparatus. But when a French

Morgan then proceeded to the English camp. His mission was to give advice of the movements of the enemy, and deceive them as to the projects and resources of the Americans. He had not been long with the English, when Cornwallis sent for him, and questioned him, in the presence of Tarleton, upon the means General Lafayette might have of crossing south of James River. Morgan replied, according to his private instructions, that he had a sufficient number of boats, on the first signal, to cross the river, with his whole army. "In that case," said Cornwallis to Tarleton, "what I said to you cannot be done;" alluding, in all probability, to an intended march upon North Carolina. After the arrival of the French fleet, M. de Lafayette, on his return from a reconnoitring party, found in his quarters six men dressed in the English uniform, and a Hessian dressed in green: Morgan was amongst them, bringing back five deserters and a prisoner: he no longer thought his services as a spy could be of any use to his country. The next day, the general offered him, as a recompence, the rank of sergeant. Morgan thanked him, but declined the offer, saying that he thought himself a good soldier, but was not certain of being a good sergeant. Other offers were also refused. "What can I then do for you?" inquired the general. "I have only one favour to ask," replied Morgan. "During my absence, my gun has been taken from me; I value it very much, and I should like to have it back again." Orders were given that the gun should be found and restored to him: this was the only thing he could be prevailed on to receive. Mr. Sparks, who published this anecdote, "says he heard it related, fifty years after it had occurred, by General Lafayette, who still expressed great admiration for that soldier's noble feelings and disinterested conduct."—(Washington's Writings, vol. viii., p. 152.)

fleet takes possession of the bay and rivers, and we form a land force superior to his, that army must, sooner or later, be forced to surrender, as we may get what reinforcements we please.

Adieu, my dear general; I heartily thank you for having ordered me to remain in Virginia; it is to your goodness that I am indebted for the most beautiful prospect which I may ever behold.

TO MADAME DE LAFAYETTE.

Camp, between the branches of York River,
August 24, 1781.

THE residence of Virginia is anything but favourable to my correspondence. I do not accuse public affairs of this evil; and as I find so much time to think of my affection for you, I could doubtless find some, also, to assure you of it; but there are no opportunities here of sending letters, and we are obliged to despatch them to Philadelphia and expose them to many hazards; these dangers, in addition to those of the sea, and the increased delay they occasion, must necessarily render the arrival of letters far more difficult. If you receive a greater number from the French than from the Virginian army, it would be unjust to imagine that I have been to blame.

Your self-love has, perhaps, been gratified by the part I have been obliged to act: you may have hoped that I could not be equally awkward on every theatre; but I should accuse you of an egregious degree of vanity (for all things being in common between us, there is vanity in rating me too highly) if you have not trembled for the perils to which I have been exposed. I am not speaking of cannon balls, but of the more dangerous master-strokes with which I was threatened by Lord Cornwallis. It was not prudent in the general to confide to me such a command. If I had been unfortunate, the public would have called that partiality an error in his judgment.

To begin, even from the deluge, I must speak to you of that miserable Portsmouth expedition. General Rochambeau had intended sending a thousand Frenchmen there, under the Baron de Viomenil. You must have heard that the French squadron gained a great deal of glory, whilst the English attained their desired end. Admiral Arbuthnot will since have informed you that I was blockaded; but, although we were not sailors, that blockade did not detain us four hours. You will have learnt, afterwards, that General Phillips having made some preparations at Portsmouth, we marched in all haste to Richmond, where we arrived nearly at the same time; but I arrived first. They then came from New York and Carolina to unite with the Virginian troops; the whole was commanded by the formidable Lord Cornwallis, who abandoned his first conquests to fulfil the ministerial plan by the conquest of Virginia. It was not without some difficulty that we avoided the battle he wished for; but, after many marches, we became stronger than we were at the commencement, and we pretended to be stronger than we were; we regained what we had lost without risking a battle, and, after two trifling affairs, the hostile army proceeded to Portsmouth, which it has since evacuated, and whose fortifications we have destroyed. That army is now in York River, whither they repaired by water. If the naval superiority which we are so fully expecting should arrive, I shall rejoice at the campaign closing by the English army's assuming that position.

The French and American troops before New York are under the orders of the generalissimo. My friend Greene has had great success in Carolina, and that campaign has taken a far better turn than we had any reason to expect or hope. *It may perhaps end in a very favourable manner.* It is said that the British ministry are sending here the Governor of Virginia; I fancy they have founded rather too many hopes upon the success of their army. The Pennsylvanians, who were to have joined them, are at present here with us. But for the virtue, zeal, and courage of the regular troops who were with me, it would have been impossible for me to have saved myself. I cannot sufficiently express my gratitude to those with whom I have undertaken this fatiguing campaign. The militia have done all they could. I have been well pleased with our little army, and only hope it may have been also pleased with me.

I must speak of my health, which is a monotonous subject,—for I need only repeat favourable accounts of my own constitution: the sun of Virginia has a very bad character, and I had received many alarming predictions; many persons, in truth, have had fevers; but this climate agrees with me as well as any other, and the only effect fatigue has upon me is to increase my appetite.

TO M. DE VERGENNES.

Camp, between the branches of York River,
August 24th, 1781.

When a person, sir, has Lord Cornwallis in front and is flying through the sands of Virginia, he must depend upon others to give circumstantial news of America. Ever since the guidance of this army has been entrusted to me, I have found myself five hundred miles from any other troops, and all accounts of the war, of General Washington, and of congress, are an immense time in reaching me; but you have the Chevalier de la Luzerne, and you could not have a better informer. There is only one point on which I cannot depend on any person to speak for me,—and that is when I am assuring you of the affectionate and devoted attachment I shall feel for you during the remainder of my life.

To execute the gigantic project which his court has planned, Lord Cornwallis was obliged to leave exposed both the Carolinas. General Greene took ample advantage of this circumstance. It is true that the hostile army bore on every point upon us, and all depended upon our having the good luck to avoid a battle: fortune served us well, and after a few junctions, our little army regained all the ground whose conquest had occasioned so many sacrifices. In the other states we manœuvred rather than fought. Lord Cornwallis has left us Portsmouth, from whence he communicated with Carolina, and finds himself at present at York, which would be a very advantageous station for us, if we possessed a naval superiority: if that should by chance arrive, our little army would enjoy successes which would amply compensate for this long and fatiguing campaign: I should not, in that case, regret our last movements having placed us in our present situation.

I can only speak to you of myself, sir, or of the English army, for all other accounts will reach you at Versailles almost as soon as they do me in this remote corner of Virginia. It is reported that you are going to make peace, but I am not very credulous on this point, and I fancy that they will at least await the end of this campaign.

This is a large packet, sir, but I do not fear taking advantage of your kindness, as I well know the full extent; I flatter myself I merit it as much as it is possible for any person to do so, by the feelings of confidence and respectful affection with which I remain, &c.

I beg you to present my kind compliments to the Countess de Vergennes, and to your sons.

TO M. DE MAUREPAS.

Camp, between the branches of the York River, August 24th, 1781.

WHILST I am thus, sir, more than ever separated from the rest of the world, I am not less occupied with the persons I love, and who honour me with their kindness and attention. I owe you so much gratitude, and feel so much attached to you, that I wish to recal sometimes to your recollection the rebel commander of the little Virginian army. Interested for me, sir, as I know you are, you would have been alarmed by the important part my youth has been called upon to act: five hundred miles from any other corps, and without any resources whatever, I was placed to oppose the projects of the court of St. James's and the good fortune of Lord

Cornwallis. Until the present moment, we have not met with any disasters; but, in a time of war, no person can tell what events may occur on the following day. Lord Cornwallis pursued us without succeeding in taking us, and after a variety of movements, he is now in the good York harbour; who knows whether his manœuvres may not end by making us prisoners of war?

As I do not know what vessel may bear this despatch, I will neither dwell upon our projects nor our hopes; the Chevalier de la Luzerne, who knows every opportunity for France, will inform you of all that passes here; for my part, I am lost in the sands of Virginia, living only by my wits, and corresponding with Lord Cornwallis only. This letter, sir, is merely intended to recal me to your remembrance, and to offer you the assurance of my respectful and affectionate regard.

Will you permit me, sir, to present my respects to the Countess de Maurepas and Madame de Flamarens?

TO GENERAL WASHINGTON.*

(ORIGINAL.)

Holt's Forge, 1st Sept., 1781.

My dear General,—From the bottom of my heart I congratulate you upon the arrival of the French fleet. Some rumours had been spread, and spy accounts sent out, but no certainty until the admiral's

* Washington having finally adopted the project of uniting the land and sea forces against the army of Cornwallis, which had so fortunately stationed itself in the position most favourable to a naval attack, it was still important and difficult to prevent him from reaching Carolina, and thus ruining the campaign of the allied powers. It was to attain this end, that Lafayette

despatches came to hand. Inclosed I send you his letter, and that of M. de St. Simon, both of whom I request you will have translated by Tilghman or Gouvion alone, as there are parts of them personal, which I do not choose to shew to others. Thanks to you, my dear general, I am in a very charming situation, and find myself at the head of a beautiful body of troops; but am not so hasty as the Count de Grasse, and think that, having so sure a game to play, it would be madness, by the risk of an attack, to give anything to chance.

It appears Count de Grasse is in a great hurry to return; he makes it a point to put upon my expressions such constructions as may favour his plan. They have been pleased to adopt my ideas, as to the sending of vessels into James River, and forming a

had despatched troops to the south of James River, under pretence of dislodging the English from Portsmouth; this movement had also the good effect of uniting to the corps of the army the troops and artillery who could escape by Albemarle Sound on the arrival of the Count de Grasse. With the same view, he detained troops on the south of James River, on pretence of sending General Wayne and his Pennsylvanians to the southern army to reinforce General Greene. No person was in the secret, and the enemy could not, therefore, be undeceived. It was at that period that he sent them the pretended deserter, Morgan. In short, after having manœuvred for several months to lead his opponent into the spot that would best allow him to take advantage of a naval co-operation, he manœuvred at last so as to prevent his enemy from withdrawing when he became conscious of his danger. His precautions in this respect were more necessary from Lord Cornwallis knowing that a large French fleet was expected in North America. The moment the Count de Grasse arrived, Lafayette marched on rapidly to Williamsburg, and effected a junction with a corps of three thousand men belonging to the Marquis de St. Simon. As soon as he landed at Jamestown, he crossed the river, united Wayne's corps to his own, and assembled, on the other side of York River, opposite to Gloucester, a corps of militia. The junction at Jamestown. I wish they may also force the passage at York, because then his lordship has no possibility of escape.

The delay of Count de Grasse's arrival, the movement of the grand army, and the alarm there was at York, have forced me, for greater security, to send a part of the troops to the south side of James River. To-morrow and the day after will be employed in making dispositions for covering a landing, which will be done with continentals discumbered of baggage; and on the 5th, agreeable to the count's desire, a junction will be made of our troops. I shall then propose to the French general the taking of a safe position, within ten or twelve miles of York; such a one as cannot be forced without a much greater loss than we could suffer.

English army thus found itself enclosed on every side, and no possible means of safety were left to Lord Cornwallis but by his undertaking a very perilous enterprise. He reconnoitred, however, the position of Williamsburg, with the intention of attacking it. It was a well chosen station: two creeks, or small rivers, throwing themselves, one into James, the other into York River, almost enclosed the peninsula on that point; it was necessary to force two well defended passages; two houses and two public buildings of Williamsburg, both of stone, were well placed to defend the front. There were five thousand French and American troops, a large corps of militia, and a well served campaign artillery. Lord Cornwallis thought he ought not to hazard an attack. He might have crossed over to Gloucester, or have ascended York River, the Count de Grasse having neglected to place vessels above that point, but he must have abandoned, in that case, his artillery, magazines, and invalids, and measures had been taken to cut off his road in several places; he determined, therefore, to await the attack. He might have had, in truth, the chance of a combat, if Lafayette had yielded to some tempting solicitations. The Count de Grasse was in a hurry to return; the idea of waiting for the northern troops and generals was intolerable to him; he entreated Lafayette to attack the English army, with the American

And, unless matters are véry different from what I think they are, my opinion is, that we ought to be contented with preventing the enemy's forages, and fatiguing them by alarming their picquets with militia, without committing our regulars. Whatever readiness the Marquis de St. Simon has been pleased to express to Colonel Gimat, respecting his being under me, I shall do nothing without paying that deference which is due to age, talents, and experience ; but would rather incline to the cautious line of conduct I have of late adopted. General Portail must be now with Count de Grasse. He knows your intentions, and our course will be consulted in our movements.

Lord Cornwallis has still one way to escape ; he may land at West Point, and cross James River,

and French troops that were under his command, offering, for that purpose, not only the detachments which formed the garrisons of the ships, but also as many sailors as he should demand. The Marquis de St. Simon, who although subordinate to Lafayette from the date of his commission, was much his senior in point of age and service, joined earnestly in the admiral's request. He represented that Lord Cornwallis's works were not yet comp eted, and that an attack of superior forces would soon, in all probability, take Yorktown, and afterwards Gloucester. The temptation was great for the young general of the combined army, who was scarcely four-and-twenty years of age; he had an unanswerable pretence for taking such a step in the declaration made by M. de Grasse, that he could not wait for the northern generals and forces ; but this attack, which, if successful, would have been so brilliant, must necessarily have cost a great deal of blood. Lafayette would not sacrifice to his personala mbition the sold ierswho had been confided to him ; and, refusing the request of the Count de Grasse, he only endeavoured to persuade him to await the arrival of General Washington, accompanied by the Generals Rochambeau and Lincoln, seniors of Lafayette ; by this means the reduction of the army of Cornwallis became a secure and by no means costly operation. (Note extracted from Manuscript, No. 2.)

some miles below Point of Fork; but I thought this part was the most important, as the other route is big with obstacles. However, to prevent even a *possibility*, I would wish some ships were above York.

The governor* was with me when the letters came; he jumped upon a horse, and posted off to his council. I gave him a memorandum, demanding provisions of every kind for the fleet and the combined army. We may depend upon a quantity of cattle, but flour ought to be sent from Maryland and Pennsylvania. Chevalier d'Annemours, the French consul, is here, and will take a method to have his countrymen supplied without starving us.

Upon a particular inquiry of the country, and our circumstances, I hope you will find we have taken the best precautions to lessen his lordship's chances to escape; he has a few left, but so very precarious, that I hardly believe he will make the attempt; if he does, he must give up ships, artillery, baggage, part of the horses, all the negroes; he must be certain to lose the third of his army, and run the greatest risk to lose the whole, without gaining that glory which he may derive from a brilliant defence.

Adieu, my dear general, the agreeable situation I am in is owing to your friendship, and is, for that reason, the dearer to your respectful servant and friend.

* The governor of Virginia, Jefferson.

TO GENERAL WASHINGTON.

(ORIGINAL.)

Williamsburg, September 8, 1781.

My dear General,—I had the honour to write you lately, giving an account of everything that came within my knowledge. I was every hour expecting I might be more particular; but if you knew how slowly things go on in this country; still I have done the best in my power; I have written and received twenty letters a day from government and from every department. The governor does what he can: the wheels of his government are so very rusty that no governor whatever will be able to set them free again. Time will prove that Jefferson has been too severely charged. The French troops, my dear general, have landed with amazing celerity; they have already been wanting flour, meat and salt, not so much, however, as to be one day without. I have been night and day the quarter-master collector, and have drawn myself into a violent head-ache and fever, which will go off with three hours' sleep, the want of which has occasioned it. This, my dear general, will apologize to you for not writing with my own hand. The French army is composed of the most excellent regiments: they have with them a corps of hussars, which may be of immediate use. The general and all the officers have cheerfully lived in the same way as our poorly provided American detachment. I think a letter from you on the subject will have a very good effect. Last night by leaving our own baggage, and accepting of our officers' horses, we have been able to move to a position near Williamsburg: it is covered along the front with ravines; the right flank is covered by a mill-pond, on the road to Jamestown; the left by Queen's Creek, small rivulets, and marshes. We have militia still in front of our right and left, and a good look out on the river. Our provisions may come to the capital landing. Williamsburg and its strong buildings are in our front. I have upon the lines General Muhlenberg with one thousand men, four hundred of whom are Virginian regulars, and one hundred dragoons. In borrowing White's unequipped horses we may add one hundred hussars. There is a line of armed ships along James River, and a small reserve of militia, which may increase every day: there are in Gloucester county eight hundred militia driving off stock. I had recommended, with proper delicacy, to Count de Grasse to send some naval forces up York River; the French armed vessels in Pamunkey are come down to West Point. No movement of Count de Grasse has as yet taken place, except some ships below York. Your excellency's letter to him has been duly forwarded; we are under infinite obligations to the officers and the men for their zeal.

I entered into these particular accounts, my dear general, in order to show you that propriety, and not the desire to advance, has dictated our measures. We will try, if not dangerous, upon a large scale, to form a good idea of the works; but, unless I am greatly deceived, there will be madness in attacking them now with our force. Marquis de St. Simon, Count de Grasse, and General du Portail, agree with me in opinion; but should Lord Cornwallis come out against such a position as we have, everybody thinks that he cannot but repent of it; and should he beat us, he must soon prepare for another battle.

Now, my dear general, I am going to speak to you of the fortifications at York. Lord Cornwallis is working day and night, and will soon work himself into a respectable situation: he has taken ashore the greater part of his sailors; he is picking up whatever provisions he can get. I am told he has ordered the inhabitants in the vicinity of the town to come in, and should think they may do him much good. Our present position will render him cautious, and I think it a great point. No news as yet in this camp of the fleet of M. le Comte de Barras.*

I will now answer you that part of your letter respecting provisions for the troops under your immediate command.

With respect to a proper place for the debarkation of your troops, it is the opinion of the Marquis de St. Simon, and mine, that it must be in James River, but we have not had an opportunity yet of fixing on the best spot: it appears, however, that it must be at or near Williamsburg or Jamestown.

With the most affectionate regard and esteem, I am, dear general, &c.

* Marshall speaks of the departure of the Count de Barras for the Chesapeak, and of his arrival with the artillery of the siege; that the admiral had received a letter from the minister of the marine, the Marshal de Castries, who, informing him of the orders given to M. de Grasse to proceed to the coasts of the United States, left him free to make a cruise on the banks of Newfoundland, not wishing to oblige him to serve under his junior, to whom the minister had entrusted the command. But M. de Barras nobly determined to convey himself and the artillery to Rhode Island, and to range himself, with all his vessels, under the command of an admiral less ancient than himself.—Manuscript, No. 2.)

TO GENERAL WASHINGTON.*

(ORIGINAL.)

Camp before York, October 16, 1781.

My dear General,—Your excellency having personally seen our dispositions, I shall only give an account of what passed in the execution.

Colonel Gimat's battalion led the van, and was followed by that of Colonel Hamilton's, who commanded the whole advanced corps; at the same time, a party of eighty men, under Colonel Laurens, turned the redoubt. I beg leave to refer your excellency to the report I have received from Colonel Hamilton, whose well known talents and gallantry were on this occasion most conspicuous and serviceable. Our obligations to him, to Colonel Gimat, to Colonel Laurens, and to each and all the officers and men, are above expression. Not one gun was fired, and the ardour of the troops did not give time for the sappers to derange them, and, owing to the conduct of the commanders and the bravery of the men, the redoubt was stormed with uncommon rapidity.

Colonel Barber's battalion, which was the first in the supporting column, being detached to the aid of the advance, arrived at the moment they were getting over the works, and executed their orders with the utmost alacrity. The colonel was slightly wounded: the rest of the column under General Muhlenberg and Hazen advanced with admirable

* It was the 13th of September that General Washington had operated his junction with General Lafayette, and the 28th the place of York was invaded. The assault was given on the 15th of October.

firmness and discipline. Colonel Vose's battalion displayed to the left, a part of the division successively dressing by him, whilst a second line was forming columns in the rear. It adds greatly to the character of the troops that, under the fire of the enemy, they displayed and took their rank with perfect silence and order. Give me leave particularly to mention Major Barber, division inspector, who distinguished himself, and received a wound by a cannon ball.

In making arrangements for the support of the works we had reduced, I was happy to find General Wayne and the Pennsylvanians so situated as to have given us, in case of need, the most effectual support.

I have the honour to be, with the most perfect respect, &c.

TO M. DE MAUREPAS.

Camp, near York, October 20th, 1781.

THE play, sir, is over—and the fifth act has just been closed; I was in a somewhat awkward situation during the first acts; my heart experienced great delight at the final one—and I do not feel less pleasure in congratulating you, at this moment, upon the fortunate issue of our campaign. I need not describe the particulars of it, sir, because Lauzun will give them to you in person; and I only wish him the same degree of good luck in crossing the ocean that he had in passing through a corps of Tarleton's legion.

M. de Rochambeau will give you a full account of the army he commands; but if the honour of having commanded for some time the division of

M. de St. Simon gives me any right to speak of my obligations to that general and his troops, that right would be much valued by me.

Will you have the kindness, sir, to present my respectful compliments to the Countess de Maurepas, and Madame de Flamarens, and to accept, yourself, the sincere assurance of my affection, gratitude, and respect.

TO M. DE VERGENNES.

Camp, near York, October 20th, 1781.

Allow me, sir, to offer you my congratulations upon the good leaf that has been turned over in our political tablets. M. Laurens will give all particulars; I rejoice that your Virginian campaign should close so well, and my respect for the talents of Lord Cornwallis renders his capture still more valuable to me. After this commencing stroke, what English general will ever think of conquering America? Their southern manœuvres have not ended more fortunately than their northern ones, and the affair of General Burgoyne has been again renewed.

Adieu, sir; I have so short a time for writing, that I can only add at present the assurance of the respect and sincere attachment of, &c.

TO MADAME DE LAFAYETTE.

On board *La Ville de Paris*, in Chesapeak Bay,
Oct. 22, 1781.

This is the last moment, my dearest love, allowed me for writing to you; M. de Lauzun is going to join the frigate and return to Europe ; some business I had to settle with the admiral affords me the pleasure of thus giving you some news of me two days later ; what relates to public affairs will be detailed to you by M. de Lauzun. The close of this campaign is truly brilliant for the allied troops ; our movements have been all remarkably well combined, and I must, indeed, be difficult to please, if I were not completely satisfied with the close of my Virginian campaign. You must have learnt all the trouble that Lord Cornwallis's talents and superior forces gave me,—the good luck we had in regaining the ground we had lost,—and, finally, our drawing Lord Cornwallis into the very position that was necessary to enable us to capture him : at that precise moment all the troops rushed upon him. I count as amongst the happiest epochs of my life, that in which the division of M. de St. Simon remained united to my army, and that in which I alternately commanded the three field-marshals, with the troops under their orders. I pity Lord Cornwallis, for whom I have the highest respect ; he is kind enough to express some esteem for me, and after having allowed myself the pleasure, in the capitulation, of repaying the incivilities of Charlestown, I do not intend to carry my vengeance any farther.

My health is extremly good, and I met with no accident during our encounter.

Present my most affectionate respects to Madame d'Ayen, and the Marshal de Noailles ; a thousand kind regards to all my sisters, the Abbé Fayon, and M. de Margelay. I embrace ten thousand times our beloved children. Adieu, adieu.

THE MARQUIS DE SEGUR TO M. DE LAFAYETTE.

December 5th, 1781.

The king, sir, having been informed of the military talents of which you have given such multiplied proofs whilst commanding the different corps of the army that has been confided to you in the United States; of the wisdom and prudence that have guided you in the various decisions you were called upon to take respecting the interests of the United States; and of the great confidence with which you have inspired General Washington; his Majesty has desired me to tell you, that the praises you have so justly merited on such various occasions have fixed his attention, and that your conduct and successes have made him, sir, conceive the most favourable opinion of you; such a one as you might yourself desire, and from which you may depend on his future kindness. His Majesty, in order to give you a very flattering and peculiar mark of this intention, renews to you the rank of field-marshal in his armies, which you are to enjoy as soon as the American war shall be terminated, at which period you will quit the service of the United States to re-enter that of his Majesty. In virtue of this decision, sir, you may be considered as field-marshal from the date of the signature of the capitulation, after the siege of York-town, by General Cornwallis, the 19th October, of this year, on account of your fulfilling at that time the functions belonging to that rank in the troops of the United States of America.

His Majesty is disposing at this moment of his regiment of dragoons, of which he had kept for you the command until the present time.

I beg you to be convinced of the pleasure I experience in this act of his Majesty's justice, and of the wish, I feel to prove to you, on every occasion, the sincere attachment with which I have the honour of being, &c.

SÉGUR.

TO GENERAL WASHINGTON.

(ORIGINAL.)

Alliance, off Boston, December 21st, 1781.

MY DEAR GENERAL,—I am sorry to think we are not yet gone, and there still remain some doubts of our going to-morrow. This delay I lament not so much on private accounts as I do on the account of our next campaign, in the planning of which your opinion, as I shall deliver it, must be of the greatest use to the common cause. As to the department of foreign affairs, I shall be happy to justify the confidence of the congress, by giving my opinion to the best of my power, whenever it is asked for; but the affair of finances will, I fear, be a difficult point for the American minister, in which, however, I shall be happy to help him with my utmost exertions. The moment I arrive in France, I will write to you minutely how things stand, and give you the best accounts in my power.

I have received every mark of affection in Boston, and am much attached to this town, to which I owe so many obligations; but, from public considerations, I have been impatient to leave it and go on board the frigate, where I receive all possible civilities, but where I had rather be under sail than at anchor.

I beg your pardon, my dear general, for giving you so much trouble in reading my scrawls; but we are going to sail, and my last adieu, I must dedicate to my beloved general. Adieu, my dear general: I know your heart so well, that I am sure that no distance can alter your attachment to me. With the same candour, I assure you that my love, my respect, my gratitude for you, are above expression; that, at the moment of leaving you, I felt more than ever the strength of those friendly ties that for ever bind me to you, and that I anticipate the pleasure, the most wished for pleasure, to be again with you, and, by my zeal and services, to gratify the feelings of my respect and affection. Will you be pleased to present my compliments and respects to Mrs. Washington, and to remember me to General Knox and General Lincoln.

Adieu, my dear general, your respectful and tender friend, &c.

ADDITIONAL CORRESPONDENCE.

INSERTED ONLY IN THE

AMERICAN EDITION.

TO HIS EXCELLENCY GENERAL WASHINGTON.

(ORIGINAL.)

At Robins's Tavern, half past four, 26 June, 1778.

DEAR GENERAL,—I have received your excellency's favor* notifying your arrival at Cramberry, and am glad to have anticipated your orders in not going too far. I have felt the unhappy effects of the want of provisions, for I dare say if we had not been stopped by it, as we were already within three miles of the enemy's rear, we would very easily have overtaken them and fought with advantage.

I have consulted the general officers of the detachment, and the general opinion seems to be that I should march in the night near them, so as to attack the rear guard when on the march. We have also spoken of a night attack. The latter seems dangerous. The former will perhaps give them time of escaping, as it is impossible I would move quite close by them, at least nearer than three miles.—Col. Morgan is towards the right flank, Gen. Dickinson is a little upon the left, Gens. Scott and Maxwel have insisted upon going further down than we are now; for Wayne's and Jackson's corps they have not had pro-

*The letter referred to does not appear in Sparks' "Writings of Washington;" but there is a letter of instructions in vol. 5, p. 417 of that work addressed to Gen. Lafayette by Gen. Washington, dated the 25th June 1770, in relation to the service upon which the former had been detached; some account of which is to be found in the preceding "Memoirs," ante p. p. 51, 52. See also, the letters of Gen. Washington to Gens. Lee and Lafayette, in Sparks'. "Writings &c." p. p. 410, 419.

visions at all but will be able to march in the night. I beg you would let me know your intention and your opinion of the matter, my motions depend much upon what the army will do for countenancing them. I beg you would be very particular upon what you think proper to be done and what your excellency will do. I wish indeed you would anticipate the different cases which may happen according to the place where the enemy lays.—Gen. Wayne, Col. Hamilton and several officers have gone to reconnoitre it. I fancy they will lay about seven or eight miles from here. Your excellency knows that by the direct road you are only three miles further from Monmouth than we are in this place.

The enemy is said to march since this morning with a great confusion and fright. Some prisoners have been made, and deserters come amazingly fast. I believe an happy blow would have the happiest effect, and I always regret the time we have lost by want of provisions.

I beg you would answer to me immediately, and with the highest respect I have the honor to be, &c.

TO GENERAL WASHINGTON.*

(ORIGINAL.)

At Cranbarry, 5 o'clock, June, 1778,

DEAR GENERAL,—I have received your orders for marching as just as I could and I have marched without waiting for the provisions tho' we want them extremely. Gen. Forman and Col. Hamilton sat out last night to meet the other troops and we shall be together at Hidestown or somewhat lower. Gen. Forman is firmly of opinion that we may overtake the enemy,—for my part I am not so quiet upon the subject as he is, but his sentiment is of great weight on account of his knowledge of the country. It is highly pleasant to me to be followed and countenanced by the army that if we stop the enemy and meet with

* In answer to the letter of instructions mentioned in the preceding note.

some advantage they may push it with vigor. I have no doubt but if we overtake them we possess a very happy chance. However, I would not have the army quite so near as not to be quite master of its motions, but a very little distance may do it.—I have heard nothing of the enemy this morning. An officer of militia says, that after they had pitched their tents yesterday night, they struck them again. But I am inclined to believe they did not go farther, and that the man who brought the intelligence was mistaken. I expect some at Hidestown which I will immediately forward to you. I beg when your excellency will write to me, that you could let me know the place you have reached, that I might govern myself accordingly.

With the highest respect I have the honor to be, &c.

TO GENERAL WASHINGTON.*

(ORIGINAL.)

Half past ten, 28th June, 1778.

Dear General,—Your orders have reached me so late and found me in such a situation that it will be impossible to follow them as soon as I could wish. It is not on account of any other motive than the impossibility of moving the troops and making such a march immediately, for in receiving your letter I have given up the project of attacking the enemy, and I only wish to join Gen. Lee.—I was even going to set out, but all the Brigadiers, Officers, &c. have represented that there was a material impossibility of moving troops in the situation where ours find themselves—I do not believe Gen. Lee is to make any attack to morrow, for then I would have been directed to fall immediately upon them, without making 11 miles entirely out of the way. I am here as near as I will be at English Town. To-morrow at two o'clock I will set off for that place.

I do not know if Morgan's corps, the militia, &c., must

*In answer probably to Gen. Washington's letter of the 26th June. Sparks' Washington, vol. 5, p. 419.

be brought along with the other part of the detachment. Gen. Forman who don't approve much of that motion, says, that our right flank must be secured, unless to incur the most fatal consequences for the whole army.

I beg your pardon sir, if my letter is so badly written, but I want to send it soon and to rest one or two hours.

I have the honor to be, &c.

Be so good as to send a speedy answer of what you think proper to order me.

TO GENERAL WASHINGTON.

(ORIGINAL.)

Cranbarry, half past nine o'clock, 29 June, 1778.

DEAR GENERAL,—Inclosed I have the honor to send you a letter which Colonel Hamilton was going to send me from this place when I arrived with the detachment, and which may give you an idea of the position of the enemy. I will try to meet and collect as soon as possible our forces, tho' I am sorry to find the enemy so far down that way. We will be obliged to march pretty fast, if we want to attack them. It is for that I am particularly concerned about provisions. I send back immediately for the purpose, and beg you would give orders to have them forwarded as speedily as possible, and directed to march fast, for I believe we must set out early to-morrow morning. The detachment is in a wood, covered by *Cranberry* Creek, and I believe extremely safe. We want to be very well furnished with spirits as a long and quick march may be found necessary, and if Gen. Scot's detachment is not provided, it should be furnished also with liquor; but the provisions of this detachment are the most necessary to be sent as soon as possible, as we expect them to march.

If any thing new comes to my knowledge, I will immediately write to your excellency, and I will send an express in the morning.

I have the honor to be, &c.

I wish also we could get some axes, but it should not stop the so important affairs of provisions.

TO THE COUNT DE VERGENNES.

St. Jean d'Angely, June, 1779.

Sir,—I learnt before I left Paris, that a loan, negociating in Holland for England, and which was to have been completed the coming autumn, would be stopped, because the lenders had demanded one per cent more interest. This loan was undertaken by a banker of English origin, who has apportioned it among a great many persons, and had become lender-general to the English government. I am told that some profits over and above the commission might help America to this sum, amounting to above forty millions. I communicated this information to the Chevalier de la Luzerne to be imparted to you; but having discharged that duty towards the Americans, I feared lest M. Necker would not share in my earnestness. I have already appropriated twenty millions to bank stock, ten to an expedition, and ten to pay the interest until the final reimbursement.

I received at the moment I was coming away a letter from America, dated in the month of January, in which the President informed me in behalf of Congress, that they had changed their determination respecting the joint expedition to Canada. The reasons assigned are, the slight probability of Rhode Island and New York being evacuated next winter, the uncertainty of the enemy's movements next spring, and therefore the impossibility of promising their quota of the troops, fixed in the plan that I was intrusted with. I have the honor to be, &c.

TO THE COUNT DE VERGENNES.

Havre, 9 July, 1779.

Sir, If my letter from America had contained any interesting information, I should not have delayed a moment to acquaint you with it; but it is only a confirmation of what you heard, and we have some later news by the way of England. It will be injurious to commerce for the British to have the command of James River, and while they can coast along those shores with impunity, their transient descents will almost always succeed. If they should establish themselves in their new profession, to drive them out would be the more accordant to the plan I spoke to you about; as, in Virginia, November and even December are good campaigning months. The arrival of M. Gerard will certainly supply you with many details of American affairs, the Swedish ambassador has sent me, in the name of his king, the most flattering assurances, and well suited to awaken my gratitude, but the vessels are not forthcoming, and if we go to America, we must go under the Spanish or French flag. I think if our Southern allies should engage alone in a similar expedition, they would do more harm than good by it.

I wish I could send news that the English fleet was beaten in good earnest; and whilst I wait that event with as much interest, as if I was at the head of the fleet, the army and the whole ministry, I do not forget that your time is precious, and so I shall content myself with presenting to you the homage of my respect and my attachment.

TO THE PRESIDENT OF CONGRESS.

Havre, 7th October, 1779.

Sir,—As from their minister in France, any European intelligence will be properly conveyed to congress, I beg only the leave of paying them a due tribute of my respect and heartfelt assurance of my unbounded zeal, love and gratitude: so sensible I am of their goodness towards me, that I flatter myself they will kindly receive this letter from one who will ever boast in the name of an American soldier, and whose delight has been long ago, in sharing the same fortune as the American people, never to be considered but as a countryman of theirs.

land has been obliged to make, the terror that has been spread along her own shores, while her naval forces were flying in the channel before our fleet, and suffering themselves to be insulted by our van guard frigates, and at length the obligation our fleet was under, to repair into the harbour of Brest for getting provisions and water, are events which will be more accurately reported by Mr. Franklin's dispatches. The Ardent, man-of-war of sixty-four guns has been taken by two French frigates. Captain Jones's small American squadron had the good luck of taking lately a fleet from the Baltic, and displaying Continental colours along the coasts of Scotland.

Since I had the honor to write to your excellency, I have ever been with Count de Vaux's army, which was divided in two corps at St. Malo and the Havre, and consisted of thirty thousand men. Another body has been stationed in Flanders, and two thousand dragoons are to embark at Brest.—The project of invading England was at first retarded by a difficult meeting of the French and Spanish fleets on account of contrary winds, by useless efforts to bring out the enemy to an engagement, and the necesssity of repairing into the harbour of Brest. How it will be possible to bring out the expedition in the autumn is yet undetermined, but it will be perhaps delayed until next spring, though the ministry seem very anxious of acting in this campaign.

Suppose the taking of Gibraltar, which they are going to attack with the greater vigor, was the only European conquest for this year, the large expenses France has made will yet be of a great use to the common cause, as it has exhausted England and detained at home forces which would have done mischief in the other part of the world.

The loss which the enemy have sustained in the East Indies has been very severly felt by them, and from their negociations in Europe they cannot procure themselvès any allies.

Count d'Estaing's arrival on the American coasts will, I hope, have produced such an effect as we earnestly desire. How truly concerned, how truly unhappy I am in being confined to mere wishes, Congress, from the knowledge they have of my sentiments will better feel for me than I might myself express. The furlough they were pleased to give me was unlimited, no one could imagine the campaign would take such a turn, and till the month of June I was in hopes of rendering myself, in this part of the world, of a more immediate use to the United States. The expedition against England had been afterwards fixed upon, and my services were thought useful to my country and the common cause: So that I hope Congress will approve of my conduct.

Whatever may be the success of the campaign in America, it will certainly bring on new projects for the ensuing year. The sense I have of the favors conferred on me by congress, and the marks of confidence which I have obtained in many occasions, give me the freedom of reminding them that the moments where I may find myself under American colours, among my fellow soldiers, and take orders from our great and heroic General will ever be considered as the happiest ones in my life.

If there is any thing in France where not only as a soldier, but as a politician, or in whatever possible light, I may employ my exertions to the advantage of the United States, I hope it is useless to tell that I will seize the happy opportunity and bless the fortunate hour which shall render me useful to those whom I love with all the ardor and frankness of my heart.

The inestimable sword which Congress have generously added to their so many favors, I have received from their minister with such honorable services as by far exceed any merit I may ever boast of. This present has been also graced by Mr. Franklin's politeness in offering it, and I could not help repeating again to Congress some assurances of those sentiments which for ever will animate my grateful heart.

With the warm feelings of one whose first ambition and delight is to be known in this and to be called in ages to come a *lover of America*, who is bound to his representatives by the most respectful and tender attachment and gratitude, and with the highest regard for your excellency.

I have the honor to be your's &c.

Paris, 9th January, 1780.

SIR,—You were too busy yesterday for me to communicate to you the answer of M. de Montbarrey to the request for powder and guns which I had taken it upon me to make. I spoke in my own name, and the advice which I took the liberty of giving was not ill received. M. de Montbarrey told me that he would speak to you about it. He promised me an early answer; and as you favor my request, I hope that we shall soon obtain the powder and the fifteen thousand complete sets of accoutrements, which we would add to the clothes bought with the king's money. You are conferring a great obligation upon America, and affording her great additional means of contributing to the advancement of the grand common cause. Every citizen must be strongly interested in the fate of our islands, and must fear the effects, which would follow if an expedition should go out from New York. It is enough to know that country, whose independence is so important to the honor and safety of France, to desire that it may be not forgotten in the plan of the campaign, and to regret the loss of the time which might be employed in giving it assistance. But the extensive operations are beyond my sphere, I shall merely ask for my guns, and assure you of the strong affection and respect with which I have the honor to be, &c.

TO GENERAL WASHINGTON.*

(ORIGINAL.)

Peekskill, July the 20th, 1780.

DEAR GENERAL,—Having heard of an express from Rhode Island being going through the Continental village, I sent for him as it would not delay him more

* This letter was written by General La Fayette, while on his journey to Newport, R. I., whither he had been sent with full instructions to concert measures of co-operation with the French Generals De Rochambeau and De Ternay. A copy of these instructions is given in Sparks' History of Washington, Vol. 7, App. III. See also the answer of Washington to La Fayette, ib. p. 117.

than an hour. Inclosed I have the honor to send you the letter from Gen. Heath, which I have opened, and also two letters from the French generals to me. It seems, my dear General, that they have anticipated the desire you expressed yourself of our plans in a private conversation. That way indeed will do better than a hundred letters. In case (what however I don't believe) they would wish to speak to yourself, I shall immediately send an express to inform you of it; but I dare say they will be satisfied with my coming.

I am glad to hear they are hunting after the Cork fleet, and those frigates being out will also apprise them of the enemy's naval motions.

Adieu, my dear General. With a heart full of hopes, and I think of well grounded expectations, I have the honor to be very tenderly and respectfully, &c.

P. S. It is much to be lamented that Paul Jones did not come in the first envoy. In case there is nothing to fear from the enemy, I will send the clothing to New-London. Be certain, my dear General, that though by serious reflexions and calculations which I can prove to be right, I have great hopes of success, I shall however look upon and speak of all the difficulties that may present themselves. I have on public and private accounts many reasons to feel the consequence of the plan in question, and to take the greatest care in considering by myself and explaining to others our circumstances. The delay of the small arms I don't consider as equally hurtful to our affairs as will be the deficiency of powder. But as (even at the so much overrated calculations) we have enough of it for one month, I will try to get a supply from the fleet, and then it will come to the same point. You will hear from me as soon as possible after my arrival.

TO GENERAL WASHINGTON.

(ORIGINAL.)

Danbury, July the 21st, 1780.

As I find an express going from Hartford to General Greene, I send this letter to him that you might hear something further about the recruits of Connecticut. From the Colonel who under Gen. Parsons is intrusted with the care of forwarding them, I hear that by the first of August two thousand of them will be at West Point; but I had put in my head that they were to bring arms with them, and I find it is not the case.

Gen. Parsons and myself will meet at Newtown, where, in mentioning again to him the necessity of hurrying the recruits to West Point, I will apprise him that you have been disappointed in the expectation of some powder, and desire him to write to you how far, in case of an emergency, you might be provided for with that article from his state.

In case Gen. Parsons thought that my waiting on the governor and council might answer any purpose, I would go three or four miles out of my way to preach to them some of my old sermons.

With the help of French horses whom I make free with on the road, I hope I will arrive very soon at Rhode Island. Nothing about Graves' fleet; but I am happy to think that they will find our people ready to receive them at Newport.

When I wrote you, my dear General, that my heart was full of flattering expectations, it is understood that I suppose a sufficiency of arms and ammunition, which I thought so far useless to explain, as I hope you believe I have some common sense. But I had an idea that the recruits would be armed, and I yet think (though I had no reason to be particular on that head) that you have many small arms in your stores. For what relates to the powder, I hope that what you will get from the states, and what I flatter myself to borrow from the French fleet, will put you in a situation to wait for the alliance. You may remember that the second division is to come before, or very little after, the beginning of our operations.

I however confess it is impossible not to be very angry at captain Jones's delays, and much disappointed in our expectations. The only thing I want to know, is *if you depend on a sufficiency of arms and ammunition for the first thirty days*. Be certain that before settling any thing, my great basis will be, *when and how does the second division come, and how far may we depend on the arms and ammunition coming with them.*

I have the honor to be, respectfully, &c.

TO GENERAL WASHINGTON.

(ORIGINAL.)

Hartford, July the 22d, 1780.*

MY DEAR GENERAL,—I hasten to inform you that the missing transport is safely arrived, on the 19th, at Boston. She is said to be a two-decker, and to have on board a vast deal of powder, with pieces of ordnance, and also the baggage of the officers of *Bourbonnsis.*—The intelligence came this instant by an officer of our army who saw the men encamped on the commons, from where they were to march to Providence. Two American frigates were, I am told, ordered to convoy the ship around the Rhode Island; but as their orders were to sail by to-morrow, they will have time to receive contrary directions from the French Admiral. The inclosed newspaper will acquaint you of Graves's cruising off Block Island, and on their first appearance, Chev. de Ternay will certainly dispatch an express to Boston.

* It appears from Spark's Hist. of Washington, p. 125. n. that in his progress to New-Port, General La Fayette called on Governor Trumbull, General Parsons, Mr. Jeremiah Wadsworth, the Commissary-General, and other persons in Connecticut, to procure and hasten forward the quota of troops, and such supplies of arms and ammunition as could be spared from that State, to co-operate with the French troops upon their landing.

In a conversation which I had yesterday with General Parsons, he told me that he thought the number of your arms in stores, amounted to ten thousand, exclusive of those which are now in the hands of the men. He seems to be of opinion, and so is Col. Wadsworth, that there is no inconvenience in their State's furnishing their drafts with arms, and giving even a larger proportion if thought necessary. They say those arms may be by the 5th of August at King's Ferry. I was so particular as to make myself certain that this demand will not in the least impeach any other measure, and as it would be too distressing to fall short on that article, I will take on myself, though in a private capacity, to persuade the Governor and Council in the measure of arming every one of the men whom they send out, and forwarding the arms to King's Ferry, or West Point, as you may direct.

As to the matter of ammunition Gen. Parsons thinks that (as far as he may guess,) near fifty tons of powder might be collected. Col. Wadsworth says he can't ascertain the quantity. They have three mills, and from what I can collect, I am certain that if you attack New York, this State will do all in their power. I will foretell the Governor, that he will have a large demand of ammunition, and let you know how much we are to depend upon, as far as I may guess from his answer. Massachusetts have, say they, a vast deal of powder.

I intend to breakfast at Newport the day after to-morrow, and as soon as I can make out any thing worth the while, from my conversation with them, I will let you know every matter that may be interesting.

With the highest respect and most tender friendship, I have the honor to be, dear General, &c.

I am told that the French are in a great want of vegetables. I think it will be agreeable to them to forward their waggons and horses as much as possible.*

* The answer to the above letter appears in Spark's Writ. of Washington, Vol. 7, p. 125. See also ib. p. 127, note.

TO GENERAL WASHINGTON.

(ORIGINAL.)

Lebanon, July the 23d, 1780.*

MY DEAR GENERAL,—I had this morning the honor to wait on His Excellency, the governor, and took the liberty, though in a private capacity, to inform him of our circumstances. The result of our conversation I will therein transmit to you, and to be more certain of conveying the governor's ideas, I am writing at his own house, and will show him my letter before I fold it up.

To begin by the article of powder which is so much wanted, and which, from unforeseen circumstances may, by its deficiency ruin all our expectations, I am, by the Governor, desired to tell you that you may depend upon: 1stly. Fifty four tons for the present. 2dly, Fifteen tons to be made up in the course of August, by the three Connecticut Mills. 3dly, Twenty tons, which in case of an absolute necessity, will be found out in this State; the whole amounting to eighty-five tons, which he would try to encrease, if possible, to ninety. How far that may fulfil your expectations, I don't know, but his Excellency will wait for a letter from you on this subject.

As to the balls, shells, &c., the Governor cannot as yet ascertain the quantity to be expected, but thinks this State may go a great length.

His resources for arms have been, it seems, overrated by General Parsons, and other gentlemen, whose opinions I had communicated to your Excellency. The Governor thinks that it would be difficult to arm the whole of the recruits. He will, however, if requested by you, do any thing in his power, and might have a good prospect of succeeding for the half part of them.

* This is one of the letters referred to in Gen. Washington's letter of 26th July. Spark's Writ. of Wash. v, 7, p. 128.

Tho' I had no orders for this interview with Governor Trumbull, and from the knowledge of our circumstances, took upon myself the freedom of disclosing them to him, I heard your Excellency's sentiments on one point so often, so strongly, and so repeatedly expressed, that I could with all certainty assure him, that you would not ask from the State more than is necessary to answer our great purposes, and in delivering the country from the danger of ruin and the disgrace of a shameful inability, to turn this decisive crisis to the honor and safety of America.

I took also the liberty of mentioning something about clothing the officers, and assured the Governor that you thought the measure to be highly necessary. He entirely agrees in opinion with me, and does not doubt but that at the first meeting of the Council a sufficient sum in hard money will be delivered for that purpose. The knowledge I have of Colonel Wadsworth's zeal and activity makes me desirous that he be intrusted with that business.

As to the clothing from the fleet, it seems the Governor wishes it to be sent into Connecticut river, and I will engage the French Admiral into that measure; for I am very warm in this opinion, my dear General, and so I know you are, that as less trouble as possible must be given to the people whose exertions should be entirely thrown in such channels, as are of absolute necessity; but if we can't send the clothing around without an eminent danger of its being taken, then his Excellency the Governor will send it with all possible dispatch and by pressed waggons from the boundaries of Rhode Island to any place on the North River, which is mentioned in Mr. Olney's instructions.

I have the honour to be, dear General, &c.

Your's, &c.

P. S.—I have read my letter to the Governor and he agrees with the contents. He will immediately give orders about the Mills, and collect four hundred french arms he had in stocks.*

TO GENERAL WASHINGTON.

(ORIGINAL.)

Newport, July 26th, 1780.

MY DEAR GENERAL,—Every private intelligence from Long-Island, and also the letters from General Howe, and the officer on the lines do agree with the note I have received from Colonel Hamilton, and are all positive upon it that General Clinton, with a great part of his army, is coming to attack the French troops.

In consequence of this Count de Rochambeau is fortifying both Islands, and making preparations of defence. He has requested our calling immediately a body of militia, which demand has been complied with by General Heath.

After many intelligences had been received, I did yet persist in disbelieving the report, but they now come from so many quarters, that I am obliged to yield to the general idea, and expect them in a little time.

I have no doubt but that in the course of the day we will receive some orders, and some intelligences from head-quarters. The French Generals have asked me if your army was in a situation to make a diversion, or if a part of it would not be marched immediately to our relief. My answer was, that if you was able to do one or the other, you would certainly not lose a minute, but that I could not tell them any thing positive ; that however, I thought you would come nearer to New-York than you was when at Preakaness.

* For the answer to the above, See Spark's Writ. of Wash. v. 7, p. 124.

All the last day has been employed or in viewing the camp with Count de Rochambeau, or in helping General Heath in his arrangements. This morning the Count is gone to reconnoitre the grounds on the Island. We dine together at the Admiral's, and I will, if possible, begin our conversation, our affairs exclusive of what we are now expecting from the enemy.

In case you was to send some troops this way, I wish I might get notice in such a time as to have some clothing kept on the road, but in all cases we should take some well looking and well dressed men; that, I only mention as a mere supposition.

If the enemy mean regular approaches the French Generals say that they would give time for a succour to come. In all suppositions I don't think the French will be able to form a junction before some time, as they can't leave the Island before the fifteenth of next month, (in supposing that they are not attacked.) They have many sick, but I will soon be able to tell you more about it, and had not those intelligences been so pressing, I might have by this time fully spoken on our affairs with the French Generals.

For my part, my dear General, till orders from you fix any thing I am to do, I will stay here under General Heath's orders, and help him to the best of my skill. As soon as any thing important comes to us I will send you an express.

From private inquiries I hope the fleet will furnish us with some powder. As to the militia who are called by General Heath, the French army will spare to them such provisions as may be wanted.

I have the honor to be with the most perfect respect and tender affection, Yours, &c.

TO GENERAL WASHINGTON.

(ORIGINAL.)

Newport, July the 26th, at Seven o'clock, P. M.*

MY DEAR GENERAL,—I had this morning the honor of writing to you by Genl. Heath's express, and informed you that we had from every official and private quarter minuted accounts of the enemy's coming in great force to attack this island. For my part I have been a long time a disbeliever of the intelligence; but so many letters came to hand that at length I was forced to take the general opinion about their intended expedition. But, tho' I wrote you in the morning, I know you are anxious of hearing often from this quarter, and will therefore desire General Heath to send an other express.

Nothing as yet (the ships of war excepted) has come in sight; but the French Generals who have not the smallest doubt about their coming, are hurrying their preparations of defence.

General Heath and myself were invited to a meeting of the French General Officers, wherein, to my great satisfaction, the idea of holding both Connecticut and Rhode Island was abandoned, as it is assured that from the first one the enemy cannot annoy our shipping, if in a certain position. Count de Rochambeau, Chevalier de Chattelux, and myself, went afterwards to dine with the Admiral, and the two French Commanders have agreed to the following plan:

The transports to be put in the harbour of Newport; the shipping to anchor along the shore from Brenton's Point, going Northward, where they are protected by batteries, a frigate and a cutter to be stationed in Sekonnet Passage; the army to encamp at its usual place, but upon the appearance of the enemy, to be in readiness to

* For the answer to this letter, See Spark's Writ. of Wash. v. 7, p. 128.

attack them at any point where they may disembark, and, if unsuccessful, to retire to the position which was once occupied by the enemy. There they want also to place some militia. Count de Rochambeau cannot hear of the idea of evacuating the island, and says he will defend this post to the last man. I could not help advising him very strongly and very often to erect works, and keep a communication open with the Continent by Howland's Ferry or Bristol Point, that matter will, I hope, be attended to in the course of the next day.

General Heath will inform you of the measures he has taken, in which, as the second officer, I am only to help him to the best of my power. The Count's urging request, made it, I think, necessary to call for Militia.

The number of sick is such that by the return given before me to Count de Rochambeau, it appears they will have but three thousand six hundred men fit for duty if they are attacked within a few days. The fleet has a great proportion of sick men and the ships are therefore poorly manned for the present.

Count de Rochambeau asked me so often if you would not send a body of Continental troops to their relief; if, in the course of twelve days from this they could not be arrived, or that I knew he wanted me to write to you about it, and at length he told me he did not want it. But this must be *between us*. The Count says he will stand a storm; but if the enemy wanted to make a long work of it that a corps of Continental troops in their rear would have the best effects. That in this case the enemy would be much exposed on the Island, and that the circumstances which would follow their re-embarking, would be so fatal to them as to facilitate our operations for the campaign. All this, my dear General, I was in a private manner desired to hint to you.

We could not speak of our grand operations, and they are wholly taken in their expectations of the enemy. But what might be an inducement to send a corps this way is, that in any case the French will not be able to march before the 15th of August.

A return of the clothing has been promised to me for this evening, but tho' I am sorry to be the news-bearer of so many disappointments, I must tell you that from what they said to me nothing but a small part of the clothing has been intrusted to them, and that not only nothing new has been done, but what I had settled has been undone by those arrangements of the alliance which I can't conceive. In case you was to send troops this way, I think their route to Providence should be known, so that they might meet the clothing on the way.

What you will do, my dear General, I don't know, but it seems Count de Rochambeau is determined to defend Newport, at all events.

With the most perfect respect and tender sentiments, I have the honor to be, Yours, &c.

TO GENERAL WASHINGTON.

(ORIGINAL.)

Newport, July the 29th, 1780.

My Dear General,—Your letter of the 22d* came to hand last evening, and I hasten to answer at least to a part of its contents. I shall begin by the disagreeable disappointment I met with on account of our clothing. Inclosed, my dear General, you will find the return of what has been put on board of the fleet, which I have sent by a vessel to Providence, and which will be forwarded to head-quarters. I can't tell you how much I feel for that shoking arrangement of clothing, but as it is not quite so essential to arms and powder, if we have no clothing. I shall be the forwardest to advise our acting without it. I am apt to blush for neglecting

* See Spark's Writ. of Wash. vol. 7, p. 117.

improvements that are within my reach, but I readily do without those which are not in our power.

As to the affair of arms I spoke this morning to the Count, and am sorry to find that he has but the most necessary articles of exchange which are to answer to the daily broken arms, &c., his superfluous armament is coming in the second division, and for the present there is nothing to expect from that quarter. The only way, my dear General, will be to request the States to pick up arms for their recruits. Governor Trumbull, (as you may have seen by my letter from Lebanon,) thinks there is a great deal of difficulty in this matter; but many other Gentlemen from the State assure that it can be done. I will desire Colonel Wadsworth to manage that affair with the Governor, and I will also write a private letter to Mr. Bowdoin and Governor Greene.

As to the powder, my dear General, I hope the Navy will give us some, not however a great deal. You cannot conceive how difficult it is for the present to speak with them on offensive plans. They expect Clinton at every minute, and say his success will decide our operations, I had however this morning a conversation with the Land General, and was to see in the evening the Admiral, who, I am told, cannot come, so that I must delay it to be done to-morrow.

Connecticut will, I think, furnish you with a much greater quantity than you expected. How far it will fulfil your purpose I hope to hear from you; but I cannot flatter you to get so much from the fleet as two hundred, even as hundred tons.

I have fully considered, my dear General, the idea of those French Generals, and made myself acquainted with every thing that has past since my departure from France. A great mismanagement in the affair of transports, has prevented the whole coming here at once; but as the French and Spaniards have a superiority, there is no doubt but that if they join together as was intended, the second division will be here in less than three or four weeks. The fleet on this Continent will, I hope, be commanded by Mr. Duchoffaut, and will be very superior to that of the enemy. If by an unlucky chance the junction was prevented, the second division would yet certainly come in the autumn, and be in a situation to act during the winter; but I have all reasons to believe that they will be here in three weeks, and you may depend upon it that they will at all events be here for the winter. From what I have been intrusted with I have a pretty certain ground to hope that my letter will produce upon Count de Guichen, the desired effect, and after an expedition which I can't trust to paper, will be concluded, you may, I think, depend upon his coming this way with a good part of his fleet.

In a word, the French Ministry are determined to keep here during the war a land and naval force which will act on the Continent till a peace is concluded, and to support it with all their power. They look upon Rhode Island as a point to be kept for receiving their fleets and their reinforcements of troops, and want the defence of it to be such an object as will insure the basis of our operations.

Before settling any thing the French Generals want to hear from their second division. *Don't fear by any means* their acting rashly, and be assured that you may very far depend on their *caution*; but our wants of arms and ammunition have made me also very cautious. If the States furnish us with a sufficiency of the first article, and almost a sufficiency of the second, which we will make up with the fleet, then I am most strongly of opinion that waiting for the second division is all together wrong and unwarrantable.

I have, however, brought Count de Rochambeau to this, viz.:—That if the second division comes we must attack. That in all cases, if we are masters of the water, we may attack; and that we may do it if the Admiral thinks that we can secure the passage by batteries, and if each part is equal to the whole of the enemy.

We must now see what the Admiral has to say. What he wrote about the harbour of New York don't please me. If Duchoffaut comes, I answer for any thing you wish. To-morrow I will speak with the two Gentlemen, so at least I hope, and will let you know their answers.

If the second division comes in time we shall certainly act and succeed. Then we will have our arms, powder, clothing, &c.

I never thought, my dear General, that Clinton would come this way; nor do I think it now, but every body says he is coming. Governor Clinton has it as a certainty, and upon his letter received this morning they have altered the arrangement; I had settled to dismiss the extraordinary militia. I hate troubling all these people, and taking them away from their harvest. Gen. Heath is of my opinion, but the intelligences are so particular, so authentic, that he dares not to neglect to gather as many men as possible. Before you receive this you will certainly know the truth of those reports.

If you think, my dear General, that Clinton is coming, and if he disembarks upon Rhode Island, I am clearly of opinion that three or four thousand Continental troops and the militia landing on his rear, while the Count would sally from Newport, would ruin the British army, and that the taking of New York would be but a trifle after such a stroke.

In case you adopt the measure, I think that the communication with the main is very important. I went yesterday to the North end of the Island, and had the works repaired in such a way (at least they will be soon so) as to keep up a communication by Howland's Ferry for eight or ten days after the enemy will possess the Island. I have also desired Colonel Greene, in case they appear, to run up the boats to Slave Ferry. Signals have been established from Watch Point to Connanicut; all those arrangements I have made with the approbation and by the orders of General Heath.

You will by this express receive a letter from Genl.

Heath, who applies for, and most ardently wishes a leave of repairing to his command in the grand army.

For my part, my dear General, I will, I think, wait your answer to this, and want to know if by the situation of your arms and ammunition, there is a possibility of your acting before the second division comes. If from the answers of the States you think *such a proportion* of powder from the fleet will be sufficient; then I will be more positive. If, however, after my conversations, I was to see that the second division must be waited for at all events, then I need not be waiting for your answer to this. I will, therefore, my dear General,

1st, Or arrange with them a beginning of operations before the second division comes, and then wait for your answer about arms and ammunition, or the prospects I may have by myself to fix it entirely.

2d, Or fix our plans for the moment the second division comes, and then I will, as soon as possible, repair to head-quarters.

They seem rather doubtful of the possibility of landing safely, and having a sufficiency of boats to carry them under the protection of our Westchester batteries, and I beg you will give me such a note about it as I might show to them.

With the highest respect and most tender friendship, I have the honor to be, dear General,

Yours, &c.

All the officers and soldiers of the army have a great desire to join the grand army, and hate the idea of staying at Rhode Island.

TO GENERAL WASHINGTON.

(ORIGINAL.)

Newport, July the 31st, 1780.

MY DEAR GENERAL,—In consequence of a note from me the Admiral came to last evening, and defensive ideas gave way to offensive plans. Our conversation was long, and it is not yet ended, but I hasten to write you a summary report of what past between the Count, the Chevalier, and myself.

I first began, in my own name, to give them a pretty exact account of the situation we were in three months ago, of the supernatural efforts which the country had made for the purpose of an immediate co-operation. I told them that by the 1st of January our army would be dismissed; that the Militia was only to serve for three months. I added, that for the defensive they were useless to us; nay, they were hurtful, and that I thought it necessary to take New-York before the winter. All that, my dear General, was said in my own name, and therefore in a less delicate way than when I am your interpreter.

I then told them that I was going to speak of you, and after many compliments, assurances of confidence, &c., I went on with your plan, beginning with the importance of possessing the harbour, and going on about the three ways which you have directed me to point out as to be hereafter regulated by circumstances.

As to the possessing of the harbour the Chevalier told that he did not believe his ships might go in; but that if superior at sea, he would answer by cruising off to protect the landing, the transportation, and prevent an evacuation; indeed to blockade the harbour.

The French General, with the advice of the Naval Commander did not hesitate to prefer the going in transports to the point you know of. Both were of opinion that nothing could be undertaken unless we had a naval superiority, and as I know it is your opinion also, (tho' it is not mine,) I durst not insist on that article.

There was another reason which made me wait for the reinforcement. I knew we had neither arms nor powder. I know we would be at least a long time to get them; but as they did not think of making me the objection I put my assent to the others on the account of my private confidence in their superior abilities; told them that you also thought we should have a naval superiority, and added, in my own name, that however we must, any how, act before the winter, and get rid of a shameful defensive.

The summary of the arrangement will, I presume, be this: That as soon as we hear of a naval reinforcement we go where you know, and establish what you intend to fix; that, if possible, we get where I want you to be; that immediately the French will embark and go where you wish them to be, or thereabout; that a number equal to the enemy's whole force be stationed in that part; that they don't want there more than ten pieces of our heavy cannon; that after every thing will be disembarked, three weeks, in their opinion, will do the business on their side; that proper means will be taken by sea to keep up the communication and prevent an evacuation; that we must not give up that plan if we may begin in August or September; that fascines and other apparatus must be ready on the opposite shore; that they will take for us all the boats belonging to the Continent which will be at Providence; that as soon as our clothing, &c., arrive, it will without entering any harbour be sent to W. C. or thereabout.

Their superiority at sea, will, I think, take place in the course of this month; they have two ways to depend upon it:—1st, Unless of an absolute impossibility the second division, consisting of four other regiments and the remaining part of Lauzun's, with the Alliance and all other stores, and with a strong convoy of ships of the line, will be here very soon. When they will be heard of on the coast, Chevalier de Ternay will, at all events, go out and meet them. 2dly, the Gentleman I wrote to on my arrival has full liberty to send here reinforcements, the Admiral has already applied to him, but I am going to make him write other letters *in my way*, and will send them to-morrow or the day after to Chevalier de la Luzerne, whom I beg you will immediately desire to secure three fast sailing vessels for the West Indies.

I am going this evening to fix plans with Pilots, and also to speak of the entrance of the harbour. Dobs and Shaw are here, and I will have a full conversation with them and the Admiral, both for the entrance of the harbour and the navigation of the Sound. To-morrow I call, with as much secrecy as possible, a number of Pilots for the harbour of Halifax and River St. Laurence.

Inclosed, you will find a letter from Count de Rochambeau. He requests you will have the goodness of letting the Minister know what the French army is about, as he had no time of writing to him; it is, I believe, very important. 1st, To send every where to meet the reinforcement, and give them proper directions. 2dly, To have some vessels ready for the West Indies.

The French set more value upon Rhode Island than it is worth. I however got them to promise that in case of an operation they will not leave here a Garrison, and that their Magazines would be sent to Providence.

You know, my dear General, I did not expect Clinton, and tho' I could not stand alone in my opinion, I ever lamented the calling out of the Militia. I am happy to inform you that they have been dismissed. Nothing can equal the spirit with which they turned out, and I did not neglect letting the French know that they have done more for their allies than they would have done for the security of their own continental troops on a similar occasion.

As to the three month men, the French General wants them to establish the communication with the main; but I will soon request him to let them go to the grand army, and will, in the same time, get from this State as many arms and powder as possible. I have written to Massachusetts for the same purpose.

After I will have sent the Pilots, and made calculations with the Commander of the Artillery and the first Engineer whom the Count will consult, I shall draw a plan which I will get their answer to, and repair with it to head-quarters. In the meantime I will receive answers from Boston and from Governor Greene.

The Admiral cannot send to us more than thirty thousand of powder. But you see that their demands as to heavy pieces are small; they indeed say they do not want any on the Island, and that their twenty-ones will be sufficient. All that, my dear General, I will be more positive upon after the Commanders of Artillery and Engineers will have made with us their calculations.

I hope, my dear General, that by the 5th or 6th of August, I will have nothing more to do in this place.

The French army hate the idea of staying here, and want to join you; they swear at those that speak of waiting for the second division; they are enraged to be blockaded in this harbour. As to the dispositions of the inhabitants and our troops, and the dispositions of the inhabitants and the Militia for them, they are such as I may wish. You would have been glad the other day to see two hundred and fifty of our drafts that came on Connecticut without provisions or tents, and who were mixed in such a way with the French troops, that every French soldier and officer took an American with him and divided their bed and their supper in the most friendly manner.

The patience and sobriety of our Militia is so much admired by the French Officers, that two days ago a French Colonel called all his officers together to desire them to take the good examples which were given to the

French soldiers by the American troops. So far are they gone in their admirations that they find a great deal to say in favor of General Varnum, and his escort of Militia Dragoons, who fill up all the streets of Newport. On the other hand, the French discipline is such, that chiken and pigs walk between the tents without being disturbed, and that there is in the camp a cornfield, from which not one leaf has been touched. The Tories don't know what to say to it.

Adieu, my dear General. To-morrow, I hope having the pleasure of writing you another letter, and am with the most tender friendship, dear General,

Your most obedient humble servant, &c.

I beg, my dear General, you will present my compliments to the family.*

TO GENERAL WASHINGTON.

(ORIGINAL.)†

Newport, August the 1st, 1780.

My Dear General,—Your letter to Count de Rochambeau mentioning the enemy's embarkation, and your future movements against New-York, a positive letter from Governor Trumbull, and a positive one from General Parsons, have once more altered the dispositions, and such of the Militia as had been dismissed have been again sent for.

In consequence of these expectations my offensive arrangements have been entirely cut short, they are wholly taken in their preparations. My letter of yesterday has been detained with the hope that some intelligence might be added to it; but I will send it this morn-

* The answer to this letter appears in Spark's Writ. of Wash. v. 7, p. 135.
† See Spark's Writ. of Wash. vol. 7, p. 126.

ing, and if it is possible to obtain from the Admiral some hour's conversation with Captains Dobs and Shaw I shall to-morrow morning dispatch another express.

The dispositions of defence are, I believe, these; the French to occupy the English lines; General Heath to command a corps of militia on the Tivertown side; I to have his van-guard on the Island, and to watch the enemy's motions almost all around the Island, which is not a small affair.

If the enemy land I will try to oppose it, and the French will come in columns to attack them with fixed bayonets. If this attack do not succeed they will retire behind the lines, and take with them fifteen hundred Militia, when with the few ones that may stay, I will retire to Butt's Hill, and secure the communication with General Heath.

As you did not write to me, my dear General, I could not know what you want me to do. If you think seriously of entering on the Island of New-York, I am extremely sorry to stay here. If on the contrary you send troops this way, (which, if the enemy land, would be fatal to them,) I will not be to lament my being away from the army. I shall feel very unhappy to be with some Militia while the Light Infantry is acting under you, and had I been sent for, I would have joined you very fast; but if you can take New-York I will heartily forget that I could have been there, and feel nothing but joy; if, however, there was time enough, I'd beg you will send for me. If you send troops this way I believe they may strike a great blow.

The wind is against them, so that they won't be here before the day after to-morrow. Adieu, my dear General, with the highest respect I have the honor to be,

Your's, &c.*

* For the answer to the above, approving the measures of La Fayette, See Spark's Writ. of Wash. v. 7, p. 141.

TO GENERAL WASHINGTON.

(ORIGINAL.)

Elizabeth Town, October the 27th, 1780.

My Dear General,—From what you have heard from Dr. Hagen about the boats when on your way to head-quarters, I don't believe that you may have kept any hope for our success. The boats have been, it seems, reduced to five, and from the time when they were yet at the Little Falls you may see that they could not be here at the appointed hour.

I will not permit myself to reflect on this moment upon the many blunders committed on that affair by the Quarter-General's department. I was too certain of some brilliant success, and military glory is too much idolized by me, not to be rather severe on the occasion. I will content myself to say that from the report and common agreement of all the spies and guides collected together by Major Lee, from the negligence of the enemy, the circumstances of the tide and a thick foggy weather, not one of those whom I led into the matter had the least doubt upon your success.

The only advantage I have got from it has been to convince myself that our troops are particularly fit for such an expedition, on account of their patience and silence; and that if the other business could be supported upon a large scale, I would answer to carry it. I have written upon both roads to the commanding officer of the brigade of the line that our expedition was relinquished, and that I would advise him not to give to his men the trouble of going farther. I have also requested him to speak of this movement as if it had taken place on account of some intelligence that the enemy meant to come out into the Jersey's to attack us.

I have taken my position between Elizabethtown and

Connecticut Farms. General Clinton has not the time of making any disposition against us. To-morrow at nine or ten I will march to our position of Crane's Town, and the day after to-morrow to Cotawa, unless I receive contrary orders.

Newark Mountain was rather too far to march it this night, and too near for to-morrow, because our men being in want of blankets will like better to join their tents again.

If your Excellency approves of this arrangement, I beg you will order our baggage to wait for us on our position of Crane's Town; if you dislike the disposition your orders may reach us on the road.

I beg, my dear General, you will please to communicate our ill success and disgraceful disappointment to the Minister, who said he would not leave Morris Town until he hears from me.

Had I any thing to reproach to myself on the occasion, I would be inconsolable. I undertook the business because I thought myself equal to it; I wish the people in the Quarter Master's Department had done the same for their plans.

I am, my dear General, your's, &c.

TO GENERAL WASHINGTON.

(ORIGINAL.)

Light Camp, October 27th, 1780.

My Dear General,—I am sorry to hear from Major Gibbs that my letter of last night did not reach you before your departure from head quarters. It had been written at one o'clock, as soon as I took my position for the night, and intrusted to Colonel Ogden, who promised to send it by an officer acquainted with the roads.

Depending upon your communication of the sad intelligence to Chevalier de la Luzerne, I did not send to Morristown where he was to wait for the news of the success.

Among the many blunders which have been committed, I shall extract from that complete assortment some instances (not for this glorious occasion that is forever lost) but on any future one.

You may remember that after a long time Colonel Pickering assured to you that the boats were in complete readiness whilst they had no oars,—he afterwards positively told that he had only three boats with him at Camp when two hours before I had seen five of them with my own eyes. The sending of those five boats two hours after that which you had appointed, you have been early apprized of, but you don't perhaps know that instead of being at Dod's the night before last the boats from Suffrans arrived there last evening about sunset, to this report the man who received them eight miles this side of Suffrans adds that they wanted their double trees and spread chains, so that he was obliged to lose about two hours in taking those things from Continental wagons and the inhabitants; when our affairs will be thus managed your best projects cannot fail of being defeated.

Had Mr. Pickering followed the example of General Knox, every thing would have been here in proper time and proper order, as was the artillery from the Park.—I confess, my dear General, that I cannot reconcile my feelings to the idea that by this neglect I have lost a most happy opportunity, blessed with all the little circumstances which may insure success. Our expedition has taken the most foolish turn in the eyes of any one who is unacquainted with this circumstance of the boats.

When I was in hopes of seeing in time at least five of them, I gave up the watering place to think only of Richmond; but when I saw that we could not be there before the break of the day, I did not hesitate to relinquish an expedition which on that footing would have occasioned a great profusion of blood for little or no purpose, but you will easily guess what I have felt on the occasion. I never have been so deeply wounded by any disappointment.

By Mercereau and Colonel Ogden, I hear that the enemy are collecting boats and intend a forage into the Jerseys. I would be very happy to know if you have got the like intelligence. Suppose they were to come out in force and at a distance from us, would not this be an opportunity to execute your grand plan?

I beg you will let me know this evening if I am to march to-morrow to our old ground to Cotawa; if the enemy were likely to come out, or if you thought of a certain plan, I would advise to keep Major Lee for some days, as in both cases he will be a capital man, — he is a most charming officer.

Arnold has issued a second proclamation wherein he invites the officers and soldiers of our army to join him, promising to them equal ranks to those they hold in the American service.

I am told expresses were sent to me to acquaint me of the delay of the boats; but excepting Doctor Pagen I have not seen one of them, — the boats have been sent to the two bridges by Major Gibbs, I had brought them up with me, and in passing by them both conductors and wagoners have received the curses of every officer and soldier in the division. The men marched last night very fast with such silence, good order and desire of fighting as would have highly pleased you. The activity and resources of Major Lee have been on that occasion displayed in such a way as entitles him to my eternal esteem and gratitude. I felt not only for me but for all the officers and men who had promised themselves so much glory on the occasion.

With the most tender affection and high respect I have the honor to be, my dear general, yours, &c.

Colonel Ogden has remained behind to get intelligences; so that being uncertain if my first letter has reached you, I would be happy to know in the course of the night if I am to march to-morrow morning to the old ground.*

TO GENERAL WASHINGTON.

(ORIGINAL.)

Philadelphia, December 4, 1780.

MY DEAR GENERAL,—I will for this time write a very short letter to you and cannot be more particular either on public or private business, until some few days stay in this city have enabled me to get further information.

I have been greatly disappointed in my not meeting Mrs. Washington. I have been very angry with my bad fate which led me into another road at the only moment when I could miss her—this has been the more the case, as I knew you was uneasy about her, and I wanted both to send you an express and to advise her to the best way of meeting you as soon as possible.

The southern news are expected this evening. Leslie has re-embarked and will probably go to Charleston; the southern members are pleased to like my going towards their country. However I cannot for the present be determined, as I don't yet know if the campaign will be active, and if succours are to be expected from France.

* The two preceding letters relate to a descent upon Staten Island, which was projected, and was to be executed by La Fayette, who was now in command of a Light Corps, consisting of battalions, stationed in advance of the main army, and was anxious to effect some important enterprise before the campaign should be brought to a close; but this expedition, as well as an attack proposed in his letter of the 30th October, ante upon the upper part of New York Island, was rendered impracticable by the want of boats and other necessary preparations. See Sparks' Writ. of Wash. v. 7, p. 280, and App. No. 9.

By a vessel from there who left Lorient before the middle of October, we hear that nothing material had happened except the taking of the merchant fleet. Both naval armies were in port. There was an expedition of, I think, ten ships of the line and five thousand men ready to sail—this vessel came in company with Jones, who is daily expected; but a very little part of our clothing will be on board, some will come on board the Serapis, Jones, who mounts the *Ariel* had dispatches from the French Court, for as he however might have been detained by a storm off the French coast which separated the little convoy. In the vessel arrived was a Mr. Ross, who, I hope will give me some account of the clothing, and Baron d'Arent, who got rid of his rupture, has a star with a cross and a ribbon, and is upon very good terms with the King of Prussia.

Congress have debated a motion about your being desired to go to the southward, but have determined that you would better know than they do if it was more useful to go or to stay. I am more than ever of this last opinion.

On my arrival I found one of the salt meat vessels sold and the other to be sold to day. I have spoken on the subject to almost every member of Congress, who promised that they would take the best measures in their power to get these provisions.

Chevalier de la Luzerne has communicated to me in *the most confidential way* a Spanish plan against St. Augustine, upon which I am building a letter for the Generals of this nation, and using the best arguments in my power to engage them either to send twelve ships of the line to take us and conduct us to Charleston, as to render their operations as useful as possible to General Greene. To-morrow I will write you about it. If I have time before the departure of the confederacy who is going to the West Indies, I will send you the original, if not a copy of my letter. This is entirely *confidential*, as I have not the Chevelier's permission to mention it.

Adieu, my dear General, your's, most respectfully.

A letter dated Cadiz, September 23d, mentions that Count d'Estaing commands the combined fleet, and is gone to sea. In this case his going with sixteen ships could not be true. I will endeavour to ascertain this matter.*

Mr. Carmichael writes that Spain has sent a hundred and thirty thousand dollas. It is not a great deal, the dispositions of that court are very satisfactory. Portugal does every thing we want, letters are just arrived from St. Domingo but not desciphered.

TO GENERAL WASHINGTON.

(ORIGINAL.)

December the 5th, in the Evening, 1780.

My Dear General,—However acquainted I may be with your intentions, I thought, upon the whole, that I should better wait for your approbation before I present any opinion of yours to the Spanish and French Generals in the West Indies. I will, I know, lose the opportunity of the confederacy, but many vessels are going that way, and if my letters meet with your approbation I shall send them by triplicates. I impatiently wait for your answer.

I will write to General Greene to let him know of this intended expedition, which, tho' uncertain as all human events are, may be, however, in a great measure depended upon.

I confess that I don't hope to prevail upon the Spaniards to come here; but if you will, you, Count de

* The Light Infantry corps which La Fayette had commanded was broken up when the army went into winter quarters, and he now entertained the desire of transferring his services to the southern army under General Greene, and had applied to Washington for his advice. See Sparks' Writ. of Wash. vol. 7, p. 316.

Rochambeau, and Chevalier de Ternay, may try. In that case I wish you would write to both of them. My letter will, at all events, give some remote chance of their doing what I wish, and insure their communicating with General Greene. For political reasons I also wish to draw them into this correspondence.

Chevalier de la Luzerne wishes his packet to Count de Rochambeau to be forward as soon as possible.

Adieu, my dear General, your's most respectfully and affectionately.*

TO GENERAL WASHINGTON.

(ORIGINAL.)

Philadelphia, December the 16th, 1780.

MY DEAR GENERAL,—Your favor of the 8th instant never came to hand before last night. My former letters will have explained to you my sentiments relating to a journey southward. I must heartily thank you, my dear General, for the kind and friendly letters you have been pleased to send me. I am so happy in your friendship that every mark of your affection for me gives me a degree of pleasure which far surpasses all expressions.

As I have written to you before, my dear General, there is an intelligence of some ships and troops having been put in readiness at Brest; there is a possibility of a Spanish officer waiting on you for the sake of a co-operation. We are also to expect news from my friend the new Minister of the French Navy, and before they arrive you would not like my departure.

Two other reasons have weight with me; the first that if the enemy make this detachment, without which nothing material will happen in the Southward, and if

* For the answer to this letter, See Sparks' Writ. of Wash. v. 7, p. 322.

the intelligence is true about the fast recruiting of six month men, there is (not a probability) but a possibility of some thing to be done in this quarter. The second is, that for reasons I will explain to you when we meet, a visit from you to the French army is to be much wished, and in this case you will be glad that I may accompany you.

Under these circumstances, to which is added a natural reluctance to part from you and this army, and some idea that upon the whole my staying will be more agreeable to you, I think, my dear General, that unless new intelligence comes I will soon return.

Colonel Laurens persists in refusing to go, and hopes Hamilton may be sent, whom he thinks better calculated for the purpose; but I don't believe now that this plan may be effected, and in that case I should advise Laurens to accept of the commission, provided he is merely a *messenger* and not an *envoy*, that would supersede the old Doctor.

The Assembly of Pennsylvania have passed a bill for their officers which seems satisfactory to them. Before I go I will still intrigue for the affair of filling up the battalions. Mifflin behaves perfectly well.

Adieu, my dear General, most affectionately and respectfully, Your's, &c.*

TO GENERAL WASHINGTON.

(ORIGINAL.)

Philadelphia, March the 2nd, 1781.

MY DEAR GENERAL,—Your letters of the 25th and 26th† both came yesterday to hand, which shows that the

* For the letter referred to in the commencement of this, See Sparks' Writ. of Wash. v. 7, p. 316, and see also the letter of Washington to Lafayette, Ibid, p. 322 & 339.

† For these, See Sparks' Writ. Wash. p. 430 & 439. The date of the letter is there given as the 27th.

expresses have not made great dispatch. I would have done myself the honour of writing to your Excellency had I not every minute waited for intelligence from the Southward.

Your Excellency remembers that our shortest calculation on the arrival of the troops at the head of Elk was for the 6th of March; I am happy to inform you that they will be there this day or to-morrow early, and notwithstanding the depth of the mud, and the extreme badness of the roads, this march, which I can call rapid, (as for example, they came in two days from MorrisTown to Princeton,) has been performed with such order and alacrity, that agreeable to the report two men only have been left behind; and yet these two men have embarked at Trenton with some remains of baggage. At every place where the detachment have halted, they have found covering and wood ready for them, and there has not been the least complaint made to me from any inhabitant. Every third day they have drawn their provisions; the clothing has also been distributed, and having embarked yesterday at Trenton they passed the city about two o'clock with a wind which was extremely favorable. Congress have given to their troops the advance of one month's pay which will be distributed at the head of Elk in new emission.

The Artillery, consisting of one 24, six 18, two brass 12, one 8 inch howitzer, two 8 inch mortars, in all, 12 heavy pieces; four 6 pounders, and two small howitzers, with a sufficient quantity of ammunition, will be at the head of the Elk this day and to-morrow, so that by the 4th I hope we shall be ready to sail. A quantity of medicines and instruments, and fifteen hundred pairs of shoes will be at the head of Elk before we embark. Vessels will be in readiness to receive us with thirty days provision on board. I am also assured that we will have a sufficient quantity of boats to land the detachment, and two heavy ones will be added for the Artillery, the public, and some of the private armed vessels in the Bay have been ordered to the head of Elk; two dispatch boats are there, and four more have been asked for. As a farther security to our subsistence, I have got the Minister's permission to dispose of the French flour and salt meat along the Bay in case of necessity.

On my arrival at this place I heard that M. de Tilly, the French Commander, had conferred with the Virginians, but upon seeing that nothing could be done immediately, he was undetermined whether to stay or to return to Rhode Island. Fearing that our letters might miscarry, and wishing to hurry the preparations of the Militia, I complied with the earnest solicitations of the Minister of France to send on Colonel Gouvion, and directed him to go either by land or water (as the state of the Bay would permit) on board the French squadron, and afterwards to Baron de Steuben's Camp, where he may apprise these Gentlemen of our force, our intentions, and the time of our arrival. This minuted account I give to your Excellency to show you that nothing on our part has been wanting for the success of the expedition. Our preparations have in every article fulfilled, and in the most important one, time, have exceeded what had been expected.

Your letter was sent by express to General St. Clair, who immediately came to town; but nothing having been done for the settling of the accounts, none of the promises having been complied with, and the men being much scattered, it has, (after much consideration,) been thought impossible to embark any number with us, and General St. Clair promises to make every exertion for the sending of two or three hundred in a few days whom however I am not to depend upon.

I am myself going to the head of Elk and shall arrive there this evening. It has not been possible for me to leave sooner the City, as the three days I have remained here have been fully employed in making and forwarding preparations.

Before I go I will wait on the Board of War Navy

and propose the sending of the frigates; but the Trumbull having not her compliment of men, and those of the Ariel having mutinied at sea, I am afraid we will find difficulties. The preparations made at New York; the return of the Amarila; the remasting of the Bedfort; the impossibility Mr. Destouches is under to give us any further assistance; the uncertainty of what Mr. de Tilly may have determined before he had received your letter. Such are, my dear General, the many reasons which from a pretty certain expedition have lately made a precarious one. Under these circumstances, indeed, there must always be more or less danger in going down the Bay, and venturing the low country about Portsmouth. Being unacquainted with the answer you have received from Count de Rochambeau and Mr. Destouches, I am not able to judge how far I may depend upon the same ship being ordered again to Chesapeake (in case before the reception of your letter) she had thought proper to sail. Her coming was not in consequence of your proposition; her going was relative to the difficulties of an expedition very different from ours, and I wish I might know if (tho' Mr. Destouches cannot give further assistance,) this assistance at least may be depended upon, so as to hope for the return of the ship should M. de Tilly have left the bay. The bottom of the Bedfort is said to be damaged; the Amarila was said to have been dismasted. Suppose those circumstances were true, they would be in our favour. If a detachment was to go from New-York to Portsmouth, Westpoint would be less in danger. If Cornwallis continues advancing on, perhaps our being in the neighbourhood of Arnold may be of service; I will, however, confine myself literally to my instructions, and if Colonel Gouvion writes me with certainty that M. de Tilly is gone; if I am not led to suppose he will return, I will march back the detachment; for the present I am going on because upon the increasing of the enemy's force at Gardner's Bay, you recommended dispatch to me; I hope, however, that I will hear from your Excellency. Now that the chain is established, Colonel Pickering says, that in six days I may receive your answer at the head of Elk. The hope of seeing the French ship again, or some other reason, may detain me; but your answer will determine my movements, and I can receive it by the 8th, which is about the time when it was thought we would arrive at the head of Elk.

My expectations are not great, and I think we have but few chances for us. I shall make all possible dispatch, and listen particularly to the voice of prudence; however, some hazard must be ran, if we undertake under these circumstances.

General Duportail having not left this place, I am led to hope that if we don't go I may return in time for the journey to Rhode Island. I most earnestly beg, my dear General, that you will favor me with an immediate answer.

With the highest respect and most tender affection, I have the honor to be, your's, &c.

P.S.—One of our transports from Trenton had got aground, but the troops of her will still be in time for her at the head of Elk. Some new difficulties have been made for the collecting of shoes, but I will try to get over them. From the extraordinary motions of Lord Cornwallis, whom we have not heard of these many days, and from the movements in New-York, I am led to hope that I will hear from you respecting my future conduct, and that I may be at head-quarters before you think it prudent to leave New Windsor.*

* See the letters of Washington in Sparks' Writ. of Wash. vol. 7, p. 444 & 447.

TO GENERAL WASHINGTON.

(ORIGINAL.)

Head of Elk, March the 7th, 1781.

My Dear General,—Contrary winds, heavy rains, disappointments of vessels, and every inconvenience to which we had no remedy, have been, from the day of my arrival, combined against our embarkation. I hope, however, we will be on board to-morrow morning, and as nothing certain has been heard from the French ships, no time will be lost on our part for the celerity of the expedition.

The troops will embark five miles below this place, and three miles higher up than the Point where General Howe landed. There will be more room for the arrangements of our vessels, and the shallowness of the water insures us against the enterprise of any vessel of force. In this situation we may wait for intelligence from our friends. The State of Maryland have made to me every offer in their power. I will improve this opportunity of making up some deficiencies in the Quarter-Master and Engineer's Department, of insuring to us a good stock of provisions, and upon the intelligence received that Baron de Steubens was gone with a large detachment to the Southward, I had hinted the possibility of getting some Militia from the lower countries, and repairing some cannon at Baltimore ; but having read the inclosed from the Baron, I will write again to Governor Lee, (as my letter has been gone but two days,) and save the State from any expence of that kind. To the obtaining of vessels has been joined the difficulty of getting them up the river, as they were taking every opportunity to slip them off. All the vessels, three excepted, are only bay craft, and our Admiral's ship mounts twelve guns. I have prepared some kind of orders for that fleet, but hope to be relieved from my Naval command by the arrival of a French frigate, and have, at all events, sent for Commodore Nicholson of Baltimore. Mr. McHenry has been very active in accelerating the measures of his State.

By a letter from Colonel Gouvion, dated Yucomico River, I find that after many adventures, he had landed there on the 4th, and was proceeding by land to his destination. The wind is fair enough to come up the Bay, and hope soon to hear from our friends.

The inclosed letter from the Baron having first come into my hand, and being on public service, as it was waited upon *to be forwarded with dispatch*, I took the liberty to open it, but was very sorry to have done it after a letter of the same date had came also to hand; both say the same thing (at least in every material point,) and I am happy to find that the Baron's preparations are going on rapidly.

Whatever may be the Baron's opinion upon the facility of taking, sword in hand, the fortifications of Portsmouth, I will not hazard any thing before I have considered the matter with my own eyes. Arnold had so much time to prepare, and plays so deep a game; nature has made the position so respectable, and some of the troops under his orders have been in so many actions that I don't flatter myself to succeed so easily as it may be thought. The prospect of preserving Naval superiority must, I think, decide if we are to save bloodshed by regular approaches, or to risk our men into the dangers of an assault; but I would like to destroy the works in some measure before we attempt to storm them. A conversation with the Baron, with Colonel Gouvion, and some other officers, joined to what I can see myself, will better fix my mind on the matter than it can be at present. When I left Philadelphia General Wayne was not far from hoping he could soon collect a thousand men; but I am not so sanguine in my expectations; I am, however, trying to prepare matters for this number of men, but I think that a sufficiency of vessels, (unless ours are sent back,) will not be obtained in a few days. Let General Wayne arrive in time or not, when he comes under my directions I wish to know if in case we succeed, he must be sent to Genl. Greene. Supposing he is to go there, would your Excellency think of selecting some riflemen for the grand army? It seems to me that I heard you once mentioning this matter. The State of Virginia, I am told, finds difficulties in the keeping of prisoners. Suppose something of the kind was stated to me, am I to alter any thing in what you said to me on the subject?

I am in a great hurry to go, my dear General; but let us succeed or fall in the object we have in view, I shan't be less hurried to return with the detachment to head-quarters, where I hope to be again as soon as you may possibly expect. I beg you will present my respects to Mrs. Washington, and Mrs. Hamilton, and compliments to the family. I have received Mr. Washington's answer, he is waiting for me at the Baron's quarters.

With the highest respect and most tender affection I have the honor to be, your's, &c.*

TO GENERAL WASHINGTON.

(ORIGINAL.)

Off Turkey Point, March the 9th.

MY DEAR GENERAL,—Commodore Nicholson has joined us sooner than I expected; he answers to conduct the detachment to Annapolis without the least danger, there he will wait for intelligence from me, but

* See Washington's letter in Sparks' Writ. in Wash, vol. 8, p. 449.

says that if the French fleet are below he might go with safety (if not for the vessels at least for the troops) to the point of our destination. Nicholson will be very useful to the French fleet as he knows well the bay.

I will be at Hampton to-morrow night or the day after, and three days after my arrival, if the French (whose arrival has not been heard of) consent to send a frigate, the detachment may come in two days from Annapolis.

Most respectfully, my dear General, your's &c.

P. S.—I have written to the State of Maryland to tell them we don't want any of their Militia. I have left to the Navy Board to judge of the propriety to send out the Ariel adding that it was no more essential.

TO GENERAL WASHINGTON.

(ORIGINAL.)

York, March 15th, 1781.

My Dear General,—The number of small frigates and privateers that are in the bay, made it impossible for me to carry the detachment farther down than Annapolis, and I have requested the Governor of Maryland as well as the principal officers of the detachment, to give out that we are going to join General Greene; but the object of the expedition is so perfectly well known every where, that our sole dependence to keep Arnold must be upon the apprehension he has of a French fleet being cruizing off the capes.

For my part, I came in a barge from Annapolis, and very luckily escaped the dangers that were in the way. Colonel Harrison will have given to your Excellency a minute detail of the reasons which have prompted me to this measure. I have taken his advice on the matter, and have no doubt but that your Excellency (considering the probability that no frigate would have been sent) will approve of the step I have taken to forward as much as possible both the advantage of the expedition and the honor of the American arms.

On my arrival, (yesterday afternoon) I have found that Baron de Stuben had been very active in making preparations, and agreeable to what he tells me, we shall have five thousand militia ready to operate. This, with the Continental detachment, is equal to the business, and we might very well do without any land force from Newport.

By papers found in the baggage of a British officer, (taken in a boat) it seems that General Gregory had a correspondence with the enemy. The Baron has suspended him, but he is still with the troops.

Arnold is so well acquainted with the coming of the detachment, and his object is so well known, that, as I said before, our only chance to keep him must be the idea of a French fleet being off the capes ; he is fortifying at Portsmouth, and trying to get provisions. There has been some trifling skirmishes with the militia.

To my great disappointment the French fleet have not yet appeared. If the project has not been given up they must be expected every minute ; they had double the time which they wanted, and such winds as ought have brought them in four days.

I wanted to hold up the idea of my going to the Southward ; but the Baron says that if the detachment is not announced, the militia will desert. He wanted me to take the command immediately, but I thought it more polite not to do it until the detachment arrives or operations are begun.

In your first letter to the Baron, I wish my dear General, you will write to him that I have been much satisfied with his preparations. I want to please him, and harmony shall be my first object. As in all cases, (even this of my going to the Southward and coming here to make arrangements with the Baron) I would reconnoitre the enemies ; I will take an opportunity of doing it as soon as possible. They have not as yet been reconnoitred by the Baron, and I think it therefore more necessary for me to see with my own eyes.

As I have just arrived, my dear General, I cannot give you a very exact account of matters.

This letter I send by duplicate, and have the honor to be with the highest respect and most tender affection, yours, &c.

TO GENERAL WASHINGTON.

(ORIGINAL.)

Elk, April the 10th, 1781.

DEAR GENERAL,—By my letter of the 8th your Excellency will have known of my arrival at this place, and the preparations I was making to proceed Southward. I took at the same time the liberty to inform you that the great want of money, baggage, clothing, under which both officers and men are suffering, and the hope they had of being furnished with a part of these articles from their States, would render it very inconvenient for the troops to proceed immediately by land ; they begin to be sensible of the reason which detains them here, and are uneasy about it, as they are so unprovided for the journey. I have, however, hurried on preparations, and will be able to set off to-morrow morning. The circumstances of my being ready sooner than I expected, and a letter from the Governor of Maryland telling that six ships, whom I take to be plundering vessels, were coming up the Potomac, induces me not to wait for your Excellency's answer. Not that I pretend to defend the towns of Alexandria, Baltimore and Annapolis, at a time, or to stop the depredations of the enemy's parties in a country where their naval superiority renders it impossible; but because I don't think any consideration must delay the execution of superior orders, and because, if the corps was not sent to Southward they would with alacrity march back thirty or forty miles more to rejoin the grand army.

Having received no particulars of your Excellency's journey to Rhode Island, but by the paper, a letter from you to Mr. Lund Washington, and private letters from some friends, I cannot know what change has taken place in your plans, and am not able to account for the inactivity which you foresee for the grand army. Letters from Ministers, letters from my friends, intelligences from other quarters, every thing was combined to flatter me with the hope that our grand and decisive object would be in contemplation. I then was not displeased with the dispositions of the enemy that weakened that place. It is probable that your Excellency's plans have changed, and you intend to prosecute the war to the Southward.

I had yesterday the pleasure of dining on board the Hermione, and left her under sail to go to Rhode Island, where she will probably be the day after to-morrow. Mr. Delatouche, uncle to captain Latouche, will, it is said, command the squadron of the second division. I was conversing with his nephew, on whom he has an entire confidence on the expedition against New York, and he assured me that his Uncle's plan would certainly be to take possession of the harbour, and send a force up the North River, which you know is entirely the thing that you wanted M. de Vernay to do.

Mr. Delatouche having confidentially told me that he had a great influence over Mr. Destouches, I observed to him how important it was for the common cause that the French fleet might have the greatest possible activity. We were also conversing of the difficulties we laboured under for transportation, and he told me that the next day after his arrival at Rhode Island, unless such obstacles occurred as he could not foresee, Mr. Destouches would make you an offer of the ship l'Eveillé, and the four frigates to carry twelve hundred men to any part of continent you might think proper. Those ships are too strong to be afraid of frigates, and too fast sailers to be in the least concerned by the fear of a squadron. Thinking that (particularly as Lord Cornwallis has retreated) our march would take us forty days, where desertion and sickness, occasioned by want of shoes and every other necessary, as well as by the heat of the season, would much reduce our numbers, and that these ships, with the addition of the two frigates at Philadelphia, armed *en flute*, would in sailing on the 4th or 5th of May, carry 1500 men to Wilmington, Georgetown, or any place in the rear of Lord Cornwallis or the neighborhood of General Greene, I thought it my duty to encourage this idea, which would bring us to the point of operations sooner than we could arrive by land. It would also give you the time of forming at Morristown or Trenton, a detachment well provided, agreeably to the project you had in contemplation after the return of this corps. The appointment of officers could be made without affecting the delicacy of the regimental officers, nor the honor of those already employed. While we would be operating, Mr. Destouches might keep cruizers off Charleston. These ideas, my dear General, are only thrown out in consequence of the freedom you have often ordered me to take. What Mr. Destouches may do is uncertain, and I did not think myself authorised to express to him the least wish on that head. It was my duty to relate our difficulties to you, and the chances I foresaw to see them relieved in some measure; but unless the bad weather, of which there is now a prospect, makes it impossible, I will be to-morrow at the ferry at the Susquehannah.

You may have known from Mr. de La Luzerne, that two millions and a half had been given to Mr. Franklin, and that Marquis de Castries and Count de Vergennes, were trying to obtain a sum more adequate to our wants.

This, however, the Minister of France has requested me not to mention, as it was as yet an uncertainty, and would perhaps give ill-grounded hopes, destructive of the internal efforts we ought to make. I am told that just before the departure of Mr. Dela Peyrouse, some dispatches were sent to Brest; but do not think they contain any thing relating to our operations, as Marquis de Castries writes me that the determination of the Council upon our letters will be sent by the ships who is to convoy the expected vessels.

I am very sorry I have not seen the Aid de Camp who had a verbal message from General Greene. Inclosed I send to your Excellency the letter I have received on the occasion. Perhaps, did he mean to propose an expedition towards Cape-fear or Georgetown, which might be made with the light squadron above mentioned. An additional circumstance is, that l'Eveillé will now be commanded by Mr. de Lombard, captain Latouche's uncle, who is entirely under that Gentleman's influence.

I write to the board of war to get some shoes and other parts of clothing. I will this morning speak to the commanding officers of battalions on our intended journey; but have not yet said any thing to Colonel Gimat and Major Galvan, because it is possible that new circumstances may engage you to change your dispositions. Going by water, if possible, would level most all difficulties; but if I don't hear from you, I will always proceed on. I have the honor to be, yours &c.*

* See Washington's Letters of 21st of March and 5th and 6th of April. Sparks' Writ. of Wash. volume 7. pp. 449 and 463, 8469. See also—Sparks' Writ. of Wash. vol. 8. Appendix No. 1.

TO GENERAL WASHINGTON.

(ORIGINAL.)

Susquehannah ferry April 13th, 1781.

MY DEAR GENERAL,—I received your Excellency's letter relating to Colonel Gouvion. It would have been very agreable to me to keep this officer, your orders have been sent to Philadelphia where he is for the present. However distant I may be from the scene, I am happy to find that your Excellency hopes to undertake the grand object we have had in contemplation.

By a letter just received from the board of War, it seems that representations of wants have been made which they have mistaken for objections from me to our journey southward. I have said to some officers that our proximity to the southern states was the reason which had induced your Excellency to send this detachment, but I hope I need not assure you that I never thought of intimating the least idea of alteration to your Excellency's projects, but such as you would think of making yourself after your own ideas and intelligences. Perhaps my letter to the board of War may appear disrespectful or impolite, but nothing could stop me in an instance where it might be suspected I objected to your plans, or even differed in opinion. You know me too perfectly not to think an explanation useless.

It is confidently reported that the second division is arrived in the capes of Delaware, consisting of nine sail of the line, this was the number mentioned to me by the Marquis de Castries to be in harbour, your Excellency would in that case have a brilliant Campaign to the northward.

With the highest and most affectionate respect

Yours &c.*

* See Letters of Wash. of the 11th April. Sparks' Writ. of Wash. vol. 8., p. 11.

TO GENERAL WASHINGTON.

(ORIGINAL.)

Susquehannah ferry April 13th, 1781.

MY DEAR GENERAL—Had your Excellency's answer to my letter of the 8th, been forwarded with an equal celerity that your favor of the 6th, I would have received it before this time, but whatever change my new situation could make in your Excellency's dispositions, I thought it my duty in the mean while to obey the positive orders I had received, the Troops are now crossing the ferry and will with all possible speed proceed to Richmond.

By a letter received from General Green I find that he is strongly of opinion that I must go to the southward, his intention si to carry the seat of war into South Carolina, there by preventing a junction between Arnold and Cornwallis, he gives me many excllent reasons to justify the movement and requests me to make to Richmond, and they will, if possible, increase my zeal to execute your Excellency's orders.

General Green's opinion is that Lord Cornwallis will fall down towords Wilmington, his own project is to carry the war into South Carolina. Under these circumstances a corps of Light Infantry embarked at Philadelphia on board a light squadron might have been upon the seat of war in a very short passage.

I cannot help fearing, my dear General, that our campaign will take a defensive turn which is far from answering our first plans and expectations. Major Mc Pherson is with me as a volunteer, that officer has most zealously employed himself and has been most dangerously exposed in the discovery of a plot made to furnish the enemy with provisions, he has managed this matter with infinite address, being for two days and one night with six soldiers who, as well as himself, put on the air of British, and, in company with a spy who thought them to be enemy and by a most violent gale of wind, crossed the bay in a small boat, by which means he was made sensible that a trade of flour is carried with the enemy from the western shore of Maryland, and saved a magazine of 800 barrells of continental flour which would otherwise have fallen into the hands of the enemy. In case we proceed southerly perhaps will it be possible for General Green to give Major McPherson a command in some detachment; I would be happy if he was recommended to him by your Excellency. My determination being to go on with rapidity, unless I am recalled, your Excellency may easily judge of my movements from the answer I will probably receive in a few hours. Was I to assure your Excellency that this journey is perfectly agreable to the Troops, I would not use that candor which you have so much right to expect, but their zeal and discipline insure their readiness to obey.—I shall do my utmost to prevent desertion, and unless I was recalled, I shall proceed with celerity. But I beg your Excellency to remember that experience has often taught us how much reduced has ever been the number of our troops from the time of their departure to that of their arrival at the Southern army.

With the highest and most affectionate respect,

Yours &c.

TO GENERAL WASHINGTON.

(ORIGINAL.)

Susquehannah ferry April 14th, 1781.

My Dear General—Your Excellency's letter of the 11th, has overtaken me at this place, and having given to you an account of every measure I thought proper to

TO MAJOR GENERAL GREENE.

(ORIGINAL.)

Hanover Court House, April 28th, 1781.

SIR,—Having received intelligence that General Phillips' army were preparing at Portsmouth, for offensive operations. I left at Baltimore every thing that could impede our march, to follow us under a proper escort, and with about a thousand men, officers included; hastened towards Richmond which I apprehended would be a principal object with the enemy.

Being on our way, I have received successive accounts of their movements. On the 21st, the British troops, commanded by their Generals, Philips and Arnold, landed at City Point on the south side of James River. A thousand militia under Maj. General Caroude Stuben and General Muhlenberg, were posted at Blandford to oppose them, and on the 25th they had an engagement with the enemy; the militia behaved very gallantly, and our loss, it is said, is about twenty killed and wounded. The same day, the enemy whose force it is reported to be near 2500 regular troops, marched into Petersburg. Yesterday they moved to Osburn's, about thirteen miles from Richmond, and after a skirmish with a corps of militia, destroyed some vessels that had been collected there, but have not yet attempted to cross the river. Baron de Stuben, is at the same side, and has removed to Falling Creek Church.

The Continental detachment will in a few hours arrive at this place, 20 miles from Richmond. The enemy are more than double our force in regular troops and their command of the waters gives them great advantages.

With the highest respect, I have the honor to be yours, &c.

TO GENERAL GREENE.

(ORIGINAL.)

Camp on Pamunkey River, May 3d, 1781.

SIR,—I had lately the honor to inform you of the enemy's movements towards Richmond, and the forced marches I was making to its defence. The detachment arrived on the 29th; the British army was thirteen miles distant on the other side of the river. Petersburg, Chesterfield Court House, and part of our vessels had fallen into their hands. Our regular force consisted of 900 men, rank and file; that of the enemy, of 2,300, at the lowest estimate.

The command of the water, and such a superiority of regular troops, gave them possession of our shore. There was no crossing for us, but under a circuit of fifteen miles, and from the number and size of their boats, their passage over the river was six times quicker than ours.

Richmond being their main object. I determined to defend this capital, where a quantity of public stores and tobacco was contained. General Nelson was there, with a corps of militia, and Generals Stuben and Muhlenberg, higher up on the other side. The same evening, we were by summons from General Philips, made accountable for the public stores on board vessels near the town, (which he declared) should certainly fall into his hands. Next morning the enemy moved to Manchester, opposite Richmond, where they burnt the ware-houses. Six hundred men ventured on this side, but were timely recalled, and being charged by a few dragoons of Major Nelson, flew into their boats with precipitation.

Knowing General Phillip's intention against Richmond, (orders for attack had been already given) I directed Baron de Stuben to join us, and collected our force to receive the enemy, but the same night they retreated to Osburn's, from thence to the neck of land formed by James River and Appamatox, where they have re-embarked. Col. Pleasant's and Good's battalions of militia, were sent on each side of the river and gave annoyance to their troops and boats. The enemy have lost some men killed, prisoners and deserters. Since the British army landed at City Point, (some flour excepted at the Court-house) no public property has been destroyed. Yours &c.

TO GENERAL WASHINGTON.

(ORIGINAL.)

Camp near Bottom's Creek, May 4th, 1781.

My Dear General,—I request you will receive my affectionate acknowledgements for your kind letters. Every mark of friendship I receive from you adds to my happiness, as I love you with all the sincerity and warmth of my heart, and the sentiment I feel for you goes to the very extent of my affections.

Inclosed I send you, my dear General, two copies of letters to General Greene, which I also sent to Congress for their information. You will also find copies of the strange letters I have received from General Phillips, and the answers which, if he does not behave better, will break off our correspondence.

The leaving of my artillery appears a strange whim, but had I waited for it Richmond was lost, and Major Galvan, who has exerted himself to the utmost, cannot be with us under two days, as he never could obtain or seize horses for the artillery and ammunition waggons. It is not without trouble I have made this rapid march. General Phillips has expressed to an officer on flag, the astonishment he felt at our celerity, and when on the 30th, as he was going to give the signal to attack, he reconnoitred our position, Mr. Osburn, who was with him, says that he flew into a violent passion and swore vengeance against me and the corps I had brought with me.

I am, however, uneasy, my dear General, and do not know what the public will think of our conduct. I cannot say in any official letter that no boats, no waggons, no intelligence, not one spy could be obtained; that if once I had been manœuvring with Phillips he had every advantage over me; that a defeat would have scattered the militia, lost the few arms we have, and knocked down this handful of Continental troops. Great deal of mischief had been already done. I did not know but what the enemy meant to establish a post. Under these circumstances I thought it better to fight on none but my own grounds and to defeat the main and most valuable object of the enemy. Had I gone on the other side, the enemy would have given me the slip and taken Richmond, leaving nothing to me, but the reputation of a rash unexperienced young man. Our stores could not be removed.

No orders from General Greene have as yet come to me. I cannot conceive the reason of his delay in answering my letters. In the meanwhile, Phillips is my object, and if with a thousand men I can be opposed to three thousand in this State, I think I am useful to General Greene. In a former letter he tells me that his object is to divide the enemy, and having no orders I must be regulated by his opinion.

The enemy are gone down the river. I have detached some militia to Hoods where I mean to make a fort. Colonel Hennis, with another corps of militia, is gone towards Williamsburg. His orders are in case the enemy land there, to annoy them, and in case they mean to establish a post, he is to disturb them until I arrive. This position is 16 miles from Richmond, 42 from Williamsburg, 60 from Fredericksburg. I have sent an officer at Point Comfort, and established a chain of expresses to know if they appear to turn towards Potomac. Should it be the case, Fredericksburg will have my attention, having missed Mr. Hunter's works at Fredericksburg must be their next object as they are the only support to our operations in the southward. Your first letters, my dear General, will perhaps tell me something more about your coming this way. How happy I should be to see you, I hope I need not express. As you are pleased to give me the choice, I shall frankly tell my wishes. If you co-operate with the French against the place, you know I wish to be at head quarters. If something is co-operated in Virginia, I will find myself very happily situated for the present. In case my detachment remains in this State I wish not to leave it, as I have a separate and active command, though it does not promise great glory ; but as you gave me leave to do it, I shall in a few days write to you more particularly on my private concerns. It is not only on account of my own situation that I wish the French fleet may come into the bay. Should they come even without troops, it is ten to one that they will block up Phillips in some rivers, and then I answer he is ruined. Had I but ships, my situation would be the most agreeable in the world. Adieu my dear General, you will make me happy to write me sometimes. With the highest respect and most tender affection, I have the honor to be, yours, &c.*

* See Letters of Wash. of 31 May.—See Sparks' Writ., v. 8., p. 60.

TO GENERAL WASHINGTON.

(ORIGINAL.)

Richmond, May the 8th, 1781.

My Dear General,—There is no fighting here unless you have a naval superiority, or an army mounted upon race-horses. Phillips' plan against Richmond has been defeated; he was going towards Portsmouth, and I thought it should be enough for me to oppose him at some principal points in this State. But now it appears I will have business to transact with two armies, and this is rather too much.

By letters from North Carolina, I find that Lord Cornwallis, who I had been assured had sailed from Charleston, is advancing towards Hallifax. In consequence of letters from the same quarter, General Phillip's has altered his plans, and returned to a place called Brandon on the south side of James river, where he landed the night before last. Our detachment is under march towards the Hallifax road, his command of the water, enabled him to land where I could not reach him. The brigade at Petersburg is destroyed, and unless he acts with an uncommon degree of folly, he will be at Hallifax before me. Each of these armies is more than the double superior to me. We have no boats, few militia, and less arms. I will try to do for the best, and hope to deserve your approbation.

Nothing can attract my sight from the supplies and reinforcements destined to General Green's army. While I am going to get beaten by both armies or each of them seperately, the Baron remains at Richmond where he hurries the collection of recruits, and every other requisite. I have forbidden every department to give me any thing that may be thought useful to General Greene, and should a battle be expected (an event which

I will try to keep off,) no consideration will prevent our sending to Carolina 800 recruits who, I hope, may be equiped in a fortnight. When General Green becomes equal to offensive operations, this quarter will be relieved. I have written to Wayne, to hasten his march, but unless I am very hard pushed, shall request him to proceed south-ward. The militia have been ordered out, but are slow, unarmed, and not yet used to this business. General Green, from whom I had as yet no letters, was on the 26th, before Camden, but did not think himself equal to the storming of the works. My respects, if you please, to Mr. Washington, and compliments to the family. Most respectfully and affectionately.

Yours &c.

TO GENERAL WASHINGTON.

(ORIGINAL.)

Welton, north side of James River, May 18th, 1781.

MY DEAR GENERAL.—Having been directed by General Greene to take command of the troops in Virginia. I have also received orders from him, that every account from this quater, be immediately transmitted to Congress, and to your Excellency; in obedience to which I shall have the honor to relate our movements, aud those of the combined armies of the enemy. When General Phillips retreated from Richmond, his project was to stop at Williamsburg, there to collect contributions which he had imposed, this induced me to take a position between Pamunkey, and Chikahomany rivers, which equally covered Richmond, and some other interesting parts of the State, and from where I detached General Nelson with some militia towards Williamsburg.

Having got as low down as that place, General Phillips seemed to discover an intention to make a landing, but upon advices received by a vessel from Portsmouth, the enemy weighed anchor, and with all the sail they could croud, hastened up the river, this intilligence made me apprehensive that the enemy intended to manœuvre me out of Richmond where I returned immediately, and again collected our small force, intelligence was the same day received that Lord Cornwallis (who I had been assured, to have embarked at Wilmington) was marching through North Carolina, (this was confirmed by the landing of General Phillips at Brandon south side of James River.) Apprehending that both armies would move to meet at a central point, I march towards Petersburg and intended to have established a communication over Appamatox and James river, but on the 9th, General Phillips took possesstion of Petersburgh; a place where his right flank being covered by James River, his front by Appamatox, on which the bridges had been destroyed in the first part of the invasion, and his left not being attackable but by a long circuit through fords that at this season are very uncertain, I could not (even with an epual force) have got any chance of fighting him, unless I had given up this side of James River, and the country from which reinforcements are expected. It being at the enemy's choice to force us to an action, which their own position insured them against our enterprizes, I thought it proper to shift this situation, and marched the greater part of our troops to this place about ten miles below Richmond. Letters from General Nash, General Sumner, and General Jones are positive as to the arrival of Colonel Tarleton, and announce that of Lord Cornwallis at Halifax. Having received a request from North Corolina for ammunition, I made a detachment of 500 men under General Muhlenberg to escort 20,000 cartridges over Appomatox, and to divert the enemys attention, Colonel Gimat, with his battalion, and 4 field pieces commanded their position from this side of the River. I hope our ammunition will arrive safe, as before General Muhlenberg returned he put it in a safe road with proper directions. On the 13th, General Phillips died and the command devolved on General Arnold. General Wayne's detachment has not yet been herd of, before he arrives, it becomes very dangerous to risk any engagement where (as the British armies being vastly superior to us) we shall certainly be beaten, and by the loss of arms, the dispersion of militia, and the difficulty of a junction with General Wayne, we may loose a less dangerous chance of resistance.

These considerations have induced me to think that with our so very great inferiority, and with the advantage the enemy have by their cavalry and naval superiority, there would be much rashness in fighting them on any but our grounds, and this side of the river, and that an engagement which I fear will be soon necessary, ought, if possible to be deferred till the Pensylvanian's arrive, whom I have by several letters requested to hasten to our assistance.

No report has lately come from near Hallifax, though a very active officer has been sent for that purpose; but every intelligence confirms that Lord Cornwallis is hourly expected at Petersburg, it is true there never was such difficulty in getting tolerable intelligence, as there is in this country, and the immense superiority of the enemy's horses, render it very precarious to hazard our small parties.

Arnold has received a small reinforcement from Portsmouth.

I am dear General, your most obedient humble servant,

Yours &c.

P. S. Injustice to Major Mitchell and Captain Muir, who were taken at Petersburg, I have the honor to inform your Excellency that they had been sent to that place on public service. I have requested General Lawson to collect and take command of the militia south of Appamatox, local impediments was thrown in the road from Hallifax to Petersburg, and precautions taken to remove the horses from the enemy's reach. Should it be possible to get arms, some militia might be brought into the field, but General Greene and myself labour under the same disadvantage, the few militia we can with great pains collect arrive unarmed, and we have not a sufficiency of weapons to put into their hands.*

TO COLONEL HAMILTON.

(ORIGINAL.)

Richmond, May 23, 1781.

MY DEAR HAMILON,—I have been long complaining that I had nothing to do, and want of employment was an objection I had to my going to the southward; but for the present, my dear friend, my complaint is quite of an opposite nature, and I have so many arrangements to make, so many difficulties to combat, so many enemies to deal with, that I am much of a General as will make me an historian of misfortunes, and nail my curse upon the ruins of what good soldiers are pleased to call the army in Virginia. There is an age past since I heard from you. I acknowledge that on my part, I have not written so often as I ought to have done, but you will excuse this silence in favor of my very embarrassing circumstances, however remote you may be from your former post of aid-de-camp, to the Commander-in-chief, I am sure you are nevertheless acquainted with every transaction at head quarters. My letters have served to report information, and I shall consequently abstain from repetitions.

Our forced march saved Richmond. Phillips was going down, and thus far I am very happy. Phillips' return, his landing at Brandon, south side of James and

* See Washington's Letter of the 31st May.—Sparks' Writ. of Wash., v. 8., p. 60.

Appamatox rivers. Had Phillips marched to Hallifax I was determined to follow him, and should have risked every thing rather to omit making adversion in favor of Greene; but that enemy took possession of Petersburg, and obliged me to stick to the side of the river whence reinforcements are expected. Both armies have formed their junction of between four and five thousand men. We have no Continentals; their infantry is near five to one; their cavalry ten to one. Our militia are not numerous, without arms, and not used to war. Government wants energy, and there is nothing to enforce the laws. General Greene has directed me to take command in this State, and I must tell you by the way, his letter is very polite and affectionate; it then became my duty to arrange the departments, which I found in the greatest confusion and relaxation; nothing can be obtained, and yet expenses are enormous. The Baron and the few new levies we could collect, are ordered to South Carolina. Is it not strange that General Wayne's detachment cannot be heard of? They are to go to Carolina; but should I have them for a few days, I am at liberty to keep them. This permission I will improve so far as to receive one blow, that being beat, I may at least be beat with some decency. There are accounts that Lord Cornwallis is very strong; others make him very weak. In this country there is no getting good intelligence. I request you will write me if you approve of my conduct. The command of the waters, the superiority in cavalry, and the great disproportion of forces, gave the enemy such advantages that I durst not venture out, and listen to my fondness for enterprise; to speak truth, I was afraid of myself as much as of the enemy. Independence has rendered me the more cautious, as I know my own warmth; but if the Pennsylvanians come, Lord Cornwallis shall pay something for his victory.

I wish a reinforcement of light infantry to recruit the battallions, or a detachment under General Huntington, was sent to me. I wish Lawson or Sheldon were immediately dispatched with some horses. Come here, my dear friend, and command our artillery in Virginia. I want your advices and your exertions. If you grant my request, you will most oblige your friend.

Yours, &c.

TO GENERAL WASHINGTON.

(ORIGINAL.)

Richmond, May the 24th, 1781.

MY DEAR GENERAL—The junction of Lord Cornwallis with the other army at Petersburg' was an event that, from local circumstances, and from their so great superiority, it was impoisible to prevent, it took place on the 20th, and having lost every hope to operate, a timely stroke in conjunction with the Pensylvanians, my ideas were confined to defensive measures. I therefore moved up to Richmond, where precautions were taken to remove every valuable property, whether public or private.

By an officer that was in Halifax after Lord Cornwallis, I hear he has not left any post at that place, it appears, his sick and wounded remained at Wilmington, and were reimplaced by that garison. Reports concerning the numbers are so different, that I cannot trust anything but my eyes, until such an oportunity offers, this is the order of march, in which it is said his Lordship crossed Roanoke. Col. Tarlton's legion, Col. Hamilton's corps, 23d, 71st, 33d, British regiments, 200 tories, an Hessian regiment, the light infantry and guards with six field pieces. I am told General Leslie and Genl. O'Hara are with him, I have received successive and repeated accounts, that a British fleet of transports was arrived at Hampton, they were said to consist of

14 large vessels, and 16 smaller ones, under convoy of three large frigates. Mr. Day D.Q.M. at Williamsburg, writes that on the 22nd, 12 sail of large ships; a sloop, and schooner got underway opposite James Town; those ships full of men, and some horses on board the sloop. We have no acconnts of any fleet having sailed from New-York.

Yesterday afternoon, we had an heavy rain, which Colonel Tarlton improved in surprising some militia in Chesterfield County, thirty of whom fell into his hands.

This morning at 9 o'clock the enemy moved from Petersburg towards City Point, and destroyed the bridge they had lately constructed over Appamatox. I have just received accounts, that a body of them has landed at Westover. These are said to be the men who came up the river from Hampton, previous to which General Arnold had received a small reinforcement from Portsmouth.

To my great mortification, I have heard this morning, that the Pensylvanians are not so near as I had been, by every account positively assured: General Wayne writes me he will hasten to my support, and I am confident he will not lose time at this critical moment, but before he arrives, it is impossible that 900 continentals and 40 horses, with a body of militia by no means so considerable as they are reported to be, and whom it is so difficult to arm, be with any advantage opposed to such a superiority of forces, such a number of cavalry, to which may be added, their very prejudicial command of the writers.

Our handful of men being the point to which militia may be collected, and the only check, however small it is, that the enemy may have in this state, it ought, I think, to be managed with a great deal of prudence as its preservation is so very important to the fate of operations in Virginia.

With the highest respect, I have the honor to be

Yours &c.

TO GENERAL WASHINGTON.

(ORIGINAL.)

Camp between Rappahannock and North Anna, June 3rd, 1781.

My Dear General,—Inclosed you will find the copy of a letter to General Green. He at first had requested that I would directly write to you, since which his orders have been different, but he directed me to forward you copies of my official accounts. So many letters are lost in their way that I do not care to avoid repetitions.—I heartily wish, my dear general, my conduct may be approved of, particularly by you. My circumstances have been peculiar, and in this state I have sometimes experienced strange disappointments. Two of them, the stores at Charlottesville, and the delay of the Pennsylvania detachment, have given me much uneasiness and may be attended with bad consequences. Your presence, my dear general, would do a great deal. Should these detachments be increased to three or four thousand, and the French army come this way, leaving one of our generals at Rhode Island and two or three about New York and in the Jerseys, you might be very offensive in this quarter, and there could be a southern army in Carolina. Your presence would do immense good, but I would wish you to have a large force. General Washington, before he personally appears, must be strong enough to hope success. Adieu, my dear general, with the highest respect and most tender affection,

I have the honor to be, Yours,*

P. S. If you persist in the idea to come this way you may depend upon about 3000 militia in the field, relieved every two months. Your presence will induce them to turn out with great spirit.

* This letter, and the succeeding one to Gen. Greene, was written while La Fayette was retreating before Lord Cornwallis, and as he was about to cross the Rapidan to form a junction with Wayne. See the answers in Sparks's *Writ. of Wash.* v. 3. p. 86.

TO GENERAL GREENE.

(ORIGINAL.)

Camp between Rappahannock and North Anna, June 3rd, 1781.

SIR,—I have done myself the honor to write you many letters, but least some of them should have miscarried, which I much apprehend to have been the case, I shall repeat an account of the late transactions in this state.

The junction of the enemy being made, which for the reasons I have mentioned it was impossible to prevent, I retired towards Richmond and waited for Lord Cornwallis's movements, his regular force being so vastly superior to mine.—Reinforcements from below having still increased it, and his cavalry being ten to one, I could not think to bring into action a small body of eight or nine hundred men, that preserved the shadow of an army and an inconsiderable number of militia whose defeat was certain and would be attended with a fatal loss of arms.—

Lord Cornwallis had at first a project to cross above Richmond, but desisted from it and landed at Westover, he then proposed to turn our left flank, but before it was executed we moved by the left to the forks of Chickahomony,—the enemy advanced twelve miles and we retreated in the same proportion; they crossed Chickahomony and advanced on the road to Fredericksburg. We marched in a parallel with them, keeping the upper part of the country. Our position at Mattapony church would have much exposed the enemy's flank on their way to Fredericksburg, but they stopped at Cook's ford on the North Anna river, where they are for the present.—General Wayne having announced to me his departure on the 23d, I expected before this time to have made a junction. We have moved back some distance and are cautious not to indulge Lord Cornwallis with an action with our present force.—

The intentions of the enemy are not as yet well explained. Fredericksburg appears to be their object, the more so as a greater number of troops are said to be gone down than is necessary for the garrison of Portsmouth.—The public stores have been as well as possible removed, and every part of Hunter's works that could be taken out of the way.—It is possible they mean to make a stroke towards Charlotteville; this I would not be uneasy for, had my repeated directions been executed, but instead of removing stores from there to Albemarle old Court House, where Baron de Steuben has collected six hundred regulars, and where I ordered the militia south of James River to rendezvous—It appears from a letter I received this evening that state stores have been contrary to my directions collected there, least they should mix with the Continentals, but my former letters were so positive, and my late precautions are so multiplied that I hope the precious part of the stores will have been removed to a safer place. I had also some stores removed from Orange Court House. Dispatches from the Governor to me have fallen into the enemies' hands; of which I gave him and the Baron immediate notice.

The report of an insurrection in Hampshire county, and the hurry of Lord Cornwallis to communicate the copy of a Cartel with you where it is settled the prisoners will be sent by such a time to Jamestown, are motives that gave me some suspicions of a project towards the Convention troops. The number of the rebels is said to be 700—Gen. Morgan has marched against them; I think the account is pretty well authenticated tho' it is not official.—Having luckily opened a letter from the Board of War, to the Governor whereby the Convention troops are ordered to New England, I sent a copy of it to Col. Wood and requested an immediate execution of the order. This motive and the apprehension that I might be interrupted in a junction with Gen. Wayne have induced me particularly to attend to our re-union, an event that was indispensable to give us a possibility to protect some part or other of this state. I was until lately ignorant of your orders, that the new Continentals and militia under Baron de Steuben be united with this part of your army, and the Baron intended shortly to march to the southward.—When united to Gen. Wayne I shall be better able to command my own movements and those of the other troops in this state.—Had this expected junction taken place sooner, matters would have been very different.

The enemy must have five hundred men mounted and their Cavalry noreases daily. It is impossible in this country to take horses out of their way, and the neglect of the inhabitants, dispersion of houses, and robberies of negroes, (should even the most vigorous measures have been taken by the Civil authority) would have yet put many horses into their hands. Under this cloud of light troops it is difficult to reconnoitre as well as counteract any rapid movements they choose to make.

I have the honor to be with great respect, &c.

TO GENERAL GREENE.

(ORIGINAL.)

Allen's Creek, 22 miles from Richmond, June 18th, 1781.

Sir,—The enemy's position at Cooke's ford enabled them either to return to James River or to gain our northern communication. The arms and other precious stores arriving from Philadelphia, the importance of a junction with Gen. Wayne, and other strong reasons mentioned in my last, made it my first object to check the further progress of Lord Cornwallis. Some stores at the forks of James River were under the care of the major general, the Baron de Steuben, who had five hundred regulars of the Virginia new levies, and some militia.

Col. Tarlton's legion having pressed for Charlottesville, where the Assembly were sitting, was disappointed in his purpose by proper information being given them,

One hundred and fifty arms, however, and a small quantity of powder fell into the enemy's hands.

A detachment under Col. Simcoe said to be four hundred dragoons and mounted infantry, proceeded to the point of Fork, of which the Baron de Steuben received notice. Both his men and stores were transported to the south branch when the Baron marched to Etaunton River. Simcoe threw over a few men which destroyed what stores had been left. He hazarded a great deal, but our loss was inconsiderable.

In the meantime the British army was moving to the point of Fork, with intention to strike our magazines at Albermarle old Court House. Our force was not equal to their defence, and a delay of our junction would have answered the views of the enemy. But on the arrival of the Pennsylvanians we made forced marches towards James River, and on our gaining the South Anna we found Lord Cornwallis encamped some miles below the point of Fork. A stolen march through a difficult road gave us a position upon Michunk Creek, between the enemy and our magazines, where, agreeable to appointment, we were joined by a body of riflemen. The next day Lord Cornwallis retired towards Richmond (where he now is) and was followed by our small army.

I have direeted General Steuben to return this way and a junction will be formed as soon as his distance permits.

With the highest regard, &c., &c.

P. S. The following is an extract of a letter just now received from James Barron, Commodore, dated Warwick, 9 miles from Hampton, June 17th, 1781,

"At five o'clock this afternoon anchored in the road from sea, 35 sail of the enemies' vessels ; viz : 24 ships, 10 brigs and one schooner, which I take to be the fleet that sailed from hence 13 days ago. Only 4 appear to have troops on board."

TO GENERAL GREENE.

(ORIGINAL.)

Mr. Tyter's plantation, 20 miles from Williamsburg, 27th June, 1781.

SIR,—My letter of the 18th, informed you of the enemy's retrograde movement to Richmond, where they had made a stop. Our loss at the point of Fork chiefly consisted of old arms out of repair and some cannon, most of which have been since recovered.

On the 18th the British Army moved towards us with design as I apprehend to strike at a detached corps commanded by Gen. Muhlenberg, upon this the light Infantry and Pennsylvanians marched under Gen. Wayne when the enemy retired into town. The day following I was joined by Gen. Steuben's troops, and on the night of the 20th Richmond was evacuated. Having followed the enemy our light parties fell in with them near New Kent Court House, the army was still at a distance and Lord Cornwallis continued his route towards Williamsburg; his rear and right flank were covered by a large corps commanded by Col. Simcoe. I pushed forward a detachment under Col. Butler, but notwithstanding a fatiguing march the colonel reports that he could not have overtaken them, had not Major McPherson mounted 50 light infantry behind an equal number of dragoons, which coming up with the enemy charged them within six miles of Williamsburg; such of the advance corps as could arrive to their support, composed of riflemen under Major Call and Major Willis began a smart action. Inclosed is the return of our loss. That of the enemy is about 60 killed and 100 wounded, including several officers, a disproportion which the skill of our riflemen easily explains. I am under great obligations to Col. Butler and the officers and men of the detachment for their ardor in the pursuit and their conduct in the action. Gen. Wayne who had marched to the support of Butler, sent down some troops under Major Hamilton. The whole British army came out to save Simcoe, and on the arrival of our army upon this ground returned to Winsburg. The post they occupy at present is strong and under protection of their shipping, but upwards of one hundred miles from the point of Fork.

I had the honor to communicate these movements to the executive of the state that the seat of government might be again re-established in the capital. Lord Cornwallis has received a reinforcement from Portsmouth.

With the greatest respect I have the honor to be.

TO GENERAL GREENE.

(ORIGINAL.)

Ambler's Plantation, opposite Jamestown, 8 July, 1781.

SIR,—On the 4th inst. the enemy evacuated Williamsburg where some stores fell into our hands, and retired to this place under the cannon of their shipping. Next morning we advanced to Bird's tavern, and a part of the army took post at Norrel's mill about nine miles from the British camp.

The 6th I detached an advanced corps under Gen. Wayne with a view of reconnoitering the enemy's situation. Their light parties being drawn in the pickets which lay close to their encampment were gallantly attacked by some riflemen whose skill was employed to great effect.

Having ascertained that Lord Cornwallis had sent off his baggage under a proper escort and posted his army in an opened field fortified by the shipping, I returned to the detachment which I found more generally engaged. A piece of cannon had been attempted by the van guard under Major Galvan whose conduct deserves high applause.—Upon this the whole British army came out and advanced to the thin wood occupied by General Wayne.—His corps chiefly composed of Pennsylvanians and some light infantry did not exceed eight hundred men with three field pieces. But notwithstanding their numbers, at sight of the British the troops ran to the rencontre. A short skirmish ensued with a close, warm, and well directed firing, but as the enemy's right and left of course greatly outflanked ours, I sent General Wayne orders to retire half a mile to where Col. Vose's and Col. Barber's light infantry battalions had arrived by a rapid move, and where I directed them to form. In this position they remained till some hours in the night. The militia under Gen. Lawson had been advanced, and the continentals were at Norrel's mill when the enemy retreated during the night to James Island, which they also evacuated, crossing over to the south side of the river. Their ground at this place and the island were successively occupied by General Muhlenberg. Many valuable horses were left on their retreat.

From every account the enemy's loss has been very great and much pains taken to conceal it. Their light infantry, the brigade of guards and two British regiments formed the first line, the remainder of the army the second; the cavalry were drawn up but did not charge.

By the inclosed return you will see what part of Gen. Wayne's detachment suffered most. The services rendered by the officers make me happy to think that altho' many were wounded we lost none. Most of the field officers had their horses killed, and the same accident to every horse of two field pieces made it impossible to move them, unless men had been sacrificed. But it is enough for the glory of Gen. Wayne and the officers and men he commanded to have attacked the whole British army with a reconnoitering party only, close to their encampment, and by this severe skirmish hastened their retreat over the river.—

Col. Bowyer of the riflemen is a prisoner.—

I have the honor to be, &c.

TO GENERAL WASHINGTON.

(ORIGINAL.)

Mrs. Ruffin's, August 29th, 1781.

MY DEAR GENERAL—Independent of the answer to your letter of the 15th, I have been very particular in a second letter intrusted to Col. Moriss. But at this moment wish to send you minuted and repeated accounts of every thing that passes in this quarter.

The enemy have evacuated their forts at Troy, Kemp's Landing, Great Bridge, and Portsmouth. Their vessels with troops and baggage went round to York. Some cannon have been left spiked up at Portsmouth; but I have not yet received proper returns.

I have got some intelligences by the way of this servant I have once mentioned. A very sensible fellow was with him, and from him as well as deserters, I hear that they begin fortifying at York. They are even working by a windmill at which place I understand they will make a fort and a battery for the defence of the river. I have no doubt but that something will be done on the land side. The works at Gloster are finished; they consist of some redoubts across Gloster creek and a battery of 18 pieces beating the river.

The enemy have 60 sails of vessels into York river, the largest a 50 gun ship and two 36 frigates.—About seven other armed vessels, the remainder are transports, some of them still loaded and a part of them very small vessels. It appears they have in that number merchantmen, some of whom are Dutch prizes. The men of war are very thinly manned. On board the other vessels there are almost no sailors.

The British army had been sickly at Portsmouth, the air of York begins to refit them. The whole cavalry have crossed on the Gloster side yesterday evening, a movement of which I gave repeated accounts to the militia there; but the light infantry and main body of the militia are at this place, Gen. Wayne on the road to Westover, and we may form our junction in one day. I keep parties upon the enemy's lines. The works at Portsmouth are levelling. The moment I can get returns and plans I will send them to your Excellency. The evacuation of a post fortified with much care and great expense will convince the people abroad that the enemy cannot hold two places at once.—The Maryland troops were to have set out on Monday last. There is in this quarter an immense want of clothing of every sort, arms, ammunition, hospital stores, and horse accoutrements. Should a maritime superiority be expected, I would propose to have all those matters carried from Philadelphia to the head of Elk.

The numbers of the British army fit for duty I *at least* would estimate at 4500, rank and file. Their sailors I cannot judge but by intelligences of the number of vessels. In a word this part affords the greatest number of regulars and the only active army to attack, which having had no place of defence must be less calculated for it than any garrison either at New York or in Carolina. With the highest respect and most sincere affection, &c.

TO GENERAL WASHINGTON.

(ORIGINAL.)

Holt's Forge, September the 1st, 1781.

MY DEAR GENERAL.—I am happy to inform your Excellency that Count de Grasse's fleet is safely arrived in this bay; it consists of 28 ships of the line with several frigates and convoys a considerable body of troops under Marquis de St. Simon.—Previous to their arrival such positions had been taken by our army as to prevent the enemy's retreating towards Carolina.

In consequence of your Excellency's orders I had the honor to open a correspondence with the French Generals, and measures have been taken for a junction of our troops.—

Lord Cornwallis is still on York river and is fortifying himself in a strong position.—

With the highest respect I have the honor to be,*

TO GENERAL WASHINGTON.

(ORIGINAL.)

Camp Williamsburg, Sept. 8th, 1781.

MY DEAR GENERAL.—Your letter of the 2d September is just come to hand. Mine of yesterday mentioned that the ships in York river had gone down. Inclosed is the account of an engagement off the capes. What disposition has been made for the internal protection of the bay, I do not know. James river is still guarded, but we have not as yet received any letter from Count de Grasse relative to his last movements. I hasten to communicate them as your Excellency will probably think it safer to keep the troops at the Head of Elks until Count de Grasse returns. Indeed, unless the greatest part of your force is brought here, a small addition can do but little more than we do effect. Lord Cornwallis will in a little time render himself very respectable.

I ardently wish your whole army may be soon brought down to operate.

We will make it our business to reconnoitre the enemy's works and give you on your arrival the best description of it that is in our power. I expect the governor this evening and will again urge the necessity of providing what you have recommended.

* See answer of Washington, Sparks's Writ. of Wash. v. 8. p. 156.

By a deserter from York I hear that two British frigates followed the French fleet and returned after they had seen them out of the capes. A spy says that two schooners supposed to be French have been seen coming up York river, but we have nothing so certain as to insure your voyage, tho' it is probable Count de Grasse will soon return.

I beg leave to request, my dear General, in your answer to the Marquis de St. Simon you will express your admiration at this celerity of their landing and your sense of their cheerfulness in submitting to the difficulties of the first moments. Indeed I would be happy something might also be said to Congress on the subject.

Your approbation of my conduct emboldens me to request that Gen. Lincoln will of course take command of the American part of your army; the division I will have under him may be composed of the troops which have gone through the fatigues and dangers of the Virginia campaign; this will be the greatest reward of the services I may have rendered, as I confess I have the strongest attachment to these troops.

With the highest respect I have the honor to be,*

TO GENERAL WASHINGTON.

(ORIGINAL.)

Williamsburg, 10 Sept. 1781.

MY DEAR GENERAL,—Gourion is just arrived, he says you may be on your way. We hasten to send to the commanding naval officer in the bay. Hitherto I had no way to write to you by water, but Count de Grasse being at sea we request the officer he has left to have every precaution taken for the safety of navigation. It is probable they are taken, but I would have been too

* See Letter of Washington, Sparks's Writ. of Wash. v. 8. p. 157. A plan of operations in Virginia at p. 158.

uneasy had I not added this measure to those that have been probably adopted.

I wrote several letters to you; the surprising speedy landing of the French troops under the Marquis de St. Simon; our junction at Williamsburg; the unremitted ardor of the enemy in fortifying at York; the sailing of Count de Grasse in pursuit of 16 sail of the line, of the British fleet, were the most principal objects. I added we were short of flour, might provide cattle enough. I took the liberty to advise James River as the best to land in, the particular spot referred to a mor particular examination, the result of which we shall s nd to-morrow.

Excuse the haste that I am in, but the idea of your being in a cutter leaves me only the tim to add that I am, &c.

TO GENERAL WASHINGTON.

(ORIGINAL.)

Camp before York, September 30th, 1781.

MY DEAR GENERAL—You have been so often pleased to ask I would give my opinion on any subject that may occur, that I will this day take the liberty to mention a few articles.

I am far from laughing at the idea of the enemy's making a retreat. It is not very probable, but it is not impossible, indeed they have no other way to escape; and since we cannot get ships at York I would be still more afraid of a retreat by West Point than any thing else. The French hussars remaining here, our dragoons and some infantry might be stationed somewhere near West Point, rather on the north side. I see the service is much done by details, and to use your permission would take the liberty to observe that when the siege is once begun it might be more agreeable to the officers and men to serve as much as possible by whole battalions. Col. Scamel is taken: his absence I had accounted for by his being officer of the day. I am very sorry we lose a valuable officer, but tho' Col. Scamel's being officer of the day has been a reason for his going in front, I think it would be well to prevent the officers under the rank of generals or field officers reconnoitering for the safety of their commands from advancing so near the enemy's lines.

There is a great disproportion between Huntington's and Hamilton's battalions. Now that Scamel is taken we might have them made equal and put the eldest of the two Lieutenant Colonels upon the right of the brigade.

I have these past days wished for an opportunity to speak with your Excellency on Count de Grasse's demand relative to Mr. de Barrass's fleet. This business being soon done, we may think of Charleston, at least of the harbor or of Savannah. I have long and seriously thought of this matter but would not be in a hurry to mention it until we knew how long this will last. However it might be possible to give Count de Grasse an early hint of it in case you agree with him upon the winterly departure of the whole fleet for the West Indies. One of my reasons to wish troops (tho' not in great number) to be sent to Glocester county by way of West Point is that for the first days it will embarrass any movement of the enemy up the river or up the country on either side, and when it is in Glocester county it may be thought advantageous by a respectable regular force to prevent the enemy's increasing their works there and giving us the trouble of a second operation, and in the same time it will keep from York a part of the British forces.

With the highest respect and most sincere affection I have the honor to be, &c.*

* For a "Plan of the Siege of Yorktown," see Spark's Writ. of Wash. v. 8. p. 186.

TO GENERAL WASHINGTON.

(ORIGINAL.)

November 29th, 1781.

MY DEAR GENERAL,—Inclosed you will find some numbers, a copy of which I have kept, and which contains some names that may probably occur in our correspondence. I need not tell you, my dear General, that I will be happy in giving you every intelligence in my power and reminding you of the most affectionate friend you can ever have.

The goodness you had to take upon yourself the communicating to the Virginia army the approbation of Congress appears much better to me than my writing to the scattered part of the body I had the honor to command. Give me leave, my dear General, to recall to your memory the peculiar situation of the troops who being already in Virginia were deprived of the month's pay given to the others. Should it be possible to do something for them it would give me great satisfaction.

I will have the honor to write to you from Boston, my dear General, and would be very sorry to think this is my last letter. Accept however once more the homage of the respect and of the affection that render me for ever—

LAFAYETTE.

END OF VOL. I.

APPENDIX I.

A SUMMARY OF THE CAMPAIGN OF 1781,

TO SERVE AS EXPLANATION TO THE MAP.

After the combat of MM. Destouches and Arbuthnot, the project on Portsmouth was abandoned: the French sailed for Rhode Island; the militia were dismissed, the regular troops proceeded to the north. Arnold was afterwards reinforced by Major-general Phillips, and the conquest of Virginia became the true object of the English during this campaign. The allied army, under the Generals Washington and Rochambeau, proceeded towards New York; that of General Greene attacked the posts which had been left in Carolina, both about five hundred miles from Richmond: Major-general the Marquis de Lafayette was charged with defending Virginia.

April and *May*.—From preparations made at Portsmouth, he conceives that the capital was the proposed aim; a forced march of his corps from Baltimore to Richmond, about two hundred miles; he arrives in the evening of the 29th of April; the enemy had reached Osborn; the small corps of militia assemble in the night at Richmond; the next morning the enemy at Manchester, seeing themselves forestalled, re-embark at Bermuda Hundred, and re-descend James River.

The Americans at Bottom's Bridge, a detached corps in Williamsburg; General Phillips receives an *aviso*, and reascends the river, landing at Brandon; second reinforcement from New York; Lord Cornwallis, who was reported to have embarked at Charlestown, advances through North Carolina.

The Americans at Osborn, to establish a communication on James and Appomattox, are forestalled by the march of Phillips to Petersburg, the 10th, at Wilton; the 18th, cannonading and reconnoitring on Petersburg, which, by assembling on one point, the hostile parties permit a convoy to file off for Carolina; the 20th, at Richmond; junction of Lord Cornwallis with the troops of Petersburg; the great disproportion of the American corps, the impossibility of commanding the navigable rivers, and the necessity of keeping the important side of James River, do not allow any opposition.

Having sent a portion of the troops to Portsmouth, Lieutenant-general Lord Cornwallis selected for himself an army of about five thousand men, three hundred dragoons, and three hundred light horsemen; crosses to Westover. The Americans had only about three thousand men, formed of one thousand two hundred regulars, fifty dragoons, and two thousand militia. All the important forces had evacuated Richmond; our troops at Wintson's Bridge; a rapid march of the two corps, the enemies to engage an action, the Americans to avoid it, and retain the heights of the country with the communication of Philadelphia, which is equally necessary to our army and to the existence of that of Carolina.

June.—The magazines of Fredericksburg are evacuated; the Americans at Mattapony Church; the enemy at Chesterfield Tavern; heavy rains, which will render the Rapid Ann impassable; Lord Cornwallis marches to engage the front; our troops hasten their march, and repair to Racoon Ford, to await General Wayne, with a regular corps of Pennsylvanians.

Despairing of being able to engage in action, or cut off the communication between Wayne and Philadelphia, Lord Cornwallis changes his own purpose, and endeavours to defeat that of the Americans; he suddenly directs his movements against the great magazines of Albemarle Court-House; a detachment of dragoons strives to carry off the Assembly of State at Charlottesville, but does not accomplish this end; another detachment bore upon Point-of-Fork, where General Steuben formed six or seven hundred recruits; he evacuated that point, and thought he ought to retire in the direction of Carolina; some objects of slight importance are destroyed. The passage of the Rapid Ann was necessary, to avoid being embarrassed by Lord Cornwallis; the communication with Philadelphia was indispensable. It was impossible to hope, even by fighting, to prevent the destruction of the magazines before the junction with the Pennsylvanians. Lafayette takes, therefore, the resolution of waiting for them, and, as soon as they arrive, regains the enemy with forced marches.

The 12th, the Americans at Boswell's Tavern; Lord Cornwallis has reached Elk Island. The common road, which it is necessary for him to cross to place himself above the enemy, passes at the head of Bird's Creek; Lord Cornwallis carries thither his advance-guard, and expects to fall upon our rear; the Americans repair, during the night, a road but little known, and, concealing their march, take a position at Mechunck Creek, where, according to the orders given, they are joined by six hundred mountaineers. The English general, seeing the magazines covered, retires to Richmond, and is followed by our army.

Various manœuvres of the two armies; the Americans are rejoined by General Steuben, with his recruits; their force then consists of two thousand regulars, and three thousand two hundred militia. Lord Cornwallis thinks he must evacuate Richmond; the 20th, the Marquis de Lafayette follows him, and retains a posture of defence, seeking to manœuvre, and avoiding a battle. The enemy retires on Williamsburg, six miles from that town; their rear-guard is attacked in an advantageous manner by our advanced corps under Colonel Butler. Station taken by the Americans at one march from Williamsburg.

July.—Various movements, which end by the evacuation of Williamsburg; the enemy at Jamestown. Our army advances upon them; the 6th, a sharp conflict between the hostile army and our advance-guard under General Wayne, in front of Green Spring: two pieces of cannon remain in their hands; but their progress is arrested by a reinforcement of light infantry; the same night they retire upon James Island, afterwards to Cobham, on the other side of James River, and from thence to their works at Portsmouth. Colonel Tarleton is detached into Amelia County; the generals Morgan and Wayne march to cut him off; he abandons his project, burns his wagons, and retires with precipitation. The enemy remaining in Portsmouth, the American army takes a healthy station upon Malvan Hill, and reposes after all its labour.

August.—The Americans refusing to descend in front of Portsmouth, a portion of the English army embarks and proceeds by water to Yorktown and Gloucester. General Lafayette takes a position at the Fork of Pamunkey and Mattapony River, having a detached corps upon both sides of York River. The Pennsylvanians and some new levies receive orders to remain on James River, and think themselves intended for Carolina. An assembly of militia on Moratie or Roanoke River; the fords and roads south of James River destroyed on various pretences; movements to occupy the attention of the enemy. As in the event prepared by Lafayette, the means of escape would remain to the garrison of Portsmouth, Lafayette threatened that point. General O'Hara thinks he ought to nail up thirty pieces of cannon, and join the largest part of the army. The whole was scarcely united, when the Count de Grasse appears at the entrance of Chesapeak Bay. General Wayne crosses the river, and places himself in such a manner as to arrest the enemy's march, if he should attempt to retreat towards Carolina. The French admiral is waited for at Cape Henry by an aide-de-camp of Lafayette, to report to him the respective situations of the land troops, and ask him to make the necessary movements to cut off all retreat to the enemy. He anchors at Cape Henry, sends three vessels to York River, and fills James River with frigates; the Marquis de Saint Simon, with three thousand men, lands at James Island or Jamestown.

September.—The river thus defended, General Wayne receives the order to cross it; the Marquis de Lafayette marches upon Williamsburg, and assembles together, in a good position, the combined troops, to the number of seven thousand three hundred men. He had left one thousand five hundred militia in the county of Gloucester, and sends to hasten some troops coming from the north. This station, which closes all retreat to Lord Cornwallis, (our advance posts nine miles from York,) is retained from the 4th to the 28th of September. Lord Cornwallis reconnoitres the position of Lafayette, and despairs of forcing it.

The 6th September, the Count de Grasse, quitting the defended rivers, goes out with the remainder of his fleet, pursues Admiral Hood, who had presented himself, beats him, and sinks the *Terror;* he takes the *Iris* and *Richmond* frigates; the 13th, he joins, in the bay, the squadron of M. de Barras, which had sailed from Rhode Island, with eight hundred men and the French artillery: the fleet of the Count de Grasse consists, at this period, of thirty-eight ships of the line.

Admiral de Grasse and General Saint Simon, commanders of the French under Lafayette, urge him to attack Lord Cornwallis, and offer him a reinforcement from the ship garrisons. He prefers acting on more secure grounds, and waiting for the troops from the north. General Washington succeeded in reality, in completely deceiving General Clinton as to his intentions; he was advancing towards Virginia with an American detachment, and the army of the Count de Rochambeau embarked at the head of Chesapeak; they proceeded, upon transports, to Williamsburg. The 28th, they march upon New York, and the combined army commences investing it; the 29th, reconnoitring the place; the 30th, the enemy evacuates the advance posts, and retires into the works of York.

October.—The 1st, a new reconnoitre; the 3rd, a skirmish between the legion of the Duke de Lauzun and that of Tarleton, in which the former gained the advantage. That legion and eight hundred men from the ships under M. de Choisy had joined the militia at Gloucester. The night of the 6th, the trenches were opened; that of the 11th, the second parallel. The night of the 14th, the redoubts of the enemy's left were taken, sword in hand, the one by the grenadiers and French light horsemen, the other by the light infantry of the Americans. The first attack directed by the Baron de Viomenil, a field-marshal; the second by the Marquis de Lafayette. The morning of the 17th, Lord Cornwallis asked to capitulate; that same evening the firing ceased. The English army, reduced to eight thousand men, comprising nine hundred militia, gave themselves up as prisoners of war.

APPENDIX II.

TO THE COUNT DE VERGENNES.

Havre, 18th July, 1779.

Sir,—You ask me for some ideas respecting an expedition to America. As it is not a fixed plan which you require, nor a memorial addressed in form to the ministry, it will be the more easy to comply with your wishes.

The state of America, and the new measures which the British appear to be adopting, render this expedition more than ever necessary. Deserted coasts, ruined ports, commerce checked, fortified posts whence expeditions are sent, all seem to call for our assistance, both by sea and land. The smallest effort made now, would have more effect on the people than a great diversion at a more distant period; but besides the gratitude of the Americans, and particularly of the oppressed states, a body of troops would insure us a great superiority on that continent. In short, sir, without entering into tedious details, you know that my opinions on this point have never varied, and my knowledge of this country convinces me, that such an expedition, if well conducted, would not only succeed in America, but would be of very essential service to our own country.

Besides the advantage of gaining the affection of the Americans, and that of concluding a good peace, France should seek to curtail the means of approaching vengeance. On this account it is extremely important to take Halifax; but as we should require foreign aid, this enterprise must be preceded by services rendered to different parts of the continent; we should then receive assistance, and, under pretext of invading Canada, we should endeavour to seize Halifax, the magazine and bulwark of the British navy in the new world.

Well aware that a proposition on a large scale would not be acceded to, I will diminish, as much as possible, the necessary number of troops. I will say four thousand men, a thousand of them to be grenadiers and chasseurs; to whom I will add two hundred dragoons and one hundred hussars, with the requisite artillery. The infantry should be divided into full battalions, commanded by lieutenant-colonels. If commissions of higher rank should be desired for the older officers, you are aware that the minister of marine has it in his power to bestow such, as when the expedition returns to Europe, will have no value in the land service. We want officers who can deny themselves, live frugally, abstain from all airs, especially a quick, peremptory manner, and who can relinquish, for one year, the pleasures of Paris. Consequently we ought to have few colonels and courtiers, whose habits are in no respect American.

I would ask, then, for four thousand three hundred men, and, as I am not writing to the ministry, allow me, for greater ease in speaking, to suppose myself for a moment the commander of this detachment. You are sufficiently acquainted with my principles to know that I shall not court the choice of the king. Although I have commanded, with some success, a larger body of troops, and I frankly confess I feel myself capable of leading them, yet my intention is not to put forth my own claims; but to answer for the actions of a stranger would be a folly, and as, setting talents apart, it is on the political conduct of the leader, the confidence of the people and of the American army, that half the success must depend, I am obliged, reluctantly, to set forth a character that I know, in order to establish my reasonings upon some basis.

Leaving this digression, I come to the embarkation of these four thousand three hundred men. As the coasts of Normandy and Brittany have been much harassed, I should propose sailing from the Island of Aix; troops and provisions might be obtained in the vicinity. The ports between Lorient and the channel would furnish transport vessels.* Lorient has some merchant ships of a pretty

* I hear that you have, at Lorient, three vessels of the India company, of forty guns and eight hundred tons. These caracks, if I recollect rightly,

large burthen. The caracks of the channel are still larger, and these vessels have, moreover, guns of large calibre, which may be of use, either in battle, or in silencing batteries on shore; besides, they might be ready in a very short time. I would embark the soldiers, a man to every two tons, and would admit the dragoons, with their cavalry equipage only. There are many details I would give if the project be decided upon, but would be superfluous to mention here. After the experience of Count d'Estaing, who found himself straitened with biscuit for four months, and flour for two, I would take the latter, adding biscuit for six months, which would make in all eight months' provision for the marine and the troops. As to our escort, that must be decided upon by the marine; but our transports being armed vessels, three ships of the line, one of fifty guns for the rivers, three frigates and two cutters, would appear to me to be more than sufficient. As the expedition is especially a naval one, the commander of the squadron should be a man of superior abilities; his character, his patriotism, are important points. I have never seen M. de Guichen, but the reports I have heard of his worth and modesty prepossess me strongly in his favour. Being then at the Island of Aix with our detachment, and the squadron that is to transport it, the next question is how to act, and our movements must depend entirely upon circumstances. According to the first project, we were to sail by the first of September, and by the second to remain here until the last of January;* it might, however, be possible to sail in October. This even appears to me better than remaining until the close of January; but the different operations are included in the other plan. The enemy's

are fifty-gun ships, of nine hundred and sixty tons burthen. A small number of vessels would be sufficient; they might soon be got ready, and their force would diminish the required escort. As for frigates, you will find in readiness, at Lorient, the *Alliance*, the *Pallas*, and others. However, if you are determined to employ the vessels which are fitted out in the expedition against England, it would be necessary to take ours from St. Malo in preference. (Note from M. de Lafayette.)

* Virginia and Carolina would be the scene of our operations during the months of December and January, and we should pass the remainder of the winter at Boston. I greatly prefer this project to waiting until the last of January.

fleet is to be reinforced, and, as we are assured that four or five weeks' preparation will be sufficient for the transports and the troops, there is nothing unreasonable in forming our projects for this autumn, and even for the month of September.

The advantages of commencing our operations in that month would be, first, to deprive the enemy of Rhode Island; secure to ourselves, till spring, a fine island and harbour, and have it in our power to open the campaign when we please. Secondly, to establish our superiority in America before the winter negotiations. Thirdly, if peace should be desired, to place an important post in our side of the balance. Fourthly, in case the enemy should have extended their forces over any one of the states, to drive them away with the more ease, as we should take them by surprise.

A few days before our departure, and not sooner (to prevent the consequences of an indiscretion), three corvettes should be despatched to America, with letters to M. de Luzerne, to congress, and to General Washington. We might write that the king, desiring to serve his allies, and agreeably to the requests of Dr. Franklin, intends sending some vessels to America, and, with them, a body of land forces; and that, if congress is in want of their assistance, they will willingly lend their aid to General Washington, but otherwise they will proceed to the Islands. This form will be perfectly appropriate. On my part, I would write, in my capacity of an American officer, more detailed letters to congress, and to General Washington. To the latter I would say, confidentially, that we have almost a *carte blanche*, and unfold my plans, and request him to make the necessary preparations. It should be reported at our departure that we are destined as a garrison to one of the Antilles, while the troops of these islands act on the offensive, and that, in the summer, we shall be ordered to attempt a revolution in Canada.

The squadron sailing before the 10th of September, would arrive at Sandy Hook, off the coast of Jersey, early in November, one of the finest months of the year in independent America. Our fleet would then seem to threaten New York, and we should find, on our arrival, pilots for different destinations, and the necessary signals and countersigns.* If Rhode Island should be the proper point of attack, of which I have no doubt, we would steer southward towards evening, and, putting about during the night, land at Block Island, and lay siege to Newport.

There are some continental troops, who might reach Bristol in a day. There are militia at Tivertown, who might also be mustered. Greenwich having also a body of troops, must have flat-bottomed boats; those at Sledge Ferry would be sent down. All these we should find on the spot. To escape the inconveniences experienced the last year, the naval commander should send, without a moment's delay, two frigates, to occupy the eastern channel, and force the middle one, a thing of trifling danger. The vessels found there should be destroyed; and as the enemy usually leave at Conanicut Island a body of from six to fifteen hundred men, we might easily seize it, and make our land rendezvous there. If the wind should be favourable, the vessels might return the same night, or the end of the squadron might join them; all these manœuvres, however, will depend on circumstances. Thus much is certain, that the same wind which brings us to land will enable us to make ourselves masters of the eastern channel, so as to assist the Americans at Bristol and Tivertown, and, if possible, to secure the middle channel; at all events, however, it is easy to effect a landing in the manner I describe.†

Newport is strongly fortified on the side towards the land, but all the shore that is behind the town offers great facilities for landing; it is, besides, too extensive to admit of being defended by batteries. There the French troops might easily disembark, and, reaching at day-break the

* To deceive the enemy, pilots might be assembled from different parts, under pretence of sending them to the Islands, at the request of the French. This business, as well as the preparations and signals, might be entrusted to a lieutenant-colonel of the royal corps of engineers, an officer of great merit at the head of the American corps of engineers, who, under cover of working to the fortifications of the Delaware, might remain near Sandy Hook.

† The frigates or vessels necessary to protect the landing, either real or pretended, of the Americans, should anchor in those channels. The enemy would then be obliged either to disperse among the forts, and thereby to weaken their lines, or else to leave the field open to the Americans, who, by a diversion upon the lines, would force the enemy to have them fully manned, and prevent them attending to their rear.

heights which command the town and the enemy's lines, might seize their outworks and storm all before them, protected, if necessary, by the fire of the ships. The enemy, scattered and confounded by these false attacks on both sides of the island, would suppose that the system of the past year was re-adopted. The bolder this manœuvre appears, the more confident we may be of its success.

You are aware, moreover, that in war all depends on the moment; the details of the attack would be quickly decided on the spot. I need only say here, that my thorough knowledge of the island leads me to think that, with the above-mentioned number of troops, and a very slender co-operation on the part of America, I might pledge myself to gain possession of the island in a few days.*

As soon as we are in possession of the island, we must write to the state of Rhode Island, offering to resign the place to the national troops. Unless the state should prefer waiting for the opinion of General Washington, our offer would be accepted, and we should be invited to establish ourselves there during the winter. The batteries upon Goat Island, Brenton's Point and Conanicut Island, would render the passage of the harbour the more secure to us, particularly with the aid of our vessels, as the British are not strong enough to attack us there, and would never attempt it in an unfavourable season. We should be supported by the country, and although it is said to be difficult to procure provisions, I should endeavour to preserve our naval stores, and should obtain more resources than the American army itself.

The same letter that announces to congress our success in Rhode Island, of which, as far as calculations may be relied on, there is little doubt, should also mention our proposed voyage to the West Indies, and inquire whether our assistance is further needed. Their reply would open to new fields of service, and, with their consent, we would leave

* It is necessary, however, to consider all the unfortunate contingencies that may occur. If the expedition to Rhode Island should be prevented, or if it should not succeed, or if nothing can be attempted at New York, we ought then to proceed on our expeditions against Virginia, or Georgia, or Carolina, and winter afterwards at Boston, leaving Rhode Island to the next season, as proposed in our plan of sailing in the month of October.

the sick in a hospital at Greenwich, and the batteries manned by the militia, and proceed to Virginia. It might be hoped, without presumption, that James River Point, if still occupied, would yield to the united efforts of our troops and those of the Virginians. The bay of Chesapeak would then be free, and that state might bend its whole force against its western frontiers.*

It is impossible to estimate here the posts which the British occupy in America. Georgia and Carolina appear to need our assistance, and the precise operation against Rhode Island must be decided on the spot; but to give a general idea, it is sufficient to say that the months of December and January should be employed at the south. As the English are obliged to station some of their vessels, frigates, merchant ships, or transports, in each of their ports, they would amount in the whole to a considerable loss.

In the month of February we would return to Newport, where we might employ ourselves in interchanges with New York; and the French sailors, exchanged for soldiers, might be sent under a flag of truce to M. d'Orvillers. Political interests might be treated of with congress, and the commander of the detachment go to Philadelphia to make arrangements with the minister plenipotentiary for the next campaign, and to lay some proposals before congress and General Washington. I should propose sending for deputies from the different savage nations, making them presents, endeavouring to gain them over from the side of the English, and to revive in their hearts that ancient love of the French nation which, at some future day, it may be important for us to possess.

It is needless to say here, that if we should wait until the month of October, the season would be too far advanced to think of Rhode Island, but the southern operations would be equally practicable, and their success more certain, as we should take the enemy by surprise.

In that case, instead of proceeding to Newport, we should winter at Boston, where we should be well received, and provided with every accommodation. We could open

* If the capture of the Bermudas, or some expedition of the kind, should be considered necessary, the rest of the winter might be employed in carrying it into effect.

the campaign when we pleased, and might make preparations beforehand for a great expedition against Rhode Island, procuring, at the same time, from the inhabitants of the ports of the north of Boston, and especially that of Marble Head, all the information they may have acquired about Halifax.

But let us suppose ourselves established at Newport. The campaign opens by the close of April, and the British will be in no haste to quit New York. The fear of leaving himself unprotected on our side will prevent his executing any design against the forts on the North River. It may even be in our power to assist General Washington in making an attack on New York. Count d'Estaing, before his departure, thought that he had discovered the possibility of a passage through the Sound. This question I leave to naval officers; but, without being one myself, I know that Long Island might be captured, the troops driven off, and, whilst General Washington made a diversion on his side, batteries might be erected that would greatly annoy the garrison of New York. At all events, preparations should be made to act against Halifax in the month of June. With the claims which the other expedition would give us, I will pledge myself that we should be assisted in this by the Americans. I could find at Boston, and in the northern parts, trust-worthy persons who could go to Halifax for us, and procure all the necessary information; the town of Marble Head, in particular, would furnish us with excellent pilots. The inhabitants of the north of New Hampshire and Cascobay should be assembled under the command of their general, Stark, who gained the victory at Bennington, ready to march, if circumstances require it, by the route of Annapolis. The country is said to be inhabited by subjects ill affected to British government;* some of them have entered into a correspondence with the Americans, and have given assurances that they will form a party in our favour.

With regard to ourselves, I suppose that we sail the 1st of June, and that we are accompanied by some conti-

* The last time I was at Boston, I saw there a respectable man, a member of the council in Nova Scotia, who had secretly entered into the service of General Gates, and who assured us of the favourable disposition of the inhabitants.

nental frigates, and such private vessels as might be collected in Boston. Congress would undoubtedly furnish us with as many troops as we should require, and those very brigades which lately belonged to my division, and whose sole object at present is to keep the enemy at Rhode Island in check, having no longer any employment, would be able to join us without impairing the main army. They would come the more willingly, as the greater part of the regiments belonging to the northern part of New England would be averse to crossing the Hudson River, and would prefer a service more advantageous to their own country.* We should find at Boston cannon and mortars. Others, if necessary, might be sent from Springfield, and the corps of American artillery is tolerably good.

The enemy would suspect our designs the less, as their ideas run wholly upon an invasion of Canada; the movements of the militia in the north would be considered as a plan for uniting with us at Sorel, near the River St. Francis, as we ascended the St. Lawrence: this opinion, which, with a little address, might be strengthened, would awaken apprehensions and excite disturbances at Quebec;† and if a vessel of war should by chance be at Halifax ready for sea, they would probably despatch it to the threatened colony.

I have never seen the town of Halifax, but those persons who, before the war, were in the English service, and had spent most of the time in garrison, inform me that the great point is, to force to the right and left the passage of George's Island, and that a landing might be effected without difficulty, either on the side towards the eastern battery, in order to seize that battery and Fort Sackville, or, which appears to be a shorter way, on the side towards the town. The northern suburb, where the magazines are, is but slightly defended. The basin, where vessels are repaired, might also be secured. Several officers, worthy of confidence, have assured me, that Halifax is built in the form us of an amphitheatre; that all the houses might be can-

* General Gates, who is popular in New England, and perfectly acquainted with Halifax, has often proposed to make an expedition, in concert, against that town, with French and American troops combined.

† In the present harassed state of the English, I doubt if they will have in port any vessel capable of joining the squadron.

nonaded by the vessels that had forced the passage, and, in that case, the town would compel the garrison to surrender. As the troops might destroy all the works on the shore, and the vessels of war easily carry the batteries on the islands, I am well persuaded, and the accounts of all who have been there convince me still more, that Halifax would be unable to withstand the united power of our forces and those of America.*

The idea of a revolution in Canada is gratifying to all good Frenchmen; and if political considerations condemn it, you will perceive that this is to be done only by suppressing every impulse of feeling. The advantages and disadvantages of this scheme demand a full discussion, into which I will not at present enter. Is it better to leave in the neighbourhood of the Americans an English colony, the constant source of fear and jealousy, or to free our oppressed brethren, recover the fur trade, our intercourse with the Indians, and the profit of our ancient establishments, without the expenses and losses formerly attending them? Shall we throw into the balance of the new world a fourteenth state, which would be always attached to us, and which, by its situation, would give us a superiority in the troubles that may, at some future day, agitate America? Opinions are very much divided on this topic. I know yours, and my own is not unknown to you; I do not, therefore, dwell on it, and consider it in no other light than as a means of deceiving and embarrassing the enemy. If, however, it should at any time be brought under consideration, it would be necessary to prepare the people beforehand; and the knowledge which I was obliged to obtain when a whole army was about to enter that country has enabled me to form some idea of the means of succeeding there. But to return to Nova Scotia: part of the American troops, who will accompany us, and such of the inhabitants as take up arms in our favour, might be left there as a garrison. It would be easy to destroy or take possession of the English establishments on the

* I have not made any allowance for the diversion in the north, of which, however, I feel certain, and if the troops should not go to Annapolis, would, at least, compel a part of the British garrison, and such of the inhabitants as adhered to the royal party, to remain in the fort.

banks of Newfoundland, and after this movement we should direct our course according to circumstances. Supposing that we could return to Boston or Rhode Island during the month of September, and that New York had not yet been taken, we might still be enabled to assist General Washington. Otherwise St. Augustine, the Bermudas, or some other favourable points of attack, might engage our attention; on the other hand, if we should be ordered home, we might reach France in three weeks or a month from the banks of Newfoundland, and alarm the coasts of Ireland on our way.

If the September plan, which combines all advantages, appears too near at hand, if it were decided even not to send us in October, it would be necessary to delay our departure until the end of January. In this case, as in the former, we should be preceded fifteen days only by corvettes; we should pass the month of April in the south, attack Rhode Island in May, and arrive at Halifax the last of June. But you are aware that the autumn is, on many accounts, the most favourable time for our departure; at all events, you will not accuse me of favouring this opinion from interested motives, as a winter at Boston or Newport is far from equivalent to one spent at Paris.*

These views, in obedience to your request, I have the honour to submit to your judgment; I do not affect to give them the form of a regular plan, but you will weigh the different schemes according to circumstances. I trust that you will receive these remarks with the greater indulgence, as my American papers, those respecting Halifax excepted, are at Paris, and, consequently, almost all my references are made from memory; beside, I did not wish to annoy you with details too long for a letter, and if you are desirous to converse more freely on the subject, the impossibility of leaving the port of Havre, at present, will allow me time to spend three days at Versailles.

* Fifteen hundred or two thousand select troops thrown into America might aid General Washington, and enable him to act on the offensive, by supplying him with good heads to his columns, and by uniting the French with an American division for combined operations. This plan would be of some use, but it appeared to me that you wished for one offering results of greater importance.

I am thoroughly convinced, and I cannot, without violating my conscience, forbear repeating, that it is highly important for us to send a body to America. If the United States should object to it, I think it is our duty to remove their objections, and even to suggest reasons for it. But on this head you will be anticipated, and Dr. Franklin is only waiting a favourable occasion to make the propositions. Even if the operations of the present campaign, with the efforts of Count d'Estaing, or some other fortunate accident should have given affairs a favourable turn, there will be a sufficient field for us, and one alone of the proposed advantages would repay the trouble of sending the detachment.

A very important point, and one on which I feel obliged to lay the greatest stress, is the necessity of perfect and inviolable secrecy. It is unnecessary to trust any person, and even the men who are most actively employed in fitting out the detachment and the vessel need not to be informed of the precise intentions of government. At farthest, the secret should be confided to the naval commander, and to the leader of the land forces, and not even to them before the last moment.

It will certainly be said that the French will be coldly received in that country, and regarded with a jealous eye in their army. I cannot deny that the Americans are difficult to be dealt with, especially by the Frenchmen; but if I were intrusted with the business, or if the commander chosen by the king, acts with tolerable judgment, I would pledge my life that all difficulties would be avoided, and that the French troops would be cordially received.

For my own part, you know my sentiments, and you will never doubt that my first interest is to serve my country. I hope, for the sake of the public good, that you will send troops to America. I shall be considered too young, I presume, to take the command, but I shall surely be employed. If, in the arrangement of this plan, any one, to whom my sentiments are less known than to yourself, in proposing for me either the command or some inferior commission, should assign as a reason, that I should thereby be induced to serve my country with more zeal either in council or in action, I took the liberty (putting aside the minister of the

V.

Mrs. Shelley's New Work.

FALKNER—A NOVEL.

BY MRS. SHELLEY.

Authoress of "Frankenstein," "The Last Man," &c.

VI.

MEMOIRS OF MRS. HEMANS,

BY H. F. CHORLEY.

2 vols. beatifully Illustrated.

VII.

Mr. Grant's New Work.

THE GREAT METROPOLIS.

BY THE AUTHOR OF

"*Random Recollections of the Lords and Commons,*" *&c*

Fourth Edition.

VIII.

Mr. Bulwer's New Drama:

THE DUCHESS DE LA VALLIERE

A Play in Five Acts.

Second Edition.

IX.

Mr. Willis's New Work.

INKLINGS OF ADVENTURE.

BY N. P. WILLIS, ESQ.

Third Edition.

X.

LUCIEN BONAPARTE'S MEMOIRS,

(*Prince of Canino.*)

WRITTEN BY HIMSELF.

CPSIA information can be obtained
at www.ICGtesting.com
Printed in the USA
BVHW040303010219
539214BV00003B/386/P

9 781290 514767